ISLAM AND URBAN LABOR IN NORTHERN NIGERIA

OTHER BOOKS IN THIS SERIES

ISLAM AND URBAN LABOR IN NORTHERN NIGERIA

The Making of a Muslim Working Class

PAUL M. LUBECK

Merrill College, University of California, Santa Cruz

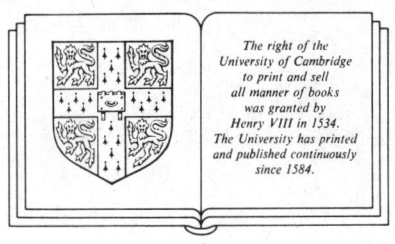

The right of the
University of Cambridge
to print and sell
all manner of books
was granted by
Henry VIII in 1534.
The University has printed
and published continuously
since 1584.

CAMBRIDGE UNIVERSITY PRESS

CAMBRIDGE
LONDON   NEW YORK   NEW ROCHELLE
MELBOURNE   SYDNEY

Published by the Press Syndicate of the University of Cambridge
The Pitt Building, Trumpington Street, Cambridge CB2 1RP
32 East 57th Street, New York, NY 10022, USA
10 Stamford Road, Oakleigh, Melbourne 3166, Australia

First published 1986

Printed in Great Britain at the University Press, Cambridge

British Library cataloguing in publication data

Lubeck, Paul M
Islam and urban labor in Northern Nigeria: the
making of a Muslim working class. – (African
studies series; 52)
1. Labor and laboring classes – Nigeria,
Northern – History 2. Muslims – Nigeria,
Northern – History 3. Social classes –
Nigeria, Northern
I. Title II. Series
305.5′62   HD8831.Z8N6/

Library of Congress cataloguing in publication data

Lubeck, Paul M.
Islam and urban labor in northern Nigeria.
(African studies series; 52)
Bibliography.
Includes index.
1. Labor and laboring classes – Nigeria, Northern.
2. Social classes – Nigeria, Northern. 3. Islam and
labor – Nigeria, Northern. I. Title. II. Series.
HD8831.Z8N635 1986   305.5′62′096695   86-6867

ISBN 0 521 30942 5

Contents

Maps

Source for all maps: K. M. Barbour, J. S. Oguntoyinbo, J. O. C. Onyemelukwe, J. C. Nwafor (eds.) 1982. *Nigeria in Maps*. New York: Africana
Publishing Co.

Tables

List of tables

Preface

The embryonic idea for this book began when I discussed returned migrants' visits to Kano and coastal cities while living as a rural development worker in a Hausa-speaking village in Niger Republic. Having recently taken a course on nineteenth-century European social history, I wondered what the process of industrialization and working-class formation would be like in Muslim West Africa. From there, I undertook the problem of the relationship of industrialized Europe to underdeveloped West Africa first with Ivor Wilks and John Paden and then with Ackie Feldman, Janet Abu-Lughod, and Alan Schnaiberg. All are at Northwestern University, and all deserve my esteem and gratitude for their patient support.

I am also grateful for the support of Nigerian Universities whose staff, faculty, and students contributed to the completion of this work. At Bayero University, members of the history and social science faculty were most supportive of the project. John Lavers, Phil Shea, Murray Last, Musa Abdullahi, Michael Mortimer, Yacub Adam, and Shehu Galadanci were especially helpful in many diverse ways. Ahmadu Bello University's faculty and resources were also important, as were those of the Nigerian Institute of Social and Economic Research and the University of Ibadan. Peter Waterman has championed the project from its inception, as have Gavin Williams, Robin Cohen, Sharon Stichter, Sara Berry, John Walton, Jean Copans, Joseph Gugler, Adrian Peace, and Keith Hart. Despite his reservations, M. G. Smith was most generous with critique and unpublished material.

Members of the comparative history group and the Sociology Board of Studies here at the University of California, Santa Cruz, deserve special thanks for years of support, patience, and careful criticism of the various versions and interpretations presented in this work. In the Sociology Board, Bill Friedland, Wally Goldfrank, and Bob Alford read drafts and offered insights that have improved the work immensely. At the University of California, Berkeley, special thanks go to Michael Watts whose support and enthusiasm for this project carried me through even when the task seemed overwhelming. My warmest gratitude to Terry Burke for his support during crucial periods and, together with Ira Lapidus, for correcting my more idealistic theorizing with their historical understanding of Muslim societies.

To the legion of students, both Nigerian and American, who worked on data collection, translation, and analysis, I want to express my thanks. In Nigeria, Usman Muktari and Ahmed Bako deserve special mention, as do the interviewers for the industrial survey: Haruna Al-Rashid, Aliyu Ilu, Haruna Ungogo, Garba Yusuf, Garba Mohammed, Usman Hasan and Ali Abbas. At Santa Cruz, Alan Zabel's dedication to composing statistical tables qualifies as truly heroic; Abdel Salem Magroui, Mark Beittel, Dana Priest, Elaine Draper, and Mike Webber were tireless in their researching and proofing. And Wendy Fassett, Brian Folk and Carole Lindner deserve mention for their typing and editing.

While in the field the dedication and unselfish effort of Deborah Phillips Lubeck in organizing the coding of the industrial survey and in conducting the Tudun Wada housing survey is gratefully acknowledged. Her methodological expertise and advice were also extremely valuable during the data analysis phase of the project. Besides Deborah's support, the loyalty and dedicated effort of Mallam Ibrahim Garba Bici of Tudun Wada enabled the book to be completed. His contribution was extraordinary and invaluable.

From its inception through its conclusion, the research for this book was supported by the Social Science Research Council's Joint Committee on African Studies, the Spencer Foundation, the National Science Foundation, the National Endowment for the Humanities, and the Academic Senate Committee on Research of the University of California, Santa Cruz. Their support is acknowledged and sincerely appreciated.

Paul M. Lubeck
August 1986

1

Islam and class formation: theoretical and historical background

THE CENTRAL PROBLEM: EXPLAINING THE FORMATION OF A MUSLIM WORKING CLASS

The objective of this study is to explain the complex process of working-class formation among Muslims residing in the northern Nigerian city of Kano during the period 1966–80. Driven by the twin forces of the Nigerian Civil War and the petroleum boom, virtually all social relations, social organizations and state administrative structures were transformed by a process that I have termed the transition to semi-industrial capitalism. During this conjuncture, what had been a relatively stable Muslim mercantile city, specializing in groundnut exports, became transformed into a semi-industrial capitalist city. The transformation was profound and de-stabilizing. The city expanded spatially and demographically as migrants searched for wage employment in the burgeoning manufacturing and service industries; entrepreneurs pursued an unceasing competitive struggle to gain access to state patronage and contracts; and a wave of speculation in consumable, or wage goods – land, housing and food – undermined the moral economy and sources of subsistence for Kano's popular classes. At the end of this social transformation, that is by the fall of the Shagari administration in 1983, industrial conflict was both chronic and often violent; a segment of the marginal and/or excluded population supported a ferocious, millenarian insurrection directed against both secular and religious authorities. At the national level, budgetary austerity and foreign debt (circa $22 billion) replaced the euphoria associated with the petroleum boom, just as an authoritarian military government replaced the civilian administration of Shehu Shagari. In the face of this transformation, this study poses several questions: How did the urban working class form from these processes? How did they create a meaningful community from the social chaos and corruption that surrounded them? And finally, how did they mobilize class solidarity and popular Islamic institutions in order to 'make' their own history?

If the conjuncture is that of the transition to semi-industrial capitalism, what are the social forces that explain the formation of an urban, Muslim working class? True, while capitalist social relations of production, exchange and consumption penetrated much more deeply into Kano

1

society, the situation was far more complex than those encountered by this typically Marxist problematic, if only because the transition to semi-industrial capitalism was accompanied by a world historic revival in Islamic social movements.[1] Herein lies the anomaly: while semi-industrial capitalism was creating an urban working class, at the same time, by building upon centuries of Islamic history in Kano, an Islamic revival was creating a Muslim communal, or *ethno-nationalist*, identity. And further, the two social processes – working-class formation and the Muslim ethno-nationalism – were not only occurring simultaneously among the same population, i.e. Kano's Muslim, Hausa-speaking wage workers, but the two processes were in a dialectical relationship with each other. By co-existing with each other, the activity of one altered, either by retarding or advancing, the activity of the other. Hence in order to explain the formation of a Muslim, urban working class, one must explain the historical relationship of Islamic social processes to their capitalist counterparts in the region of northern Nigeria. Only then will one be able to explain the structure, consciousness and action of a first generation Muslim urban working class. To do so requires the analyst to grant sufficient autonomy to both Islamic and capitalist processes.

Islamic social movements among the urban popular classes is a topical subject of intellectual discourse in the eighties. But the relationship of religious-based communities to new forms of social relations based upon social class is hardly new.[2] Classical sociological thinkers such as Durkheim and Weber as well as scholars studying social change in African societies have utilized both of these concepts. However, all too often, scholars have interpreted either class or community as the exclusive basis of social identity and social action. Reality requires us to recognize that urban African workers, like the rest of us, belong to both classes and ethnic or religiously defined communities. Often, they belong to multiple and situationally defined communities. Any perspective that advances the one and excludes the other in an *a priori* manner as a basis of explanation for social action and social consciousness is surely flawed methodologically.

To return to the central problem, that of explaining the structure, consciousness and action of a Muslim working class in the northern Nigerian city of Kano, one must take into account not only the effect of participation in the labor process of capitalist accumulation but also the way in which membership in an ethno-nationalist group of precapitalist origin relates to and structures the development of an urban working class. To be sure, the relationship is a dialectical one where the outcome of the combined effect of Islam and capitalism may reinforce or dilute the cohesion and militancy of a first-generation working class. For over one hundred years, Marxist scholars have argued that it is self-evident that workers are involved in class organizations and possess class-induced forms of consciousness. Similarly, classical sociology within the liberal vein has argued for the primacy of cultural and national identities that cross-cut class relations. Obviously,

2

workers do participate in social organizations and possess forms of consciousness that arise from both social class and ethno-nationalist experiences. But the crucial task is to understand the effect of the interaction of class and nation on the structure, consciousness and activity of an urban working class rather than, as is often done, to write polemics that run past each other by denying the relevance and explanatory power of the opposing theoretical argument.

Theoretical orientation

It must be obvious to the reader by now that this work is inspired by Marxist theory and the associated discourse that has been developed by debates over the past two decades. Less obvious is the debt owed to Weber and Weberian scholarship. Concepts such as status-honor groups, charismatic authority, sultanism, bureaucratic rationalization, the 'calling' of a vocation, and style of life are used extensively to explicate the process of Muslim working-class formation.[3] Indeed, my emphasis upon the subjectivity of the actors and the application of the method of 'empathetic understanding' (*verstehen*) to individuals undergoing the process of proletarianization is inspired by Weberian sociology. Nonetheless, most of the assumptions, arguments and propositions developed for empirical verification are drawn from the Marxian theoretical tradition. For this contentious discourse, I have drawn from three distinct schools: classical Marxism, the articulation of modes of production school and the world systems/dependency school.

Initially the study was inspired by Edward Thompson's *The Making of the English Working Class*, only in this instance the initial focus was upon Kano's industrial workers.[4] Hence, classical Marxian concepts such as the labor process, labor as a commodity, the commodification of wage goods (e.g. subsistence goods), class consciousness and class struggle offered the best theoretical constructs to explain the processes under investigation.[5] Two observations generated a creative intellectual tension, one that ultimately led me to apply the concept of the 'articulation of the modes of production' to the study of the interaction of Islam and capitalism within a first generation urban working class. First, as opposed to the expectations of both Weberian and classical Marxist theory, participation in urban-industrial institutions was correlated with increased participation in Islam and what I later defined as Islamic ethno-nationalism. Indeed, not only was Islamic solidarity an active social force integrating workers from diverse ethnic groups into a new urban Muslim identity, but also it was used as a weapon in the process of class struggle on the shop floor. Secondly, while workers were class conscious and formed class organizations, as predicted by classical Marxist theory, their political consciousness in society-wide social relations was defined to a significant degree by membership in the politically defined status-honor group, the *talakawa* (i.e., the commoners), a precapitalist social identity that was determined by the social division of

3

labor in the precolonial Islamic Hausa social formation. Both of these observations forced me to analyze the social formation of the nineteenth century, when Kano was the economic center of the Sokoto Caliphate, as well as the way in which colonial mercantile capitalism interacted with and related to the clearly precapitalist Islamic Hausa social formation.

The work of P. P. Rey and the 'articulation of modes of production' school offered a framework and some insights for conceptualizing at an abstract level the relationship of semi-industrial capitalism to the Islamic Hausa social formation.[6] This approach assumes a situation where capitalism did not evolve through the secular decline of feudalism, as in the original and thus unique case of western Europe. Rather, the capitalist mode of production is violently inserted into a precapitalist mode, so that the resulting social formation (e.g. society) reflects the tensions contained in the joining of two analytically distinct, often thought to be contradictory, modes of production. The key concept applied in this study is the *articulation* of precapitalist and capitalist elements. By the term articulation is meant the way in which institutions, ideologies and social practices, proper to two different modes of production, co-exist and serve to condition one another's development. Rey's insight was that, although capitalism was dominant over the precapitalist mode, during the first phase of this articulation, the precapitalist mode was actually strengthened while at the same time its integrity was eroded by its subordination to the capitalist mode. Hence, it is readily apparent that the concept of articulation, shorn of its idealistic and unnecessarily abstract elements and oriented toward empirical analysis, is a heuristically valuable concept for explaining the complex interaction between Islam and capitalism in the formation of a Muslim working class. The task is to apply this admittedly abstract concept to empirical situations.[7]

All of the aforementioned theoretical approaches employ the nation-state, society or region as their unit of analysis. But both Nigeria's origin and social processes are conditioned by political and economic forces that are *external* to its boundaries. For this reason, the role Nigeria and northern Nigeria play in the international division of labor and in the international state system, e.g. the totality of the world system, exerts a profound influence upon the social, political and economic processes that are internal to the nation-state. For example, the state of Nigeria itself is a creation of the capitalist world system; the export crops during the colonial period reinforced regional and ethno-nationalist divisions within the polity; and the rise of petroleum as the source of over 95 percent of Nigeria's foreign exchange earnings created a foreign exchange crisis which paved the way for the military coup of 1983. Without entering the thorny debate between world systems theorists and classical Marxists over the definition of capitalism and the correct units of analysis, world systems theory represents a creative attempt to formulate some empirical generalizations governing the relationship of states to world market cycles and the effect of the role played

4

by a state in the international division of labor (i.e. core, periphery or semi-periphery) on internal political and social processes.[8]

In addition to locating region and state in the international division of labor, with all the constraints on internal social processes that this implies, world systems theory proposes a *structural* rather than a solely *cultural* theory of national community formation: *reactive ethno-nationalism*.[9] It is this concept which is employed in this study. By employing states, ethnonations and regions as units of analysis, world systems theory explains how, over the long term, formal political intervention and the international division of labor dissolves and creates ethno-nations. Concretely, when the British invaded Muslim northern Nigeria, killed the Caliph of Sokoto and forced the region to become an agro-exporter (e.g. cotton and peanuts) in the international division of labor, a reactive ethno-nationalist consciousness formed which was an interactive product of an historically evolved Muslim culture and global inequality structures of the capitalist world system. Thus, penetration by the British imperial state and incorporation into the capitalist world economy as a peripheral region intensified opposition to 'Christian' imperialists and southern Nigerian ethnic groups. Indeed, as a social force, Muslim reactive ethno-nationalism strengthened the centuries-old process of Islamization: it intensified religious nationalism among the already orthodox classes of northern Nigerian cities; it deepened Islamic practice among the commoners, in part due to colonial communications and trade; and it extended Islamic communities through colonial administrative practices into areas not formerly part of Islamdom.[10]

At the micro-level, since wage labor and the organization of industrial production are perceived as European, then this cultural division of labor within the factory is perceived by Muslim workers as both 'alien' and 'alienating'. Insofar as cultural categories of the international division of labor are reproduced within the factory, reactive Muslim ethno-nationalism often converges so as to reinforce class consciousness arising from the industrial division of labor. As the products of articulation between industrial capitalism and Islamization, class and reactive Islamic nationalism are in a complex dialectical relationship whose practical political project can only be determined empirically. That is to say, this study argues that class experience mediates the application of reactive Islamic nationalism to concrete situations. Typically, among the subordinate classes, this takes the form of Islamic populism. And any cursory examination of the political projects of the class-based Muslim groups operating in Kano verifies this assertion (e.g. from the *Tijaniyya* to the *Yan Tatsine*).

Explaining the structure, consciousness and action of a Muslim, urban working class forces one to apply an eclectic blend of theoretical tools. Marxism possesses a powerful theory to explain how one class controls labor and the state in order to accumulate capital, thus undermining precapitalist institutions, cultures and practices. But it has no theory of national or cultural community. By drawing upon Weberian and world

5

systems theory, one may explain how cultural and nationalist factors interact with the underlying structural processes of commodification, accumulation and class formation that are inevitable products of the transition to semi-industrial capitalism.

Method, units of analysis and data collection

The discussion of my theoretical orientation to the problem of Muslim working-class formation has already suggested several methodological assumptions: empathetic understanding of the actor's motive, articulation of precapitalist and capitalist modes, empirical verification and the integration of macro- and micro-level units of analysis. This study presumes that it is possible and necessary to have a social science that is historical and empirical, rather than merely descriptive and interpretative. Class and nation are presumed to be in a dialectical relationship with each other, just as capitalism and Islamization are, at a much more abstract conceptual level, articulated to each other. And, given the propensity of social scientists to reproduce their own ideology as data and to avoid testing their most treasured theoretical assumptions, empirical verification through qualitative, quantitative and historical methods is an absolute necessity, if one is to show how the articulation of Islam and capitalism explains the structure, consciousness and action of a Muslim urban working class.

The integration of macro-level with micro-level units of analysis is a perplexing problem for social science. Macro-level units of analysis, moreover, tend to be more abstract (e.g. world system, mode of production and national state) while micro-level units of analysis are usually observable as well as conceptually less abstract (e.g. community, working class, ethno-nation and individual consciousness). The problem of integrating macro to micro-level is resolved in this study by employing a telescoping mode of organization where a more inclusive macro unit of analysis continually shifts downward in scale to a more micro-level unit as the study unfolds. It is analogous to a series of concentric circles, in which each subsequent chapter takes on a more micro-level unit of analysis. Thus, at the world systemic level, Islamization and capitalist development are treated as expanding world historic forces that confront each other in northern Nigeria in 1900. Then structural social change is explained by the articulation of these two macro-level social forces in the northern region and in urban Kano during the period of the colonial, nationalist and first military governments (e.g. Chapters One and Two). From the regional and urban units of analysis, analytic attention then turns to the popular classes – independent commodity producers and wage workers in their workplaces, markets and communities (e.g. Chapters Three and Four). In turn, the unit of analysis shifts to the industrial proletariat at the point of production where their organization, consciousness and, most importantly, their political struggles are described and explained with reference to the articulation of Islam and

6

capitalism (Chapters Five and Six). And finally, the unit of analysis turns to differences between individual Muslim workers. Here, a statistical analysis is presented relating structural experiences and forms of social participation, both capitalist and Islamic, to class and ethno-nationalist consciousness in order to test in a positivistic manner the theoretical propositions argued throughout (Chapter Seven).

The reader will note, undoubtedly, that this methodological approach refers to concepts at several levels of abstraction and employs historical, qualitative and quantitative techniques of data collection. Because I have described the three methods of data collection and the logic of a multiple methods approach to empirical verification elsewhere, there is no need to repeat it here.[11] Suffice it to say that the multiple methods approach assumes that each method, though appropriate to a particular question, unit of analysis or level of abstraction, contains inherent bias. Hence, by employing comparative-historical, qualitative-field and quantitative-survey methods, the strength of each method of data collection is brought to bear on the problem. Yet, by cross-checking and comparing findings from each, the reliability of each method is enhanced. A detailed description of the method, logic and data collection techniques used in this study is available in Appendices One and Two.

ISLAM AND CAPITALISM IN NORTHERN NIGERIA: AN HISTORICAL OVERVIEW

By the end of the nineteenth century, two expansionary world historical forces – Islam and capitalism – confronted each other in what has become modern Nigeria. The term 'world historic' is appropriate because both Islam and capitalism take the world as the parameter of their respective expansion. Similarly, despite the radically opposed assumptions and purposes of Islam and capitalism, those responsible for territorial expansion in each case assume, according to allegedly universalistic criteria, that significant benefits accrue to affected peoples even though the process of penetration and incorporation into their respective system is typically violent. Further, while capitalism works through the market and Islam employs the legal and military apparatus of the state, any society incorporated by either Islam or capitalism experiences a social transformation in the areas of polity, culture and economy.

Simply stated, the transformation associated with Islamization is primarily political and cultural though economic transformations also occur. The objective of Islam is the creation of a universalistic, openly recruited community of belief that is organized around the principles of Islamic law (*Shari'a*).[12] Such a goal requires an Islamic state to safeguard the community and to implement Islamic law. Materially, the rulers of an Islamic state must have sources of wealth, which they obtain in accordance with Islamic law by taxing subjects whose relationship to the ruling class is determined by

7

membership in politically defined status groups which may also form precapitalist classes. While Islamization is associated with merchant capital (e.g., long-distance trade, credit and literacy) and extensive rather than technically innovative processes of production, the primary effect of Islamization is at the political and cultural level. Most importantly, Islam creates an open and universalistic community. When Islamic communities exist within a defined territory, usually under an Islamic state, those communities form a Muslim *nation*, one that is located within a particular region yet with acknowledged linkages and responsibilities to the world Muslim community – Islamdom.

If Islamic transformation creates a distinct political community that may take the form of a regionally bounded Islamic nation, what is the corresponding effect of capitalist penetration into a precapitalist society? Divorced from the peculiarities of the European societies and cultures from which it emerged, capitalism is a process whereby the production of objects for maximum profit in a market (that is, commodities) overcomes any political, cultural or social obstacle to the realization of unrestrained commodity production. One may periodize capitalist development so as to distinguish between mercantile and industrial capitalism.[13] The former exists when merchants accumulate capital through exchange, but where the actual process of production is only partially capitalist or is completely precapitalist. The latter exists when industrial capitalists accumulate capital through the production of commodities by wage labor as well as when the creative activities of the wage laborers are monitored, reorganized and transformed by labor-saving technologies. To the detriment of precapitalist culture, capital accumulating activities promote commodity relations between all individuals as determined by the objects that they exchange rather than by the values of a precapitalist culture. Accordingly, the complex division of labor that is generated by the socially unrestrained process of commodity production and commodification of social relations creates objective social classes which are determined in larger part by the relationship of each class to the capitalist mode of production, exchange and consumption.

If Islamization creates a politically defined community which in northern Nigeria takes the form of a regionally bounded Islamic nation, and capitalism creates classes by promoting the unrestrained production of commodities for profit in a market, the central question is: how do Islam and capitalism relate to each other so as to determine the structure, consciousness and action of a first-generation Muslim working class in urban Kano?

To answer this question, one must step back from the contemporary situation in order to grasp the exact manner in which these two world historic forces confronted each other in northern Nigeria at the end of the nineteenth century. From about A.D. 1000, northern Nigeria gradually became a cultural but not an economic or political periphery of the North African empires of central Islamdom. Hence, the division of labor, state structures and forms of exchange were not subordinated to the exactions of the central states of Islam. Yet, once the region was transformed by the *jihad* (i.e. holy war against syncretist and non-Muslims) into the Sokoto Caliphate by indigenous African militants, as an expanding Muslim state it possessed the political and economic autonomy that allowed it to expand throughout the wider region while, at the same time, remaining a cultural periphery of central Islamdom. Expansion of the Caliphate state was accompanied by social, political and economic transformations which contemporary Islamic nationalists believe would have united the region under Islam had the technically superior Europeans not intervened to introduce colonial capitalism. That a geopolitical struggle existed is reflected in the observations of the imperial adventurer Richard Burton when he described the strength of Islamic elites in Lagos as the British were making their first territorial conquest of Nigeria. According to Burton, Lagos contained 'some 800 Moslems though not yet 2,000 as it is reported. Though few they have risen to political importance; in 1851 our bravest and most active opponents were those wearing turbans.'[14] Just as Burton viewed Muslims as rivals, so too officials of the Sokoto Caliphate defined themselves as part of Islamdom and thus accepted the geopolitical rivalry between European Christian states and Muslim states in a manner unlike non-Muslim African states. For example, when the British explorer Clapperton visited Sokoto in 1830, he recorded that: 'he was regarded as a spy in Sokoto and that it was the talk of the town that Europeans intended to take Hausaland as they had taken India.'[15]

In order to grasp the historical relationship between Islamdom and European capitalism, it is necessary to review the process of Islamization in northern Nigeria, the formation of the Sokoto Caliphate, the social and economic transformations that occurred when a Muslim state ruled according to Islamic law (*Shari'a*), the nature of precapitalist urban social relations in Kano and the way in which Islamic ideology and institutions resisted British imperial penetration. After examining the consequences of incorporation as a peripheral region into the capitalist world economy, we turn to the class alliance between British administrators and Muslim aristocrats, and the social consequences of the articulation of Islam and capitalism. In addition, the emergence of colonial Kano as a groundnut exporting center, the role of Islamic ideology and institutions in the formation of Kano's mercantile bourgeoisie and the anti-imperialist nationalist movement among the *talakawa* (commoners) are also examined.

ISLAMIZATION IN HAUSALAND: THE EMERGENCE OF KANO AS A MUSLIM CITY STATE

The geographical area of interest, Hausaland, is situated between the Sahara desert and the woody savanna regions of central and southern Nigeria. The Hausa are not an ethnic group that claims descent from a common ancestor; rather they are a linguistic group sharing a common culture, one that was formed by waves of migration, often from the north, and by interaction with neighboring societies such as the Songhai and the Kanuri.[16] Ecology exerted a determining influence on the formation of city states, the use of cavalry for conquest and the siting of city states near rivers so that water was available after the short rainy season varying from three to five months long.[17] Since archeological studies have yet to be undertaken, it is impossible to estimate accurately the origins of Hausa towns (*gari/ garuruwa*). Kano, for example, is estimated to have been founded by A.D. 600; iron-smelting was introduced into Hausa towns by the first millennium and Islam was introduced into Kano by the fourteenth century at the latest and probably earlier.

The transition from towns, where authority was based upon kinship relations, to cities (*birni/birane*), where authority was based upon the control of territory, marked the process of state formation. Further, it marked the establishment of the basic social cleavage between the ruling groups (*sarauta*) and the *talakawa*. The walled city reflects the division of labor between city and countryside and the transfer of wealth (taxation) from the agrarian producers to the king (*sarki*) and his officials residing in the walled cities. A ruler of the early Hausa states was faced with many obstacles: rival lineages of landholding families threatened both his rule and the continuity of his dynasty; the authority of the state needed to be exercised against recalcitrant rural producers and invading groups; and the demands of the non-agricultural urban residents also had to be considered, for without them, trade, luxury goods and valuable manufacturing skills would be lost. With the emergence of the walled city, the *sarauta–talakawa* cleavage and the division of labor between the city and the countryside, the embryonic social structure of the Hausa social formation appeared and continues until the present period. The talakawa included craft producers and merchants as well as agricultural producers. In exchange for protection, the talakawa paid a portion of their labor or product to the sarauta.

Kano: the transition to an Islamic state

Oral tradition holds that Kano was founded by Bagauda who legitimated his rule by mediating with spirits associated with a sacred grove of trees. As the city prospered and as the division of labor evolved to include long distance trade, the state apparatus became differentiated into distinct offices whose holders collected a land tax from the rural producers as early as the thirteenth century. In the same century Islam was introduced, probably from a variety of sources including Wangara from Mali, Arabs from North Africa and scholars from Kanem-Borno. While Islam has exerted an influence on Kano's rulers since its introduction, Mohammed Rumfa (1463–99) 'was the *sarki* who appears to have applied himself seriously to the problems of ruling a multireligious community in accordance with

10

Islamic law'.[18] Though Rumfa established Islam as the state religion, built mosques and schools, attacked pre-Islamic shrines and institutions and centralized the state in accordance with Muslim tradition, his achievements were eroded after his death by wars, famines, increased corruption and tyranny and the re-emergence of syncretist religious practices.

It was this tension between a pre-Islamic society rooted in the rural areas and a centralizing, urban-based Muslim state which depended increasingly on trade that set the stage for the *jihad* of the populist reformer Usman dan Fodio in the eighteenth century. Traditional accounts of the *jihad* emphasize, as the victors always do, the moral corruption of the Hausa kings that provoked the *jihad*, Recently, Murray Last has suggested a brilliant materialist explanation of the tension between Islam and indigenous Hausa religion, as well as associated material and social forces that shaped the history of Hausaland prior to its incorporation into the capitalist world economy (1900).[19] To summarize a complex and erudite argument, Last begins by noting how pivotal city-states involved in trans-Saharan trade, and in particular in the gold trade, moved in a southerly direction from the desert to the savanna states. Thus, he argues, the appearance of the Wangara as mentioned in the Kano Chronicle refers to the emergence of Muslim, perhaps Malian-origin, gold traders who purchased gold at Kano that had been produced in central and southern Nigeria. The southerly shift of gold entrepôts in the West African end of the trans-Saharan trade indicates the greater material, agricultural and military strength of savanna societies in contrast with the desert states. Food, population, iron and military materials were far more plentiful in the savanna areas than in the desert.

The city-state of Kano, therefore, was bifurcated between two opposing social and economic forces, each with its own religio-political system. For defense, agricultural production and labor, the Hausa *sarki* depended upon the rural population, the officeholders and the spirit priests associated with the indigenous religious system. In order to maintain his legitimacy with the agrarian communities, the *sarki* had to participate in, or at least to tolerate, the rituals of pre-Islamic Hausa society because his subjects associated his ritual participation with successful agricultural production. On the other hand, with the introduction of Islam and with the involvement of Kano in trans-saharan trade, the Hausa *sarki* became dependent to some degree on the urban, Islamic scholar-merchant community which linked the city-state to the wider world governed by the networks and norms of Muslim mercantile capitalism. Not only did trans-Saharan trade offer a ruler great wealth, luxury goods, technical innovation and access to superior weapons, but it also offered a superb ideology of centralized state building, with a powerful written legal tradition as well as a literate stratum of scholars and students who strengthened a state's administration. Opposed to the urban-Islamic gold-trading faction were rival aristocratic lineages whose social base was agrarian and pre-Islamic.

11

What followed from this structural antagonism between Islamic and pre-Islamic social forces was a series of conflicts, even civil wars, in which one or the other was hegemonic for a period. While the overall trend toward increased Islamization and the gradual penetration of Islam into the countryside prevailed, especially among scholar-traders, there was a marked tendency for rulers to attempt to bridge the gap between the two antagonists by participating in the activities of both. Hence, syncretism became common. More importantly, from the perspective of Muslim reformers, syncretism was backsliding, un-Islamic government and thus a justification for *jihad*; that is, an Islamic political revolution whereby the *Shari'a* would become institutionalized within the social and cultural fabric of Hausa society.

The jihad, Shari'a *and the Sokoto Caliphate*

By the end of the eighteenth century the religious syncretism and social injustice of Hausa society provoked a populist social upheaval that was led by a charismatic preacher named Usman dan Fodio.[20] Faced with the material interests that supported syncretism, Fodio sparked a religious revival inspired by the goal of establishing a state ruled in accord with Muslim law, the *Shari'a*. His biography and the history of the *jihad* is well known so it would be superfluous to repeat it here. It is noteworthy that he was influenced through his teacher by Wahabbite reformist doctrines of Arabia, that he began as a wandering preacher engaged in Islamic scholarship but soon emerged as a social reformer who communicated to large popular audiences. His preaching aroused the fear of Hausa kings who persecuted his followers. Then in classical emulation of the *hijra* of Mohammed, Fodio established a separate community, issued written manifestos calling for the establishment of Muslim law, the end of illegal taxation and social injustice and used Islamic networks such as the Qadiriyya brotherhood to extend his Islamic revolution.[21] When his holy war was completed, this humble preacher had founded the largest, in terms of territory and population, and most complexly organized state system in precolonial West Africa, if not Africa generally.

The *jihad* and the Sokoto Caliphate built upon the economic growth of the eighteenth century, the popular expectation that an Islamic reformer would appear at the beginning of a new century according to the Muslim calendar (e.g. November 1785) and the hostility generated by the Hausa kings' taxation of traders and teacher-scholars (*mallam/mallamai*, from Arabic *alim/ulema*). Once conquered by the followers of Fodio, Kano became a quasi-independent emirate under the Sokoto Caliph to whom it paid tribute. More importantly, the Fulani clans who formed the new ruling class of Kano became integrated into a self-conscious, Caliph-wide ruling class which continues to exist. It was committed to the establishment of *Shari'a* and to its collective ruling class interest which superceded the

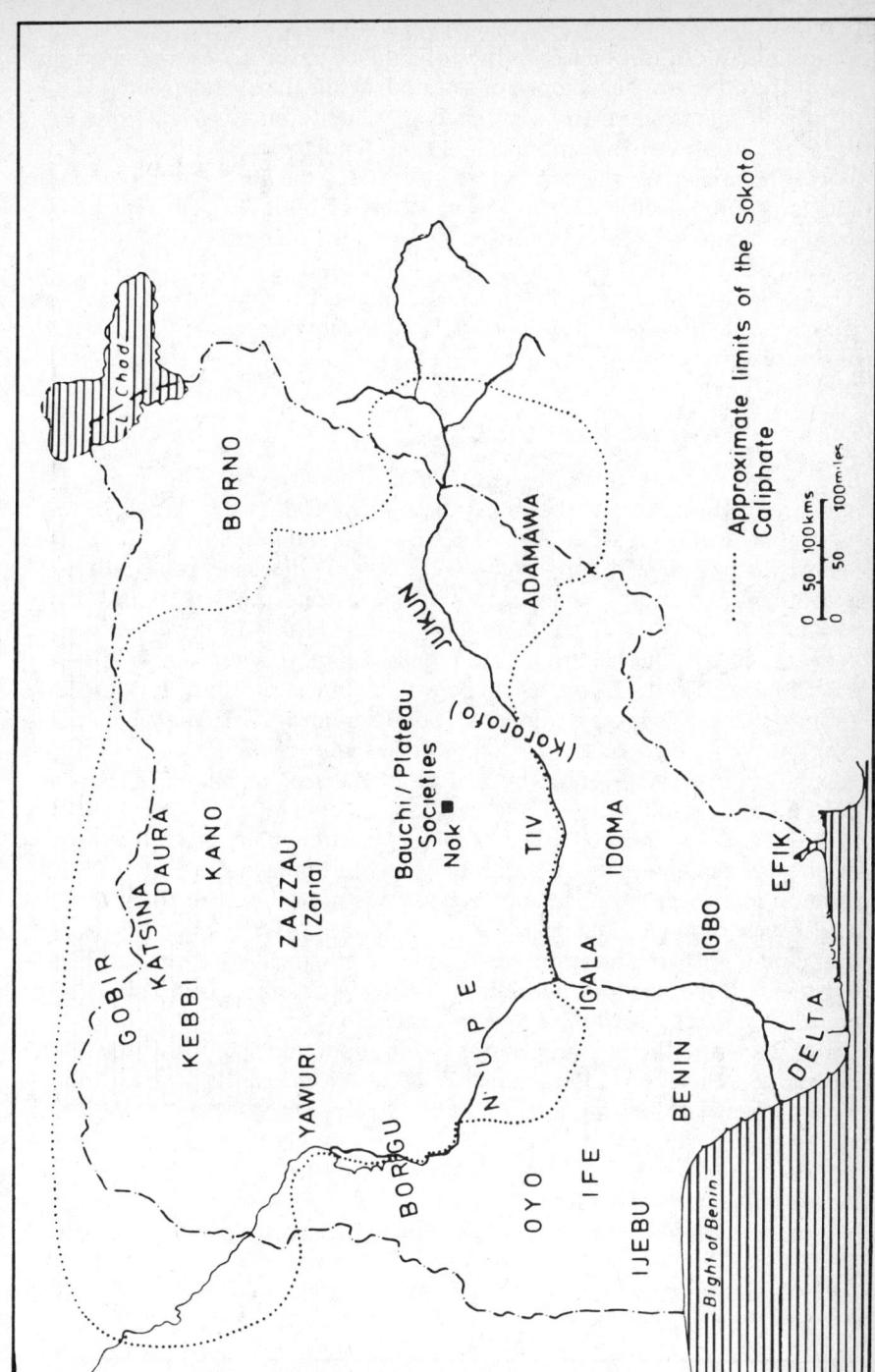

1. The Sokoto Caliphate within West Africa

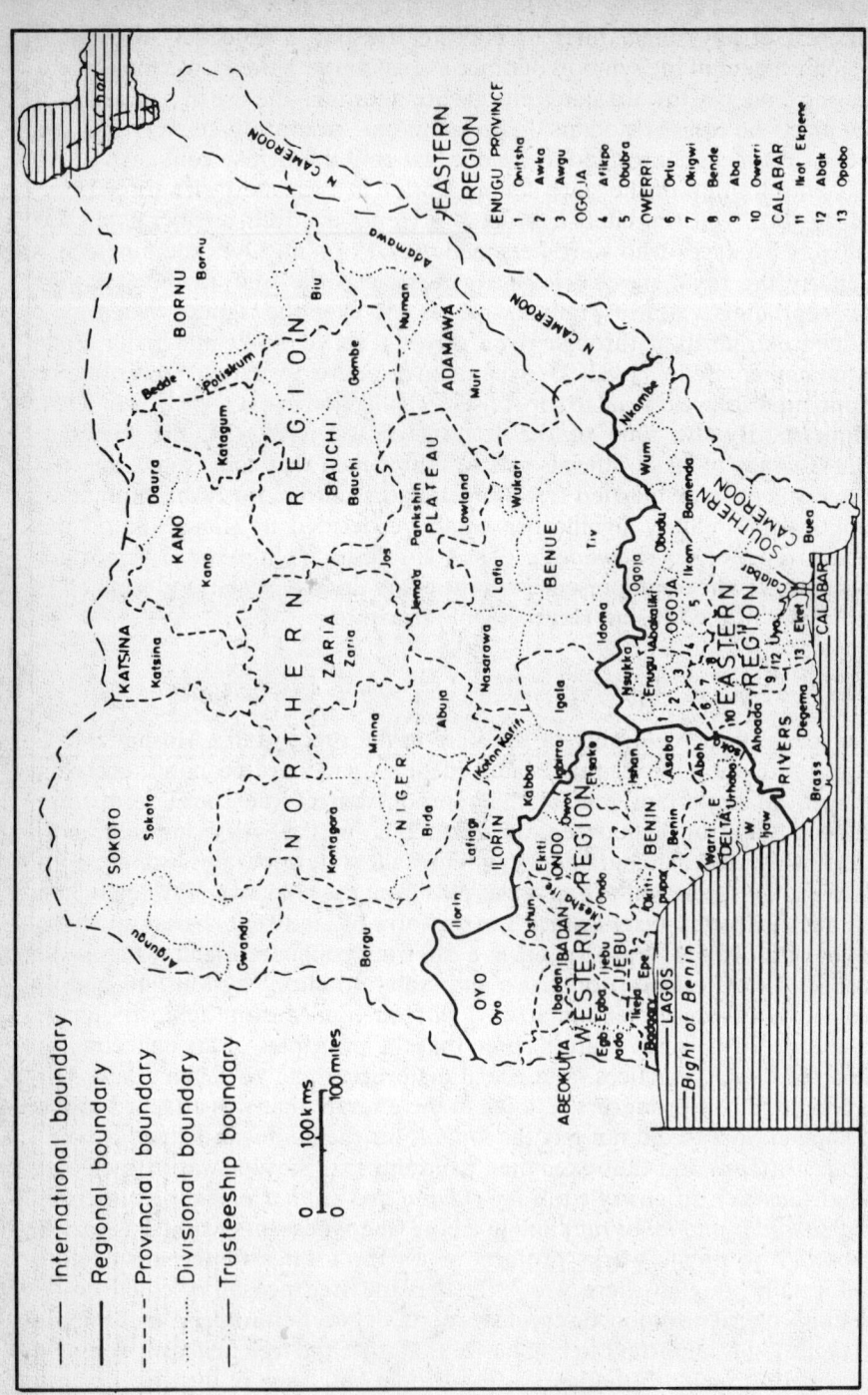

14

2. Colonial Nigeria: Regional, Provincial and Divisional Boundaries, 1954

International boundary
Regional boundary
Provincial boundary
Divisional boundary
Trusteeship boundary

0   100 kms
0   100 miles

EASTERN REGION

ENUGU PROVINCE
1 Onitsha
2 Awka
3 Awgu

OGOJA
4 Afikpo
5 Obubra

OWERRI
6 Orlu
7 Okigwi
8 Bende
9 Aba
10 Owerri

CALABAR
11 Ikot Ekpene
12 Abak
13 Opobo

NORTHERN REGION

SOKOTO
Sokoto
Gwandu
Argungu

KATSINA
Katsina
Daura

KANO
Kano
Katagum

BORNU
Bornu
Biu
Beddie
Potiskum

BAUCHI
Bauchi
Gombe

ADAMAWA
Muri
Numan

PLATEAU
Pankshin
Lowland
Jos
Jemaa

BENUE
Lafia
Wukari
Idoma
Nasarawa
Tiv

NIGER
Minna
Bida
Kontagora

ZARIA
Zaria
Abuja

ILORIN
Ilorin
Lafiagi
Kabba
Borgu
Igala
Kotonkarfi

WESTERN REGION

OYO
Oyo
Ibadan
Ekiti
ONDO
Ondo

ABEOKUTA
Egba
Egbado
JEBU
Ijebu
Ijebu Remo
Epe

BENIN
Benin
Asaba
Aboh
Owan
Kukuruku
Ishan

DELTA
Warri
W Ijaw
Urhobo

LAGOS

RIVERS
Degema
Brass
Ahoada

EASTERN REGION
Nsukka
Enugu
Abakaliki
Ogoja
Obubra
Calabar
Ikom
Uyo
Eket
Opobo

N CAMEROON

SOUTHERN CAMEROON
Nkambe
Wum
Bamenda
Obudu
Buea

Lake Chad

Bight of Benin

interest of any single ruler or emirate. Despite a tendency toward re-establishment of the symbols of office associated with the Hausa kings and a strong tendency toward state centralization through the use of palace slaves in place of free aristocrats (e.g. sultanism, according to Weber), the political system conformed to Islamic law until the British conquest.

Centralization of the state administration is associated with Emir Dabo (1819–46).[22] He initiated a process of replacing free aristocrats as fief holders by slaves who were personally loyal to him. Over the nineteenth century the royal slaves (*cucunawa*) displaced the free aristocracy, thus appropriating tax farms, military offices and even the right to own slaves. State centralization through royal slaves reached its zenith under Emir Mohammed Bello (1882–93) when, in response to a revenue crisis, he appointed a slave official to supervise tax collection in over 400 fiefs in Kano Emirate. By the time of the Kano civil war (1893–5), the sultanate bureaucracy of slave officials was so entrenched that their sons inherited their offices, they married free women and according to Fika, 'nothing of political or military significance could be decided in Kano without the concurrence of key *cucunawa*'.[23] The centralization of the state is important because of the omnipresence of the state in the social and economic processes of the Muslim Hausa social formation.

The Muslim state: modes of surplus extraction and social structure

To speak of the centrality of the state in the precapitalist Muslim Hausa social formation means that Islamic ideology and extra-economic coercion played an important role in the reproduction of the social formation. Indeed, the struggle between free aristocrats and the emirs' slave officeholders, while critical to our understanding of the state apparatus, was merely a struggle over the right to extract surplus from the talakawa.[24] Actually, the sarauta extracted taxes, which were a form of land rent, based upon the right of an Islamic state to collect a tax from conquered land (*kharaj*), to collect a tithe (*zakkat*) on crops and crafts produced by Muslims and to collect a tribute-protection levy (*jizia*) on non-Muslim subjects of the emirate. Virtually all sources agree that the principles of tax collection, if not the actual practices, were legitimate according to Islamic law. For example, direct producers residing in the emirate that was attached to the Caliph at Sokoto did not pay the *kharaj*, for the land was defined as *wakf* (*Dar al Islam*) and thus exempted from this tax. Surplus was extracted in kind (*zakkat*), in cowry-currency (*kharaj* and *zakkat* on non-grain crops called *kudin shukka* or *rafi*) and in labor, where peasants worked as *corvee* laborers on public works projects or on the estates of the aristocracy. Informally, though there was little that the free peasantry could do to redress illegal taxation or the extortions of the fief-holders' messengers (*jakadu*), it is important to emphasize that since the free talakawa were not attached formally to the land as in serfdom and since productive farmers

15

were desired by other fiefholders and other emirates, migration was frequently an effective tactic of resistance to exploitation. Further, the intensity of competition among officeholders and the importance of an officeholder's reputation for correct Islamic administration acted as additional checks on exploitation.

Slavery represented an additional source of revenue for the officeholding aristocracy.[25] In this instance, the spiritual obligation of waging holy war against infidels converged neatly with the material interest of the sarauta as a land-controlling class. *Jihad* produced slaves for sale and settlement on slave estates within their fiefs. Further, after 1807, when the Atlantic slave trade was outlawed and external demand for slaves from the capitalist world economy declined, the tendency for settlement of slaves on estates within the Caliphate and in *ribats* on the frontiers of the Caliphate increased accordingly. A *ribat* was a fortified frontier post where slaves were placed as settlers in the interest of strengthening and extending the boundaries of Islamdom. In turn, this coerced urban-development policy brought more of the region's population into the forms of commodity production and Muslim mercantile capitalism that governed the exchange economy. Some talakawa, such as merchants and farmers, owned slaves, but death taxes and the prominent role of the aristocracy in producing and utilizing slaves meant that slave-holding was predominantly the domain of the officeholding sarauta.

Once settled upon the slave estates of the aristocracy, additional burdens were placed upon slave producers as opposed to the free talakawa. But once they became Muslims, settled slaves were not usually sold, though they might have paid an additional levy, even during the colonial period. Women of child-bearing age were at a premium, for they could be legally taken as concubines by a freeman, and the sons of such a union were not only free but inherited equally with those born of free-born women. A woman who gave birth to a son was also freed. Culturally, the Islamic ideal conferred great prestige upon an aristocrat who freed his slaves upon his death, but little is known about the frequency of such acts of generosity. More particular to the Hausa Muslim system of slavery, further distinguishing it from the plantation slavery of the new world, was the institution of *murgu* whereby a slave could ransom himself through earnings from his private economic activity; indeed, a slave could even pay a fixed fee in order to be free during the dry season to take up a craft or trading occupation. In theory, slaves also had the right to petition the court if they were maltreated by their masters.

Earlier I described the situation of the royal slaves, who could own slaves, accumulate wealth and offices and even marry free women. Thus slave status in itself did not determine one's relationship to the means of production (i.e., an objective class location in a system of production); rather, that would be determined by whether one was incorporated into the sarauta or the talakawa. Together, the relatively powerless position of the

16

free talakawa, the tendency for the state to encourage slave assimilation into Muslim society, the state's emphasis on settlement of productive labor for revenue purposes and the tendency for large slave estates to be divided upon the death of the founder mitigated against the evolution of any permanent slave class. Indeed, historians have recorded no slave revolts. Similarly, my field data indicate no permanent stigma in contemporary Kano arising from precolonial slave status.

Theoretically, with regard to class structure, how does one characterize the sarauta–talakawa cleavage? Instead of defining this cleavage as a fully developed class system, a definition that is reserved for a mature or semi-industrial, capitalist society in this study, the concept that best describes this relationship is that of a 'class-like, status-honor system', where a politically defined relationship to the Muslim state acts to mediate to a profound degree the effects of a cleavage arising from the social division of labor.[26] The term 'class-like' is appropriate because the sarauta–talakawa cleavage reflects the division between the direct producers and the ruling class who exploited them. To be sure, for certain purposes these strata may be defined as objective, though not subjective, classes. But when one examines the situation of the talakawa, one discovers that it is an occu-pationally heterogeneous political status group, defined by its relationship to the state rather than by a common objective location in the social division of labor. For example, wealthy merchants, farm slaves, full- and part-time craft producers and free agricultural producers are defined and identify as talakawa. Moreover, state extraction of taxation-rents did not reinforce objective class relations. Because of the baroque system of fragmented fiefholding, adjacent villages sharing a common social existence paid taxes to different officeholders. Further, institutionalized patron–client relations, referred to as *chappa*, allowed certain talakawa households to pay taxes to, and thus acknowledge the protection of, an officeholder who did not possess local territorial rights.

Therefore, the system of surplus extraction was characterized by pecu-liarly customary rights and individualized mediation with state authority, all of which encouraged the formation of vertical patronage links rather than the horizontal bonds of class cohesion that arise from commodity relations characteristic of capitalist society. Hence, because the labor process of precapitalist talakawa producers did not integrate communities (often originating from diverse ethnic and regional groups), into manifold rela-tions with each other, and equally important, because the relationship of exploitation arising from surplus extraction tended to be peculiarly custom-ary and even negotiated, the term 'class-like status-honor group' is more appropriate than social class in its fullest sense. The manner in which the sarauta and the Islamic state extracted surplus and reproduced the social formation in general obscured the potential maturation of class relations and class consciousness. For, in order to extract surplus and to reproduce the state in accordance with the *Shari'a*, the Islamic state recognized and thus legitimized a myriad of distinct status groups, including servile and non-Muslim groups and ethnic communities of distinct social origins, all of whom might claim prerogatives derived from their status. By reinforcing these forms of status consciousness and the vertical linkage of patronage between superior and inferior, an arabesque system of status relations emerged that mitigated against the formation of a talakawa consciousness corresponding to the material relations of exploitation. And finally, talakawa social protest took the form of Mahdism, migration or hostility toward the behavior of a particular ruler rather than toward the inequality of the system as a whole.

STATE, SOCIETY AND ECONOMY: MATERIAL CONSEQUENCES OF THE *JIHAD*

The achievement of the *jihad* was the Muslim state: the Sokoto Caliphate. By remaining *external* to the processes of the capitalist world economy, thus avoiding the socially divisive consequences of peripheralization, the Caliphate gained a century of autonomy to consolidate Muslim society under the *Shari'a*.[27] At the same time, though the Caliphate could be called a cultural periphery of the North African states of central Islamdom, the ecological barrier of the Sahara and European imperialism there insured it did not become an economic or political dependent of central Islamdom. Thus the Caliphate gained advantages of *Shari'aization* in terms of state formation, the legal basis of Muslim mercantile capitalism, literacy and some technological innovation but avoided the costs of subjugation either to central Islamdom or European capitalism. Cultural incorporation into Islamdom meant that economic and cultural contact through the trans-Saharan trade and the *hajj* to Mecca respectively, integrated Caliphal society into a universalistic, global civilization that had been combating European expansion for centuries already. From this integration into Islamdom, reactive Muslim ethno-nationalism emerged when British forces invaded the Caliphate.

The *jihad* created an emirate system stretching over a vast territory that was governed by an integrated aristocracy which ruled through the application of Muslim law. Sokoto appointed emirs in accordance with consensus and local custom, thus allowing for some autonomy. The consequences at the political level are clear: the Caliphate was the largest and most completely organized state system in precolonial West Africa. But what of social and economic consequences in the area of the division of labor, in the transformation of the unit and technical means of production, in the area of exchange and in the social relations of production?

In answering these classic materialist questions, one can not emphasize enough the degree to which state structures and *jihadi* ideology penetrated the economic process of production, exchange and consumption. The centralized, Muslim state was hegemonic ideologically, politically and to a significant degree, economically. While the Muslim ruling class may have encouraged a wealthy merchant class, wage labor and intense commodity production during the prosperous nineteenth century, neither of these practices nor the merchant class challenged the hegemony of the *jihadi* state. In order to answer those classic materialist questions, one must conceptualize state and ideological structures as deeply embedded in and not separated from the specifically economic structures. The state and ideological structures of the Sokoto Caliphate determined the specific forms of extra-economic coercion and means of surplus extraction which distinguished it as a particular precapitalist mode of production.

Just as before the *jihad*, the basic unit of production remained the household employing mostly family, some slave and occasionally wage labor. Yet the formation of the Sokoto Caliphate and the application of the *Shari'a* altered the social division of labor especially in the areas of exchange and consumption and to some degree at the level of production. Under the obligation of *jihad* against resistant non-Muslim communities, state officials expanded the productive territory of the Caliphate with the establishment of *ribats*. Here they incorporated as slave producers both skilled and unskilled laborers who, by assuming responsibility for much of the arduous agricultural labor, freed the skilled talakawa to pursue more productive and lucrative tasks. Hence the military activities of the state had a direct material effect on the parameters and scale of agricultural production, the size of the internal market and the skill and size of the labor force. Also, the surpluses in currency and in kind extracted from the talakawa by the sarauta had the effect of increasing the circulation of commodities within the Caliphate for, like slaves, surpluses were sold on the open market.

In Kano, moreover, it is certain that the emirate pursued a fiscal policy that had the effect, presumably intentional, of encouraging productive activity. Land taxes were not fixed but depended upon access to a market; in order to encourage cultivation, valuable land such as that used for wheat production was taxed annually according to its potential productivity, irrespective of whether wheat was grown on the plot.[28] Most importantly, with the exception of dye pits and smithing, craft production was not taxed. Shea interprets this fact as evidence for a state fiscal policy supporting the export-oriented textile industry by Kano Emirate.[29]

The symbiotic relationship between Islam and mercantile capitalism has been noted earlier.[30] The state promoted long-distance trading and the accumulation of merchant's capital. At the same time, the sarauta, together with their dependants and clients, constituted an enormous market for common and luxury goods carried by the merchants. Sarauta activities, such as tribute, the cementing of political alliances, the rituals of office and the maintenance of the sarauta lifestyle, required large numbers of gowns, turbans, leather products and imported luxury goods. At the same time, among the talakawa and the non-Muslim population, those who wished to enter trade discovered that participation in the symbolic piety and rituals of

Islamic organizations such as brotherhoods brought material rewards. In a society lacking efficient policing organizations and credit control mechanisms, where long-distance trade required the allocation of wealth for months if not years before repayment or profits, Islamic rituals and brotherhoods maintained social control over debtors. When traveling beyond their own community, Muslim traders depended upon *ulema*-controlled networks for commercial information and introductions into new communities, for establishing their credit-worthiness and for access to literate scribes, Islamic judges and introductions to political authorities. Hence the movement for Islamic reform, the obligations and material needs of the Islamic state and the Muslim entrepreneurial preference for commerce over fixed investments in land or capital goods all converged so as to create a mutually supportive relationship between Islamization and mercantile capitalism.

Because of *Shari'a*'s support for private property, commodity production and inheritance rights for sons and daughters in a nuclear family, Islamization is correlated reciprocally with mercantile capitalism. Conversion, therefore, involves obvious material benefits besides tax-reductions. To convert to Islam in a serious way requires that rural producers abstain from the brewing and consumption of beer. Islamization, therefore, increased the supply of grain surpluses, from the reduction of beer brewing, available for regional trade by dry-season peasant-traders (*fatauci*). Conversion to Islam increased the demand for woven cotton cloth to be used for gowns and turbans and for clothing women in accordance with the norms of Islamic modesty. Islamization stimulated the production and marketing of rams for ritual purposes (naming ceremonies, festivals, etc.), a service that was provided by nomadic Fulani and Tuareg herdsmen who had supported the *jihad* or had migrated into the Caliphate subsequently. Note that animal husbandry increased in this period, thus creating an ample supply of transport animals, raw material for the leather handicraft industry and long-distance trade in leather goods, which was second in importance after textiles. Since the puritanical standards of *jihadi* Islam discouraged the use of stimulants other than the kola nut, the growth of kola nut consumption stimulated the expansion of merchant capitalist networks, mostly from Kano, across West Africa and into the Asante kingdom (Ghana), where kola nuts were purchased in exchange for Kano's handicrafts, salt, natron and cattle.

The material consequences of the *jihad* are most evident in the domain of mercantile capitalism, luxury good and craft production and appropriate styles of Muslim consumption such as the choice of kola nut over beer. But the intensification of Islamic practices also affected household agricultural production. Land, for example, was allocated by the Muslim state to free peasants and to officials and clients of the state in order to establish slave estates which brought bush and marginal lands into cultivation. Islamic scholarship, necessary for the reproduction of the Muslim state, also

20

contributed to peasant household security and the labor requirements of craft production destined for the caravans of Muslim mercantile capitalists. Inspired by Fodio's injunction that Islamic learning be extended to all, a tradition of wandering Islamic scholars evolved which linked towns and countryside.[31] Scholars were supported by alms from the rural communities for a limited period of time in exchange for teaching village children and ministering to the spiritual or ritual needs of the community. Students varying in age from children to young adults attached themselves to a peripatetic mallam and accompanied him as he traveled to villages, along trade routes and even into large cities such as Kano. Finally, ecology and material existence bolstered this Islamic network. By drawing children and youths from the villages to centers of trade and, perhaps, to dry-season agriculture, precious food was conserved for household workers during the rainy season, thus contributing to the reproduction of the basic unit of production.

To support themselves through the obligation of almsgiving, students (*almajirai*) possessed craft or trading skills acquired at home or during their wandering that enabled them to function as a surplus labor category in centers of dry-season economic activity. Shea refers to them as a 'floating labor pool' because they were available at a cheap price relative to the cost of clientage among craft workers. *Almajirai* could be employed in menial tasks assisting craftsmen or as skilled craftsmen in the indigo-dyeing industry where, typically, an unexpected demand for dyed cloth from a caravan or trader increased the demand for a surplus labor category. Indeed, Shea cites an example from Sudawa ward in Kano City where a mallam established a dyeing center (pits) in order to provide employment for his *almajirai*.

Space does not permit a complete elaboration of the ways in which the Muslim state and the process of *Shari'aization* altered and transformed economic processes and relations of production. The extension of literacy in the last example shows how Islamization contributed to Muslim mercantile capitalism; literacy is necessary for keeping accounts, allocating credit and for the rational calculation of profit. An effective if cumbersome monetary system did exist, consisting of gold, Maria Teresa dollars and cowry shells.[32]

Kano: urban society and rural linkages

All precapitalist social formations are predominantly agrarian and rural. Caliphal society was composed of hierarchically organized layers of hamlets, villages, towns and cities, with Sokoto functioning as the religio-political apex and Kano as the economic apex. Within this hierarchy, socially produced surplus flowed from countryside to city while political power and ideology flowed in the opposite direction. The division of labor between city and countryside distinguished each but did not isolate them from each other. Craft production, in particular, integrated rural and urban areas.

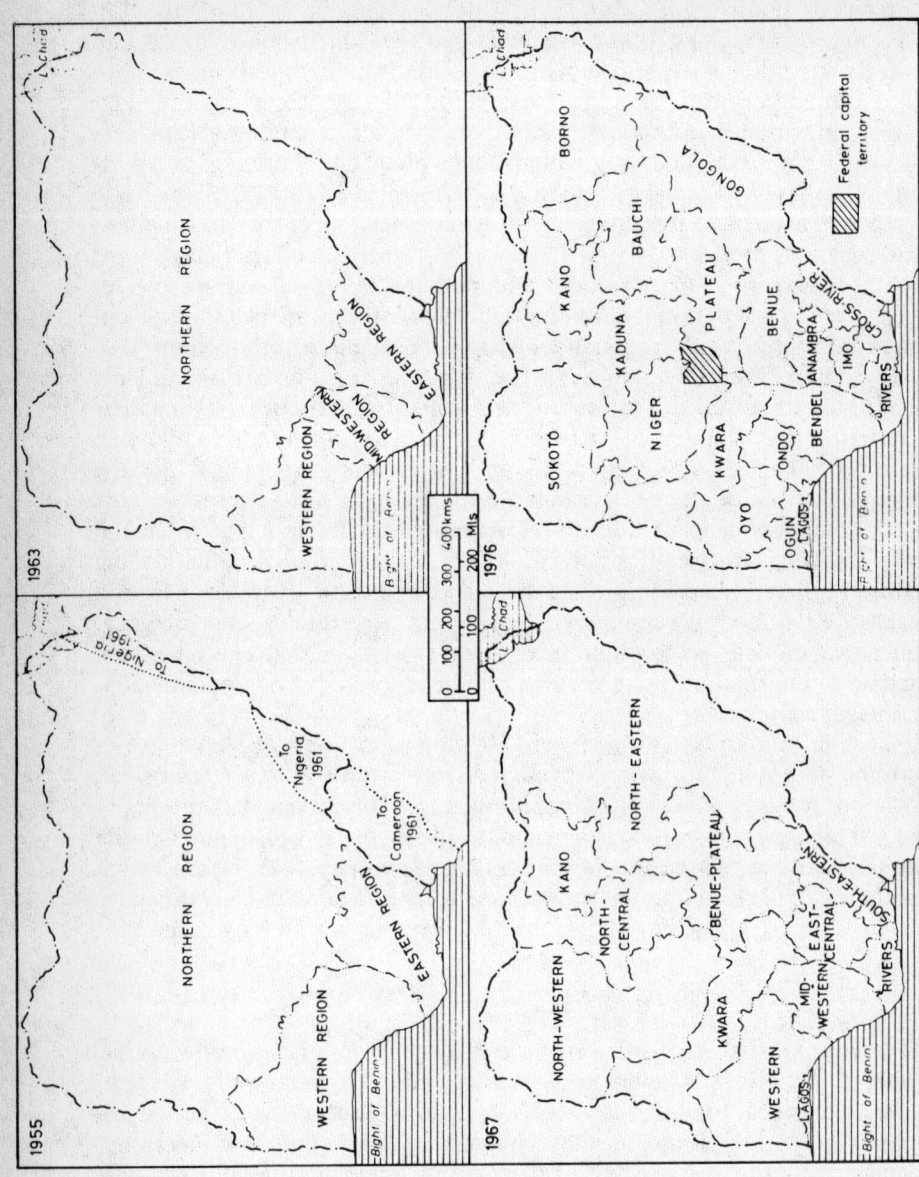

SOURCE: Barbour et al. (1982), p.39

Administrative divisions of Nigeria, 1955–1976

22

Though a walled city functioning as a fortress and political center, Kano served as the financial and commercial center of the Caliphate in that it possessed the most advanced merchant class.[33] The sarauta–talakawa cleavage was reproduced spatially because the wards of the city were segregated by occupation, region or ethnicity. Each ward had a wardhead appointed by the emir. Compared to urban communities of Western Europe, autonomous corporations were unknown,[34] for there was no intermediate, autonomous body that acted between the community and the emir. Thus, no corporate group checked the centralized authority of the emir. The only legitimate check on illegitimate action rested with the *ulema*, whose support was required before implementing controversial policies. Here the sarauta–talakawa cleavage was also obvious. The sarauta controlled judicial, Islamic studies as well as administration and military offices while the talakawa engaged in commerce, craft production and farming. The talakawa specialized in Muslim law, in order to bolster their claims for protection against illegal seizures (*wasau*) by the followers of sarauta households. At the same time, the sarauta of Kano valued their merchant class, the productivity of craft producers and the prosperity that they brought to the emirate.

Merchants and Muslim mercantile capitalism

Kano's geographical location meant that, more than other emirates, it was protected from invasions and border warfare. Together with encouragement from the emirate's fiscal policies, this location encouraged Muslim merchants to settle in Birnin Kano. Barth's (1851) comment that the combination of trade and handicraft production was responsible for Kano's prosperity may be true. But because recent research has emphasized the rural location of much of Kano's handicraft production, one is on surer ground if one emphasizes the entrepôt and commercial function of urban Kano and its linkages to centers of rural craft production. As a commercial center, urban Kano surely had no rival, for its preeminence rested upon three levels of commercial intercourse: (1) as the southern terminus of the trans-Saharan trade and the northern trade in salt, grain, leather and indigo-dyed cloth; (2) as the entrepôt for the West African regional trade, especially for the kola trade to Asante but also for the natron trade with Borno and the southern and eastern trade with Yoruba states and central Africa; and (3) as a center for local trade in handicrafts, foodstuffs and export-oriented cloth and leather products from within Kano and the adjacent emirates. The latter trade was determined more by location on trade routes and environmental factors (water sources) than by the political boundaries of the emirates. Since trade on all three levels flowed through Kano, merchants active at any one level could purchase goods from another level, at wholesale prices, for trans-shipment into their own trading networks. Moreover, given the constraints presented by the awkward and inflated cowry currency, which often necessitated exchange of goods or

23

slaves whose value was calculated in cowries, the wide choice of goods available at Kano reinforced its natural advantages as the Caliphate's unrivaled center of Muslim mercantile capitalism. When one examines the more successful merchant capitalists, one encounters diversified entrepreneurial activities: long-distance trading ventures organized by clients, which could last for years before realizing a profit; the financing and brokerage of short-term and local ventures; the production or processing of commodities valued for long-distance trade, such as leather products and indigo-dyed cloth, in a production process that involved combinations of wage, slave and household labor; and, by acting as landlords, the financing and management of trading activities for alien traders. Further, though evidence is poor, merchants also may have accumulated through hoarding and usury. If a merchant developed a close relationship with the emir or his powerful officials through gift giving (*gaisuwa* or *girma da arziki*), then he could gain access to land, settle his slaves and produce for his household as well as for the market. Though this last practice was common, the relative insecurity of landed property granted through a personal relationship with political authority, the high death duties (50 percent) levied by the state and the tendency of Maliki laws of inheritance to fragment property all mitigated against any secular tendency for the merchant class to become a land-owning, commodity-producing class. Indeed, for a Muslim merchant, long-distance trade was preferred since it not only involved liquid assets but also because portable property was more secure from state confiscation than land or industrial-fixed assets.

As the term Muslim mercantile capitalism suggests, Islamic institutions were crucial for the expansion and prosperity of Kano's merchant class whose religious authority was personified in the office of *Baban Mallamai* of Madabo ward.[35] Islamic networks are the key to understanding the integrity and social relations of Muslim mercantile capitalism. Faced with the monopoly of political power by the sarauta, the talakawa merchants mobilized as political resources Islamic law, brotherhoods and styles of life such as undertaking the *hajj*, as well as the sponsorship of Islamic scholarship and mosques. The talakawa *ulema* not only strengthened credit relations, met ritual needs in the form of astrological services and provided literate accounting services, but in situations of warring magistrates, they could arrange safe passage for merchants' caravans. Acting together, *ulema* networks complemented and sometimes overlapped with those of the merchant class.

CRAFT PRODUCTION: NETWORKS, CLASS CONFLICT AND THE LIMITS OF DIFFERENTIATION

Craft production occurred during the dry season within a household unit of production, mostly in rural centers that were linked to caravan routes or to cities. The fear of famine, the limitations of agrarian technique and the short rainy season forced most craft producers to farm during the rainy season. This was an obvious barrier to increased specialization in the social division of labor. Nonetheless Kano's dense mercantile networks, its dry-season water resources (e.g. dyeing), its intensely cultivated lands and its skilled population attracted investment and thus created a transportation-cost advantage for craft production to locate in the southern Kano-Zaria region. The portrait that emerges is one of intense, commodity production in numerous and highly specialized craft production centers, with slaves and non-Muslims engaging in unskilled labor and food production, while the Muslim talakawa specialized in skilled handicraft and commercial occupations. Both rural and urban handicraft production centers were integrated by Muslim mercantile capitalist networks to markets extending across the Caliphate to North and West Africa.

Two craft industries stand out from the others: the indigo-dyed textile and the blacksmithing industries.[36] Fortunately, Shea's original work illuminates the changes that occurred in the textile industry during the nineteenth century. He documents, for example, the change from smaller dye pots to larger dye pits in response to increases in demand and in accordance with the logic of economies of scale. The social organization of production also changed during the course of the century in a way that complemented the technical innovation represented by the choice of dye pits over dye pots. According to Shea, by the end of the century dye pits were bought, sold, and rented as commodities. But more importantly, 'wealthy businessmen not only owned ten or more dyepits but . . . also owned all of the cloth dyed in these pits . . . and had large guest houses' where these merchant capitalists financed, entertained clients and transacted the cloth business.[37] By the end of the century, therefore, merchant capitalists had achieved a high degree of integration involving the production of raw material, weaving, dyeing and sales of the cloth. Shea notes: 'wage labor became more and more important and capital equipment was increasingly owned by people other than those who used it.'[38] Just as one would expect where merchant capital begins to own the means of production and displaces independent producers, class conflict erupted in the dyeing center of Kura over the piecework price that dyers would be paid by merchants for dyeing the latters' cloth. As a result, merchant capitalists withdrew their support from the Kura dyers and sent their cloth elsewhere to be dyed. Here is a clear example of embryonic class conflict erupting between merchant capital and handicraft labor, one which is quite exceptional for precolonial Africa.[39]

While indigo-dyed textile production lacked craft organization of any significance and was subsumed under the control of merchant's capital by the end of the century, blacksmithing exhibits a very different pattern. Since ironworking and blacksmithing were necessary for the defense of the state it is not surprising that an office (*Sarkin Makera*) was established by the Emir, that the *Sarkin Makera* possessed a slave estate on rather valuable land in the peri-urban area and that the urban-based blacksmiths, while personally exempted from taxation, collected a tax in-kind from their rural counterparts.[40] Hence this craft association was neither autonomous nor self-

25

governing but rather an apparatus created by a centralized state for tax collection and defense. The labor process of production was based upon the individual household, and only under exceptional circumstances would the smiths cooperate on a large-scale project such as defense or a large order of weapons from the palace. Thus the blacksmiths became artisan-clients of the state, replete with several offices appointed by the Emir. Again, Shea argues that by establishing an office complete with a slave estate and by exempting urban blacksmiths from taxation, Kano Emirate pursued a policy of protecting and encouraging crafts that were necessary for security and prosperity.

As the most technically and economically sophisticated emirate, Kano exhibited the most advanced features of Muslim mercantile capitalism. These included credit and long distance trading, craft production based upon free, slave and wage labor as well as incidents of class conflict and a state administration that encouraged commodity production and merchant capital accumulation. Slavery co-existed with wage labor. Indeed through the system of *murgu* a slave could ransom himself or pay a flat fee to his master in order to trade or sell his labor to another. Yet, on the eve of the British conquest, both ecological, political and ideological constraints appear to have dampened any transition to deeper forms of capitalism along the lines of early modern Europe or Tokugawa Japan. In addition to those constraints derived from Muslim law, transportation costs, for example, were a major limit to the circulation of commodities and thus the accumulation of capital.

Incorporation and resistance: Mahdism

Once British troops conquered the Caliphate and killed the Caliph with 600 followers at Burmi (1903), the fate of Muslim northern Nigeria was inextricably linked to that of southern Nigeria. Yet the processes of incorporation into the capitalist world economy were very different in the south. The latter had participated in the slave and palm oil trade; returned 'Saro' slaves acted as missionaries and as a 'proto-bourgeoisie'; and while Kano was under siege, a railway was being constructed between Lagos and Ibadan, the south's largest city. The gradual incorporation of the south through informal empire and Christian missionaries, contrasted sharply with the incorporation of the Sokoto Caliphate. Instead, it was swift, violent and resisted.[41]

As argued earlier, from the northern Muslim perspective the British were Christian invaders who had conquered the Muslim states of India and Egypt. Throughout the crisis of incorporation, the invaders were always described as Christians by the authorities. The question remained: what was the appropriate response? After refusing to sign treaties that would have transferred and thus debased the sovereignty of the Muslim state according to the *Shari'a*, the ruling groups chose to flee to the east toward Mecca in search of the promised Mahdi. Mahdism is based on the belief that the end of the world is imminent (e.g. a profound crisis) and that a redeemer will appear to defend Islamdom and to establish a period of peace and justice just prior to the end of the world. Similar Mahdist uprisings occurred in Ghana, the Caucasus, the Anglo-Egyptian Sudan and Algeria.

After pursuing the Caliph who resisted until death, the British experienced both talakawa and sarauta resistance to their rule. Once they established rival lineages in power as emirs who accepted the authority (e.g. protectorate status) of the British, Mahdism again erupted (1906) at the village of Satiru near Sokoto. In fact, successive village heads had declared themselves Mahdi in 1904 and again in 1906. After the first uprising was put down, the second actually defeated the British force, killing the British Resident and two other officers along with 25 mounted cavalry. Losses also included rifles and a maxim gun to the rebels. Of course, since the railway was only completed to Kano in 1912, the fear of a generalized Muslim insurrection under a Mahdist movement alarmed the British so they asked for aid from their newly appointed emirs of Zaria, Bauchi, Bida and Kano. Though not asked to do so, the latter emirs sent cavalry forces who, together with British forces, killed the entire population of the village. By 1906, the emirs recognized the advantage of collaboration with their new overlords just as earlier they had feared that their 'subjects and people who are within the boundaries of our land would certainly throw off their allegiance to us on hearing the news' of the British conquest.[42] The obvious point here is that the class cleavage of sarauta-talakawa was foremost in the minds of the ruling class even when the crisis had provoked a reactive wave of Muslim nationalism against the Christian conquerors. M. G. Smith's interpretation supports this view: 'Thus revolt at Satiru changed relations between the British and the ruling Fulani from superordination based upon force to near parity based upon common interests.'[43]

COMMON INTERESTS, AND RULING CLASS ALLIANCE

These 'common interests', of course, cemented a class alliance that gave the British a peaceful colonial order, revenues to fund the colonial state, an experienced, ruthless yet comparatively inexpensive administrative class and, for metropolitan economic interests, markets for surplus industrial exports as well as raw materials in the form of groundnuts, cotton and tin. In return for their loyalty to the colonial state, the new sarauta-administrators, who were drawn from rival lineages, received a salaried office, the technical and military support of the most powerful state in the world at that time and the opportunity to exploit and to dominate the talakawa in a myriad of ways both old and new. One key to understanding this transition is contained in the British pledge not to interfere with the practices of the Islamic religion nor with the sacred prerogatives of Muslim office, except for particularly outrageous practices such as 'slave-raiding' and the slave trade. In practice, the sarauta defined virtually all of their prerogatives as Islamic, thus assuring the continued, though now technically superior, modes of domination and exploitation over the talakawa, but without the traditional checks on the

27

abuses of office. Indeed, under the British, Muslim district heads were forced upon non-Muslim ethnic groups who had successfully resisted the raids of the nineteenth century. Also important for the integration of the Muslim ruling class in the Northern Region was the incorporation of Borno, an older Muslim state that had resisted the *jihad*, into the emirate system of colonial northern Nigeria. And finally, under the agreement that initiated the class alliance, the British blocked any Christian proselytization in Muslim areas, a practice that was undoubtedly popular and legitimate but also had the consequence of eliminating for the talakawa virtually any opportunity to acquire western education. The ability of the sarauta to manipulate the domain of Islamic practice and interpretation gave them great leverage over the 'Christian' colonial administrators, who always feared a Muslim-inspired uprising.

Conscious of the same class contradictions represented by the talakawa and the slaves of the sarauta, Lord Lugard's solution was to formulate a policy of indirect rule which he hoped would lower the cost of administration in the eyes of the colonial office. At the same time as he was concerned about the cost of administration, Lugard was anxious over the material welfare of the sarauta as a ruling class. The pressing question concerned the status of slavery and in particular the economic dependence of the sarauta on farm slavery. Allegedly, the justification of conquest was to abolish slave-raiding, trading and slavery in general, but Lugard feared that wholesale emancipation of the sarauta's slaves 'would create a state of anarchy and chaos ... [that] would dislocate the whole social framework of the Moslem states and result in pauperizing and destroy the ruling class which it was the object of Government to preserve and strengthen'.[44] Accordingly, in order to strengthen the class alliance that would direct Nigeria well into the period of formal independence, Lugard discouraged 'wholesale assertion of freedom' and instructed his colonial officers to refuse to grant land to runaway slaves.[45] To be sure, while slavery as a large scale system of labor control gradually declined because of the abolition of slave-raiding and trading, M. G. Smith's re-analysis of Rowling's evidence on land tenure shows that as late as 1949 descendants of slaves worked on lands formerly belonging to an officeholder in order to gain access to land for their private cultivation, i.e. a form of sharecropping maintained by extra-economic coercion.[46]

The taxation of export crops (cotton and groundnuts) and the community tax became the new source of revenue for the colonial state. Here the sarauta were quick to grasp the importance of export income among the peasantry for it provided the specie to pay taxes. Certainly, the sarauta maintained actual control over the peasantry no matter what the intentions of the benign British administrator. Given the scarcity of European administrators to rule over an extensive and densely settled area, the responsibility for day-to-day administration was carried out by indigenous officials of the Native Authority (N.A.). For example, for a population numbering over two and one-half million in Kano Emirate, the normal complement of European administrators was eleven; during World War II the number fell as low as five.[47] Moreover, whenever a resident or colonial officer went on tour, he was accompanied by a representative of the emir, so it was unlikely that N.A. abuses would be reported by the talakawa in front of the emir's representative. M. G. Smith's account of Zaria about 1950 confirms the existence of widespread extortion, corruption and 'fear and awe' on the part of the talakawa toward the aristocracy 'even where they are not remote from British administrative centres'.[48] Even if well-intentioned colonial officers developed the linguistic, cultural and political skills necessary to entrap Native Authority officials in the acts of corruption their number was too few, and their dependence upon the sarauta for administration too strong to effect any significant relief for the talakawa. Corruption, moreover, was necessary to supplement the income of the officeholders who were threatened by the rising wealth of the merchant class.

The class alliance necessary for administering indirect rule along 'native lines' required the extraction of labor through extra-economic coercion well into the independence period. Indeed, it was one of the central organizing issues promoted by the talakawa political party, the Northern (Nigerian) Elements Progressive Union (NEPU). Ignoring for a moment the travesty of western ideals that this policy represented, one cannot emphasize enough how the class alliance strengthened the coercive hold of the sarauta while increasing the burdens borne by the talakawa. This burden of extra-economic coercion and associated fears for life and property carried during the colonial period, weigh heavily on the consciousness of Kano's urban working class especially those recently emigrating from the authoritarian countryside.

Corruption by the Native Authority administrators was an unrelieved theme in the memoirs and reports of the British officials. It included: using forced labor on sarauta farms, absconding with wages intended for N.A. laborers, holding back tax receipts, using state revenues to speculate on export crops, engaging in usury in collusion with merchant capitalists and simply extorting money from fearful talakawa peasants.[49] The illegitimacy of the colonial state, undoubtedly, contributed to the scale of corruption since a Muslim patrimonial official could hardly be expected to uphold the standards of a Christian administration imposed by force.

Education of the sons of the ruling class was deemed to offer a solution to corruption and maladministration. But universal education and worse still, the acceptance of Christian missionaries, was unacceptable for it would undermine the Muslim aristocracy, educate the talakawa and thus threaten the stability of the ruling class alliance. After a debate over whether traditional Islamic education or modern western education should be implemented, the latter was chosen albeit in the gentry tradition of an English public school where elite sports (polo, rounds and fives) and gentlemanly habits were encouraged. By 1920, therefore, criticism of the traditional Islamic education forced the founding of Katsina Training College, an institution which, after some early resistance, reproduced the next generation of

29

sarauta. With a mandate to teach the sons of the aristocracy 'to rule along native lines', Katsina Training College (now Barewa College, Kaduna) practised gross ethnic, class and religious discrimination: between 1921 and 1936 not a single non-Muslim was admitted even though non-Muslims comprised an estimated one-third of the population of the northern provinces; between 1921 and 1931, 68 percent of students admitted were sons of N.A. officials; and as late as 1939, the British resident of Niger Province complained that Katsina should not allow boys of 'good birth' to be 'elbowed out' by clever students of peasant origin.[50] Hubbard's work on this subject documents the class bias and gentry origins and/or aspirations of the education officers who implemented these policies. Finally it is important to emphasize that the class alliance was a step backward in educational opportunity for the majority of the Northern Region's population, compared to the precolonial, Islamic system.

THE COLONIAL ECONOMY: EXPORT CROPS, STATE REVENUE AND PEASANT HOUSEHOLDS

Unlike white settler or mineral exporting colonies, neither the sarauta nor the peasantry were displaced by the colonial state. Under indirect rule, however, the colonial state had to reproduce both the export sector to meet the needs of metropolitan interests, while at the same time, reproducing the peasantry at a minimal level of subsistence. The class alliance required the sarauta to mediate between the colonial state and the peasantry. Early during the colonial period, Lugard's suggestion that the sarauta be transformed into a land-holding gentry with a tenant class of peasant producers was rejected out of fear of producing landlessness and social instability. Instead, the views of Temple and Girouard prevailed. Land was nationalized under the control of the colonial state. This decision had immense consequences for colonial capitalism.

By vesting land in the state rather than defining land as a marketable commodity to be bought and sold in densely populated areas like Kano during the precapitalist period, colonial policy blocked agrarian capitalism as an avenue for accumulation for either the merchant class or the sarauta. Instead the sarauta's main source of income derived from the taxation and illegal exploitation of an impoverished peasantry whose productivity and technical capacity stagnated. Thus, as a result of this decision, the control of state office, the extortion of talakawa producers and the bilking of state coffers (rather than productive investment in agriculture or industry), were the only available routes to wealth or accumulation for the new administrative class. Hence, the land tenure guaranteed the hegemony of merchant capital in the economy of northern Nigeria. The articulation of these two modes through indirect rule required that the colonial state first guarantee the accumulation of capital, via merchant capital in this instance, in favor of the interests of the accumulating classes of the British state and in accordance with the constraints imposed by the capitalist world economy. Meanwhile, the colonial state was required to build an infrastructure such as railways and motor roads to transport export crops; to maintain social and economic services for the small enclave of international firms (e.g. Unilever) and Levantine residents; to finance the political-administrative and minimal social services for the colonized population; and to collect sufficient revenue to reproduce materially the colonial state.

At the onset of colonial rule therefore, capitalism, in the form of mercantile capital subordinated to industrial capital in the metropole, was but a thin veneer superimposed upon a transformed yet largely intact Muslim Hausa social formation. The relationship (i.e. articulation) between these two modes of production – precapitalist and capitalist – involved the conservation, dissolution and reinforcement of certain aspects of the precapitalist social formation with regard to production and exchange, political relations and culture, especially Islam. Hence, for the colonial state it was an awesome responsibility to reproduce a social formation containing a precapitalist mode that was, at the same time, subordinated to the needs of an externally controlled capitalist mode. The colonial state's situation was one replete with contradictions, self-deception and human misery.

Until recent research documented the high cost paid by the talakawa for their participation in colonial export crop production. Hogendorn's sanguine analysis of the effects of the groundnut trade on Hausa society established the orthodox view.[51] Hogendorn's research emphasizes the importance of the railway in overcoming the transportation constraint which had truly limited growth in the precolonial economy. Local initiative on the part of peasants and merchants determined that groundnuts rather than cotton, in spite of the efforts of the British Cotton Growing Association, would become the basic export staple for northern Nigeria. Following a theory advanced by Myint, Hogendorn argues that the northern Nigerian groundnut trade was relatively costless, since the railway allowed access to the world market for peasant production and thus represented a 'vent for surplus' in which the peasants employed surplus labor and land to export groundnuts to the world economy.[52] The implied argument herein is that the peasantry voluntarily substituted income for previous forms of leisure and thus benefited materially, yet without altering existing levels of subsistence production and the material security of the peasant household.

Recent research by Watts and Shenton simply demolishes this naive neoclassical analysis of the colonial groundnut economy.[53] In opposition to Hogendorn's view, they argue that groundnut and, to a lesser degree, cotton exports subjected the peasant household to the ecological and food scarcity crises inherent in a precapitalist economy as well as to those arising from dependence upon income from exports to a cyclical world market. Their evidence and argument rests upon several interrelated factors. To summarize, Watts analyzes the peasant household during the precapitalist and colonial capitalist eras in order to show that the land and labor invested in

31

the production of export crops greatly increased risks to the simple reproduction of the peasant household. In order to understand why this was true, the effect of the colonial state's taxation policy on the household must be factored into the analysis. That is, the political and economic conditions of peasant production must be analyzed as a totality. Export crops were grown in order to pay newly imposed colonial taxes, which were collected *prior* to harvest in most instances. Thus the peasant was forced to sell export and grain crops during the time when prices were at their lowest or, worse, to mortgage them prior to harvest to a money lender. By monetizing the *zakkat* tax rather than collecting in-kind, the colonial state increased the real rate of taxation but decreased the local availability of grain (millet and sorghum). Whereas during the precolonial period the *zakkat* provided a grain reserve that could be distributed during cyclical drought and famine, no such reserve existed in the colonial era. Hence, peasants paid a higher proportion of the labor time and land allocations for taxes, and with increased cotton and groundnut exports, less of the cultivated land was used to produce food crops. Additional factors include the rigidity of the tax rate as compared to the flexibility of the precolonial period, and the arbitrary and unequal distribution of taxes by the N.A. officials. Clearly, the revenue needs of the colonial state forced the peasant to produce more export and grain crops for the market (i.e., exchange values) and less for household subsistence (i.e., use values).

Commodization of production, exchange and consumption, increases in debt and intensification of cultivation without increases in productive technique explain both the obvious poverty of the Hausa peasant and the deleterious consequences of the colonial export economy for household security. Watts, moreover, provides detailed descriptions of famines and rising food prices during the colonial era: for example, two years after the railway began exporting groundnuts from Kano, a drought occurred causing fatalities of 40,000 in Kano Province alone, 100,000 if migrants from Niger are included. Subsequent famines occurred during 1927, 1942–3 and 1950. Watts interprets the famine of 1927 as pivotal, for after that disaster, the peasantry no longer resisted production of cash crops for the world economy.[54] Consequently, the Hausa peasantry experienced greater commoditization of life, increased indebtedness and greater dependence on price fluctuations of the world economy.[55]

Driven by the revenue demands of the colonial state, by the scarcities inherent in the ecology and by the eroding tentacles of merchant capitalism, the peasant household had no choice but to produce for the world economy with all the insecurity, instability and dependency that such involvement portends. If one surveys the evidence for the peasant's production response to world market prices, one is struck by the fact that when the terms of trade shifted against the direct producers, as in the depression of the thirties, peasant production of groundnuts and cotton increased significantly.[56] Under the burden of taxation and debt, therefore, peasants were forced to produce export crops for cash, often to the neglect of household subsistence crops, but the vicissitudes of the world market meant that they became increasingly impoverished by shifts in the terms of trade against the peasant.

As a result of this devastating trio – colonial taxation policies, cyclical natural crises usually arising from a fragile and increasingly overburdened ecology, and subordination to international and local merchant capitalists who linked peasants to the crises of the world market – the material situation of the rural talakawa declined precipitously. What were the long-term consequences? Famine, mortality, increased indebtedness, labor migration and increased involvement in commodity production have already been mentioned. But new assaults on the autonomy of the peasant household followed: increased commoditization of land through leasing, pledging, sharecropping and disguised forms of land sales. All evidence indicates that the extended household production unit, the *gandu*, was and continues to be in decline, largely due to commoditization, the inability of the household head to provide for dependents, and the fact that craft production gave way to labor migration.[57] Most importantly, the process of commoditization stimulated by this trio of factors generated increased and widespread differentiation within the Hausa village into clearly defined income groups measured in terms of land ownership, the commodification of bride price, the relationship to wage labor and access to capital and trading opportunities.[58] Accordingly, the consequences of these three destructive factors should be remembered when the patterns for labor migration to Kano are analyzed in Chapter Three.

Kano: urban development under colonial capitalism

Kano was unique among the Caliphate's urban centers, for while the incorporation of the region into the capitalist world economy altered regional patterns of trade and 'underdeveloped' the thriving handicraft manufacturing sector, the railway and the groundnut trade enabled Kano to retain its role as the region's unrivaled economic center.[59] Nonetheless, under colonialism, motor roads connected with railway centers in such a way that precolonial urban networks were radically altered. Although the groundnut and cotton export economy eventually (though not immediately in the case of cotton cloth) destroyed the vitality of Kano's handicraft manufacturing sector and forced many rural producers to migrate for work during the dry season, urban Kano did benefit significantly from the colonial economy. Rather than absorbing merchants' capital for months or years before realizing a profit from long-distance trade, the railway revolutionized the time necessary to complete a circuit of capital, since the one-way to Lagos took as little as fifty-four hours rather than several months. Further, bolstered by the decline of rival urban centers, the siting of British colonial administrative and technical departments and the commercial growth afforded by the groundnut economy, Kano became the most populous and most commercially advanced city as well as the wealthiest Native Authority in the Northern Region.

British policy toward the urban administration of Kano followed from the dual-mandate dogmas derived from indirect rule.[60] Accordingly, the city was divided between the jurisdictions of the Native Authority and the Township. The walled city, the Birni, and Fagge, a walled area formerly used as a caravan and warehousing service center outside the Birni, were administered by the N.A. Meanwhile, the Township was organized on the principle of racial segregation to include Bompai and Nasarawa for European settlement; Fagge TaKudu or Syrian Quarters for alien Arabs who were mostly traders, and Sabon Gari for non-native Africans (e.g., Christian southern Nigerians). Though it is true that Kano's Muslim community wished to remain undisturbed and separate from alien and non-Muslim residents, British policy institutionalized racial, ethnic and class segregation patterns that have largely endured into the semi-industrial era (see Chapter Four).

During the colonial period, the physical and social organization of the Birni changed little: wards were rationalized as tax collection units; a market and a new mosque as well as the emir's palace were constructed; and some sanitation improvements were made, such as piped water and drainage. Outside the Birni (Waje), the demand for literate and skilled labor enabled Sabon Gari to grow as a residential area for southern Nigerians and to provide liquor, entertainment and brothels for the urban population at large. British policies which ossified Islamic institutions to preserve the 'traditional' not only blocked the development of an urban land market but, by following strict segregation of Nigerian ethnic groups, actually contributed to the ethnic animosities and riots that took place in Kano during 1953 and 1966. After the first of these riots, Sabon Gari residents of northern origin were moved eastward to a village called Gwagwarwa, which became identified with migrant ethnic groups, both Christian and Muslim, originating from the Northern Region. By 1959, this area expanded into the village known as Gawuna (now Gamar Tudu), and a new similarly constituted social area was created by compensating the peasants and allocating rather than selling plots to those who qualified on ethnic criteria. Earlier, in 1940, Tudun Wada was established as a residential area for soldiers and retired Native Authority laborers (see Chapter Four). And finally, prior to independence, two industrial estates were established: the first to the east of Sabon Gari within the township, and the second at Bompai.

Throughout this period land remained controlled by the state. Plots were allocated through personal networks, by auction or to those who could prove that they possessed the resources for improvements. In theory, only the improvements, and not the land, were sold, although a secondary land market for plots once allocated did develop. Besides being yet another example of British paternalism that blocked the development of capitalist relations of production and reinforced ethnic antagonisms, the land policy also strengthened the position of the sarauta, who used their control over land to maintain leverage over the rising financial power of the merchant capitalist class.[61]

Islam and merchant capital: The rise of the urban bourgeoisie

Though less visible than the alliance between the sarauta and colonial administrator, a parallel class alliance evolved between representatives of international firms and the Muslim merchant capitalist class around the import-export trade.[62] Indigenous merchant capital expanded rapidly during the colonial era. Initially involved in the groundnut trade, international competition deflected it to the kola, cattle and food trade until the end of World War II, when they garnered their share of licensed buying agents from the Groundnut Marketing Board (established 1939). Meanwhile, indigenous merchant capital continued to distribute imported cloth, salt and necessities to peasant consumers. From the very beginning of colonial rule then, Kano's merchant capitalist class expanded in number and economic strength so as to represent a new social force in the political life of the emirate. By the end of the colonial era, moreover, Kano's bourgeoisie had gained membership on the emir's council, financed the Northern People's Congress (NPC) – which was but a political party expression of the Native Authority and the sarauta class – and exercised their new political power in order to advance the economic interests of the northern bourgeoisie.[63]

In order to comprehend the transformation of the bourgeoisie and their subsequent rise to dominance during military rule, one must discover how they were able to overcome obstacles to obtaining formal political power, specifically those arising from the sarauta's claim that Islamic law and tradition legitimized their monopoly of political power and office. The answer does not lie in the vulgar materialist interpretation that the bourgeoisie purchased high office, for even though the sarauta became increasingly involved in mercantile activity, the process is far more complex. The colonial state too, played a role as broker to the marriage of political and economic power. For instance, in his memoirs, appropriately entitled *But Always As Friends*, then Resident Sharwood-Smith describes in detail his efforts to convince the emir and his advisors to appoint the Alhassan Dantata, the undisputed leader of Kano's bourgeoisie, to the Emirate Council.[64] According to Tahir, the appointment of Dantata presaged a 'bourgeois revolution' through which the merchant industrialist fraction of the bourgeoisie would achieve political hegemony during the era of military rule, when, for example, merchants from talakawa origins would displace titled aristocrats and form a majority on the Emirate Council (1973).

Given the prestige of the sarauta, how does one explain the legitimacy of the merchant capitalist's entry into political and religious life? The changing role and use of Islamic institutions provides an explanation. Both Tahir and Paden marshal much evidence to show that the Tijaniyya brotherhood transformed Islamic ritual and social practice in Kano during the colonial period.[65] Paden argues that *sufi* rituals and brotherhood organization allowed multi-ethnic forms of social participation to develop across ethnic

35

groups and classes that had been isolated earlier. By offering a more materialist analysis from a Weberian perspective, Tahir's work charts the way in
which mercantile capitalist growth, the dramatic efflorescence of *sufi*
brotherhood participation (particularly in the Tijaniyya) and the contradiction inherent in the sarauta-colonial administrator class alliance converged to shift the balance of power in favor of the bourgeoisie and away from
the sarauta.

According to Tahir, Kano's merchant class opposed the aristocracy's
policy of passive resistance and class collaboration in favor of a traditional
Mahdist-*jihadi* ideology that advocated overt resistance to Christian
imperialism. This is exactly how the Tijaniyya had resisted French imperialism in the Senegal valley, and while the precise date of the introduction of
Tijani practice into Kano is debated by historians, there is no doubt that the
refugees from the Senegal valley arrived in Kano around the time of the
Christian conquest and thus reinforced the process of reactive Islamic
nationalism directed against British rule. The political ideology and practice
of the Tijaniyya strengthened the merchants' cultural resistance to imperialism and distinguished them from the aristocracy who tended to follow the
Qadiriyya during the early phases of colonial rule. Further, conversion to
the Tijaniyya sect also offered concrete material benefits to the wealthy but
status-deprived bourgeoisie. Note that the followers believe that Tijani
membership confers upon them a unique quality that assures economic
success. Hence this belief acts as a kind of Islamic analogue to Calvinism's
concept of 'the elect', such that religious belief and participation reinforce
capital accumulation.[66] The reorganization of mercantile capitalist activity
under colonial rule and the post-war use of modern banks, credit institutions
and joint stock companies were not blocked by Tijani leaders but, rather,
were encouraged and even personally guaranteed by Tijani mallams.
Apparently, economic liberalism did not contradict Islamic mysticism.
Hence, not only did the Tijaniyya provide – through its exclusivity, its
promise of economic success and its ritual networks – a cultural and organizational framework for the expansion and integration of the northern bourgeoisie centered at Kano, but it also gave the bourgeoisie sufficient autonomy from the cultural and religious hegemony of the aristocracy who were
associated with the British.

Moreover, throughout this period, despite the efforts of the British to
protect their allies – the sarauta – from the tradition-eroding influence of
capitalism, the bourgeoisie gradually became the dominant patrons of
Islamic institutional activity, a role that formerly belonged to the sarauta:
e.g., mosque building, supporting schools, paying *zakkat* to the *ulema* and
their students, sponsoring mallams and participating in the *hajj* to Mecca. By
the onset of the nationalist period, the Tijaniyya had become the dominant
sect in Kano, its membership including the Emir. Important linkages were
formed throughout Nigeria and even extended to the charismatic Shaiyk
Ibrahim Niasse of Koalack, Senegal.

THE TALAKAWA'S RESPONSE TO THE NATIONALIST MOVEMENT: NEPU
AND ISLAMIC POPULISM

In the face of the colonial class alliance's vision of a unified, 'holy', orderly and changeless north, Kano gave birth to a radical political movement that expressed talakawa nationalism. That Kano should be the center of radical, anti-imperialist, Islamic populism was predictable given the economic, social and religious changes that urban Kano experienced during colonialism. The city had grown from less than 40,000 to over 300,000 inhabitants by the military coup of 1966.[67] Not only had the talakawa-origin bourgeoisie emerged as both wealthy and powerful, but elements of a radical, petty bourgeois culture, clothed under the rubric of Islamic reform, were gaining influence among the urban traders, craftsmen, salaried employees and above all the talakawa *ulema*. What of the bourgeoisie? With few exceptions, because of their need for state patronage in the form of N.A. contracts, appointments as licensed buying agents and allocations of land and other state-controlled resources, the large-scale bourgeoisie had no choice but to support the NPC, thus aligning themselves with the sarauta.

The alliance of the leading members of the merchant bourgeoisie and the sarauta in the NPC marks the maturation of a fully developed social class system, one that became differentiated out of the class-like status-honor system that existed in the precapitalist social formation of the nineteenth century. Two structural processes explain the transition to a fully developed class system. First, the systematic intrusion of the revenue-hungry state into the lives of the talakawa, together with the unchecked abuses by the sarauta, created a shared sense of class deprivation among the increasingly integrated talakawa. This intrusion, moreover, was illegitimate in terms of Islamic culture, unchecked by traditional institutional mechanisms and unmediated by the complex web of privileges, exemptions and clientage relationships so characteristic of the nineteenth century, precapitalist social formation. Secondly, at the economic level, surplus-extraction by the sarauta, the colonial state and merchant capital compelled the peasantry to allocate land, labor and productive activity for the world market (e.g. exchange values), thus intensifying the process of commoditization in the areas of production, consumption, credit (usury) and labor. Equally important, the latter processes stimulated the geographical mobility of the talakawa via labor, Koranic and petty trading networks. In turn, such activities propelled peasants seasonally and permanently into towns where communication among formerly isolated and regionally distinct talakawa communities was intensified. Thus in towns and cities a radical Islamic and overtly political ideology had a radicalizing impact on the social consciousness of the talakawa. Bearing in mind the evidence cited earlier concerning usurous forms of debt, famine and the intensification of commodity relations, linked to a political system that exercised extra-economic coercion with impunity, it is not surprising that by the onset of the nationalist era economic differen-

37

tiation had created distinct economic strata within villages most integrated into the colonial export economy and/or the internal market economy.

However oppressed and exploited the rural talakawa might have been by these political and economic processes, it was in urban centers like Kano, Zaria and Gusau and in smaller towns situated along modern motor and rail roads where talakawa consciousness and the economic basis of class differentiation was most developed. Here, of course, NEPU was the strongest.[68] The relative openness of urban centers, where colonial officials checked the ruthlessness of N.A. police and thugs, allowed the intermediate layers of Hausa society – traders, tailors, Koranic teachers, bicycle repairers, teachers, clerks, civil servants and employees of international firms – to form a leadership cadre and to organize a broadly based talakawa social movement whose organizational expression was NEPU.

As the center of the colonial export economy, Kano's differentiated occupational structure, its commercial superiority, exemplified by the Kano bourgeoisie, and its large diversified class of independent traders and commodity producers provided the social structural foundation for an anti-authoritarian, radial petty bourgeois political culture that invoked Islamic symbols to legitimize itself. Interwoven within this occupational structure were permanent and temporary resident mallams and their students, whose complex yet informal networks served as organizational and communication links across cities, towns and villages. Given the fact that the sarauta and leading officials of the N.A. as well as the NPC legitimized their rule by claiming descent from an eighteenth century peripatetic mallam (e.g., Usman dan Fodio), talakawa mallams claimed the same prerogative in order to criticize social injustice and to preach social reforms advocated by NEPU. While mallams and their students could be and were suppressed, to do so exposed the N.A. to the risk of infuriating comparatively non-political yet devout Muslims who supported and valued the peripatetic mallams and their spiritual services. Finally, though wage labor outside the N.A. among Hausa-speakers was largely seasonal prior to the opening of Kano's Bompai industrial estate, Koranic school networks often introduced youths to the urban labor market and thus to urban talakawa social life and culture. Again, just as in commerce, Islam and wage labor became interwoven within the urban lower class.

The Northern Elements Progressive Union was formed in Kano in 1950. Ideologically, the NEPU manifesto employed Marxist rhetoric to proclaim class struggle between the talakawa and the sarauta; but their goal was socialism of the social democratic variety. Soon 'Mallam' Aminu Kano, a Fulani school teacher descended from a prominent scholarly family, came to personify NEPU and became its unchallenged leader, even though he was clearly sarauta in terms of social origin.[69] As an urban-based movement whose class base was the rural peasantry, the N.A. authoritarian grip over the rural talakawa occupied NEPU from its first campaign against forced labor until the collapse of the First Nigerian Republic. Although the radical

38

slogan of 'freedom' (*Sawaba*) and the rhetoric of class struggle, anti-imperialism and socialism appealed to youths and the literate urban intelligentsia, Aminu Kano discovered that 'NEPU could not be effective by preaching Laski to the talakawa'.[70]

Given the hiatus between militant ideology and popular consciousness, NEPU turned to a strategy which I have labeled 'Islamic populism', which is the concrete expression of Islamic nationalism among the popular classes. Using the authority flowing from his esteemed scholarly pedigree, Aminu Kano launched an attack on the un-Islamic basis of sarauta domination by emphasizing what he termed the 'Anglo-Fulani' alliance, the positive traditions of egalitarianism and democracy contained within Islam and the popular mobilization of the talakawa *ulema* in support of NEPU's objectives. And, of course, given the talakawa's burden as victims of forced labor, corruption and abuses of power, the Islamic populist strategy made a deep impression on the popular consciousness of the talakawa, both rural and urban; even though major electoral victories eluded NEPU until the Second Nigerian Republic, when Aminu Kano's party was renamed the People's Redemption Party (PRP). Most importantly, Islamic populism translated radical concepts into the cognitive language of the talakawa experience: hence, radical nationalism and populist socialism became meaningful. It is worth noting that NEPU propaganda overtly employed Islamic symbols associated with martyrdom, such as portraits of Caliph Ali and the traditions of the first four caliphs of classical Islam. Furthermore, although the Tijaniyya never formally associated itself with NEPU, a branch that prayed with crossed arms rather than in the orthodox way with arms parallel to the torso became so identified with NEPU that public prayer with crossed arms was interpreted as a symbolic rejection of the authority of the sarauta to lead the Muslim community.

What is important about the Islamic populist ideology and the symbolic actions of Mallam Aminu Kano is that this strategy transcended the differences between the rural and the urban talakawa situation. It provided the talakawa with an anti-imperialist and class-conscious interpretation of their situation, in conformance with a talakawa interpretation of regional nationalism and Islamic justice. Again, one must emphasize that the social impact of Islamic populism cannot be measured by the very limited success of NEPU's electoral victories. Rather, NEPU's contribution over the long term lies in reinterpreting classical Islamic doctrines so as to legitimize the talakawa's struggle against an imperialist class alliance that allowed social and economic exploitation on a vast scale. Yet, as I shall show in the concluding chapter, the strengths of Islamic populism rest upon its oppositional and 'anti-feudal' thrust, rather than on a positive, workable socialist alternative.

Though NEPU was crushed in the 1964 elections by the overwhelming and illegitimate force of the NPC, history confirms that NEPU was gaining strength while the policies of the NPC at the regional and federal levels were

increasingly self-destructive. As a consequence, NEPU garnered many supporters 'of the heart' who, nonetheless, feared economic ruin or physical
harm to themselves or their families if they publicly supported NEPU.[71] Yet
popular sympathy for the ideals, Islamic reforms and leadership of NEPU
made a profound impression on the consciousness of the talakawa,
especially in Kano State. In class terms, NEPU confirmed the degree to
which classes that had become differentiated out of the status-honor system
of the precapitalist social formation could be mobilized by urban petty bourgeois leadership to oppose an essentially political (i.e., extra-economic)
system of exploitation. Over the long term, NEPU's mobilization of talakawa consciousness means that embryonic classes such as the urban working
class carried with them a sense of political awareness that structured their
perception of class allies and the political interconnectedness of economic
exploitation.

It is beyond the scope of this study to analyze the events and policies
that resulted in the collapse of the First Nigerian Republic, but it is
irrefutable that the contradictions inherent in the Northern Region played
a significant role. Clearly, even with British support the 'holy' north not
only seethed with its own class tensions, but the differences between
regions were so extreme that the federal state was unable to survive the
grafting of three or more radically different social formations whereby
each controlled a semi-autonomous regional government. Historically, the
causes of the civil war originate in British decisions to administer Nigeria
as separate colonies, to reinforce the powers of the most repressive and
backward classes in the north in order to maintain cheap administration,
and to continue to manipulate their romantic alliance with the traditional
ruling class as a counterweight to the demands of more radical southern
nationalists.

Summary

As an introduction to the process of urban working class formation among
Muslim workers of northern Nigeria, this chapter argues that the articulation of precapitalist and capitalist elements is key to understanding the
relationship of Islamic nationalism and class formation. Rooted in a populist Islamic reform movement of the eighteenth and nineteenth century,
Muslim workers call upon Islamic ideologies and institutions in order to
defend their interests. Further, the political status of the talakawa as well
as their relationship to the state during the precolonial and colonial epochs
also contributes to the consciousness and practice of Kano's working class.
Finally, it is only by understanding the consequences of the sarauta-British
class alliance that the contradictory consciousness and uneven development of Kano's popular and working classes can be comprehended. Let us
examine the impact of the Nigerian Civil War and the petroleum boom on
urban Kano.

2

The political economy of urban Kano: the transformation of state and capital, 1966–79

THE TRANSITION TO SEMI-INDUSTRIAL CAPITALISM

The objective of this chapter is to describe the reorganization of state structures and processes of capitalist development that transformed Kano from a groundnut exporting center, largely governed by Muslim mercantile capitalism, to a semi-industrial capitalist city when Nigeria returned to civilian rule. I will describe how the reorganization of the state apparatus, the new forms of capitalist accumulation and the new relationship to the world economy brought about by the petroleum boom structured the social conditions that gave rise to a Muslim, urban working class. The transformation of state and capital initiated Kano's transition to semi-industrial capitalism, a process that witnessed enormous population growth, a massive infusion of wealth from petroleum rents, a new ruling class alliance, a completely new relationship with the federal center and a deepening of capitalist social relations at the levels of production, exchange and consumption.

The transition to semi-industrial capitalism brought more than an increase in industrial production and rapid growth of the industrial proletariat. A bureaucratic state, functioning at both the federal and local levels, intervened into the economic, social and political life of Kano's residents to an unprecedented degree. International capital became more deeply embedded in the economic life of the city, whose prosperity became dependent on the price of petroleum in the world market. Local capital, nurtured by state sponsorship, extended its activities from trade and transport to the manufacturing of commodities as it never had previously. Inflation and the intense competition for material objects of consumption altered and internationalized the consumption patterns of virtually all classes. Competition for the means of subsistence on the part of salaried and wage workers transformed consumption patterns such that it became possible for a class to accumulate capital by providing wage goods to these classes. The historical pace of life, the quality of community relations and the styles of consumption of Kano's inhabitants were transformed to such a degree during this period that urban social life no longer resembled that of a mercantile Muslim city dependent on the seasonal export of groundnuts and the commercial distribution of commodities. The sum total of these changes

41

in the activities of state and capital marks Kano's transition to semi-industrial capitalism. For even though industrial production remains a small portion of economic and social life, the rapid and extensive development of commodity relations, the intensity of the struggle for the means of subsistence, the penetration of society by bureaucratically organized state institutions and the gulf between rich and poor generated changes that can be described only by the term semi-industrial.

Organizationally, in order to provide a basis for analyzing the emergence of an urban working class from the occupationally diverse talakawa, I intend to describe first the reorganization of the state at the federal, state and local government levels. Next, the impact of the new petroleum economy will be discussed with reference to structural changes in Kano's relationship to the world economy and to the federal state apparatus. Important here is the impact of this transformation on the region as a whole. Third, the role of the state and capital in the transition to industrial capitalism will be described and assessed. Fourth, the micro- and macro-level processes of capital accumulation will be described with the purpose of measuring the impact of these urban social processes on the behavior and consciousness of Kano's laboring population. And finally, I shall explain in schematic fashion how these transformations have altered the urban class structure of Kano.

THE FEDERAL MILITARY GOVERNMENT (FMG): THE DECLINE OF SEMI-AUTONOMOUS REGIONS

From 1966 to 1979, Nigeria was ruled by an oligarchy composed of military officers, civil servants and politicians, of whom the latter were often drawn from the First Republic's opposition groups, such as Aminu Kano and Obafemi Awolowo.[1] As is well known, Gowon was the head of state until July 1975, when he was overthrown in a bloodless coup by a Kano-born aristocrat, General Murtala Mohammed. In February of 1976, Murtala was assassinated in an abortive coup. He was succeeded by General Olusegun Obasanjo, who remained head of state until the return of civilian rule. Gowon's rule was successful in that he waged the civil war, introduced a state system to replace the four semi-autonomous regions and, in general, brought the states of the former Eastern Region back into the Federation without exacting a crippling reparations burden. On the other hand, the failure of Gowon to curb excessive corruption among his close allies, the inability of his regime to conduct a reliable census necessary to distribute petroleum rents and his postponement of a promised return to civilian rule are certainly important reasons for his subsequent unpopularity and eventual removal. In effect, the policies of the Murtala and Obasanjo governments were sufficiently similar to be treated as continuous.

During the political crisis and civil war, Gowon initiated state centralization at the federal level, at the expense of the once semi-autonomous regions. Murtala Mohammed's government went on to centralize authority at the federal level even more decisively. Immediately upon assuming power (July, 1975), Murtala acted swiftly to resolve divisive issues that had been simmering for years: he established a constitutional commission that was empowered to draft a constitution initiating a transition to civilian rule; he rejected the controversial and apparently inaccurate census of 1973; he realigned Nigerian foreign policy in a nationalist and anti-imperialist direction by, for example, recognizing and financially aiding the MPLA government in Angola; and he continued to expand and centralize the role of the federal government in the society and economy of Nigeria. Let us review the process of state centralization during the period of military rule, bearing in mind the pre-war situation, wherein regional governments controlled exports via marketing boards, courts, police and education.

One may distinguish two dimensions of federal intervention. The first involves absorbing administrative authority for activities previously controlled by the region and centralizing this authority at the federal level. Thus, police and courts, produce and agricultural marketing boards, universal primary education, university administration, land tenure and even local government administration were either taken over by the federal government or else vested in state governments under federally determined guidelines. The second dimension is more innovative in that the federal state has become a dominant economic actor and, in many cases, has become directly involved in the process of commodity production as well as in the accumulation of capital.[2] For instance, by 1979 the federal government owned a majority share of the petroleum industry and had established a para-statal corporation empowered to produce and distribute petroleum products; it managed numerous large-scale irrigation projects involving hundreds of thousands of peasant farmers; it purchased controlling interest in financial institutions such as banks and insurance companies as well as in subsidiaries of multinational corporations; and it introduced an indigenization of industry decree that, despite debates over its efficacy, was designed to increase Nigerian participation at all levels and in all types of industry. Hence, compared to the situation in 1966, when the regions were paramount and controlled the surplus of the produce marketing boards, there has been a dramatic shift in political and economic power toward the federal center. In turn, federal state centralization has increased the status enjoyed by the federal state apparatus and (as events since the 1979 election unequivocally illustrate), encouraged opposition groups who gained control over state governments to use the 'state's rights' argument to direct their opposition against the federal government.

Petroleum revenue and state centralization

While a political crisis brought about by a civil war often encourages increased state centralization, it was the petroleum revenue flowing from

43

the historic OPEC price increases of 1974 that literally financed the process of centralization. Membership in OPEC (1971), the technical requirements of petroleum production, and federal jurisdiction over offshore oil deposits enabled federal rather than state government to determine the allocation of petroleum revenues. Note that this situation is the opposite of the case during the First Republic, when each regional government controlled large amounts of capital within their respective produce marketing boards. But by increasing the number of subnational units first from four to twelve and later from twelve to nineteen, the federal policy makers were able to co-opt powerful local elites by offering them control over state-level offices. Nonetheless, without the petroleum revenue, funding of nineteen state governments would have been impossible.

The tension between the federal center and the states is nowhere more evident than in the debates surrounding the distribution of petroleum revenue.[3] If one examines the history of petroleum distribution under the military regime, it is easy to decipher the pattern of state centralization that occurred. Before April of 1975, following the regional principle of derivation of income, oil-producing states received 45 percent of onshore mining income, the FMG received 5 percent, and the remaining 50 percent went to a Distribution Pool for use by all states. Subsequently, the FMG claimed all offshore revenues, while the distribution of onshore revenues was altered such that the state of origin's share was reduced to 20 percent with the remaining 80 percent going to the Distribution Pool. This meant that the total state revenues and the total statutory allocations to the states by the FMG increased by approximately 120 percent from 1974–5 to 1975–6. While much revenue was redistributed to the states by the federal center, the authority to control petroleum revenue shifted to the FMG. In 1978, the FMG accepted many of the recommendations of the Aboyade Committee Report, produced by a committee of powerful senior civil servants, such that the revenue allocation system was altered once again in favor of the federal government. As a result, after April of 1978, 60 percent of all revenue was allocated to the federal government, 30 percent was allocated to state governments, and 10 percent went to the newly created local governments. Over time, the criteria used to distribute petroleum revenue will become a contested issue, but federal control remains the most significant change since 1966.

Federal control over petroleum revenue enabled the federal civil service to go beyond mere administrative centralization. Since the onset of military rule, a burgeoning state capitalist sector has emerged in control of basic industries, an innovation that places state technocrats in a position to manage productive agricultural and industrial enterprises directly. Of course, critics quite correctly note the inefficiency of para-statal agencies, underscoring their dependence upon foreign capital for technical expertise, capital goods and even management contracts; furthermore, one must question whether the Nigerian civil service in its present form possesses the discipline and expertise to fulfill its mandated responsibilities.[4] Also, it is true that mismanagement is rampant, to the degree that there is little evidence of a rational technocratic bureaucracy that plans and accumulates capital. But whatever the merits of this debate, it is a fact that the state capitalist sector has emerged, that it will probably expand its influence and expertise during the next decade and that it must be taken into account when analyzing the role of the Nigerian state in the process of capitalist development. Indeed, Nigerian para-statals possess formal control over large areas of the Nigerian economy. For example, areas in which they are involved or are the sole producer include: petroleum and natural gas, mining, automotive assembly and production, paper, sugar, petroleum refining and petro-chemical manufacturing, fertilizers, cement and building materials, as well as several consumer-oriented manufacturing concerns. Again, the entry of the federal government into the production of raw materials and manufacturing goods is a major innovation as compared to the First Nigerian Republic.

KANO STATE UNDER MILITARY RULE

Kano State was created by amalgamating the Emirates of Kano, Gumel, Kazaure and Hadejia. When the federation was expanded to nineteen states, Kano became Nigeria's most populous state and, equally important, the one with the largest proportion of its population professing Islam. Because the FMG rejected the census of 1973 as unreliable, it is difficult to ascertain the exact population of Kano State. The 1973 census figure of nearly eleven million is certainly too high, for in order for this figure to be true, Kano's population would have to have grown by nearly 89 percent since the 1963 census.[5] Note that according to the 1973 census, Lagos State, clearly the most rapidly growing and congested area in the federation, registered a growth rate of only 71 percent. A conservative estimate, based upon the 1963 census and noting a growth rate of 2.5 percent, yields a population of eight million in 1975 and ten million in 1980. Even with this conservative correction, however, Kano State is larger than a majority of existing African states, including the Ivory Coast, Mali, Cameroon and Burkina Faso.

The period of military rule witnessed an increased differentiation between urban Kano and the rural area such that nearly all public and private investment occurred in urban centers, mostly in Kano, while the rural areas suffered relative or, in some cases, absolute economic decline. Of course, the bias of state and private investment toward urban Kano accelerated the emigration of unskilled rural inhabitants to urban Kano in search of employment. However, the drift of population to urban Kano actually resulted from the convergence of several other factors, including the Sahelian drought which brought emigrants from the northern states as well as from Chad and Niger; the collapse of the groundnut economy which reduced rural income opportunities; and, most importantly, the disproportionate state and private investment in urban Kano which generated a temporary construction boom that absorbed a sizeable proportion of unskilled emigrants. Without a reliable census, one can only estimate the rate of urban growth and the size of the urbanized area. Throughout the period after the civil war, most observers estimate that urban Kano's population grew at an annual rate of 6 to 8 percent, and by 1980 the urban population was estimated at 1.1 to 1.4 million inhabitants, up from nearly 300,000 in 1963.

Such a surge in population growth altered the ecological form of the city, causing an expansion into the peri-urban area at a rapid rate, especially along all major roads, i.e., the routes to Zaria, Katsina, Wudil and Hadejia. Much of the new growth occurred around the northeast area, but the state plans increased growth in the southwest along the Kano-Zaria road. The neat ethnic segregation patterns of the late colonial and pre-war period remain to some degree, but competitive market forces have brought greater heterogeneity to once segregated areas. Class differences in the new areas are reflected rather starkly, as costly, modern cement-block construction gives way to mud-constructed housing for the new rural emigrants adjacent to the Bompai and Nasarawa areas. At the same time, rapid urban growth has increased the density of existing areas as owners add more levels and build on vacant space. Despite the enormous increase in population, no adequate drainage or sewer system has been constructed. Public health conditions for the majority of the urban population are increasingly squalid, and the incidence of and potential for epidemic diseases such as cholera remain exceedingly high.[6]

During the period of military rule, Kano State was headed by two military administrations that correspond to the Gowon and Murtala-Obasanjo governments at the federal level: Audu Bako (1967–75) and Sani Bello (1975–9). Just as was the case at the federal level, state administration was shared among former politicians, prominent merchant-industrialists and professional civil servants. Bako was credited with initiating large-scale irrigation projects that are now under federal control, with encouraging industrial investment and with expanding public sector infrastructure, especially roads and highways. Subsequent official investigations indicate that Bako enriched himself at the public's expense in the process, yet at the same time he is remembered as a governor who advanced Kano's agriculture and industry. Given the increased state centralization that was implemented under the Murtala government, as well as his highly publicized purging of the civil service for incompetence and corruption, most of the innovations that occurred in Kano State under the Bello administration were initiated by the federal center at Lagos.

Kano's fiscal dependence on the federal center

The creation of nineteen states from four semi-autonomous regions, coupled with a dramatic redefinition of federal government administrative and economic prerogatives, did indeed constitute an organizational revolution within the Nigerian state apparatus. Clearly, nineteen national sub-units with decreased powers, directed by inexperienced administrative personnel, were no match for the centralizing coalition of military officers, politicians and ambitious civil servants. But the relative ease with which centralization was implemented can only be explained by the fortuitous rise in petroleum revenues after 1973/74 which allowed the centralizing coalition to buy off any local opposition to centralization through the generous allocation of petroleum revenues to the states. While I wish to avoid any suggestion of crude 'commodity determinism', it is nevertheless true that the particular character of petroleum production encourages a close working relationship between central state bureaucrats and multinational oil firms, a relationship that provides the material basis for state centralization at the expense of subnational units. In the case of Kano, moreover, not only did dependence upon federally mediated petroleum revenues reduce local political autonomy, but equally important, the switch from groundnut exports to petroleum dependence made the state profoundly dependent upon the vagaries of the international oil market and the politics of OPEC's pricing policies.

Let us briefly examine the impact of petroleum revenues on the Nigerian economy and on Kano State in particular. By 1975, petroleum revenues accounted for nearly 93 percent of Nigeria's export earnings, 75 percent of its foreign exchange earnings, 87 percent of total government revenues and 45 percent of its gross domestic product.[7] Within the period of military rule, the price per barrel increased from less than $2 to a high of $40. Prior to the historic OPEC price increases of 1973/74, total federal government expenditure was budgeted at ₦1,562 million. By 1979/80, the budgeted figure had increased roughly six times, to ₦9,510 million. Again, I must emphasize that petroleum revenue fluctuates with regard to the level of world economic activity, the degree of pricing cooperating among OPEC states and the technical capacity of Nigerian oil production itself, so that even though total petroleum revenues during 1980 were expected to approach 25 billion dollars, a glut on the world oil market during 1981 forced Nigerian production to sink below 1 million barrels a day from a high of around 2.3 million. By 1986, when oil fell as low as $8 per barrel, the dependence on petroleum revenue produced a local depression.

If one examines the impact of federally controlled petroleum revenues on the recurrent revenue of Kano State, the material basis of state centralization becomes visible. In 1971/72, total revenue amounted to ₦33,214,000, of which ₦284,000 – 21.9 percent – was derived from local Kano State sources and ₦25,930,000 – 78.1 percent – was derived from the federal government. By 1975/76, the corresponding figures were: total revenue ₦133,256,000 of which ₦17,369,000 – 13 percent – was derived from Kano State and ₦115,887,000 – 87 percent – came from the federal government.[8] Assuming that the trend continues, as I do, by the end of the decade well over 90 percent of Kano State's revenues will come from federal sources.

47

Rhetoric of federalism and state's rights aside, Nigeria has become a centralized state during the period of military rule and the petroleum boom. Furthermore, given the dependence of both federal and state government on petroleum revenues, the net economic effect has been to draw once relatively autonomous regions like Kano more closely into greater dependence upon the workings of the capitalist world economy.

From patrimonialism to popular democracy: local government reforms

It will be recalled from Chapter One that the Native Authority system was the preserve of a patrimonial aristocracy, the sarauta, who economically exploited and politically dominated the rural talakawa. Some reform of this odious system occurred during the Gowon regime, including the federalization of courts and police. But it was the local government reforms of 1976 that ended the era of complete autocratic rule by the rural aristocracy and the urban local government authorities. Interestingly, the FMG's reorganization of land tenure and its policy of vesting land allocation in the hands of the state governments further limited the power of the aristocrats within the local government who had previously controlled land allocation. At the same time, it is important to bear in mind that the inflationary impact of the petroleum economy and the huge fortunes amassed by the merchant-industrial bourgeoisie meant that the office-holding aristocracy could not remain competitive in the status-honor system of Kano by relying solely on the traditional exploitation of the talakawa. The rural talakawa were simply too poor and too inefficient as producers to provide revenue at the level required by the local government officials to maintain an appropriate aristocratic lifestyle during the period of rapid capitalist growth associated with the transition to semi-industrial capitalism.

The local government reforms introduced under the Bello administration in 1976 were the most innovative.[9] These federally promulgated reforms abolished the provincial and divisional administration subsequently creating twenty local government authorities under Kano State's Ministry for Local Government. Local governments now possess authority over markets, public order and all essentially local affairs. Thus, in addition to the statutory grant from the federal government (which in 1976 amounted to 10 percent of federally collected revenues) and with financial grants from Kano State, these new authorities are expected to raise additional revenue for services such as health and education. Nevertheless, though undermining the earlier system, the reforms did not abolish the powers of the traditional aristocracy: the district head and village head systems continue to parallel the local government authorities, and the Emir of Kano continues to appoint the district heads, whose salaries will be paid by the local authorities.

One cannot underestimate the potential effect of introducing popular democracy into the rural areas of Kano State, especially if the populist PRP government returns in a future civilian government. While the reforms promise to end precapitalist (i.e., Muslim patrimonial) forms of peasant exploitation, it is certain that state-nurtured capitalist social relations will be accelerated, which nonetheless allows the possibility of democratic, popular governments to exist for the first time in Kano's history. To be sure, the rural aristocracy have not been eliminated, for they continue to hold the district headships. Moreover, they are personally exceedingly adroit at manipulating their limited powers and popular esteem in order to preserve their interests in spite of the structural reforms and the PRP victory. The problem of rural class relations depends upon the transition to capitalist agriculture, a process that is in its infancy in selected areas of the state.

KANO REGION AND THE WORLD ECONOMY

Thus far I have argued that the restructuring of the state at both the federal and local levels was facilitated by the enormous increase in Nigerian petroleum revenues after 1973/74. At the same time, the petroleum boom established a new relationship for Kano with the world economy. Since 1912, peasant-produced groundnuts had provided the material link between Kano and the world capitalist economy, but after 1974/75 petroleum revenues controlled by a centralizing federal state provided the material link as well as, one should emphasize, the material basis for capitalist growth in Kano. Certainly the decline of the groundnut trade was caused by factors other than the distortions attributed to the petroleum boom: the drought of the early 1970s, disease and unusual weather conditions, and state mismanagement of produce-buying operations, for example. Yet factors associated with the petroleum boom and subsequent federal government policies, made possible only by the large petroleum revenues, contributed to the decline of the groundnut trade to such a degree that toward the end of the 1970s Kano's groundnut oil millers were importing groundnuts in order to produce oil. Groundnut production was significantly affected by the petroleum boom in the following ways: a lower producer price for groundnuts relative to the inflated price received by peasants for food crops marketed to the burgeoning urban population; the urban bias of state infrastructural investments which stimulated an enormous demand for unskilled peasant labor in the construction sector, thus raising the cost of labor and thereby reducing the cultivation of cash crops like groundnuts; and the federally funded Universal Primary Education program which orientated youths away from rural industry and agriculture and toward urban centers that allegedly promised jobs for primary school leavers.

With regard to the *external* dimension of capitalist development in Kano, it is important to emphasize that the shift from the groundnut to the petroleum economy had critical consequences for the autonomy of the region *vis à vis* the capitalist world economy. When contrasted with the present situation, wherein Kano is dependent upon petroleum revenues controlled by a centralized federal government, the groundnut economy contained inherent qualities that made Kano *relatively* less dependent upon the price fluctuations of the world market. For peasants, groundnuts possessed both *use* and *exchange* value: they could be eaten or traded in local markets if the price was too low. For local industrial capitalists, groundnut milling offered investment opportunities in light manufacturing that were appropriate to existing technical and capital resources. For state bureaucrats, groundnut sales produced marketing board surpluses that were accumulated and controlled by the political and bureaucratic elites of the northern states. This relative level of regional autonomy contrasts sharply with the effects of the petroleum economy on local autonomy. Furthermore, though the petroleum economy brought unprecedented wealth to the dominant classes, increased state investment and new investment opportunities for Kano's bourgeoisie, it also brought a devastating rate of inflation and linked the material welfare of an increasing proportion of Kano's urban population more directly to the fluctuating price of petroleum in the world market.

More indirectly, the rural population was affected too.[10] Urban-centered inflation raised the price of commodities produced in or transferred through urban centers that were consumed by rural inhabitants, while the prices of peasant-produced foods as well as groundnuts were controlled by the importation of cheap foodstuffs by the federal government. The FMG's fear of urban disorder over food prices checked any proportionate increase in the price of locally produced food. Other factors, such as the rapid rise in land value in the peri-urban area and the migration of labor from the countryside into high-paying construction labor, also undermined the equilibrium of the rural economy.

Regional control over the groundnut economy contrasts sharply with the centralization tendencies inherent in the petroleum economy. Instead of management by a regional groundnut marketing board, the petroleum economy is easily managed by direct negotiations between the federal government and multinational oil companies. Instead of local industrialists processing groundnuts for local and international sales, petroleum refining and associated industries are jointly controlled by the federal government and international firms, as the petroleum complex at Kaduna clearly illustrates. The petroleum boom undermined regional economic autonomy in a fashion that parallels the process of state centralization at the political-administrative level. Measured in terms of decreased autonomy, greater dependence upon a single commodity and greater social inequity as reflected in the skewed income distribution, the transition to a petroleum economy has been a costly one for the inhabitants of Kano State.[11]

Regional development: The Kano-Kaduna axis of growth

Kano forms the northern pole of an axis of capitalist development that extends south-westward from Kano through Zaria to the industrial and

50

administrative center of Kaduna, a distance of 260 kilometers.[12] The axis formed by these three cities has attracted industrial and human capital investment in the form of advanced research and educational facilities, a capital-intensive irrigation scheme and large-scale industrial investments, as well as additional state funding for existing railway, motor road and air transport infrastructures. Of course, these investments have attracted commercial and financial capital from both local merchant capitalists and international firms. I shall compare the industrial development of Kano to that of Kaduna in Chapter Six below. It is sufficient to note here that Kano forms the northern pole of Nigeria's second largest economic and industrial growth center. Moreover, physical construction along the highway between these two cities reflects the intense level of economic activity that has taken place, especially since the petroleum boom. Even the villages along the motor route reflect this growth. Over the long run, I expect that the 260-kilometer axis will become a corridor of intense capital accumulation, given its comparative advantage with regard to access to industrial production, available markets, labor supplies and sources of agricultural and industrial raw material, such as the planned petroleum products pipeline and the Kano River Project (KRP).

Among the significant changes funded by petroleum revenues are the capital-intensive irrigation schemes such as the Kano River Project, which lies between Kano and Zaria. This is an irrigation scheme of approximately 60,000 acres which forms part of a larger irrigation scheme of approximately 200,000 acres in Kano State.[13] Though originally initiated by the Kano State government, the KRP now comes under the authority of the federal agency, the Hadejia-Jama're River Basin Authority. It represents a substantial portion of a federal government investment of at least three and one-half billion dollars designed to bring capital-intensive agricultural production to the northern states of Nigeria. Virtually all economic and social aspects of these schemes are hotly contested, so that it would be foolish to engage in a debate over the project's economic feasibility, its deleterious impact on the Kano river system's natural ecology, its cost to smallholding peasants or, finally, whether the scheme will eventually displace the pre-existing peasants in order to develop capital-intensive, capitalist agriculture. At the same time, it is certain that the schemes will help develop valuable and potentially productive agricultural land that could generate large profits if production were oriented toward feeding the burgeoning urban populations along the Kano-Kaduna axis (populations totalling around three million inhabitants). Further, since it is known that through a variety of illegal and legal mechanisms irrigated land is transferred from the original peasant proprietors to wealthy urban residents, there is a high probability that capitalist agriculture, heavily nurtured by state subsidies, will develop in the next decade. Neither space nor the objectives of this study allow for an analysis of the KRP, but the project obviously represents a radical state intervention into the traditional peasant agrarian economy, an intervention

51

that is nurturing capitalist agriculture and attracting multinational corporations such as Castle and Cooke (Bud) and the FMC.[14] More importantly for this study, the KRP represents the rural dimension of an urban-centered process that has restructured Kano's relationship to and function within the capitalist world economy.

Before returning to Kano's urban political economy, it is appropriate to inform the reader that, in addition to the KRP, joint state and World Bank interventions into the rural economy are planned for Kano State during the decade of the eighties. In May 1981, the World Bank announced an agreement with the Nigerian government to initiate a rural development project for Kano State modelled on the existing projects at Funtua, Gusau and Gombe. It is designed to increase food production, provide support services, improve infrastructure and introduce modern agricultural technology such as small-scale irrigation. This 'Green Revolution' package will cost $482.2 million and is intended to benefit 430,000 farm families whose incomes fall below the relative rural poverty level.[15] Researchers who have studied the existing World Bank projects report that, while food production increases, the bias of subsidies and technical support is directed to the larger farmers so as to increase already existing levels of rural inequality.[16] Such interventions, either through design or error, tend to make problems for smaller and less efficient peasant producers, a complex process of differentiation that usually expells surplus population into cities like Kano. Hence, for the rural population surrounding urban Kano, not only have the indirect effects of the petroleum economy undermined the pre-existing rural economy, but the state and World Bank responses to the market distortions associated with the petroleum economy will intensify the process of capitalist differentiation among the peasantry and integrate peasant communities more deeply into the fluctuations of an urban-centered national economy whose stability is determined by the price fetched for Nigerian oil in the world economy.

Urban Kano: regional role in the international division of labor

Thus far I have argued that the actions of the state and capital associated with the petroleum boom have begun to transform the area between the cities of Kano and Kaduna, thus integrating this urban axis of intense capitalist activity more profoundly into the cyclical movements of the capitalist world economy. For urban Kano proper, the external transformation associated with the shift from the groundnut to the petroleum economy has also altered the role the city plays in the international division of labor. My argument is simple: in the context of the capitalist world economy, the growth of the Nigerian market and the economic potential of Nigeria created the need for several internationalized cities (in addition to congested and chaotic Lagos), to service the needs of global capitalist organizations and institutions, i.e., to service international firms and their personnel, to manage investments, to gain a share of the market and, if necessary, to engage in industrial production. Thus, within the region formed by the northern states of Nigeria, of which Kano is the most populous and economically active, Kano city has emerged as the urban center that provides a critical link for the states of this region to the capitalist world economy. I shall discuss the *internal* transformation of capitalist development in urban Kano in the next section; here my purpose is to examine global processes that have transformed Kano into a regional outpost in a global network of cities that integrate their respective regions into the capitalist world economy.

Given the urban bias of state expenditure, the comparatively advanced communication and transport facilities located in Kano and, as compared to other Nigerian cities, the advanced level of capital accumulation achieved by the indigenous bourgeoisie, it is hardly surprising that Kano plays this role for the northern states. To examine the evidence for Kano's transition to a semi-industrial city that functions as a regional capitalist urban center within a capitalist world economy, let us begin with capital investment.

In contrast to the period prior to the petroleum boom, when industrial investment was, with the exception of leather tanning, largely limited to Asian, Levantine and Hausa entrepreneurs, multinational corporations have invested productive capital in Kano's industries. These include: Fiat (trucks and tractors), Union-Carbide (batteries), Bata (shoes), Dunlop (foam products), Imperial Chemical Industries (paints and chemicals), Lonrho (groundnut milling and tanning), Raleigh (bicycles) and CFAO (textiles). Equally important for Kano's increased integration into the networks of international firms is the increase in partnerships between indigenous capitalists and international businesses. While many of these relationships involve mere representation and distribution, often only because state policy requires some aspect of production to occur in Kano, manufacturing in Kano is advanced. Besides outright manufacturing firms, prominent international service firms such as International Telephone and Telegraph and National Cash Register now have offices at Kano. Major international banks such as Chase Merchants Bank and Bank of America (Savanna Bank) have integrated wealthy merchant-industrial capitalists into their financial networks. The crucial point is that multinational firms which once limited their activities to Lagos have moved north, restructuring and intensifying Kano's degree of integration into the world economy.[17]

Yet, as I shall demonstrate in a subsequent section, the available evidence suggests that Kano is not destined to become a center of heavy manufacturing industry. Absent are the intermediate industries that produce raw materials such as petrochemicals, aluminum or steel and that normally generate extensive backward and forward linkages in the form of new industries. When one considers Kano's transport and finance, its densely settled rural population and its investments in irrigation schemes, then it is clear that Kano's industrial specialization will be agri-

53

cultural processing and consumer-oriented industries. Tractor production by Fiat is consistent with this view. At the same time, the rapidly rising urban population in Kano and in the northern states served by Kano's distribution networks should create a gigantic market for light manufactured and consumer goods (e.g., foodstuffs, textiles, leather products and drugs).

The expansion of commercial, financial and technical services should not be ignored, nor should Kano's transportation facilities. In the case of the latter, Kano's direct flights to Western Europe and Middle Eastern cities as well as to Niamey, the capital of Niger, enhance Kano's attractiveness as a regional outpost for international financial, commercial or other service firms. Kano has also benefitted from its proximity to international motor highways. It will be the southern terminus of the trans-Saharan highway and is located on the route to East Africa. Thus, just as in the nineteenth century when Kano was a major entrepôt for merchants and pilgrims, its transportation linkages to the global economy contribute to both the internationalization of the city and the process of local capital accumulation. In this regard, one cannot overlook the trading networks of indigenous merchant capitalists, who loan enormous sums of money to their distributors, or indigenous state banks such as the Bank of the North, which is amassing billions of naira in its new 25-story office building overlooking the old city. Distribution, finance and commercial services for the northern states will continue to be centered at Kano and thus contribute to the external and internal dimensions of Kano's capitalist transition.

The transformation of Kano, from a relatively autonomous mercantile capitalist export center to a semi-industrial urban center which functions as the northern regional center in the international division of labor, has been achieved by the combination of state centralization, the distributional effects of the petroleum economy and the intervention of international firms and agencies. Clearly, these factors form the macro-level framework from which one must analyze the micro-level process of capitalist development as it emerges at the level of an urban society. While these factors exert pressure on the pre-existing social and cultural practices in a clearly capitalist direction, macro-level factors and global processes, taken by themselves, do not *determine* the process of class formation and class struggle within urban Kano. Before I analyze the micro-level processes, however, I want to emphasize how global processes influence the routine social reproduction of mercantile capitalism, how they alter existing class and status group hierarchies and how they alter lifestyles and consumption patterns.

One must bear in mind that great wealth and income inequalities existed during the era of the groundnut economy. But the scale of contemporary income inequality and the internationalization of highly visible consumption styles among the dominant classes act to create a qualitatively new situation, one which has exacerbated class tensions. What makes this change so explosive is that previous forms of inequality and consumption existed within the regional context of a Muslim patrimonial and mercantile capitalist urban situation, where the popular classes tolerated income inequality in hopes of participating in the 'traditional' redistribution processes, and where the styles of redistribution and consumption conformed to Muslim norms. During the petroleum era, however, internationalized styles of consumption among the dominant and educated classes create a profound moral cleavage between the latter group and declining members of the popular classes.

The global factors that contribute to the internationalization of Kano exert an influence that extends beyond the consumption of sumptuous homes, video products and other international luxury goods. Formal linkages with international firms and informal relations with transnational personalities have transformed the once regionally bounded merchant class into one that is affiliated with transnational capitalism and whose investments extend even beyond Nigeria. With regard to changes in the urban class structure, these formal and informal linkages are important for forming joint ventures and other avenues of capital accumulation, for introducing relevant ideological and technological models, and for consultation between transnational and local capital on political issues of mutual interest such as combatting socialism and populism. Hence, when one examines the micro-level processes of class differentiation and class formation within the urban community, one must bear in mind that, since the petroleum boom, international styles of consumption, the exigencies of the global economy and the linkages of the dominant classes to advanced capitalist states and transnational organizations shape the popular class's perception and experience of class inequality as never before.

THE INDUSTRIAL SECTOR: THE CONTRADICTIONS OF SEMI-INDUSTRIAL CAPITALISM

The discussion of Kano's transformation since the civil war and the oil boom, of the changing role of state policies and international capitalist actors, inevitably leads to Kano's industrial sector. Here one enters a thicket of debates between dependency theorists, neo-classical economists and more orthodox Marxist theorists over such issues as the technical capacity, transformative potential and national control of Nigeria's modern manufacturing industries. No consensus has yet emerged among theorists regarding correct methodology, units of analysis, the meaning of an empirical outcome for a theoretical expectation or what a reasonable expectation for Nigerian industry would be during the present conjuncture. While I want to avoid digressing extensively into this debate, certain issues do bear on Kano's transformation from a groundnut exporting center to a semi-industrial capitalist city.[18] Equally important, since industrial workers are the object of my analysis, the structural and technical features of Kano's industrial sector require comment. Let us first examine the industrial sector as it existed in 1979.

Empirically, the actual number of manufacturing industries, the absolute number of industrial employees, the number and proportion of Nigerian owners and managers and the involvement of state and federal capital have all increased significantly during the period of military rule. Several new industrial estates have been constructed at Challawa, Sharada and along the Kano-Zaria road. And, as I noted earlier, new industrial investors have included international firms. No one doubts that these increases have occurred, or that more industrial products are now produced at Kano as compared to the period prior to the Nigerian civil war. Rather, the debate centers on questions regarding the degree to which commodities are assembled rather than produced from local materials that, ideally, could be organized into backward linking industries; or whether technologies are appropriate given the surplus urban population and the need for skill development in the labor force; or whether such industries serve to accumulate capital for self-sustaining industrialization within Nigeria or, alternatively, whether the current industries increase Nigerian dependence on external economies, thus leading to the accumulation of capital overseas instead of in Nigeria. Nationalists and other critics, arguing from the dependency position, dismiss the indigenous bourgeoisie as technically backward, as dependent upon state patronage and contracts and as mere 'fronts' or silent partners for foreign capital.[19] Finally, the same critics argue that the state has intervened on behalf of international firms in that its joint ventures with these firms, such as Fiat in Kano, only reduce opportunities for local capitalists and place state monopoly power behind international firms which Nigerians neither control nor possess the technical capacity to manage effectively. Of course, this position reflects the standard dependency critique of industrialization under international capital (i.e. multinational corporations) in peripheral capitalist countries.

Recently this position has received criticism from more orthodox Marxists, not so much because the situation described by dependency theorists is empirically incorrect, but rather because their position lacks an acceptable theory explaining capitalist development under the contemporary conditions of the world economy; that is to say, the dependency approach cannot explain comparatively successful states such as Brazil or South Korea. Secondly, Marxists argue that the transition to capitalism is a contradictory and highly uneven process, where new regions and cities may grow and rural areas stagnate or decline; and further that social disorder and human misery of the kind described so forcefully by dependency theorists are integral to, rather than deviant from, the process of capitalist transformation.[20] Hence, one cannot attribute uneven development, social misery and public corruption solely to the dependent nature of Nigerian industrialization. Furthermore, Marxists point out that the current situation in Nigeria contains positive elements in that modern technology is transferred and that supportive capitalist economic institutions and highly socialized urban laboring classes are also created. In turn, it is argued, internal markets are created for wage goods, small-scale capitalists expand to supply this market, and as a result precapitalist forms of production and distribution are eroded or destroyed, only to be replaced by more modern 'capitalist' forms.

At the same time, Marxist theorists acknowledge the reality of contemporary imperialism in the form of multinational corporations and core state agencies that distort and manipulate peripheral economies by extracting exorbitant rents from new technologies, by transferring local earnings back to the home office (through such devices as transfer prices) and by attempting to integrate peripheral economies into a dependent position within a cartelized global economy. All of the latter may be correct, but these empirical conditions do not explain the success or failure of the process of capitalist industrialization in states like Nigeria, a process that is occurring under the conditions of external capitalist domination (i.e., imperialism). From this perspective, attention centers on the ability of the state, acting with the support of local capitalists, to use nationalist ideology to mobilize support for a transition to industrial capitalism, a process that can only reflect the contradictions of industrial capitalist accumulation under imperialism. According to Marxist critics, such a policy calls for limiting international capital's access to the Nigerian market, for supporting the local bourgeoisie only insofar as they invest in desirable and productive enterprises and for establishing the maximum conditions for accumulation by private and state actors through the elimination of non-productive expenditure and the political influence of backward precapitalist groups. In order for this policy to be implemented, of course, new class coalitions around the state would have to be formed.

Let us now apply these debates more specifically to the Nigerian situation. While it is true that Nigerian industrial production is dependent upon imported technology, inputs and technical personnel, it is difficult to see how it could be otherwise, given the low level of technical education and the effects of British colonial policy that discouraged industrial investment, as well as the need for any newly industrializing state to import intermediate and capital goods. One problem is the tendency for nationalist critics to compare the current situation with the experience of advanced industrial states during a different era in the history of the capitalist world economy. During the current conjuncture it is clear that international firms which control the most modern, productive technologies and associated expertise in marketing, finance and industrial organization will be involved in most newly industrializing states. Further, international firms are no longer associated with a single nation-state, nor are they tightly controlled by the government of their state of origin, as the behavior of American energy firms in the American economy so clearly illustrates. The functioning of the contemporary world economy creates an international division of labor

57

where production processes for a single commodity may occur in several nation-states depending on costs and incentives offered by competing states. All economies, whether located at the periphery or the core of the world economy, are increasingly influenced by global competition and global forces which, during the current crisis in core state economies, seek to reduce costs by producing overseas. Hence it is exceedingly unlikely that any peripheral capitalist state during the present conjuncture will experience successful capitalist industrialization by pursuing an autonomous or self-reliant model of development.

Acceptance of the reality of the internationalization of capital does not mean that the description of Nigerian industrial underdevelopment offered by dependency critics and nationalists is unfounded, nor that the predicted outcome (i.e., stagnation) is inevitable. Rather it means that the process of capitalist development in Nigeria must be viewed as one where international firms and agencies will play a significant role in transferring technology and in establishing basic industries. But the involvement of international capital does not necessarily mean that international capital must exert inexorable control over the process and determine the structure of industrial development, for it is certain that states and firms from the 'core' are in competition with each other. Both the policy makers and the technocrats located in the state apparatus as well as the capital-accumulating bourgeoisie in the private sector possess the potential, if not the will, to control access to the Nigerian market, to coordinate international investment so as to deepen and rationalize backward and forward linkages within the Nigerian economy, to monitor the external flow of profits and to locate capital accumulation within Nigeria for the West African region as a whole.

To conclude, then, problems with Nigerian industrialization cannot be explained solely or in large part by the role played by international capital, for it is difficult to see how international capital benefits from the chaos and inefficiency described by critics. Viewed within the framework of a new international division of labor, Beckman has persuasively argued that international capital has much to gain from a deepening of industrialization as measured by increasing productivity and profitability. He argues further that a corrupt and inefficient state sector, as now exists in Nigeria, hardly benefits international firms that depend on state infrastructure and services.[21] Moreover, at the level of the global ideological struggle between capitalism and socialism, the interest of international capital is not served by the chaos and corruption exhibited by its chief ally in the region. Hence, one must look beyond the demon of international capital for the complete explanation of Nigerian industrial underdevelopment.

State intervention on behalf of the Nigerian bourgeoisie

Internally, assuming Nigeria continues to pursue a capitalist path, the only economic and political actors capable of affecting Nigerian industrialization are located in the state apparatus and in the private bourgeoisie. One of the problems encountered by the political alliances of these regionally based capitalist classes arises from their lack of national integration. The absence of an authoritarian state or a strong national bourgeois alliance creates a 'disarticulated' economy where political and economic power are separated from each other. But as strong as the forces of regional competition may be in Nigeria, in themselves they do not explain the absence of the coalition of capitalists and state bureaucrats that would be necessary if Nigeria were to rationalize and to deepen its industrialization process. Another clear problem is that the state-controlled oil revenue centralizes wealth and capital in the state apparatus. From the point of view of capital accumu-lation, political and bureaucratic controllers disperse this wealth in irrational ways, in order to maintain the support of their networks and coalition members, as well as their personal accumulation needs. Petroleum wealth distributed by the state in the form of contracts, grants, incentives and privileges to the state- and private-sector bourgeoisie maintains the coalition in power, either military or civilian, by buying off other threaten-ing groups such as Nigerian entrepreneurs and urban wage earners. But taken as a whole, these policies waste capital resources, destroy the discipline of the market and the potential rationality of the state bureau-cracy and, instead, create a distorted and irrational economy from the point of view of capitalist industrialization. The portrait that emerges is one in which state revenues are usurped for private needs because no single, ideologically coherent capitalist coalition has yet coalesced to guide Nigeria towards the process of capitalist industrialization. By itself, public sector corruption does not necessarily inhibit the deepening of the industrial-ization process. Were the beneficiaries of the legal and illegally gained wealth to invest in productive industry, they would form an economically based political group that could potentially at least, force discipline and rational capitalist planning on the state policy makers. Problems such as these become clear if one examines state intervention on behalf of the Nigerian bourgeoisie.

Within such contradictions, the federal government has promulgated a policy of industry indigenization that reserves certain low technology industries and commercial services for Nigerians; it requires at least 40 percent Nigerian ownership in all industries and 60 percent in some more complex industries, including banking. While this policy has expanded Nigerian participation in the economy largely at the expense of petty bourgeois aliens (i.e., Indians and Lebanese) and has increased the role of the state in basic and intermediate industries, the sale of shares in international firms' subsidiaries to Nigerians has absorbed a significant portion of national capital that could have funded indigenous accumulation instead of providing local financing for international firms. In addition to drawing national capital toward the financing of local subsidiaries of international firms, indigenization has enabled many Nigerian entrepreneurs to accept state funding while avoiding actual management and control over industrial production in several ways: by allowing them to act as fronts for foreigners, by accepting ownership of equity in return for performing political services for foreign firms and by not following the strict provisions of the indigenization decree.[22] In some cases, the state simply does not enforce the decree. Hence, while the indigenization decrees increased Nigerian ownership in absolute terms, they failed to stimulate innovative entrepreneurship and competent technocratic management as was originally intended by policy makers. In fact, this line of reasoning has been used by critics to argue that the net effect of the decrees has been greater dependence of the Nigerian industrial bourgeoisie on the networks of foreign firms. Yet, in spite of the fact that the positive benefits for Nigerian private capital were limited to a small yet politically influential group of businessmen, indigenization did result in greater participation and greater opportunities for Nigerian businessmen to accumulate capital. This financial expansion and control is extremely important. However, Nigerian businessmen are clearly subordinate to and, in general, dependent upon the management, technical expertise and planning services of international firms in the industrial sector. Hence, one must look to the state sector for Nigerian industrial leadership.

State capital: an assessment

The performance of the state sector during military rule is typified by two contradictory processes. On one hand, the state has extended and deepened its role in the administration, management and production functions of the national economy, especially in the areas of petroleum production, refining and processing, automobile assembly, mineral extraction, steel production and other basic and intermediate kinds of industries. On the other hand, in virtually all instances the state has proven incapable of transforming the vast rents realized from the petroleum industry into productive industrial activities where capital is accumulated by a disciplined, technocratically competent bureaucracy that plans and executes production decisions for the purpose of realizing profit (capital) in a market economy. Note that the planners who implemented the policy which increased state intervention were aware of the shortcomings of state industries. According to Rimmer, state planners 'remarked on the gross inefficiency in these enterprises, the mediocrity of their personnel, the fraudulence of some of their operations, their vulnerability to partisan political pressure, and the insensitivity to the wants of users of the services or products they supplied'.[23]

Furthermore, the recently published report of the Public Accounts Committee (PAC), which was established at the end of military rule to review the accounts of the Federal Military Government, provides more evidence for the dismal performance of the state sector. The PAC reports that the Customs and Excise Board could not account for the 160 payment vouchers which totalled more than ₦8 million; the Ministry of Finance, charged with managing the federal government's portfolio of investment shares of companies that were recently indigenized, could not produce a list of such investments nor provide audited accounts for those investments which totalled more than ₦2 billion; and with regard to the accounts of the Nigerian Police Force, the committee held 'the view that if a similar situation were to have been found in another department, the police would have been called in for investigation'.[24] One could continue, for there is a bevy of financial scandals and examples of gross mismanagement in the state sector. Even more depressing is the fact that informal reports of the activity of the civilian regime indicate that the abuses remain unchecked and that the National Assembly was incapable of generating the will to oversee public accounts. Finally it should be noted that the failure of the public sector to manage industrial development competently is not due to lack of investment capital: the total amount of public sector investment during the first two years (1975–7) of the Third National Development Plan totalled ₦5,043 million, as compared to the ₦148 million invested from 1962 to 1967. By the end of 1976, the cost of public sector investment envisioned in the Third Plan had risen to ₦26.5 billion.[25] Hence the problem is organizational and motivational, and the solution necessitates a deep structural transformation within the Nigerian state at both the political level, in terms of class discipline and coalitions, and the bureaucratic level, in terms of organizational discipline and efficiency.

It is too early to conclude whether state investments in basic industries, whose effective control rests in the hands of foreign consultants or personnel, will serve as the material foundation of self-sustaining industrialization. But there is virtually no evidence regarding the competence and effectiveness of the state bureaucracy that encourages one to be sanguine about such an outcome. Clearly, if the state is to hold broad economic powers, it must possess the capacity to exercise state power. Currently, however, the state is incapable of halting smuggling operations that involve customs officials, thus discouraging foreign investment industries because of this effective 'open market'. What discipline existed before the petroleum boom has been dissipated by the excesses that accompanied the boom. Given the record of the state sector, one must assess the opportunity costs of massive state intervention into the economy, for not only have the controllers of the Nigerian state wasted an unprecedented opportunity and a unique source of capital for industrialization, but the state has also displaced private capitalist initiatives, both Nigerian and foreign, from those markets and sources of capital accumulation. Even more alarming, the overextension of the state discourages private capitalist investment by creating uncertainty about the state's next intervention or its capacity to fulfill its current obligations even at the level of infrastructure (such as electric power service). And of course such a situation only encourages Nigerian private capital to pursue *compradore* activities and contracting roles, while awaiting further patronage from the state. Such flagrant waste in a situation of extreme poverty and widespread deterioration of urban public health, social order and public services only exacerbates the already abundant social and political tensions present in contemporary Nigeria.

THE POLITICAL ECONOMY OF URBAN CAPITALIST ACCUMULATION: ISSUES AND CONCEPTS

In order to explain the structure, consciousness and action of Kano's Muslim working class, one must move from the analysis of macro-level forces – essentially state and capital on a global scale – to the micro-level processes that determine capital accumulation, class formation and class struggle within a rapidly growing community. Thus, while the Nigerian state, the global economy and the internationalization of consumption all condition and intervene in the process of urban differentiation and class formation, such macro-level processes by themselves cannot explain the social transformation of urban Kano during the period of military rule. Rather, only a micro-level approach that focuses upon the process of capitalist differentiation and the *articulation* of capitalist and precapitalist elements (i.e., organizations, institutions and ideologies) will explain this critical problem. *Most importantly, I shall argue that participation in the urban social processes of a semi-industrial capitalist city such as Kano acts as a material social force in a manner analogous to the way in which participation in the labor processes of capitalist production structures and informs the consciousness of the laboring and popular classes*. To comprehend this thesis, one must conceive of the semi-industrial capitalist city at the periphery of the capitalist world economy as composed of a set of structured urban social processes that determine urban social relations, constrain life chances and income opportunities and socialize wage earners into an urban working class identity.

With this thesis in mind, let us begin with the problem of analyzing the semi-industrial capitalist city. If one compares metropolitan Kano before the civil war and the petroleum boom to the urban society that witnessed the return to civilian rule, the most obvious visible changes are its extensive spatial expansion and its enormous population growth. True, state investment policies, Kano's linking function to the world economy, and its commercial-financial role in the regional economy explain part of this growth. But in order to explain the relationship between the transition to industrial capitalism and rapid urbanization, one must first confront the question of why industrial capitalism always generates vast urban agglomerations that require extensive transport and communication networks as well as public sector investments in medical care, education and other services. That is to say, how does Kano's spatial and demographic explosion relate to the transformation of a once mercantile and administrative center into a semi-industrial capitalist city? In order to answer this

question, one must review the contributions of the existing urban socio-
logies.

The Chicago school's human ecology approach is useless because, in the
words of Castells, it confuses an effect with a cause.[26] That is to say, the
physical and ecological form of the industrial capitalist city is a product of,
and thus is determined by, the process of industrial capitalist accumulation. Hence, one cannot explain urban social organization and culture by
reference to physical forms and environments that are created in response
to the class structure and accumulation needs of an industrializing capitalist
society.

The Marxist sociological tradition also addresses this question. Marx, for
example, noted the spatial dimension of capital accumulation: 'capital
grows to a huge mass in a single hand in one place, because it has been lost
by many in another place. This is centralization proper, as distinct from
accumulation and concentration'.[27] Elsewhere he argues that a mass of
capital attracts other capital and that 'centralization supplements the work
of accumulation by enabling industrial capitalists to extend the scale of their
operation'.[28] Taking off from Marx on this line of reasoning, the French
urban theorist Lojkine argues cogently that, 'far from being a minor
phenomenon, urbanization in our opinion plays as important a role in the
general development of capitalism as does the increased use of mechanical
labor power in the production unit'.[29] Subsequently, Lojkine links his
analysis with several of Marx's observations. The first point addresses
Marx's concern with the *general conditions* of capitalist production: 'The
revolution in the modes of production of industry and agriculture made
necessary a revolution in the *general* conditions of the social process of
production, i.e., in the means of communication and transport'.[30] According to Lojkine, the concentration of population and capitalist production
units in a centralized urban society increases efficiency, and thus the rate of
profit, because the density and proximity afforded by large urban agglomerations reduce transport and communication costs between suppliers and
producers and between production units and consumers. At both the urban
and regional levels, furthermore, investments in modern transportation,
such as motor roads in Nigeria, reduce the turnover time that lapses
between capital advanced for production costs, the sale of the product and
the actual receipt of profit for reinvestment (i.e., the circuits of capital).
Hence, large centralized cities with urban-centered transportation systems
that link the city with the secondary markets in the hinterland reduce the
turnover time in the circuit of capital, thus increasing the efficiency and
raising the potential rate of profit. For Lojkine, therefore, concentrated
urban agglomerations, such as Kano, and their transportation systems
function to attract and to serve the needs of capital by providing immediate
markets, lowering production costs and reducing the turnover time between
investment and the realization of profit.

Though Kano's transition toward semi-industrial capitalism is in its

63

infancy and exceedingly uneven in its social effects, Lojkine's insights are valuable for explaining the time/space relations and the material basis for the increased 'speed' of Kano's urban life. According to Lojkine, the capitalist city takes 'a spatial form which, by reducing indirect costs of production, and costs of circulation and consumption, speeds up the rotation of capital'.[31] Bearing in mind the urban bias of Nigerian state investment, note that new transport and communication investments exert their effect on the social processes of urban Kano. In turn, the process of capital accumulation in this semi-industrial capitalist city is enhanced by the transformation of communication and transportation facilities and the concentration of population around these facilities.

Let us follow the analogy of the labor process of capitalist production one step further: just as is the case in the capitalist enterprise (where the labor process and the use of cost-reducing technology are constantly transformed to increase profitability), the spatial form in the semi-industrial city, the class location of housing and the 'speed' of urban social relations are constantly being renovated and reorganized in order to maximize the profitability of its spatial form, to reduce indirect costs and to increase the productivity of its laboring population. It is in this sense that the *urban social processes* of a semi-industrial capitalist city exert a distinct and independent influence on the class structure and forms of consciousness among Kano's laboring and popular classes.

Lojkine extends his urban sociology by developing a second Marxian concept: the concentration of workers in a worksite allows them to cooperate in production, and in this way a number of useless expenses are reduced, all of which lowers the capitalist's reproduction costs incurred in maintaining a productive labor force over several generations. In applying this observation to the capitalist city, Lojkine argues that in addition to the obvious advantage accruing to capital from having an abundant supply of labor, the dense urban agglomeration necessarily creates concentrated institutions which he terms the *collective means of consumption*: e.g., schools, universities, hospitals, sports centers and cultural centers. Having concentrated population in the urban center, the capitalist city must ensure the reproduction of urban capitalist society and in particular the labor supply, especially its skilled and technocratic members. In order to ensure reproduction of the urban capitalist society, therefore, a capitalist city creates collective means of consumption which, according to Lojkine, are 'material supports of the activities devoted to the extended reproduction of labor power'.[32] That is to say, in a dense urban agglomeration, the material, cultural and social needs of the labor supply must be met, and further, care must be taken to ensure that the social contradictions of the urban capitalist society do not inhibit labor from performing its productive function for capitalist industrialization in its broadest sense. Thus Lojkine argues that the development of the collective means of consumption in a mature industrial capitalist city is, increasingly, a factor which produces higher labor productivity in diverse ways: by maintaining physical and mental health, by avoiding disruptive criminal and social unheavals and by educating labor so as to enable it to perform at its maximum efficiency.

The theoretical value of Lojkine's analysis lies in his linking of the prerequisites of capital accumulation and the dynamic of capitalist growth to the spatial form and settlement patterns of a semi-industrial capitalist city. Viewed from Lojkine's perspective, Nigerian state investments in communications, transportation and the collective means of consumption correspond to and advance the process of capital accumulation in semi-industrial urban centers. To be sure, the processes that are the object of Lojkine's theoretical analysis are only beginning to emerge and to shape the urban social processes of Kano. But they do exist. For example, new motor roads are reducing the time taken for transportation between Kano and other regional cities; motorized transport, using new roads that have drastically restructured communication patterns in the ancient walled city of Birni, has replaced human-powered carts for intra-urban transportation of goods; and state investments in the collective means of consumption, especially educational facilities, have restructured settlement patterns, as have the physical sitings of state services ranging from administration and health to economic infrastructure. Therefore, insofar as state investments (in transportation and communication, as well as in the collective means of consumption), structure urban class relations and influence class segregation patterns and the speed at which urban social interaction flows, one may develop a thesis that explains the process of urban class formation as the product of *participation in the diffuse urban social processes* arising from residence and consumption in a semi-industrial city as well as from *participation in the labor process* of capitalist production.

URBAN SOCIAL PROCESSES: CAPITAL ACCUMULATION AND COMMODITY RELATIONS

If, as I have argued, participation in the urban social processes of a semi-industrial city socializes wage earners into a working class identity, then it is important to describe such processes in detail, to measure their growth during the period of interest and to explain how these processes are crucial to understanding urban class formation. At the same time, not withstanding the rapidity and scale of the capitalist transformation that has occurred during military rule, urban Kano remains a Muslim city. This means that precapitalist elements (i.e., institutions, ideologies and organizations) remain in some complex relationship to emerging capitalist forces. One should expect that, while capitalist processes of capital accumulation and commodity relations are on the ascendancy, in actual empirical reality they are always found in a complex relationship (e.g., articulation) to their precapitalist counterparts. In subsequent chapters I shall describe in detail how the two articulate with each other, but in this section my purpose is to

65

analyze at the micro-level the *internal* social processes of urban capitalist development so as to illustrate how participation in these diffuse urban processes makes an independent contribution to urban working class formation.

To speak of capital accumulation on the ascendancy requires some explanation. Firstly, during the period of interest the activities of Kano's dominant indigenous classes have been directed increasingly toward acquiring private ownership of the means of producing goods and services and objects of value: e.g., shops, land, houses, state contracts and finance, and consumer goods for sale and consumption. Secondly, besides mercantile-finance capitalist activities, which have expanded both in scale and in concentration, the production of goods and services by these same classes has increased significantly through the garnering of government contracts, private investment in factories, access to state-sponsored financing, and joint ventures with international firms. Not only has wealth been invested in income-generating capitalist projects, which of course generate more wealth, but wage labor increasingly has replaced more personal forms of clientage as the dominant form of remuneration within these productive organizations. That is to say, wage labor, either formally as in a large factory or informally as in the local construction industry, increasingly became the dominant way in which profit and thus capital were accumulated.

The process of capital accumulation, therefore, has advanced from one primarily based upon commerce, trade and 'Muslim finance' to one based upon ownership and/or participation in industrial production, obtainment of lucrative state contracts for construction and other services, acquisition of land for real estate speculation or the erection of houses for new urban immigrants, and increasingly, at the experimental level, agricultural investments in land, machinery and improvements. To a marked degree, capital accumulation has moved toward productive enterprises employing wage labor or directly productive services such as housing construction and large-scale transportation, as well as toward indirectly productive financial and commerical services. In comparison to the period preceding the civil war, therefore, the process of capital accumulation by the dominant classes has transformed the social relations of urban Kano in several ways: by undermining Muslim cultural values and institutionalized restraints on capital accumulation; by creating marketable commodities out of formerly natural and household objects; by intensifying competition, and thus socio-economic differentiation, among residents for the acquisition of valued commodities; and by entering increasingly into the production of industrial and agricultural commodities for consumption as wage goods by urban wage earners and other consumers.

In order to be successful in the competitive scramble for capital accumulation, the perspective of Kano's accumulators, the bourgeoisie, must change such that objects are viewed not for their natural qualities or their symbolic or ritual (i.e., Islamic) significance but as commodities, that is, objects that are produced or taken from a natural situation to be sold on the market for a profit. As Marx states so clearly, the essence of capitalism is contained in the *commodity relation*, the process whereby all objects, including human labor, are treated as marketable, as having some price and thus as a source of potential profit if the constraints on their 'commodification' can be eliminated, be they precapitalist, religious, sentimental or political.[33] Given the atmosphere created during such an intense, competitive period of capital accumulation as exists in contemporary Nigeria, it is readily apparent that human labor also becomes a commodity (i.e., labor power), that the relationship between buyers and sellers of objects, including human labor power, takes on the quality of the commodities exchanged, and that human relationships in the most generalized sense take on the character of commodity relations, leading to the gradual demise of the precapitalist cultural values (i.e., Islamic) that once restrained the full development of commodity relations.

At the micro-sociological level then, the period of interest witnessed intense capital accumulation: new magnates and greater concentrations of capital emerged; the process of capital accumulation penetrated new fields of activity; and human social relations increasingly took on the character of commodity relations. Viewed as underlying social forces, capital accumulation and commodity relations find their concrete expression as an urban social process in the increasing use of the impersonal market to hire labor, to purchase the means of subsistence and to satisfy human needs. Amongst many urban social processes, the most important class socializing experience for urban laborers arises from competition for limited work in the urban labor market. It is here that individuals confront the impersonality of commodity relations and the objective reality that, in order to survive, they must find someone to purchase their labor power.

Land as a commodity: primitive accumulation in a semi-industrial city

During the colonial period, a truly capitalist land market was blocked by colonial authorities who feared the inequities and social differentiation that speculation and rentier capitalism would create.[34] Prior to the civil war, land was vested in the authority of the Emir and was distributed, not sold, through the local government authority. Demand, though increasing, was comparatively limited by state action and by the mercantile capitalist character of the groundnut economy. With the civil war and the petroleum boom, however, an unprecedented scramble for land erupted in three areas: first, in the urban area, where a secondary land market already existed; second, in the peri-urban area adjacent to the city and especially along major routes such as the Kano-Zaria-Kaduna road; and lastly, in more distant rural areas, in part for commercial agriculture but mainly for speculative investment.

67

Nurtured by a huge increase in the money supply, by the petroleum revenue and by an annual average inflation rate of between 20 and 50 percent during this period, the search for land investments by the various fractions of the bourgeoisie and the salaried middle class was feverish. Land prices spiralled in the secondary land market to reach thousands of naira per plot by the middle of the 1970s. Moreover, state infrastructural facilities (e.g., airports, army bases, schools and government administration) required large tracts of land in the peri-urban area surrounding Kano. Similarly, the new industrial estates at Sharada, Challawa and the Bompai extension also urbanized large tracts of land to which the peasantry once held usufructuary rights. Irrespective of the scale of land transfers from the peasantry to the state for infrastructure and 'the collective means of consumption', the voracity of the land grab is most evident in the private acquisition of land for private housing and commercial purposes.

Here one observes how the bureaucratic bourgeoisie and the private bourgeoisie collaborate in the process of primitive accumulation, a process involving the forcible, even violent, appropriation of valuable peasant land without paying the fair market value. Because the peasant holder of undeveloped land did not legally own the land but only possessed usufructuary rights, once peasant land was confiscated and declared a 'settlement area', the state (i.e., the local government authority) paid the former peasant landholder only a disturbance fee. Afterwards, the state reallocated the peasant's land to a new owner who could afford to make the necessary urban improvements. The new owner paid the state only the disturbance fee and not the true market value of the land. In 1973 the compensation or disturbance fee was ₦120 per acre everywhere in the urban area. Given the low value of this fee, the critical question concerns the manner in which state officials reallocated peasant lands. After researching this question extensively, Frishman concluded that farm land on the urban fringe sells for 1.7 to 5 times the compensation fee; residential land in the built-up area sells for 66 to 333 times the compensation fee; and commercial sites sell for 200 to 1,000 times the fee. Frishman concluded his essentially neo-classical economic analysis with this comment:

> The government power of declaring an area a 'settlement area' and paying compensation, therefore, is disruptive of the secondary market for land, and is a method of transferring expensive land from farmers to 'respected' urban residents at a devalued rate. In effect, the government is taxing the poorer farmers and subsidizing the richer urban resident.[35]

The role of the state in expropriating the peasantry and in advancing land tenure as a commodity relation requires elaboration. In the case of Kano's land tenure system, precapitalist and colonial institutions inhibited the development of a capitalist land market in the western sense. This policy reinforced the power of their clients, the sarauta, and constrained the development of land as a commodity. But under the conditions of semi-industrial capitalism, the process of primitive accumulation is very much in evidence. The state is used by the bourgeoisie to control and to own land that had been available to urban residents on the basis of *need* during the precolonial and most of the colonial periods. By confiscating peasant lands and paying a disturbance fee below the market price, state policy rewards real estate speculators and capitalist classes, yet uses the traditional authority of the state to legitimize the allocation of land in the name of the community. Again, as the process of primitive accumulation extends spatially into the peasant communities of the peri-urban area, the newly landless are expelled into the urban labor market as unskilled workers, where they are forced to struggle for subsistence.

The housing market: urban rentier capitalism and wage goods

The question of housing relates closely to the previous section, for Kano's population grows both by the emigration of rural inhabitants and by the spatial expansion of the city, which literally engulfs peasant villages, appropriates their lands and forces them to become dependent upon urban income sources for their livelihood. Note that since the population densities surrounding urban Kano have already reached 1,400 per square mile, the engulfment of such villages adds significantly to the rate of urban population growth.[36] In any event, all migrants to the city and even some engulfed and expropriated peasants are forced to seek shelter in Kano's urban housing market. Of course, the latter is quite differentiated with regard to price, quality, and degree of ethnic and class segregation. Elite housing for the upper classes is in great demand and is so expensive that it is common for tenants to be required to pay rent several years in advance.

My concern is with the housing market of the lower income groups and especially the wage-earning classes. As stated earlier, the conditions wrought by the civil war and the petroleum boom generated an enormous demand for housing, especially for state- and private-sector wage earners. In the face of this seemingly insatiable demand for shelter, housing became a lucrative investment for all fractions of the bourgeoisie and the more affluent salaried classes. In Chapter Four, I shall devote space to issues surrounding rentier capitalism, absentee landlords and the quality of amenities in Kano's oldest working class area – Tudun Wada – but here it is suggested, at a more abstract level of analysis, how the rise of rentier capitalism relates to the transition to semi-industrial capitalism in Kano.

The expansion of rentier capitalism, as well as the impersonality of the transactions, reflects the tendency under semi-industrial capitalism for goods like housing, that are necessary to meet the human needs of wage earners and independent commodity producers (i.e., craftsmen and petty traders), to become a source of profit and hence capital accumulation. Thus, in a short time, even some relatively small-scale traders advanced to become owners of dozens of quickly constructed houses in the lower-

69

income areas of Kano. What had formerly been a part of a household economy, whose price was not necessarily rationally calculated as it was often rented for a nominal price to relatives, friends or business associates, now became a valuable commodity. More importantly, housing is a wage good whose cost enters into the cost of production of manufactured commodities and services. In this sense, housing expenditures are moving out of the informal household economy and entering the circuits of semi-industrial capitalism as a cost of labor power and thus as a cost of modern sector goods. Further, the emergence of rentier capitalists, whose source of profit depends on the income of wage earners, not only reduces the role of household producers but puts them into an intimate, more integrated relationship with business cycles that govern the demand for manufactured foods, which, in turn, are linked to the national and world economy.

Note further that the sale of houses by owners is becoming increasingly impersonal and commodified, as compared to an earlier era when it was customary, especially in the more conservative Birni, to retain houses within the family. For example, when Frishman conducted a survey (1973) of housing sales in the Birni (N=145), he discovered that sales to 'relatives' accounted for only 15.9 percent of transactions, while the equivalent figures for categories such as 'don't know seller' and 'an acquaintance' accounted for 28.3 percent and 36.6 percent, respectively.[37] Again, allow me to emphasize that this level of impersonality is found in the Birni, not in a migrant area of the Waje where commoditization of housing is far more advanced. (See Table 4.3 for comparable data in Tudun Wada.)

Here one should reflect for a moment on the process that I have described in the last and present sections. The appropriation of peasant land, the expelling of the inhabitants into the urban labor market, and the urban housing market are ideal examples of urban capitalist social processes that socialize recent migrants into the urban working class. The gradual erosion of patrimonial household relations, the subsequent decline in the charitable allocation of shelter to the indigent and the expansion of the market for inflated wage goods like housing are critical to understanding the role of urban social processes in working class formation. The worker's struggle to obtain housing is particularly important, for it penetrates the family and imprints the experience of commodity relations into the consciousness of the next generation of urban workers.

The struggle for the means of subsistence and the means of collective consumption

Like housing, food is a wage good on which urban workers, the laboring poor and independent commodity producers spend a large portion of their income. Again, just as in the case of housing, food processing and distribution are moving away from small-scale household processors and

Table 2.1 *Food prices and industrial wages in Kano, 1971–80*[a]

	November 1971	November 1975	Increase 1971–5[b]	November 1978	Increase 1971–8[b]	December 1980	Increase 1971–80[b]
Millet (measure)	0.17	0.50	(1.94)	1.10	(5.47)	1.20	(6.05)
Rice (measure)	0.83	1.60	(0.92)	2.50	(2.01)	5.50	(5.62)
Sorghum (Guinea Corn) (measure)	0.21	0.50	(1.38)	1.00	(3.76)	1.00	(3.76)
Beef (kilo)	0.93	—	—	2.50	(1.68)	3.50	(2.76)
Palm oil (beer bottle)	0.17	0.70	(3.11)	1.55	(8.11)	1.00	(4.88)
Groundnut oil (beer bottle)	0.25	0.85	(2.40)	1.25	(4.00)	0.70	(1.80)
Pepper (measure)	0.33	—	—	1.00	(2.03)	3.50	(9.60)
Starting wage for industrial worker	0.87	1.75	(1.01)	2.25	(1.58)	3.85	(3.43)

[a] Wages and prices in naira (one naira=approximately $1.65)

[b] Rate of increase $= \dfrac{\text{(Price at given year)} - \text{(Price November 1971)}}{\text{(Price November 1971)}}$

increasingly falling under the control of industrial capital. Of course, this is a relative statement, for female-organized household production and processing of foodstuffs remains high. But the shift in popular consumption away from traditional grains like millet and sorghum, which require great quantities of labor to prepare, and toward refined white flour or locally produced bread is apparent. Aside from the net loss in nutrition that this shift in taste represents, the trend reflects the increasing role of industrial capital (i.e., flour milling and bakeries) in the production of wage goods and therefore in the material reproduction of the laboring and popular classes.

For a number of reasons – civil war, cyclical drought, state investment policies, urban wage rates and urban migration – food production in Nigeria has failed to keep up with demand. So serious is the food deficit in Nigeria, where approximately 70 percent of the labor force is located in agriculture, that Nigeria's food import bill reached three billion dollars in 1980.[38] Combined with speculation and hoarding, inflation has driven up the price of food relative to the unskilled wage rate for industrial workers. Table 2.1 illustrates the relationship between the starting wage for an industrial worker and the cost of basic foodstuffs from 1971 to 1980. Note that all foodstuffs listed have increased at a rate well beyond the rate of wage increases. The situation, one should emphasize, is far worse for casual workers, informal-sector wage workers, marginal peddlers and the laboring poor, who do not earn the comparatively high wages offered to beginning industrial workers. Again, the struggle to obtain food is a primary antagonism for urban wage workers and members of the urban talakawa, who depend on the market for subsistence. When discussing the socializing effects of participation in the urban social process on working class formation, it is to this constant struggle for the means of subsistence in the

71

face of unprecedented opulence and internationalized consumption styles among the affluent classes that I refer. As I shall illustrate in Chapter Seven, participation in the urban social processes of a semi-industrial city has a strong effect on a worker's evaluation of the fairness of his wages, which, of course, determines his consumption standard.

At this point, I wish to consider for a moment what effect inflation has on the struggle for the means of consumption and, over the long term, on the process of urban class formation. In the case of Kano, the transition from mercantile to semi-industrial capitalism occurs during a period of rapid inflation (20 to 50 percent annually) that is fuelled by the petroleum boom, contradictory state policies and the importation of inflation from the world economy, to which, of course, OPEC pricing is a major contributor. While the transition to semi-industrial capitalism is destructive of institutions and values associated with mercantile Muslim capitalism and the livelihoods of independent commodity producers, inflation makes the consequences of this transition even more devastating for the majority of Kano's inhabitants. Unless urban consumers have access to a source of income that is automatically indexed to the inflation rate, real income falls and consumers must compete more intensely with each other in order to maintain the same real level of subsistence. Inflation, as Castells observes, 'hits the least favored categories of the population; and encourages the purchase of goods already on the market'.[39] Not only does this increase the struggle over urban consumption, but: 'Inflation makes people more consumption-oriented at the same time as it differentiates them according to their capacity for consumption'.[40] Even conservative researchers such as Bienen and Diejomaoh agree that income inequalities have widened during the period of interest.[41] More specifically, a recent World Bank study (1982) estimates that 52 to 67 percent of Kano's urban population remain at the 'absolute poverty level', i.e., less than $472 per capita per annum; and 48 to 62 percent fall into the 'relative poverty level', i.e., below $402 per capita per annum.[42] Hence, while the transition to semi-industrial capitalism displaces the weaker independent commodity producers and small-scale entrepreneurs in favor of the bourgeoisie who obtain the monopoly of the state, the conjunctural effect of high and continual inflation increases the intensity of the dislocation experienced by the urban lower classes and sharpens the antagonistic features of urban class formation.

In theory, the state has allocated funds for the development of educational and medical facilities (i.e., the means of collective consumption) for all urban inhabitants regardless of class or income level. But in reality urban workers and the urban talakawa do not have equal access to quality medical care or western education. This is especially true for entry into post-primary schools, which, with the huge expansion of primary education financed by the FMG's Universal Primary Education Program, is the gate-keeping mechanism for entry into skilled or salaried employment for the urban lower classes. In Chapter Five, I shall analyze industrial workers' views regarding equality of access to secondary school for their sons.

While the state follows the program described by Lojkine in that it continues to invest in the collective means of consumption, access to quality medical care is class-determined. The hospitals are riddled with corruption and incompetence, such that drugs often must be purchased from the hospital personnel, and bribes must be paid to obtain a hospital bed. Experienced urban residents are aware of this and if possible they seek, as do the upper classes, medical treatment from private clinics and missionary hospitals. Like so many legal rights and privileges granted as formal social rights to Kano's urban lower classes, access to quality medical care, even at a standard that is appropriate to the material and social development of the society, is largely a fiction. Hence, to the struggle to obtain the means of subsistence must be added the struggle to gain access to the means of collective consumption. Both of these struggles, while outside of the labor process of capitalist production, are primary experiences that socialize workers into the class perspective of the urban lower classes. Such constant daily struggles are part of the urban social process of a semi-industrialized capitalist city, a process which reinforces class inequalities at the worksite and in the urban labor market. Organized movements of lower class urban dwellers around issues governing individual and collective consumption are rare at Kano. Instead, expressions of protest are more likely to take the form of food riots or millenarian movements, though, as I shall describe in Chapter Four, informal forms of community protest against individuals who betray community trust in the allocation of housing plots have also occurred.

Urban social processes and working class formation

To the list of changes that weigh upon the consciousness of urban workers one should add the effects of huge and increasing inequalities between the urban lower classes and the upper classes with regard to access to state patronage and privileges, increasing differentiation in material culture, lifestyles and recreational activities and (as I suggested in the section on global economy), the internationalization of consumption among Kano's urban bourgeoisie. Unlike housing, food, land, education, health or participation in the urban labor market, the aforementioned inequities are neither material experiences nor daily struggles. Yet to reside in a semi-industrial city that links the periphery to the centers of the world economy is itself a powerful socializing force for both recent migrants and the popular classes. Why? Residence requires even the most insulated and backward entrants to urban life to participate in the urban social processes I have described. At the same time, individuals are exposed to the mechanisms of state power; they observe the contradiction between ideological promise and the real activity of the wealthy and powerful in a way that rural residents cannot. In this sense, exposure to the urban social processes of a semi-industrial city demystifies state power, which, of course, may lead to cynicism and despair as well as to class consciousness and political action.

Earlier I alluded to the transfer of taste and the internationalization of consumption that resulted from Kano's role as a linking urban center to the larger capitalist world economy. Clearly, the period of military rule witnessed no change more dramatic than the internationalization of consumption by the bourgeoisie. It is not so much the extravagance and luxury that civil war contracting and the petroleum revenue brought, nor the bevy of electronic consumer items (televisions, stereos, tape decks and video recorders) and regular shopping tours to European cities, nor the enormous expansion of automobile ownership that explains the tension arising from the internationalization of consumption.[43] Rather it is the stark contrast between the consumption styles of a tiny minority of the urban population and those of the overwhelming majority of the inhabitants, whose living standards have either declined or only marginally improved. And, of course, this statement says nothing about the extraordinary decline in the quality of urban life: traffic congestion, increased public health hazards, increased pollution, spiralling theft, increasing criminal violence and the loss of community solidarity and deeply sentimental ties that once informally ordered the quality of urban Muslim cultural life. All of this occurred recently and rapidly during the last decade. It cannot be emphasized too strongly that to grasp the hiatus that separates the consumption standards of the two extremes, one must imagine the consciousness of a recent migrant, perhaps recently 'liberated' from his ancestral land in the peri-urban area, as he walks through Nasarawa area, where strongly guarded, neatly gardened, multi-story mansions contrast so sharply with his own home and community in the recently expanded area of Dakata or Tudun Murtala where refuse water running through irregular gutters forms cholera-breeding pools and where he rents a single, mud-constructed room for his family of four. However depressing the contrasts of contemporary Kano may be, it is important to remember that participation in the urban social process is a dialectical experience in that it contains the seeds of human emancipation as well as the culture of class domination and despair.

One of the positive aspects that participation in the urban social processes offers to the urban lower classes is the opportunity to acquire literacy in western script, if not literacy in English, the language employed in the modern international sector. As will be illustrated in Chapter Five, Muslim workers quickly learn the importance of literacy in western script for surviving in the semi-industrialized city. Such literacy enables them to obtain higher-paying employment, to participate in political and trade union activities more effectively, to communicate among themselves and to raise their level of self-esteem and their aspirations for themselves and their children. To offer a concrete example, I recall a poignant moment during an interview with an illiterate, a recent migrant factory worker, when he described his shame 'as feeling like a donkey' when he had to ask passers-by to read the street signs and house numbers so that he could report for a new job. Literacy, moreover, marks a rite of passage into the communication system of semi-industrial and even world capitalist culture. It is surprising to note that a proportion of workers acquire Hausa literacy in western script through night school and informal training from literate friends. Viewed as a tool of entry into the cultural and communication system of semi-industrial urban capitalism, literacy should be recognized as an attribute that reflects an individual's integration into and ability to cope effectively with the struggles inherent in a semi-industrial capitalist city.

It has been argued that many aspects of the urban social processes that are related to, yet distinct from, the role an individual plays in the social relations of production make an independent contribution to the process of class formation, class consciousness and, at a more general level, the formation of a populist political consciousness. For reasons of clarity, the description and analysis of the urban labor market has been postponed until the following chapter where there will be sufficient space to provide the necessary empirical material. Discussion of the labor market necessitates an understanding of the urban class structure and the manner in which precapitalist elements articulate with emerging semi-industrial capitalist elements so as to give force and direction to the political movements struggling to control the state apparatus in Kano State. Let us turn to the class structure of urban Kano.

Urban class structure in transition: accumulation and articulation

Thus far I have emphasized how urban Kano has been transformed by the transition to semi-industrial capitalism, a process that involves state struc-tures, global economic relations and micro-level urban social processes. Yet, as dramatic as the transition to semi-industrial capitalism may be, neither the scale nor the intensity of this process has completely abolished precapitalist organizations, practices, institutions and ideologies. Rather, the outcome is highly uneven, where prior social forms exist side by side with emerging forms and expressions of semi-industrial capitalism. Nonetheless, it would be a serious conceptual error to presume that ideal-typical dual societies have emerged or that dualism (i.e., modern and traditional sectors) offers a solution to analyzing urban class formation during a period of rapid tran-sition. In contrast to dualism, I shall argue that one must take account of the totality of social relations that structure Kano as an urban social formation. And further, one must examine precapitalist and semi-industrial capitalist elements as they intertwine and relate to each other. That is to say, one must examine how precapitalist and capitalist elements *articulate* with each other in contradictory as well as complementary ways, giving shape and expres-sion to the increasingly dominant process of semi-industrial capitalism.

75

In order to develop this conception of class analysis in the following chapters, it is important to emphasize that semi-industrial capitalism is hegemonic and continually increasing in strength, whether from external or internal sources of capital accumulation. But hegemonic does not mean solely determinant. In actual reality, the logical development of capitalism in Kano is constrained by the resistance and influence of precapitalist ideologies, political organizations and status-honor groups, household economic organizations, redistributive practices of precapitalist origin, and cultural modes that govern the timing and discipline of everyday life. Conversely, although the contradictory tension between precapitalist and capitalist processes is most visible, under certain conditions precapitalist elements (be they ideologies, institutions or organizations) may articulate with capitalist processes so as to *advance* the logical purpose of capitalism. The outcomes may not be linear in direction. Empirically, therefore, one might observe precapitalist elements joined with a capitalist organization or interwoven into an emerging social class, which acting in combination may serve to intensify either the process of capital accumulation or that of class struggle. Viewed from this dialectical perspective, the articulation of precapitalist to capitalist elements means that they co-exist out of necessity, not choice, and in so doing they act either to reinforce or to constrain the logical development of each other.

Note that oftentimes co-existence means that precapitalist elements are necessary for the reproduction of capitalist elements. Nevertheless, despite the strength of precapitalist elements, the long-term transition of urban Kano is one in which capitalism is dominant, and thus by its very nature it gradually erodes, undermines and subordinates the autonomy of precapitalist organizations, institutions and ideologies. Theorists suggest concepts such as co-existence, unevenness, combined development and articulation, but these are abstract terms that cannot predict the specific empirical form which articulation will take or the purposes for which transitional classes will use precapitalist elements. Hence, while ancient social practices, forms of redistribution and certain cultural values appear to decline, specific precapitalist elements may be conserved, not merely as cultural curiosities but as resources for the accumulation of capital by the dominant classes. Alternatively, their social antagonists, the subordinate classes, may employ precapitalist elements as a legitimizing tradition through which they resist new forms of domination and exploitation. As applied in this study, articulation is valuable as a conceptual tool that makes one aware of the dynamic processes of class formation under semi-industrial capitalism, but it must be specified empirically in each instance. Let us turn to the issues of class structure and class analysis.

Theoretical approaches to social class

What, then, is the meaning and usage of the term social class? By class, I am referring to objective roles in the social division of labor that are determined by the productive activities required by a given system of production.[44] The production process should be understood as a social process encompassing all purposive human activity, and not merely in the technical or strictly laboring sense of the term. Internally, the solidarity of classes that fill these objective locations in a production process is determined in a positive sense by the cohesion generated through participation in mutually shared productive activities and by the common experiences of their social existence. In the negative sense, solidarity is generated by their shared opposition to antagonistic classes, either dominant or subordinate, with whom they must struggle over the division of the material surplus. The dominant classes, be they entrepreneurial capitalists, Muslim officeholders or plantation slave owners, must obtain control over the socially produced surplus, that is, over and above the amount necessary to maintain the direct producers at a historically and morally determined level of subsistence. Class, therefore, is a *relational* concept. Classes reflect common social relations among those who share the same role in the social division of labor and antagonistic social relations of exploitation between the direct producers and those who extract surplus from them. Hence, the struggle between the direct producers and the dominant classes over the control of societal surplus – rent, profit, surplus labor or payment in kind – forms one of the underlying social tensions that contribute in a major way to historical change.

As one moves from the abstract definition of social class to classes as real historical, social and political actors, theorists differ regarding their criteria for the definition of an active social class. Structuralists, employing strictly formal criteria, define classes in terms of the formal role that classes play in a labor process with reference to an abstract model of a given mode of production, itself a non-historical, Marxist ideal-type.[45] This approach is valuable for constructing models that are logically consistent and centered on production processes. In contrast to the structuralist approach, the alternative historical approach defines social classes both by the role that they play in a theoretically defined production process and by the way in which they define themselves in the actual process of class struggle as it unfolds under particular historical and contradictory conditions of *social existence*. Again, as opposed to abstract definitions of structuralist theory, historical interpreters of class analysis are interested in how classes as social and historical actors shape their own history and act out political solutions which determine to a significant degree the internal boundaries and conscious self-identity of their class. Viewed from this perspective, classes are situationally determined and are contradictory historical actors, influenced by political and even precapitalist traditions. Historical theorists emphasize that self-activity and past struggles with their antagonists determine to a significant degree the class boundaries and political objectives of a given class. Summarizing this perspective, Zeitlin states 'classes and class "interests" are both "objectively given" and themselves are dialectical historical products ... determined both by their place in a historically

77

specific ensemble of productive relations and by their own self activity'.[46]
E. P. Thompson is less strict, even anti-theoretical in his definition: 'Class
is defined by men as they live their own history, and, in the end, this is its
only definition.'[47]

What is important, then, for historical analysts is the nature of political
action undertaken by a given class and not the logical inconsistencies of a
particular class coalition as measured against an abstract model. Classes
are historical products. As such, members carry with them a sense of
solidarity with other strata or classes as well as internal cleavages that
derive from precapitalist institutions, ethnic and national identity or the
influence of the world economy. It is not that all historical theorists of class
analysis completely reject the value of abstract analysis in the vein of
structuralist mode-of-production construction, but rather that they find
that classes in their capacity as real historical actors rarely, if ever,
conform to the logically consistent and elegant theoretical categories and
ideal types put forward by structuralist theorists. To summarize, the
historical approach is concerned with the political activity of classes, how
their consciousness contains ideas drawn from disparate traditions and
social experiences and, most importantly, how class members themselves
take class action which, in turn, shapes the historical development of
capitalism.

Classes possess subjective modes of consciousness as well as objective
locations in an ensemble of productive relations. All Marxists distinguish between an objective class without consciousness of itself and a
self-conscious class that understands its collective interests and antagonists, develops an ideology and a program that defines its interests and,
ultimately, takes political action in order to realize its interests. Though
the subjective dimension of a social class is crucial to an understanding
of class-based political action, it is equally difficult to isolate and to
interpret in a meaningful manner, especially among the inarticulate and
illiterate classes. Rather than searching for an ideally typical expression
of 'true' class consciousness within the subjectivity of a particular class,
the historical approach to class analysis is interested in the contradictory
elements as well as those elements that conform to the theoretically
expected features of consciousness. What is the value of this approach?
If one examines the contradictory elements, one may observe not only
how the historical evolution of a class imprints its character but also
how the historically determined yet contradictory elements present
within a conscious class or class coalition will determine the political
movement, goals and organization of that class or class coalition. But
here the structuralist concept of articulation is valuable also, for it
allows one to locate the origins of a contradictory element of class
consciousness within the internal logic of a prior, usually precapitalist,
social formation, and thus one gains insight into the potentiality of a
given class.

78

AN OUTLINE OF KANO'S CLASS STRUCTURE: THE DOMINANT AND
INTERMEDIATE CLASSES

My objective here is to provide the framework for a detailed analysis of the
laboring and popular classes and especially of the consciousness of industrial workers, who it is argued, are the most advanced class fragment of a
broader urban working class – the *leburori*. Further, it is important to note
that the indigenous Muslim, Hausa-speaking community is the substantive
and theoretical object of this study. As indicated earlier, both the personnel
of international firms and other resident aliens are extremely important in
the advanced sectors of Kano's economy, but they are marginal to the
internal processes of class formation since they do not participate in politics,
nor are most alien entrepreneurs residents. Those issues related to Kano's
ethnic minorities will be discussed in Chapters Three, Four and Seven.

Even within a situation of intense capital accumulation, marked by new
forms of production, rapid urban growth and unprecedented kinds and
degrees of inequality, the precapitalist class-like status-honor system of
sarauta (office-holders) and talakawa (commoners) continues to exert its
influence on the structure and consciousness of emerging social classes. As I
indicated in Chapter One, during colonialism and prior to the collapse of
the First Nigerian Republic, classes, determined not by political status but
rather by the role they played in the production process, began to
differentiate themselves from the precapitalist status groups of sarauta and
talakawa. Merchant capitalists and urban wage laborers, for instance,
became more prominent, while craft producers declined in importance.
Nevertheless, one should understand that the process of capital accumulation, the extension and deepening of capitalist social relations and the
concomitant erosion of institutions, practices and values of precapitalist
origin have not erased the influence of the precapitalist elements of the
structure and consciousness of Kano's urban classes. Let us examine the
process of differentiation with each status-honor group so as to trace the
emergence of distinct social classes.

During the late colonial period, the sarauta aligned themselves politically
with the merchant capitalist classes, but within the state they limited their
involvement to administration in local, regional and national services. But
with the centralization and expansion of federal power, the reform of local
government and the enormous increase in wealth associated with the
petroleum boom, the sarauta and especially their more highly educated
sons have entered the federal and state civil service and the technocratic
state capitalist sector; here production decisions, capital investment and
managerial expertise are required, in contrast to the purely political-
administrative activities so typical of the previous generation. Together
with the sons of wealthy commoners, the new state bureaucratic class is
drawn largely from the sarauta stratum and from groups traditionally
associated with the sarauta, such as judicial families. Given the advantages

79

that accrue from their aristocratic birth, as well as their privileged education, social networks and the social graces that flow from primary
socialization into their status group, the sarauta are entrenched within the
hierarchy of the public sector. Thus, precapitalist status has a determining
effect on the formation and character of the Nigerian state-sector bourgeoisie, as was also true for their German and Japanese counterparts.

During the period of interest, however, the merchant class has emerged
as much more powerful than the sarauta, both because of the increased rate
of capital accumulation and because its leading members have become
prominent in the political life of Kano as Commissioners and office holders.
As we noted earlier, their sources of accumulation extend from trade and
finance to modern construction and manufacturing within and beyond Kano
State. Much of the capital accumulated depended upon access to state
contracts, especially during the civil war, and even included illegal activities
such as smuggling and currency manipulation. Nevertheless, as hegemonic
as the rule of capital is in Kano today, members of the wealthiest and most
powerful fractions of the bourgeoisie still acknowledge their talakawa status
by offering the customary greetings, appropriate to talakawa status, to a
prominent member of the sarauta. In some instances, moreover, members
of the more prominent families claim Fulani (i.e., aristocratic social)
origins, evidence of their recognition of precapitalist status, even during the
transition to semi-industrial capitalism.

Just as the merchant-industrialists, the most powerful and wealthiest
fraction of Kano's bourgeoisie, have become increasingly prominent in
roles once completely controlled by the sarauta (such as political activity
and state administration), the sarauta have also entered business, by
forming companies, by competing for state contracts, by serving as consultants and agents for joint ventures between local and international capitalists and, in general, by accumulating capital in the private sector.[48] Because
the sarauta families historically have controlled access to education, many
of their sons are well educated and well connected and thus are often
employed by technically advanced international firms such as banks. Yet, in
actual practice, their individual career paths move from international
capitalist firms to state enterprises and even back to private Nigerian firms,
often straddling public and private sectors. To chart such career paths offers
one a glimpse of the social relationships that integrate the two classes –
senior civil servants and the merchant-industrial bourgeoisie – who together
form the dominant class coalition. Whatever sectoral roles the sarauta-
origin bourgeoisie may hold during their career, in order to be successful
they must invest and accumulate capital through essentially capitalist
activities rather than solely through holding bureaucratic offices.

Bearing in mind the historical distinction between sarauta and merchant
members of the talakawa, which was originally a political status distinction,
Kano's emerging bourgeoisie contains both sarauta members who engage in
formally capitalist activity and merchant industrialists who wield consider-

able political power. As compared to the position held by sarauta from other traditional emirates, such as Katsina, Kano's sarauta are perceived as relatively weak when evaluated according to traditional criteria. But this evaluation is illusory. In fact, Kano's sarauta are positioning themselves to participate in the new, increasingly capitalist political order, where involvement in capital accumulation will be necessary in order to participate in the power brokerage with Kano's new aggressively capitalist magnates.

The state bourgeoisie and the relatively large-scale private-sector bourgeoisie, who are involved in finance, manufacturing, construction, wholesale trade and state contracting, form the upper tier of the bourgeoisie. Let us examine the remaining class fractions, examining first the traditional aristocracy.[49] Though not engaged directly in the accumulation of capital, and though their position and way of life is in decline, the traditional aristocracy remain members of the dominant class coalition that is increasingly taking on a bourgeois character. Within Kano, descent from a titled family remains a valuable asset. Similarly, merchant capitalists with investments in wholesale trade, transportation, real estate and medium-scale construction occupy the middle tier of Kano's bourgeoisie. This fraction lacks the capital resources, political power, international linkages and technical capacity of the economic organizations ruled by the leading members of the merchant industrial bourgeoisie. Yet the subordinate merchant fraction maintains linkages with the merchant industrialists through traditional clientage and credit relations, common religious affiliations and marriages. The dominant class in Kano, therefore, is an emerging bourgeoisie with fractions located in the state and private sectors but characterized by an informal overlap in terms of social relationships, lifestyles and political affiliations. Careers of the state bourgeoisie involve them in the affairs of international firms and present opportunities to obtain financial investments in the enterprises managed by the private-sector bourgeoisie. Again, while one may distinguish theoretically distinct classes or class fractions (i.e., merchant-industrialists, merchants, senior civil servants and the traditional aristocracy), together these groups form a class coalition whose degree of integration, lifestyle and distinction from other classes render to it the characteristics of an emerging bourgeoisie appropriate to a semi-industrial capitalist city.

The intermediate classes are made up of three strata drawn from the talakawa: a petty bourgeoisie, a salaried and educated middle class and, more marginally, a popular class of petty entrepreneurs. The new middle class, including professionals, exists objectively but is numerically insignificant and has not acted as a political force to date. Most members are employed by the state or, to a lesser degree, by international firms. The former class, the petty bourgeoisie, is numerous and therefore politically significant. It is a heterogeneous class whose members have credit and client linkages with the merchant classes. While they exist objectively as a class, they are neither wealthy enough to belong to the merchant fraction of the bourgeoisie nor powerful enough to form a class-based political party, though they are identified with the conservative faction of the PRP; nor are they so marginal as to belong to the popular stratum of petty entrepreneurs, stall owners, commission agents and successful craftsmen, whose position is in relative decline. The petty bourgeoisie own small transport companies, engage in some wholesale but mostly retail sales, often transacting business on credit rather than in cash, and may even own small-scale industrial enterprises such as cement block industries, machine repair shops or bakeries. Again, the membership of this class is characterized by a great deal of upward and downward mobility, and thus, without systematic empirical data, it is difficult to locate class boundaries during a period of rapid transition.

Finally, the popular stratum is composed of petty entrepreneurs, stall owners, taxi owners, small shopkeepers and small-scale craft producers. Fear of being crushed by competition from the merchant classes and the petty bourgoisie, and their subjective identification as members of the urban talakawa, have forced them to become allied with the populist class coalition that forms the social base of the PRP. Again, as we shall see, their rate of downward mobility into the working class is high. Hence, while the petty bourgeoisie may identify with the dominant classes and may actually achieve mobility into this class through the avenue of state patronage, the petty entrepreneurial stratum has virtually no chance of following this example. To conclude, the intermediate class, a large and diverse class, was caught between two blocs of power – the dominant classes represented by the NPN (National Party of Nigeria) and the populist coalition of the popular and working classes represented by the PRP – and therefore, as a class, it was unable to organize itself effectively and accepted the leadership of the two major blocs.

The laboring and popular classes: wage laborers and independent commodity producers

Just as membership in the sarauta status group informs the consciousness and strengthens authority within the state-sector bourgeoisie, so too membership in the talakawa influences emerging class boundaries within the class structure of urban Kano. In order to understand how talakawa status articulates within Kano's lower classes, it is necessary to know how talakawa status converges with the process of class differentiation associated with the deepening of semi-industrial capitalism. In a relative and absolute sense, the small-scale trading, craft and service groups, whom I call independent commodity producers, are declining economically and socially due to the economic, political and social changes I have described above. Independent producers who lack sufficient capital to cope with Nigeria's raging inflation rate, or who do not possess networks to state policymakers for such resources as import licenses, contracts and cheap credit, or who face the concentration of economic power and do not innovate by entering new markets or new activities have experienced relative and in some cases absolute economic decline during the period of military rule. Clearly, the increasing concentration of market activity, coupled with state sponsorship of the merchant industrialists and the large-scale merchants along with their clientage networks, have reduced the opportunities for small traders, commission agents and craft producers to maintain their relative market share. Hence, economic deprivation in terms of real income and relative status losses have shifted the social location of these groups downward toward the wage-earning and the propertyless classes and away from the intermediate classes such as the petty bourgeoisie.

In the context of intense competition, widespread inflation, increasing inequality and the internationalization of consumption which were described earlier, talakawa status has come to mean more than belonging to a powerless precapitalist status-honor group. During military rule, political domination was reduced as successive military governments eliminated the authoritarian political prerogatives of the sarauta which had allowed them to exploit the talakawa. But even more important was the extension of commodity relations associated with the deepening of semi-industrial capitalism, a process which undermined traditional clientage and integrative social networks between the wealthy and their petty trading dependants. Together, these two processes – the virtual elimination of sarauta authoritarian domination and the intensification of commodity relations – created a popularly conceived image of the talakawa not so much as powerless commoners but as an impoverished urban stratum that lacked the resources to stem their relative decline. Again, it is not the case that wealthy merchants or the petty bourgeoisie would deny their talakawa origins, but no one would associate them with the urban talakawa during a period of ruthless competition to accumulate capital, since possession of capital eliminated virtually all barriers to their economic, political and social opportunities.

During the period of interest, therefore, the talakawa label came to be associated not only with poverty but with the urban lower classes who lacked modern education, access to state patronage, or sufficient capital to keep up with the more dynamic, capital-accumulating classes. Given these changes in Kano society, the talakawa came to be identified with petty entrepreneurs and with laboring groups, that is to say, with those who worked with their hands as well as the formal wage-earning groups – the leburori. But, interestingly, the political content of the term talakawa did not disappear. In order to understand why, one must bear in mind that the economy is based upon the distribution of oil revenues directly and indirectly dispensed through the state. Thus, the urban talakawa believe that they did not benefit because of political discrimination directed against them by the dominant classes, mostly because of their poverty and their ignorance of modern skills and lifestyles (such as those associated with western education). So, under semi-industrial capitalism, the political conception of what talakawa means has changed. At the same time, most members of the urban lower classes came to see their poverty as *politically* as well as economically determined. Given the rise in political power held by the merchant industrialists, one should emphasize that the bourgeoisie are not defined by the urban lower classes as talakawa but rather as 'the rich' (*masu kudi*). Moreover, as residents of the city, the urban talakawa know that because wealth purchases political influence, the wealthy classes possess political power, either formally or informally.

These changes are based on the premise that the petroleum boom has widened the gap between the wealthiest and the poorest income groups. Virtually all sources agree that income has become less equally distributed, and as all social analysts know, income distribution studies not only fail to account for informal, entrepreneurial or illegal transfers of income but ignore the distribution of wealth as well.[50] Under these conditions, the urban talakawa became more closely identified with the wage-laboring classes, even if comparatively more secure independent producers subsisted from petty commerce or sales commissions rather than from wages. To comprehend this change in the meaning and usage of talakawa, one must understand that the upper classes have differentiated themselves in terms of amount of capital controlled, technical forms of production, distribution and credit, and in doing so they have distanced themselves from the petty entrepreneurial classes and other independent commodity producers, who cling to the values and institutions of a declining form of Muslim mercantile capitalism.

Viewed in dynamic terms, the restructuring of the class structure forces the non-competitive independent commodity producers into the newly defined urban talakawa. At the same time, those classes who have benefitted from semi-industrial capitalism, who tend increasingly to use wage labor rather than more paternalistic forms of household labor, have created a larger and more diverse wage-earning class – the urban *leburori*, who join the latter groups in the newly defined urban talakawa. What emerges then is an occupationally diverse yet politically conscious class coalition composed of two analytically distinct classes – independent commodity producers and wage laborers – who, though possessing different roles in the social division of labor and tending to an ideal-typical mode of capitalist production, nonetheless share the same *political-class* identity, that of membership in the urban talakawa. Over the long term, depending on the struggles of particular groups, many of the independent commodity producers will become wage laborers as semi-industrial capitalism exerts its effects on the class structure; that is to say, urban capitalist development will force these two classes even closer. But, for the current period, the urban talakawa form a diverse and poorly organized class coalition, unified by common roots in their talakawa status identity and by a common sense of poverty, powerlessness, exclusion from state patronage and alienation from the lifestyles of the educated and the dominant classes. Again, the transitional nature of the period means that each class (i.e., independent commodity producers and wage laborers) may act as a conscious class at their respective workplaces, but their common 'social existence', reflected by residence, social ties, the pressure of market forces and the cohesion of their talakawa identity, still directs their political consciousness toward the populist movements of the urban talakawa.

The social and material forces that hold the laboring and popular classes together and those that separate them are the object of my analysis in the next chapter. Thus I shall complete the outline of Kano's class structure here and hold the detailed empirical analysis of each class and class fraction within the urban talakawa until Chapter Three. Nevertheless, it is clear that the declining independent commodity producers and others in the petty entrepreneurial class are the aristocrats of the urban talakawa. Others, such as wage laborers, aspire to achieve a return to an independent status, whether as craftsmen or as traders. Internally, one distinguishes those engaged in different forms of craft and small-scale industrial activity from those engaged purely in sales or who live by commissions realized from selling the goods of others for a fee. Again, the diversity of this social class defies curt summary and thus requires detailed empirical description.

Following the independent commodity producers in relative status are the wage workers employed in the modern state sector. This sector is attractive to unskilled wage workers because of the comparatively high level of job security and the privileges associated with work in the modern enumerated sector (labor law, unions, wage reviews and other material and legal rights). Though also located in the modern enumerated sector, wage workers employed in the private sector in manufacturing, construction and commerical services do not share the security of all of the privileges of state-sector workers. All feel dependent upon the market and the pressure 'to produce' for a profit. Finally, wage workers located in the informal sector form the most insecure, lowest paid and often most exploited class fraction within the urban leburori. Others who share a common social existence and similar occupational career paths with wage workers are the occupationally diverse group that I have labelled *labor service* workers: e.g., hawkers, tea sellers, fingernail clippers and scavengers.[51] Though they do not work for a formal wage, a labor service worker's only actual contribution is the labor expended in carrying out his tasks, for neither does he possess petty capital nor does the task necessitate skill or entrepreneurial expertise. Often, these activities are short-lived, undertaken by individuals during the period in which they search for new employment. Again, though they do not possess the same role in the social division of labor as wage workers, nor the same relationship to capital, labor service workers are undisputed members of the urban talakawa, and many even consider themselves members of the leburori. The remaining

85

members of the urban talakawa include the unemployed, the destitute and the deviant occupations.

Summary

Kano's transition to semi-industrial capitalism was conditioned by the convergence of distinct political and economic forces: an increasingly centralized and interventionist federal state apparatus; a new, increasingly dependent, yet comparatively beneficial, relationship to the world economy via petroleum exports; and a deepening of capitalist social relations wrought by increased investment in state infrastructure, industrial production and modern housing. As compared to the era prior to the Nigerian civil war (1966), wage labor increased absolutely, commodification of social relations and wage goods accelerated so as to undermine the norms associated with Muslim mercantile capitalism, and inflation, crowding, crime and new forms of social inequality soared so as to increase social tension between the dominant and subordinate classes. Both the exigencies associated with the civil war and the fortuitous petroleum rents allowed a restructuring of state and capital within Nigeria, which in turn deepened the penetration of capitalism into all spheres of social existence.

Just as the external conditions internal sources of change, so too did macro-level forces structure micro-level processes within a peripheral capitalist city undergoing the transition to semi-industrial capitalism. To participate in Kano's social life exposed inhabitants to *urban social processes* experienced in the labor, food and housing markets and in the manner in which the state distributed petroleum-derived wealth. The impact of these macro- and micro-level processes reduced the significance of precapitalist-origin status identities and increased the salience of economic and formally capitalist attributes in determining the class structure. Though rooted in the sarauta-talakawa cleavage, the urban class structure emerging under semi-industrial capitalism coalesced into two rival class coalitions: the first, associated with the NPN, was composed of merchant-industrialists, merchants and powerful members of the state bourgeoisie, and the second, associated with the populist PRP, was composed of independent commodity producers, wage-earners and the urban poor.

With this bare outline of Kano's complex and changing class structure in mind, let us turn to sources of solidarity and cleavage within the urban talakawa and especially to how industrial workers relate behaviorally and subjectively to this occupationally diverse coalition of distinct objective classes.

3

The leburori within the urban talakawa: the social basis of a populist alliance

SOURCES OF COHESION AND DIFFERENTIATION

The urban talakawa form an occupationally diverse, politically conscious, popular stratum that is composed of two distinct classes: independent commodity producers and wage workers, the *leburori*. The former include craftsmen, small-scale industrial producers, traders, commission agents and other service workers; the leburori include state, industrial, transport, construction and informal-sector wage workers. As we saw earlier, though these two groups form distinct classes as defined by their roles in the social division of labor, they are unified by a common social existence, by popular cultural traditions, by a common yet newly defined talakawa social identity and by negative differentiating effects of semi-industrial capitalism. Collectively, they are without western education, sarauta status, access to state patronage or an independent, sizeable source of capital that would enable them to keep pace with inflation or to employ new technologies that would allow accumulation rather than mere reproduction. Social cohesion within this populist class alliance arises from several sources. The first is membership in the precapitalist-origin status group, the talakawa, which is increasingly identified with the uneducated urban poor. To identify as talakawa means that one feels solidarity with workers, petty traders and craft producers who possess a shared experience of political discrimination, personal humiliation, financial extortion and previously described forms of social injustice.

The second source of cohesion arises from the mutually shared deprivation, both relative and absolute, associated with the penetration and extension of commodity relations, primitive accumulation (land and corruption) and other features of Kano's transition to semi-industrial capitalism. Here I emphasize that both *political* forces and *market* forces converge to act against the material interests of independent commodity producers, driving them downward toward the social existence of the skilled and unskilled wage-earning class. And, finally, both classes share a comparatively powerless position in the face of *urban social processes* that increase the rate of proletarianization and concentrate capital and market shares in the hands of a small number of merchant-industrial capitalists, thus widening the distribution of income between upper and lower classes.

With these sources of talakawa cohesion in mind, allow me to review the objectives of this chapter. One objective is to describe in empirical detail the *common social existence* that generates solidarity within this politically conscious social stratum. To accomplish this objective requires a description of the production units and the occupational categories of the informal sector in which independent commodity producers earn their livelihood. The purpose here is to illustrate empirically how members of both classes – independent commodity producers and wage workers – are socially integrated, and how members of both classes overlap in terms of residential ties, occupational career histories and personal relationships (friendships), as well as how they participate in popular forms of Islam. For reasons of orderly presentation, I shall present material on the informal sector and the labor market in this chapter and material on residence and popular Islam in the next chapter.

Because any discussion of cohesion must be balanced by an analysis of cleavages, the second objective is to describe the sources of differentiation within and between these two classes. To be sure, even among Muslim Hausa-speaking groups ethnicity and occupation are obviously important. But besides these obvious sources, a major source of differentiation for both independent commodity producers and wage workers is determined by *urban status*. By urban status I refer to the degree of individual participation in the *urban social processes* of a semi-industrial capitalist city. The argument is that urban status differentiates independent commodity producers and wage workers in such a way that it is highly correlated with an individual's skill, income, occupational location and social consciousness.

Let us examine three urban status groups. Kano's urban-born residents, defined hereafter as 'urbans', are the most privileged and the most politically conscious members of the urban talakawa. Bearing in mind Kano's high rate of population growth, rural-born emigrants who now reside in the city form a second urban status group, hereafter referred to as 'migrants'. The latter are heterogeneous in origin and in exposure to the social processes of semi-industrial urban capitalist life, but at the same time they experience the greatest degree of exposure to and thus dependence on the market for subsistence, income and general social existence. Furthermore, since the semi-industrial capitalist city is expanding into the lands occupied by densely settled peasant communities surrounding Kano's urban perimeter, a third urban status group, that of 'commuters', emerges as a distinct source of differentiation within the urban talakawa. Completely dependent neither upon farming nor on similar sources of rural income, commuters engage in trade, craft production, wage labor and other urban services, while the rapidly expanding city gradually engulfs their once rural villages. For them, urbanization is a passive experience. In contrast to the urbans, commuters are the least politically conscious and most influenced by the authoritarian political relations of the rural aristocracy. And in contrast to the migrants, commuters are the most self-sufficient and thus the least dependent upon the market. Notice that urban status is an *empirical* concept rather than a theoretically deduced concept, one that is used to generalize and to describe a particular historical process in the city of Kano. Unlike theoretically defined concepts, such as capital and labor or core and periphery, there is no *a priori* reason why these particular urban status categories would describe sources of differentiation within the urban lower classes of any other semi-industrial capitalist city.

After describing the organization of the informal sector and the categories of labor that exist in the urban labor market among the leburori, attention will focus on the objective experience and subjective perspective of industrial workers as they relate to the independent commodity producers of the informal sector and to their experiences within the urban labor market. Ideally, one would want to have material on all occupational categories numbered in these two classes. But, for now, one must be satisfied with an analysis that relies upon the perspective of industrial workers drawn from distinct urban status groups as they objectively and subjectively experience the common social existence of the urban talakawa.

Accordingly, after presenting survey data that analyze the social and geographical origins and the social characteristics of Kano's industrial workers, I shall complement this objective material with more subjective material drawn from the three urban status groups in order to provide the subjective dimension of the most important sources of differentiation among Hausa-speaking industrial workers. Finally, after locating industrial workers within the urban talakawa and after examining the effect of urban status, we shall turn to the objective experience of industrial workers within the urban labor market and see how they subjectively evaluate their experiences. By stressing the subjective experience and perspective of newly proletarianized industrial workers, I wish to convey in their own words how workers experience the process of differentiation from the talakawa and, at the same time, the manner in which they redefine their new urban talakawa identity under the conditions of semi-industrial capitalism. Following Thompson's example, I wish to show how industrial workers actively create their own social world, as well as how they react to the political and economic forces associated with the advance of semi-industrial capitalism.[1]

Before describing independent commodity producers in the informal sector, let us be clear about the relationship of industrial workers to the urban working class, the leburori, and to the broader stratum referred to as urban talakawa. Industrial workers are a class fraction of the urban working class who subjectively identify with the label – leburori. Yet, at the same time as industrial workers are subjected to the disciplined labor process of the most advanced form of capitalist production existing at Kano, they are socially integrated into and identify willingly as members of the urban talakawa. As I argued earlier, though originally a precapitalist, class-like status-honor group that was determined by one's political relationship to the state, during the transition to semi-industrial capitalism talakawa has come to refer to the uneducated, impoverished and relatively declining members of the urban lower classes. Hence, while industrial workers possess class consciousness toward issues and organizations of the workplace, their membership in the talakawa weighs heavily upon their wider political consciousness in such a way that they identify with the populist political movement of the PRP.

On the one hand, one may argue that an industrial worker's class interests are neither represented nor served by the leadership of the PRP because it is drawn from the petty bourgeoisie, professional political brokers and radical intellectuals. Further, it follows that industrial workers' support for a populist class alliance, ostensibly serving the mutually incompatible interests of the urban talakawa and the petty bourgeoisie, constrains the development of a working class political movement. In this sense, talakawa consciousness inhibits the growth of a mature and powerful working class consciousness. But, on the other hand, there are positive aspects to industrial workers' support for the populist class alliance. Since current Federal policy prohibits trade union participation in politics and since industrial workers are a heterogeneous, largely illiterate, first-generation industrial proletariat, one may argue that they show no evidence of possessing the confidence or the capacity necessary for organizing a working class political movement for all the leburori. In this sense, populist consciousness is appropriate to the level of social development achieved by industrial workers and by the uneven and contradictory character of semi-industrial capitalism. Given Kano's level of economic and social development, its rapid rate of rural to urban migration and the strength of precapitalist-origin institutions, ideologies and practices, the *articulation* of talakawa consciousness to emerging working class consciousness is consistent with the level of capitalist development reached in Kano during the period of interest. Moreover, as the leburori increase in number and political maturity, their close relationship to other independent producers who also identify as talakawa will become a basis for possible class alliances in the future where the balance of power within the urban talakawa may be tilted more toward the interests of the leburori.[2]

THE INFORMAL SECTOR

In the following pages, only the broadest features of the production, distribution and service industries that make up the informal sector in which the majority of the urban talakawa earn a living and/or purchase commodities for their subsistence are described. It should be emphasized that the objective is not to describe this sector in the empirical detail that it deserves, but rather to provide the reader with the minimal empirical data necessary for an understanding of the occupational categories and institutions controlled by the urban talakawa. Closely related to this, the second objective is to describe the general social existence in which Kano's urban working class, the leburori, is immersed, as well as the occupational groups that workers are drawn from or aspire to achieve and with whom the leburori are allied in a common political movement that took expression as the PRP.

In its broadest definition the informal sector[3] defies geographical specificity, for informal producers and traders are found virtually everywhere in the urban area except in elite and new middle class residential areas. Activity is concentrated in markets, small-scale industrial areas, residences, sidewalks, streets and virtually any unoccupied urban space. The informal sector includes production, distribution, commercial services and transport activities. Surplus population, moreover, tends to concentrate around the markets, so that the destitute, the wandering Koranic students, the infirm and aged transients and the impoverished unemployed can usually be found clustered around informal sector activity.

Though within the informal sector there is a hierarchy headed by merchant capitalists among the traders and by more heavily capitalized industries using modern production techniques among small-scale and craft producers, talakawa independent producers of goods and services tend to be segmented by ethnicity, credit networks and scale of operation. Among those who identify with the urban talakawa, the informal sector could also be termed the *competitive* sector in that services, especially commercial ones, are duplicated, entry into a market is open, and profit rates are too low to provide capital to increase productivity. The more successful producers, whom I would locate among the petty bourgeoisie rather than in the stratum of independent commodity producers, often are distributing agents for large-scale firms or receive income from other investments such as real estate or state contracts. Let us examine the situation of small-scale and craft producers in the informal sector.

Small-scale industries

Frishman's research on small-scale industries provides an excellent overview.[4] His research follows up on a small-scale industrial survey conducted by the Economics Department of Ahmadu Bello University in 1972. Drawing upon a random sample taken from the original enumeration of industries located in urban Kano (approximately 4,250), Frishman found that the original survey enumerated only about one-third of existing industries; that the turnover/disappearance rate was very high, about 70.4 percent after eight years, with only 1.4 percent in existence for twenty years or more; that the initial capital investment for industries other than bakeries was low (₦305 in 1980); and that the average value of 'firms' other than bakeries was ₦1,736 in 1980. His research confirms the findings reported elsewhere in peripheral capitalist societies. Owners see insufficient capital

91

as posing the greatest barrier to expansion and survival. The workers' education and technical capacity is low, but overall Frishman estimates that Kano's small-scale industrial sector employed an estimated 32.7 percent of the urban labor force, paying a wage bill that was higher than that of large-scale industry.

Given the increase in urban population, the rise in the cost of food, labor and fuel used in preparing traditional foods and the changing tastes of urban consumers, bakeries emerged as a more highly capitalized industry, moving away from the small-scale and toward the medium-scale industrial designation. Thus bakeries illustrate how the transition to semi-industrial capitalism generates opportunities for expansion of small-scale industries and for indigenous capital accumulation as the demand for wage goods increases among the growing urban population. In this regard bakeries are exceptional among Kano's small-scale industries.

If one surveys Kano's industrial sector, both formal and informal, one is struck by the great scarcity of intermediate-scale industries employing modern technologies and wage workers. Kano's industries tend to be distributed in a bi-modal pattern with thousands of small-scale and artisan units that are poorly integrated (i.e., linked) into the heavily subsidized and protected large-scale industrial sector. Those few intermediate industrial units that either repair or produce products are rarely owned and managed by northern Muslim entrepreneurs; Asians, Levantines and southern Nigerians dominate this activity. Clearly, the absence of an intermediate industrial sector marked by backward and forward linkages to existing modern industries is a serious obstacle to the expansion of industrial capitalism in Kano. As a result, industrial production does not link up with local industries in a way that would disseminate modern skills and technologies throughout the urban economy. True, many individuals employed by international firms do initiate their own firms, but their cumulative impact has been marginal. Until now local capitalists have invested largely in trade, real estate and transport or in joint ventures with state and international capital; this is an investment posture which allows secure rates of profit but little management or technical control over the production process that could later emerge in the form of intermediate-scale industries. Hence, state intervention under a class alliance committed to indigenous production rather than dependent capitalism is necessary in order to transform the underdeveloped state of intermediate industries.

Craft production

Though Kano possessed an unrivaled reputation for craft- and handicraft-produced commodities during the nineteenth century, the impact of incorporation into world capitalism has undermined much of the autonomy and dynamism of craft production. Faced with monopolies, imported industrial products and backward technologies, many craft producers have become distributors of imported commodities that they formerly produced. Among those crafts that originated in the precapitalist and precolonial period, one may distinguish between those that have expanded and modernized to some degree, such as tailors and butchers, and those that have been devastated by modern imports or local production by modern capitalist firms, such as tanners and shoemakers. Others, such as blacksmiths, have declined significantly from their precolonial importance, yet continue to produce local ironware such as locks, hinges, farm implements and other peasant tools.[5] Further, like many craft producers, blacksmiths are dependent upon the modern capitalist sector's imports for raw materials such as iron scrap, rather than using locally produced iron. Note that blacksmiths are respected by foreign technicians, continue to produce farm implements and tools and, in my opinion, possess the potential for developing into an intermediate-scale industry. Similarly, local dyers employ factory-produced cotton cloth and imported chemical dyes in addition to the locally produced indigo-dyed cloth used mostly for tourist consumption. Hence, while many of the precapitalist crafts still exist and while their means of production can still be found, such as a tannery in the Birni or the dye pits at the Kofar Mata gate, nearly all have altered production processes such that most craft production is dependent upon inputs from the modern industrial and international economy.

Among the successful or modernizing crafts, the butchers stand out as a dynamic and powerful exception to the general decline of craft producers. They have organized a strong union which enrolls 'all who touch meat'. During the early 1960s they organized a strike to protest against the requirement that they slaughter meat only at the abattoir. One informant believes that the strike was successful because of the widespread perception among the butchers that the state would exclude their sons from the abattoir. The strike was undertaken in order to allow sons to work with fathers at the abattoir, thus enabling the butcher to endow a craft to his son. Moreover, the butchers' organization is multi-ethnic, with Yoruba as well as Hausa butchers belonging to the same union. Politically, the butchers are influential. Because they slaughter at a central place and distribute meat throughout the city to local markets and peddlers, their natural distribution networks serve as a political communication network in a city lacking modern communications for most of its inhabitants. Many senior butchers also are petty capitalists who speculate by buying cattle in rural areas for the market in Ibadan and Lagos. Part of the reason for their success is that the rapid increase in the urban population, coupled with an improving standard of living for the upper classes, assures increasing demand for meat and, therefore, for butchering services.

Traditional builders of sun-dried brick and mud mortar provide an interesting example of an ancient craft that employs large numbers of wage laborers (especially during the dry season) and one that has innovated within the traditional style by using cement and modern materials in construction. Until recently, most houses in the Birni, and to a lesser degree in Waje, were made of sun-dried bricks, sometimes plastered with cement. More affluent and newer homeowners have plastered their houses with cement, or for newer houses they have used cement blocks. Thus, what had been a local industry, using either local urban materials or donkey-transported clay from the peri-urban area and employing indigenously trained labor, has been altered by processes associated with semi-industrial capitalism. Now state-licensed contractors are building the new homes, mostly using materials either imported or produced by the large-scale industrial sector. While there is a clear preference for modern cement housing among the middle and upper classes, part of the reason for the change is explained by the large amount of wage labor that was necessary for the seasonal repair of traditional mud-brick structures. As food prices and inflation have driven up the price of wage goods and thus the price of wage labor for traditional builders, and as a landlord class which owns and rents multiple family units to wage workers has expanded, capitalist market rationality encourages landlords to use more cement blocks in order to reduce labor costs. This change eliminates employment opportunities for unskilled workers during the dry season but has the positive effect of integrating a small-scale industry into the large-scale industrial sector and away from the informal sector.

Tailors represent an ancient craft that has modernized with the latest power machinery at some levels, while at the same time maintaining older techniques of hand embroidery and manual machines. Because it is considered a clean and somewhat prestigious craft, one that is often practiced as a secondary occupation by mallams, tailoring is extremely competitive and differentiated. Medium-sized shops employ up to a dozen workers under 'sweat shop' conditions, using power machines and producing styles that cater to modern taste. At the same time, less successful and part-time tailors continue to work at home or in the street in all areas of the city. Interviews with former tailors indicate that large numbers of tailors rent their machines and thus do not own their means of production. Their income fluctuates enormously by seasonal demand, usually highest around Muslim festivals. Such a situation of easy entry, available machinery and limited skill requirements produces vicious competition and a high rate of turnover among tailors. The number of tailors who rent their machines and who do not own their means of production appears to be increasing.

There are few generalizations to be made about craft production. Many crafts, such as dyeing and indigo-beating, are in decline, and others, such as leather production and jewelry making, have become subordinated to merchants servicing tourist demand for 'traditional' handicraft products. Again, declining crafts have not disappeared completely but continue to exist in rural areas such as the peri-urban villages of the commuters, or as part-time occupations. Just as in the precapitalist period, rural producers in the peri-urban areas supply the market with traditional Hausa craft products such as cloth, baskets, straw mats, calabashes and earthenware pottery. Further, as in the precapitalist period, there is a tendency for the urban craftsmen to take advantage of rural networks and knowledge of the trade in order to become merchants who sell the rural-made products that they formerly produced. Again, because most peasants have a craft or trade in addition to farming, seasonal migration of craftsmen during the dry season and peasant production in the peri-urban area account for much of the craft production of goods consumed in urban Kano. It is also important to note that many craft and small-scale producers can be found at the large urban markets, where one may commission the production of an item such as furniture, or purchase an available item or have an item repaired. In this sense, the markets are bazaars where production and exchange are united and integrated by a common cultural milieu and by the traditions drawn from Muslim mercantile capitalism.

Within these same markets one finds new crafts whose workers are recruited from older craft traditions. One can purchase metal trunks that are made from scrap and that are produced by former blacksmiths using cold metal techniques. Outside the market and off the streets, food, woven goods, hats and other products are made within households and marketed to the immediate neighbourhood and distributed through personal networks. Household production and the division of labor within the family are discussed in greater detail in Chapter Four.

Modern crafts

The incorporation of Kano into the capitalist world economy did not produce a radical break with precapitalist production techniques, but it did introduce new skills, materials and technologies into the society. Rather than training local Kano residents for the skills of the colonial economy, colonial authorities and foreign firms reduced wages costs by employing skilled workers from the southern region. The latter were usually Christian and literate, and most had already been incorporated into the capitalist world economy or at least had had a lengthier exposure to it than had the Muslim, Hausa-speaking groups of Kano; thus modern crafts and technical occupations tend to be dominated by workers of southern origins. To be sure, given the resistance of Muslim nationalism to 'Christian' conquest, the Kanawa resisted new production processes, often exhibiting a clear preference for trade over technical craftsmanship, particularly among Kano's talakawa population. Moreover, as western education was limited to a small minority even a decade after political independence, the few skilled modern craftsmen could achieve higher and more reliable incomes by working for the state sector, usually for the Native Authority technical departments. And of course, state employment also allowed a skilled Muslim northern worker to engage in part-time work after hours. To some degree, then, this historical choice has become institutionalized as an ethnic division of labor,

95

where skilled crafts and modern small-scale industries are dominated by craftsmen and workers from southern Nigeria.

One modern craft requiring neither western education nor technical training has grown up around the bicycle industry. Kano's flat geography and its high rural-urban interaction create ideal conditions for bicycle transport. Bicycles are hired, sold and replaced throughout the city, with repair shops growing up to patch tubes and mend mechanical parts. Given the ubiquity of the bicycle, large numbers of workers are employed in this small-scale industry. Besides repairs and spare parts, the industry has specialists who decorate bicycles with paper and paint, so that distinct urban lifestyles are reflected in bicycle ownership. In addition to regular bicycles, increased incomes have brought greater use of motor-driven bicycles and motorcycles, which has also led to the growth of a small-scale industry to provide spares and repairs. It is therefore not surprising that the Raleigh Industries have opened an entire bicycle factory at Kano's Bompai industrial estate.

The informal sector of the economy must operate with low wages and cheap raw materials. In order to do so, scavenger industries have emerged which draw their raw materials from the waste of imported products and by-products of the large-scale industries. For example, lint and damaged thread from textile factories are used in the production of mattresses; evaporated milk cans are made into oil lamps; glass bottles are used for distributing household products such as palm or groundnut oil; automobile tires are stripped to produce rubber sandals, and wire is extracted to weave into household utensils. Given the extraordinary number of damaged vehicles and a high accident rate in Nigeria, the chassis of automobiles provide a nearly unlimited supply of raw materials for hand carts. Until recently, large amounts of labor were employed in producing two- and four-wheeled carts from wrecked autos. These carts were used to push goods from transport centers to markets, and because of their low wage cost, some large-scale industries contract cart pushers to return empty beer bottles from the market or to return empty groundnut oil barrels to the factories. Even at the end of military rule, these carts are still being used by night soil collectors and by workers for personal hauling. Further, as workers tend to move often in search of cheap rents, the two-wheeled carts are the main means available to the less affluent for transporting personal belongings within the city.

Despite the advantages of labor intensity and cheap raw material costs of the cart-pushing industry, however, the local government banned the use of four-wheeled carts on main arteries because of the congestion caused by the semi-naked cart pushers as they groaned and cursed their way through the city.[6] The petroleum boom has brought many automobile and van vehicle assembly plants into Nigeria. (From 1970 to 1976, for example, total motor vehicle registration in Kano state increased by over 490 percent.)[7] Thus as intraurban transport has been taken over by small vans and trucks, the cart pushers are forced to search for new wage-earning opportunities, and the city has become choked with automobiles driven by the affluent classes. The banning of four-wheeled carts in favor of motorized vehicles for intraurban transport exemplifies how new technologies fueled by petroleum wealth have advanced the forces of production and reduced the turnover time for the completion of the circuits of capital among Kano's merchant capitalists. Given the condition of low food prices during the period of Muslim mercantile capitalism, the casual labor of cart pushers was appropriate for intraurban transport. But as food prices increased and the volume of goods exchanged increased along with urban congestion, labor was replaced by capital in the form of motorized transport. Hence the elimination of cart pushers provides a clear example of the transition to urban semi-industrial capitalism.

Craft and small-scale industries share some common characteristics in Kano. The most obvious and oft-quoted characteristics are: ease of entry; labor-intensive production; low skill, capital and technological requirements; negligible accounting; high competition resulting in high failure rates; and the use of undifferentiated family and client labor where profit maximization is sacrificed for household or family employment. However widespread and useful its products may be, each successful industry is vulnerable to large-scale capitalist entry into its market. This is equally true for those dependent upon raw materials or subcontracting from large-scale industries. Further, ostensibly rational state policies may eliminate demand for some products, as in the case of carts, or prevent small-scale producers from squatting near markets, on streets or in places where the demand for their services and products is highest.

While small-scale and craft producers have low incomes and poor prospects for future security, they have all the *freedoms* associated with independent commodity production. That is to say, they are free to organize their own labor processes, to pray at the proper hour, to employ relatives and clients and to exert control over their fragile livelihoods. Yet, like others among the urban talakawa who make up the laboring and popular classes, they are without access to state patronage, a source of independent wealth, modern skills or education. Hence, their situation appears likely to remain stagnant or, worse, to decline further due to inflation. While some may enter wage employment in the large-scale capitalist sector, many will fall into labor service or peddling occupations as the rural areas continue to expel population to peripheral capitalist urban centers. Even with an increase in the proportion of the urban population employed in the large-scale capitalist sector, the demographic situation and the pattern of dry-season migration from rural areas insures that craft and small-scale production will continue for the indefinite future. Their future role in Kano's economy depends on the expansion of large-scale production into areas now controlled by craft and small-scale producers and by state policy toward intermediate-scale industries. Currently, state agencies subsi-

97

dize, protect and encourage large-scale industries while virtually ignoring the needs of small-scale industries in the informal sector.

Petty entrepreneurs: traders, brokers and commission agents

Until the very recent entry of merchant capitalists into industrial production, merchant capitalism and transport represented the highest achievement of Kano's indigenous capitalist class. From the local perspective, commerce, trading, brokerage and the general activity of buying cheap and selling dear are imprinted upon the social character and popular culture of Kano. Locating the dividing line among those who consider themselves members of the urban talakawa and who, at the same time, are sympathetic to the urban working classes is difficult to do with any degree of accuracy. Since the system depends on competitive pressure from large-scale merchants and state-affiliated capitalists who control credit, market space and access to state patronage for small and medium-sized merchants, the dividing line between the petty bourgeois class and the petty traders (i.e., independent commodity producers) of the urban talakawa will vary significantly across the market.[8] For example, even though many are linked to large-scale merchants, those who rent market stalls fear being squeezed by larger merchant capitalists and industrial capitalists who are allied with state authorities to monopolize all aspects of the wholesale and even the retail trade.

Most traders who identify with the urban talakawa are stall owners, small shop owners and even some urban wholesale traders. Included here are long-distance traders who travel to Lagos for wholesale purchases or those who sell to or buy from rural markets in Kano State or the northern towns. While they lack heavily capitalized investments such as trucks or vans, they typically own their own homes and have some investments other than their trading stock. Retail traders, unfortunately, are in internal competition with each other, remain organized around personal networks and thus are likely to decline as larger wholesale traders and more efficient distribution methods are introduced; this has already occurred in the southern areas of Nigeria. Yet, if the latter trend persists, the petty entrepreneurs and traders will probably not disappear entirely but rather will decline in relative market share and average wealth.

Unlike the wholesale merchants and large-scale interurban merchants, most retail traders *must* grant credit to their customers, a practice that involves great risk. Immersed in the culture and institutions of Muslim mercantile capitalism, credit and networks are the key to the success of traders and petty entrepreneurs, rather than expansion of the market by lowering the cost of each item sold. As Cohen has shown in Ibadan, and as Last has illustrated among recent Hausa converts to Islam, the control of risk depends on institutionalized trust and the reputation of the debtors.[9] Islamic institutions and especially the Islamic brotherhoods, therefore, are widespread among this class of merchants and traders. Islamic institutions are used to secure material relationships. Of course, urban status is still an important source of differentiation among this group. Traders from the Birni have the best networks, enabling them to gain access to capital, state contracts or local opportunities, whereas recent migrants from rural areas or from the peri-urban area do not have these advantages. Finally, my observations suggest that clientage networks between retail traders and the merchant or merchant-industrial classes have declined in importance. Though still important, wage labor and modern credit practices (e.g., banks) are eroding the hold of clientage over the commercial capitalist sector.

Below the retail traders and petty entrepreneurs are their clients, affiliated brokers and commission agents, who would claim to be traders but who, in practice, are without an independent source of capital. Thus they must depend on wealthier merchants or landlord creditors of the type described by Cohen. Many of these commission agents, who are paid according to what they are able to market, are from declining merchant families or are migrants who began trading in rural markets. Their aspiration is to gain sufficient capital, either through trading for their patron (*maigida*) or by receiving credit from a financier, to begin trading on their own. The kinds of activities, the complexity of relationships and understandings between merchant and client, and the variety of commodities traded by this dependent class of entrepreneurs are great, worthy of an extensive study and thus defy summary here. It is important to note that the situation of this group is insecure and that they are located in a sector that is flooded with competitors so that, again, personal networks determine individual success.

Outside of the physical marketplaces and long-distance trading networks, one finds petty traders who are located in neighborhoods where they sell from kiosks, tables and even tiny rooms often located within their homes. They trade in daily necessities: coffee, milk, sugar, soft drinks, soap powder, cooking oil, patent medicines and tobacco. Much of their trade is also on credit to local inhabitants, so their success is a function of their community's economy and of the income level of the neighborhood in which they operate. Better locations along main streets are perceived to offer greater opportunities for a petty trader to increase his scale of operation. In a market saturated with petty traders, much of one's success depends on personal networks, reciprocal relations with other traders or suppliers and the ability to scrutinize those to whom one extends credit. Even more insecure and impoverished than the relatively permanent stationary petty traders are the peddlers and hawkers who wander throughout the city in search of customers. Individually, they possess little or no capital and negligible entrepreneurial acumen, and thus do not qualify as petty traders but rather as *labor service* workers. Indeed, many actively identify themselves as leburori who are in search of permanent wage employment. Again, while they remain outside of wage employment and thus do not share the same *relationship to capital* as do wage workers, their historical origins, their consciousness and their *conditions of social existence* integrate them within the social milieu of the urban leburori.

Thus far I have described only the major occupational categories and activities that make up the informal sector of Kano. Together they form a loosely organized class of independent commodity producers who compete amongst each other and who are immersed in distinct social networks and credit relationships. All but the most affluent identify with the urban talakawa and the populist politics of the PRP. While capital accumulation of any substantial size is difficult, or insufficient to reproduce the careers of their offspring, independent commodity producers show no sign of declining in number or social importance. Both the historical traditions associated with Muslim mercantile capitalism and the entrepôt nature of Kano's economy ensure their presence for the indefinite future. Therefore the question of importance for the forces associated with radical political change is whether their political consciousness and activity will ally them to the petty bourgeoisie and the dominant classes or, instead, to the laboring classes in a populist class alliance that offers an alternative to the corruption and incompetence displayed by the managers of Nigeria's woefully dependent capitalist society.

THE LEBURORI AND THE URBAN LABOR MARKET: INFORMAL SECTOR LABOR

Since the remainder of this chapter is concerned with industrial labor, it is important to describe briefly the categories of labor that identify with and share the social existence of the urban leburori. After outlining these laboring categories and their position within the urban labor market, I shall focus on the social characteristics of Kano's industrial labor force and the effect of urban status in differentiating the urban leburori.

Although the workers in the state and industrial sectors are the most important political and social force within the laboring classes, all workers who labor for a wage belong to this class. Besides those who work for an agreed-upon wage for a day's labor or for a definite task such as unloading a truck, also included in the laboring classes are the heterogeneous occupations of peddler and other 'laboring' service workers. After interviewing and observing the activities of service workers, such as peddlers and hawkers, I concluded that nearly all lacked an independent source of capital or any entrepreneurial skill that distinguished them from unemployed laborers or that required training of any duration. Rather, they were unskilled distributors of commodities (e.g., blue-collar sales) whose contribution to the purchaser lay in the *labor* expended in bringing the product to the purchaser's home or work place. Hence, they are really 'labor service' workers, for their value lies in the crude laboring activity of delivery rather than in commercial skill or possession of commercial capital. Many, such as used-clothing peddlers, do not even own the commodities that they are peddling but receive a commission on each item that they manage to sell. Further, many peddlers are seasonal workers from rural areas, or semi-proletarianized peasants from the peri-urban area hawking rural produce, or unemployed wage workers who search for permanent employment while selling consumable goods outside factory gates. In other cases, peddlers and hawkers alternate daily between casual labor, such as cart pushing or unloading trucks, and peddling goods for a commission. Oftentimes, a migrant may have three distinct kinds of work, depending on the demand for his labor. Within the labor market, then, this group of labor service workers shares the common insecure conditions of the laboring poor. More importantly, they are labeled and identify themselves as members of the leburori. Often described in the literature as 'tertiarization', this is a typical feature of the class structure of peripheral capitalist urban centers, where large-scale industrial production employs few laborers relative to output, and the exchange and distribution of industrially produced commodities absorbs a disproportionate share of surplus urban labor.[10] Finally, while I recognize that labor service workers do not possess the same relationship to capital as wage workers, it is argued that their history and conditions of social existence locate them among the laboring classes.

The category of labor service workers includes others besides hawkers and peddlers of the informal sector. Within the urban neighborhoods and communities, some labor service workers wash clothing and carry water from the public tap to households. Others shine shoes and clip finger and toenails. In Kano, at least there is a complex division of services and service labor within the laboring and lower class communities themselves. Besides deviant and illegal occupations such as thieving, prostitution, pimping, drug sales and local gin sales, a number of legitimate service occupations exist within communities. Food processing and sales are major household industries in communities where single men and seasonal laborers are numerous. Clearly, the women who organize the production of food belong to the small-scale sector. But when child labor is unavailable or insufficient, they often employ younger men for cleaning and washing utensils and for hawking food. Similarly, workers from the peri-urban areas cut wood for a wage, often after they have sold a donkey-load to food producers. Hence there are a large number of service occupations which, in addition to not paying a fixed wage, involve little more than the labor expended in achieving the unskilled task. It is the insecurity and low income of these occupations that encourages service workers to seek permanent wage employment in the formal sector.

Because Kano acts as a pivotal commercial distributional center for rail, air and motor transport, large numbers of casual laborers are employed loading and unloading freight. Before they were banned by the local government, large numbers of workers pushed carts from rail and motor

101

stations to markets and to freight centers. Others work in gangs under a labor contractor who contracts with factory managers to unload raw materials from trucks. The headman's share for arranging this with management varies from one-tenth to one-third of the fee for unloading the truck. The remainder is divided among the laborers who actually unload the freight. Any center of commerce or transport attracts casual laborers who await the opportunity to sell their labor power, regardless of the exploitation by the contractor.

Craft and small-scale production also employs wage laborers at a wage rate below the state- and formal-sector minimum daily wage. Large numbers of workers are employed as day laborers for mud-brick and modern construction, though this work usually is limited to the dry season. Most peasants inherit some rudimentary craft or skill which, upon arriving in the city, enables them to work as a craftsman's helper for a wage or by piecework commissions. To be sure, many of these occupations are irregular, and a worker may combine two (or even three) occupations, such as construction worker by day and watchman by night.

Wage employment in the households of the middle and upper classes is also significant. The large expatriot community and the skewed income distribution of Kano encourage the employment of large numbers of servants. Some are skilled cooks, but most do unskilled work as gardeners, night watchmen and housecleaners. Increasingly, one finds skilled workers, technicians and merchants employing young migrants as houseboys. They perform unskilled tasks that release other household members, usually women, for more skilled and remunerative employment. Wage employment in the informal sector is great and is increasing at the expense of clientage and informal forms of remuneration.

Formal-sector wage workers

In most cases, informal-sector wage workers are aspiring to gain employment in the formal sector. Among all wage workers whom I interviewed, the security and benefits of state employment make this sector their ideal choice for employment. Not only are state-sector workers the oldest category of wage earners in Kano, thus possessing more prestige than industrial or casual labor, but the regulations of the civil service allow for trade union organization as well as the potential opportunity, through loyal service and access to powerful state-sector officials, to secure loans. Furthermore, state-sector employment is shielded from trade recessions or layoffs due to raw material shortages, and thus these workers are insulated from the insecurity and much of the alienation associated with industrial labor.[11] Within the large-scale private capitalist sector, employment in international firms is favored over local Nigerian or foreign entrepreneurial capitalist firms. This is true whether the sector is construction, commerce or industry.

Commercial firms and services such as hotels employ some wage labor-

102

ers, but since the petroleum boom, construction of roads, state office buildings, factories and modern housing has employed ever-increasing numbers of unskilled workers. Although some have learned new skills while engaged in construction, most are still employed as temporary workers; once the project is completed and the skilled workers have moved to a new site, construction firms retain few of these temporary workers. Employment in this industry, while numerically significant, fluctuates according to season, petroleum revenues and state policy. The instability of construction labor was a common reason given by former construction workers for moving to industrial labor. Let us turn now to the social characteristics and origins of Kano's industrial working class.

INDUSTRIAL LABOR: GEOGRAPHICAL ORIGINS AND SOCIO-DEMOGRAPHIC CHARACTERISTICS

Because we lack any reliable census material describing the migration patterns underlying Kano's high growth rate, the following industrial survey constitutes the best available estimate and thus may be employed in lieu of census material in order to assess Kano's patterns of labor migration. While the survey is not a random sample of all industrial workers, it is spatially *representative* of the three industrial locations in Kano. Hence, because firms from the three areas of the city – Birni-Fagge, Township and Bompai – are represented in approximate proportion to the number of industrial workers employed in each area, no unique feature of an area went undetected. Again, despite the obvious limitations, in the absence of reliable census material I shall assume that the industrial survey provides the best estimate of labor migration patterns and the social characteristics of Kano's urban working class. Finally, because of the high degree of labor circulation between the formal sector and the informal sector, I have found the industrial survey to be an approximate estimate of the social characteristics of workers and producers in the informal sector.

The first two tables, 3.1 and 3.2, present selected social characteristics of the industrial labor force by state of origin (i.e., birth place). State of origin refers to the twelve-state system which existed in Nigeria from 1968 to 1976.[12] Table 3.1, Row 1 presents the distribution of industrial labor by state of origin. Kano State contributes nearly half the labor force. Most factory workers are young, with an average age of 26.5 years, a figure that varies little by state, apart from Kano where it rises to 28.6 years. Nearly three-quarters of this work force is rural-born: most workers from the states of the former Northern Region were born in rural villages, while the proportion of urban-born workers increases among those from Kano, Mid-West, East Central, Lagos and Western States. Note that workers from the western states are from urban centers. Migrants from Kano State and adjacent northern states, as one would expect, have lived in urban Kano for much longer periods than southern migrants.

103

Table 3.1 Social characteristics of industrial labor by state of birth

	Survey total	Kano	North-East	North-Central	North-West	Benue-Plateau	Kwara	Western	Mid-West	Rivers	East-Central	Lagos	South-East
1. Distribution by state	100[a] (3036)	43.9 (1334)	19.5 (591)	6.9 (210)	2.8 (84)	6.7 (202)	8.0 (244)	3.2 (97)	5.0 (152)	0.1 (2)	0.8 (24)	0.4 (12)	2.8 (84)
2. Age – mean years	26.5	28.6	24.9	27.1	27.5	22.9	22.3	26.9	26.6	27.5	25.8	26.4	23.2
3. % born in rural villages	71.6 (2090)	75.9 (1012)	78.4 (444)	69.3 (140)	62.2 (51)	75.1 (145)	80.8 (185)	4.6 (4)	57.9 (73)	No Data	17.6 (3)	0.0 (0)	45.8 (33)
4. % born in towns	10.9 (318)	0.6 (8)	21.2 (120)	15.3 (31)	32.9 (27)	17.1 (33)	12.7 (29)	17.2 (15)	21.4 (27)	No Data	47.1 (8)	8.3 (1)	26.4 (19)
5. % born in cities	17.5 (512)	23.5 (314)	0.4 (2)	15.3 (31)	4.9 (4)	7.8 (15)	6.6 (15)	78.2 (68)	20.6 (26)	No Data	35.3 (6)	91.7 (11)	27.8 (20)
6. Migrants' years at Kano – mean	5.5	9.8	5.0	7.4	6.3	3.2	3.0	4.8	4.0	1.5	1.7	6.6	2.5
7. at Kano – median	3.2	7.4	3.3	5.7	4.8	2.2	2.3	3.1	2.8	1.5	1.1	4.0	1.5
8. Religion – % Muslim	65.6 (1987)	99.6 (1329)	46.3 (272)	52.4 (110)	97.6 (82)	22.4 (45)	35.2 (86)	38.1 (37)	12.5 (19)	0.0	0.0	58.3 (7)	0.0
9. Muslims – % with Koranic schooling	84.6 (1669)	95.5 (1261)	59.8 (162)	96.3 (105)	81.3 (65)	46.5 (20)	39.5 (34)	32.4 (12)	36.8 (7)	0.0	0.0	42.9 (3)	0.0
10. Muslims – years of Koranic schooling – mean	5.8	6.1	4.7	6.1	5.2	4.5	4.7	4.9	5.3	0.0	0.0	4.3	0.0
11. Family: % unmarried	27.9 (847)	14.6 (195)	32.3 (191)	31.4 (66)	29.8 (25)	53.0 (107)	52.0 (127)	33.0 (32)	34.9 (53)	50.0 (1)	41.7 (10)	25.0 (3)	44.0 (37)
12. % single wife	55.1 (1672)	57.0 (760)	58.5 (346)	54.8 (115)	51.2 (43)	43.1 (87)	45.5 (111)	56.7 (55)	56.6 (86)	50.0 (1)	58.3 (14)	66.7 (8)	54.8 (46)
13. % polygamous	17.0 (517)	28.4 (379)	9.1 (54)	13.8 (29)	19.0 (16)	4.0 (8)	2.5 (6)	10.3 (10)	8.6 (13)	0.0	0.0	8.3 (1)	1.2 (1)
14. Number of dependants – mean	4.8	6.5	4.0	4.0	4.0	2.7	2.3	4.0	3.9	2.0	3.5	4.5	2.8

[a] The original survey total is 3,075.
Non-Nigerians and missing cases equal 39.

104

Table 3.2 Occupational and educational characteristics of industrial labor by state of birth

Characteristic	Sample total	Kano	North-East	North-Central	North-West	Benue-Plateau	Kwara	Western	Mid-West	Rivers	East-Central	Lagos	South-East
1. Western education % none	58.0 (1760)	88.1 (1175)	57.0 (337)	47.6 (100)	60.7 (51)	22.8 (46)	10.8 (26)	8.2 (8)	6.6 (10)	0.0 (0)	0.0 (0)	8.3 (1)	7.1 (6)
2. % literate (western)	28.9 (876)	4.1 (55)	21.4 (126)	32.5 (68)	16.7 (14)	59.9 (121)	78.5 (190)	82.5 (80)	83.4 (126)	50.0 (1)	100 (24)	83.3 (10)	72.6 (61)
3. % attending primary school	32.2 (977)	11.2 (150)	41.1 (243)	48.6 (102)	35.7 (30)	65.3 (132)	71.0 (171)	39.2 (38)	41.4 (63)	50.0 (1)	25.0 (6)	50.0 (6)	41.7 (35)
4. % secondary school or above	9.8 (296)	0.7 (9)	1.9 (11)	3.8 (8)	3.6 (3)	11.9 (24)	18.3 (44)	52.6 (51)	52.0 (79)	50.0 (1)	75.0 (18)	41.7 (5)	51.2 (43)
Years of western education													
5. – mean	6.6	4.9	5.2	5.9	5.6	6.8	7.3	8.5	8.4	6.0	8.9	8.8	7.3
6. – median	6.9	4.8	6.5	6.7	6.7	7.0	7.1	8.2	8.2	6.0	8.2	7.4	7.7
Years in present job													
7. – mean	3.3	4.3	3.2	3.9	3.1	1.5	1.4	1.8	1.7	0.5	0.4	3.3	1.1
8. – median	2.0	2.7	2.2	2.3	2.0	0.9	1.0	1.7	1.4	0.5	0.1	1.5	0.7
9. % upper level supervisors	0.9 (26)	1.3 (17)	0.5 (3)	1.9 (4)	1.2 (1)	0.0 (0)	0.0 (0)	0.0 (0)	0.0 (0)	0.0 (0)	0.0 (0)	8.3 (1)	0.0 (0)
10. % lower level supervisors	6.1 (185)	4.9 (65)	4.2 (25)	9.5 (20)	7.1 (6)	4.5 (9)	7.4 (18)	21.6 (21)	11.2 (17)	0.0 (0)	4.2 (1)	0.0 (0)	3.6 (3)
11. % skilled	8.2 (249)	5.5 (73)	4.4 (26)	12.9 (27)	3.6 (3)	7.4 (15)	11.9 (29)	22.7 (22)	29.6 (45)	0.0 (0)	4.2 (1)	33.3 (4)	4.8 (4)
12. % semiskilled	24.5 (744)	20.9 (279)	23.2 (137)	29.5 (62)	31.0 (26)	42.1 (85)	30.7 (75)	7.2 (7)	20.4 (31)	50.0 (1)	33.3 (8)	16.7 (2)	36.9 (31)
13. % unskilled	60.3 (1832)	67.5 (900)	67.7 (400)	46.2 (97)	57.1 (48)	46.0 (93)	50.0 (122)	48.5 (47)	38.8 (59)	50.0 (1)	58.3 (14)	41.7 (5)	54.8 (46)

Regarding religious affiliation, approximately two-thirds of the sample are Muslim and the remaining third profess to be Christian. The data also suggest that within the northern states, such as North-Central (Kaduna), which are predominantly Muslim, a higher than expected proportion of migrants to Kano are Christian and thus originate from the Southern Zaria region. Among Muslims from the northern and Hausa-speaking states, especially Kano, a much greater percentage of respondents have attended Koranic school. This figure declines among Muslims originating from southern states. This difference may indicate that Muslims from southern states converted to Islam, or that their attendance at western school competed with Koranic education. The figures illustrate the near universality of Koranic education among northern and usually Hausa-speaking Muslims.

Marital status and dependency burdens show great variation according to the state of origin. Kano State's statistics show higher rates of polygamy and higher dependency burdens in part because of the employment of rural resident peasants (commuters) from the peri-urban area. This problem is dealt with below when the effect of urban status is examined. Yet, even allowing for the higher rate of polygamy among commuters from the peri-urban area, polygamy is practiced only by a minority of workers.

The next table, 3.2, examines the distribution of educational and occupational characteristics by state of origin. Indigenes from Kano State, by far those least exposed to western education, are at an enormous disadvantage in acquiring skilled labor positions. Similarly, while 11.9 percent of the workers from Kano State have attended western schools, only 4.1 percent were able to pass a literacy test using articles from either local Hausa or English-language newspapers. Within the former Northern Region, workers from Benue-Plateau and Kwara States possess greater opportunities to attend primary school; thus they appear to be responding to the shortage of skilled labor in Kano. But when secondary schooling is examined, the southern states show far greater levels of participation. Not surprisingly, this statistic correlates with the high proportion of urban-born migrants (see Table 3.1, Row 5) and the high proportion of skilled workers (Table 3.2, Row 11) originating from Western, Mid-West and Lagos States. Hence, the inability of Kano and other northern states to supply educated and skilled labor encourages the migration of urban-born educated workers from southern states.

When we examine skill levels and length of time at present job, it is clear that many workers of southern origin had only been employed for less than two years. This is due to the political crisis and civil war that preceded the industrial survey (1971). Workers of northern origin and especially those from Kano State, in contrast, are associated with longer employment figures, though given the difference between means and medians, there is wide variation among them. Regarding supervisors, there is a clear preference for northern upper-level supervisors as there are virtually no upper-

Table 3.3 *Ethnic distribution of industrial labor*

Hausa-Fulani	1551	50.4%
Plateau-Tiv Cluster	286	9.3%
Yoruba group	187	6.1%
Babur-Bura	246	8.0%
Ibibio	79	2.6%
Idoma-Nupe group	315	10.2%
Ibo	32	1.0%
Edo group	137	4.5%
Kanuri group	53	1.7%
Kilba & related	143	4.7%
Residual	27	0.9%
Non-Nigerian	19	0.6%
Total	3,075	100.0%

level supervisors originating from southern states. Among lower-level supervisors, a much greater than proportional number originate from Western and Mid-West states. As the education statistics suggest, the great proportion of workers originating from the northern states are engaged in semi-skilled and unskilled occupations. A far greater proportion of skilled workers originate from Mid-West, Western, Lagos and Kwara States.

Now let us examine selected demographic features of Kano's industrial labor force. Table 3.3 presents the distribution of ethnic groups from the survey. Workers of Hausa and Fulani ethnic origin make up 50 percent of the sample and about 18 percent of these report Fulani ethnicity. The clustering of ethnic groups into major categories is somewhat arbitrary and is used here for simplicity of presentation. Statistics on individual ethnic groups within the clusters are also available but are cumbersome to present.[13]

Space limitations do not permit the presentation of a detailed analysis of the industrial labor force as I have done elsewhere.[14] To summarize, one notes that over 73 percent of the survey report ages below thirty; the majority (58 percent) have been employed in their present jobs for less than two years. One interesting finding concerns the proportion of workers who remain resident in the peri-urban villages and commute to industrial labor. About 21 percent of the sample and 42 percent of those identifying as either Hausa or Fulani fall into this category. In order to determine if this high proportion of commuters arose from the peculiarities of factories sampled, I investigated the rate of participation among resident males in the peri-urban villages by examining the incidence of formal-sector tax payment (Appendix Table A.1). Rather than paying the community tax, villagers who worked in the formal sector as wage earners paid their tax at work (i.e.,

PAYE), and thus the incidence of PAYE taxpayers recorded in the districts surrounding Kano serves as an indicator of the villagers' participation in modern-sector wage labor. The tax records unequivocally confirm that the incidence of formal wage labor among villagers increased dramatically during this period. For example, in Ungogo district where most of the commuters resided, the 1966/67 records show only 0.1 percent of taxpaying males in the PAYE system, but by 1974/75 the proportion had increased to 9.6 percent. Thus the PAYE tax data confirm the reliability of the industrial survey.

When asked about the primary reason for coming to Kano, about 54 percent of those surveyed cited economic opportunity, 10 percent cited the pull of affective ties such as the family, and 3 percent cited Islamic education. When the incidence of coming for Islamic education was examined only among Hausa and Fulani ethnic groups, 13.8 percent cited Islamic education. Thus, in contrast to the ideal-typical assumptions of modernization theory, the situation in Kano is one where precapitalist institutions – Koranic school networks – *articulate* with the capitalist labor market so as to create a conscious status group that is interwoven within the industrial working class. As I have argued elsewhere, rural to urban migration through Koranic school networks reflects the complex articulation between precapitalist institutions which may generate a volatile social force capable of creating violent outbursts, such as the *Yan Tatsine* uprising of December 1980.[15]

URBAN STATUS AND SOCIAL DIFFERENTIATION: INDUSTRIAL WORKERS FROM KANO STATE

If sectoral differences within the urban working class are muted by talakawa status, social ties and market forces, then we must look elsewhere for the source of heterogeneity and uneven development within the Hausa-speaking urban working class. Kano is an anomaly when compared to the typical peripheral urban center undergoing the transition to semi-industrial capitalist production. Precapitalist urban development bequeathed both an urban lower class identity, the talakawa, and a densely settled peasantry in the peri-urban areas that has produced for and related to the urban economy during the precapitalist and mercantile capitalist eras. As argued earlier, the combination of precapitalist, colonial and international industrial capitalist patterns of urban domination and exploitation of the country-side has generated significant degrees of inequality, an inequality rooted in the division of labor between city and country but experienced in everyday life as *urban status* differences. To a great degree, therefore, urban status corresponds to one's occupational and class location within the urban talakawa. Lifelong urban dwellers of the Birni, for example, not only have better trading networks and opportunities to acquire new skills than do village-born migrants or commuters from the peri-urban area, but their

Table 3.4 *Kano State: social characteristics of industrial labor by urban status*

	Survey totals	Urbans	Migrants	Commuters
1. Distribution by urban status	100	24.4	27.6	48.0
	(1331)	(325)	(367)	(639)
2. Unmarried	14.6	19.4	15.3	11.7
	(194)	(63)	(56)	(75)
3. Single wife	56.9	61.5	61.6	52.0
	(758)	(200)	(226)	(332)
4. Polygamous	28.5	19.1	23.2	36.3
	(379)	(62)	(85)	(232)
5. Number of dependants – mean	6.5	6.1	5.5	7.2
Muslims – years of Koranic schooling				
6. mean	6.1	6.8	6.1	5.6
7. median	4.9	6.2	4.9	4.2
8. % literate (western)	4.1	10.2	5.2	0.5
	(55)	(33)	(19)	(3)
9. % attending a western school	11.9	26.8	13.6	3.3
	(158)	(87)	(50)	(21)
10. % upper level supervisors	1.3	3.1	1.1	0.5
	(17)	(10)	(4)	(3)
11. % lower level supervisors	4.9	8.6	5.4	2.7
	(65)	(28)	(20)	(17)
12. % skilled	5.5	7.7	6.5	3.8
	(73)	(25)	(24)	(24)
13. % semiskilled	21.0	32.0	22.3	14.6
	(279)	(104)	(82)	(93)
14. % unskilled	67.4	48.6	64.6	78.6
	(897)	(158)	(237)	(502)
15. Years at present job – mean	4.3	4.9	4.3	4.0

higher political consciousness and sense of self-esteem are shaped by participation in a peripheral capitalist urban center. Compared to migrants and commuters, urbans are significantly more integrated into the urban social processes of a peripheral capitalist city and have been shaped by these forces since birth.

Informal field data suggested urban status is a significant source of differentiation, and thus uneven development, within the industrial proletariat. But it was not until the industrial labor survey data was analyzed for Kano State that urban status differences within the industrial proletariat were so forcefully demonstrated and objectified empirically. Tables 3.4 and 3.5 present social and occupational characteristics and the social origins of industrial workers from Kano State, who account for approximately 44 percent of those enumerated in the industrial survey. In these tables, workers originating from Kano State are compared across three urban

Table 3.5 *Kano State: social origins of industrial labor by urban status*

Sector of father's primary occupation	Survey total	Urbans	Migrants	Commuters
1. Agriculture	55.6	16.6	63.6	70.3
	(717)	(51)	(224)	(442)
2. Manufacturing	7.5	10.4	6.8	6.5
	(97)	(32)	(24)	(41)
3. Commercial service	11.9	35.7	5.7	3.7
	(153)	(110)	(20)	(23)
4. Public service	3.0	5.5	3.1	1.7
	(39)	(17)	(11)	(11)
5. Religious service	8.5	13.3	10.2	5.2
	(110)	(41)	(36)	(33)
6. Labor service	13.4	18.5	10.5	12.6
	(173)	(57)	(37)	(79)
7. Totals	100	23.9	27.3	48.8
	(1289)	(308)	(352)	(629)
% with father having:				
8. Religious secondary occupation[a]	15.7	18.7	15.9	14.7
	(81)	(14)	(29)	(38)
9. Western education	1.8	3.5	2.2	0.8
	(24)	(11)	(8)	(5)
10. Traditional office	3.7	2.8	7.2	2.2
	(49)	(9)	(26)	(14)

[a] % is figured from those reporting father's secondary occupation.

status dimensions. It will be recalled that the criteria employed for designating urban status categories were: 1) 'urbans' – workers born and continuing to reside in urban Kano; 2) 'migrants' – workers born in rural areas and towns, who migrated to urban Kano; and 3) 'commuters' – workers born and continuing to live in the peri-urban area of Kano, who commute to factories daily.

One surprising finding was the great number of commuters found working in factories. There are nearly twice as many commuters as urbans engaged in industrial labor. Further, as Table 3.4 indicates, commuters are much more likely to have more than one wife, and their dependency burden is higher than either migrants' or urbans', all of which is characteristic of peasant households as contrasted with urban workers' family patterns. Furthermore, the peri-urban peasantry are slowly being squeezed by their own natural growth and by the gradual expansion of the urban perimeter into peasant lands. In turn, they have become dependent upon urban wage labor and other sources of urban income. Moreover, if nearly 10 per cent of the taxpaying males of Ungogo district were paying their taxes through formal-sector employment, a comparatively privileged occupational situation, one should expect that a proportion several times as great would be employed in the lower-paid informal sector. Hence, the peri-urban peasantry cannot be considered rural in the normal usage of the term; rather, they are becoming semi-proletarianized communities whose material existence is increasingly determined by the market cycles of industrial capitalism. Peasant life is eroded as their youths gradually migrate to the city for employment or as the local authority and/or land speculators gradually engulf them.

Industrial labor: social origins by urban status

One way to comprehend the historically rooted impact of urban status on an unevenly developed industrial proletariat is to examine workers' social origins. While the process of proletarianization in a semi-industrial capitalist urban center will, in the long run, homogenize differences among urban status groups, during the period of transition such differences are real and inhibit the organizational development of an urban working class. Accordingly, Table 3.5 compares the social origins of each urban status category by the sector of father's primary occupation. Rows 8–10 provide status characteristics of the respondent's father. In the case of migrants and commuters, the pattern of intergenerational occupational mobility is from the agricultural sector to the industrial manufacturing sector. Note that among these two rural-born urban status groups, there is a slight tendency for migrants to have come from higher status service occupations, such as religious teachers (mallams), public servants (i.e., sons of village heads) and commercial backgrounds.

Interestingly, among migrants the frequency of those reporting mallamic fathers is nearly twice that reported among commuters and approaches the frequency reported among urbans. Moreover, it is of interest to note that among migrants, if the frequency for a father in religious service occupations is combined with the father's secondary occupation, then 18.2 percent of the migrants originate from fathers whose primary or secondary occupation was religious. This is an extraordinary occurrence, for it surpasses the frequency achieved by the urbans and provides more evidence that there is a relationship between mallams and Koranic school networks and rural-urban labor migration networks.

When social origins of the urbans are investigated, there is a clear break with the pattern established by the rural-born migrants and commuters. Commercial service accounts for the social origins of over 35 percent of the urbans; handicraft manufacturing or craft labor accounts for over 10 percent; and labor service occupations, of which most are peddlers and hawkers, account for over 18 percent. Together, these commercial, craft and peddler (labor service) occupations account for the social origins of over 64 percent of the urbans. Here one discovers a classic situation of intergenerational downward mobility, where sons of free producers and traders are unable to maintain the occupation and status of their fathers' social

111

class positions. Furthermore, while market forces and competition from industrial production have not eroded the career opportunities of mallams' sons, as is the case for craft and commercial occupations, a significant number of mallams' sons are engaged in industrial labor. Because sons are usually trained in Koranic studies as well as for moral leadership, one discovers that mallams and Koranic students are interwoven as a status group within a first-generation industrial proletariat. This finding suggests that sons of mallams are unable to make a secure living in traditional occupations, such as tailoring or commerce, which would allow them to continue Islamic scholarship.

The statistical data confirm the importance of urban status as a source of uneven development within the industrial proletariat. Note that nearly all respondents, irrespective of urban status, are descended from uneducated, talakawa families. Thus, talakawa status is constant across the three urban status groups. Given the occupational advantages as well as the social education provided by urban living, the urbans emerge as the most advanced group within the Hausa-speaking industrial proletariat, while the commuters are the most politically backward.

The statistics for western education in Table 3.4 illustrate the virtual absence of educational opportunity for the peasantry in the peri-urban area. While lagging behind urbans in literacy and schooling, migrants fare better than commuters; and of course, just as in the case of Koranic education, urbans have much higher levels of literacy and participation in western schooling. One expects that once the Federal Government's Universal Primary Education program becomes established, far greater numbers of rural primary school leavers will be represented in the industrial labor force.

When the effect of urban status on occupational attainment is examined in Table 3.4 the correlation between industrial inequality and urban status is unambiguously present. Just as in the case of entry into the commercial occupations of the petty entrepreneurial classes, urban status determines to a significant degree the opportunities for commuters or migrants to gain entry into higher paying skilled or supervisory positions. In all positions within the skill hierarchy of the factories there is a clear linear relationship between urban status and skill attainment. For example, while slightly less than one-half of the urbans are in unskilled positions, over three-quarters of the commuters hold such positions. And further, while the mean number of years at one's present job is higher for urbans, there is less than one year separating them from the commuters. Hence, though commuters have been employed in factory labor for some duration, they have not advanced upward in the skill hierarchy. Let us move from objective characteristics to an analysis of the subjective perspectives of industrial workers within each urban status group.

Urbans: proletarianization of independent commodity producers

Apart from a tiny minority of workers interviewed, the urbans are from established urban families of the Birni. As members of the urban talakawa

112

from birth, their careers, social networks and consciousness reflect an urbanity and a level of cynical awareness that is usually absent from all but the most urbanized among their rural-born counterparts. Virtually all urban workers express a sentimental attachment to the Birni and especially to their ward, where some remember neighborhoods treating children as family members and where most attended Koranic school with children of both wealthy and poor families. Urbans hold an identity of being 'sons of Kano'. This status differentiates them from recent migrants and commuters, whom they refer to as 'peasants'. As Table 3.5 indicated, most urbans are from merchant, craft, petty trading and mallam families. Unlike the migrants or the commuters, therefore, their social networks may involve contact or a personal relationship with the affluent, the educated or the powerful. As discussed below, though many of the migrants and commuters paid a bribe for their factory job, the urbans rarely admitted paying for a job. Instead, a former patron, or a childhood friend who had advanced in the state bureaucracy, or a friend or relative who traded in the products of the firm was able to arrange employment with the manager for the urban worker. Urban status, therefore, overlaps with sectoral location, for the urbans are better integrated into the craft and entrepreneurial groups within the informal sector through residence, prior careers and social ties.

Since many urbans descend from respected trading or merchant families that are often identified with Hausa sub-ethnic groups, such as the Agalawa, their careers are classically downwardly mobile.[16] One respondent described his entry into factory work with the expression, 'I fell into this job'. Indeed, even if the urbans were not from respected urban merchant families, the success of their peers or their neighbors generates a conscious sense of downward mobility as they become increasingly proletarianized and as their peers achieve some success from Nigeria's economic growth, especially during the petroleum economy. Worse still is the loss of social esteem they associate with their downward mobility. As one former trader from an Agalawa family described his situation: 'People in our ward are traders. If you are a laborer like me, they will say that you are worthless.' When one examines their career histories, there appear to be many routes to becoming proletarianized. Among the forty-four urbans, at least five lost their trading capital as a direct consequence of the Nigerian political crisis and civil war (1966–70). One respondent was a successful cattle merchant (similar to those described by Cohen in Ibadan) who invested his capital in cattle and transport costs in order to market the cattle in Lagos; upon their arrival, however, the first coup occurred, the markets closed for fear of destruction from rioting, and the cattle soon died of sleeping sickness because they could not be sold and slaughtered in time. Still others, who were engaged in the kola trade in the former Western Region, lost houses and other investments due to communal rioting. And finally, several respondents had been traders at Kano's Sabon Gari market but lost their capital in the communal rioting that took place in Kano during 1966.

113

Not all urbans, however, are from respected merchant families. Several in the survey are from families of slave origin who describe themselves as retainers and servants to titled aristocracy. Leatherworkers and declining craft families also provide a number of workers from the Birni. When one examines such workers' careers, it is clear that they did not move directly to factory work. Instead, they tried several crafts or petty trading occupations first, but failed to become independent, self-supporting traders. Many believe that the clientage system of the past, where loyal service for an unspecified payment was rewarded by financial assistance that enabled a client to become an established trader, no longer operates unless one is related to the patron. For them, the intensification of commodity relations required career changes. Moreover, former clients are unanimous in evaluating clientage as an unlikely route to success. They point out that, for a wage of a few kwebo per day, a shop boy performs the role of the former client. Thus traders no longer uphold the obligation of financing the client. Further, many respondents complained about the lack of freedom under clientage, as compared to wage labor, and the probability that a client eventually will be dismissed for allegedly stealing from the trader. In general, then, the urbans perceive that 'modern times' (i.e., intensification of capitalist social relations), have brought greater competition between traders, greater dependence upon wage labor for services and a change in attitude by the wealthy towards the less fortunate. One worker described this change: 'Before, the wealthy would help small traders of his ward begin trading, but now the wealthy say that they must save their money in order to open a factory.' A second commented, 'The big merchants are becoming richer and crushing the market for small traders.' A third argued, 'Before, one merchant's *arziki* [fortune] brought us some benefits, now his arziki impoverishes us.' It would be difficult to find clearer descriptions of the social costs of capital accumulation for a once integrated ward-community than those contained in the urbans' statements.

Tailoring is a craft occupation that a disproportionate number of urban workers tried and failed at during earlier phases of their careers. Though some inherited the craft from their fathers, many entered tailoring from other declining craft backgrounds, such as dyers, tanners, leatherworkers or poorly trained mallams. While the demand for tailoring in a society where factory-produced clothing is comparatively uncommon is very high, so too is the competition for customers. Note that a majority of former tailors rented their hand-powered sewing machines, and when customers failed to provide sufficient income, they hired themselves out to merchants as mass producers of hats and other objects of clothing. Tailoring also attracts mallams and Koranic students. The latter begin by hand-sewing the multicolored hats worn by nearly all Muslim men in the region. The example of tailoring illustrates the futile efforts of a declining class of independent producers to survive where the market is flooded with tailors and where large-scale production using power machines and modern styles is capturing the taste of higher income groups.

If one investigates the friendship networks and residence patterns of the urbans, it is obvious how the urban status of a downwardly mobile 'son of Kano' generates opportunities denied to a rural-born migrant or commuter. Though declining in influence, the wards continue to reflect community sentiments and friendship ties. Thus, lifetime residents maintain some network relations among the wealthy and, in some cases, the powerful state bureaucrats. For example, one urban worker knew one of the African directors of his factory and claimed to have intervened with the director in order to reinstate a dismissed worker. Another urban worker, originating from a ward famous for learned Muslim scholars, reported that he greeted and occasionally socialized with a leading university administrator/scholar with whom he had developed a friendship when they attended Koranic school as children in their ward. The statistical data of Kano State in Table 4.1 (below) indicate that a significant minority of urban workers owned their homes or lived in family-owned houses. Not only are the urbans shielded from the inflationary effects of the housing market, but their social networks and residence patterns retain the quality of primary social relations, which reinforces the importance of their urban status in their own eyes. Among the urbans who rent accommodations, one finds residential patterns that are similar to those of the migrants; that is to say, they reside with wage laborers, mallams, labor service workers and lorry park ticket collectors, etc., but there is a higher percentage of state-sector workers.

Given the resources and esteem of originating as a 'son of Kano', how do the urbans view life and changes in Kano since their childhood? Virtually all urbans are critical of the decline in Muslim moral standards for women, children and obligations between friends. Many repeated the statement that childhood friendships were destroyed as one friend became wealthy and ignored his poorer friend. Others emphasized the increase in individualism and 'love of self' as well as greater competition among brothers and friends to get ahead in the world. Not surprisingly, urbans see the world as changing from one based upon Muslim values to one based upon money. One worker gave this example: 'Before, if you had a car accident, the driver stopped and asked if you were all right. Now people stop and do not ask about you, they only say, "Do not worry, I shall pay for damages".' In general, urbans volunteered that traditional standards of generosity, modesty, friendship and honesty have declined in favor of the pursuit of material goods and career advancements. Of course, this attitude corresponds to the increase in wealth and capitalist social relations in urban Kano, while at the same time it remains the perspective of those who have failed to seize their share of the new wealth.

On the positive side, urbans are aware of the importance and the value of western education and, most importantly, acknowledge that their past resistance to attending western school was a mistake. As one urban put it,

115

'When I was a child, I cried so much about attending primary school that my parents took me out. Now I cry even more because I do not have it.' Another urban worker commented that when he was a child, if you attended primary school, children called you *dan nasara* (literally, 'son of a Christian') and would not play with you. Some workers blamed their political leaders for discouraging them from attending school, while at the same time they were sending their own children to western schools.[17] Regarding positive attitudes toward recent political reforms, many urbans believed that freedom has increased for the talakawa. One cited the example of courts where previously the talakawa were required to prostrate themselves before a judge, but now they are allowed to stand and present their case to the judge. Finally, after the civil war there was a general expression of feeling for Nigerian nationalism and the criticism of ethnic conflict which, they believe, led to the civil war. Like so many participants in urban capitalist society, the urbans expressed an ambiguously felt sentiment by denouncing the materialism of capitalism while simultaneously acknowledging the value of individual freedom that the transition to semi-industrial capitalism created in the Nigerian case.

With this general understanding of the urbans in mind, we can ask the question – what do they bring to the rural-born workers within an emerging yet unevenly developed industrial proletariat? First, the urbans are aware of the alliance of wealth and state power in Kano, because of their networks and knowledge of local personalities. For example, their knowledge of personal, sexual and financial scandals among members of the dominant classes demystifies the power held by those classes. Second, since nearly all the older workers were supporters of NEPU, they understand the importance of workers organizing and participating in politics. More importantly, urbans believe that, as sons of Kano, they have the right to organize, criticize and petition authority if they believe that their rights have been violated. Moreover, compared to the rural-born, they are more intellectually agile at interpreting Islamic theory for their own class needs; they are less mystified by, and more critical of, managerial and political authority. Thus, the urbans have political awareness and network resources, a strong sense of possessing rights as urban talakawa and a cynical acceptance of the fact that contemporary conditions require workers to organize and to petition political authorities in order to improve their lot. One expects that leadership in any working class movement will be drawn from the urbans, as they possess the self-confidence and organizational experience to negotiate with managerial and political authority.

Commuters: passive proletarianization of peasant producers

If the urbans represent downwardly mobile independent producers and thus a more advanced segment of an emergent urban working class, the commuters represent their sociological opposite. Yet, together, both reflect the uneven development within a first-generation industrial proletariat. In spite of the differences between industrial capitalism at the core and at the periphery, the sizeable number of commuters enumerated in the industrial survey verifies the common need of industrial capitalism: the search for a cheap and docile source of labor. Just as was the case in English industrialization, where cheap rural labor allowed industrial capitalists to overcome the resistance offered by guild-organized urban producers, the commuters' level of social development and an authoritarian political situation act to reduce workers' demands for higher wages and the development of working class organizations.[18] This is true because the commuters reside in their original villages and continue to reproduce themselves and their families in large part by independent peasant production (i.e., farming, crafts, services and trade). Hence, unlike urban dwellers, they are less dependent upon a wage and the market for survival. More importantly, never having made a break with independent peasant life means that their morally determined consumption needs and their long-term material aspirations are much lower than those of urban dwellers (i.e., urbans and migrants). Hence, in a labor force comprised of a large number of commuters, industrial capitalists can pay a wage lower than would be the case if the labor supply consisted of urban residents who were completely dependent upon the market for inflated wage goods and housing.[19] While the socially determined standard of living of the commuters is lower than that for urban resident workers, and while the peasant household possesses income sources such as access to land, urban services and craft production, the critical difference between commuters and urban dwellers is that most commuters identify personally with rural life and accept its authority relations. Unlike the migrants and the urbans, the commuters are not conditioned by the organizational and institutional processes of urban life that I described earlier as urban social processes of a semi-industrial capitalist city. Until they are engulfed by the expanding urban perimeter, their self-identification as rural people, or peasants, precludes them for the most part from participation in the processes of urban class formation, even though they participate in the urban labor market and in the labor process of industrial capitalist production. Let us examine the conditions that maintain and reproduce the commuters as an urban status category, one that constrains the maturation of militant working class consciousness.

Compared to migrants and urbans, the commuters are immersed in poverty, patrimonial authority relations and relative ignorance as measured by either Islamic or western standards of education. The population density of the peri-urban area, the lack of available land and the expansion of the city dooms them to increasing poverty. Because the state pays only a compensation fee rather than the market price for land confiscated for urban expansion, the victims of state confiscation usually fall into the urban proletariat, the petty entrepreneurial or labor service occupations, soon after losing their land. As the city expands to accommodate industrial,

117

housing and transportation requirements, the villages of the remaining commuters are certain to be engulfed. In this sense, commuters are passive rather than active proletarians.[20] Moreover, many peasants expect to be engulfed, as many had been moved during previous expansions of the urban area. Such a situation, therefore, encourages younger commuters to emigrate to Kano when they secure a reliable position in the formal sector labor force.

When one examines the commuter's household, one understands why they report a higher number of dependants than other urban status groups (see Table 3.1), for commuters report large numbers of older, sometimes infirm family members and recently divorced women as part of their dependency burden. Many indicate that the patriarchal authority of their fathers prevents them from emigrating to the urban area. Unlike the rural-born migrants, the commuters appear to be under the domination of a multigenerational extended family which offers them social security but limits their personal freedom and their commitment to urban workers' struggles. From the perspective of security, their attachment to the extended family is understandable if one examines the household activities of the larger families. It is common for several sons to engage in modern-sector wage labor such as construction or industrial labor; others may supply urban dwellers' needs for firewood and building materials transported by donkey; an elder brother might have a stall in the urban market selling rural products or handicrafts; and all might work together with wage laborers (*kodago*) on family farms. Generally, the activities of these large households lack specialization in any one activity; instead, family members have invested their labor in several sectors in order to maximize household security against uncertain risks. Besides state confiscation of land, sales of land are more common among commuters than among migrants, and as one would expect, the larger households seem to be net purchasers. Again, while most households are poor, there were several deviant cases where, for example, the son of a village head was also a successful grain trader; a second worker's family specialized in selling groundnut oil to Lagos; and a third worker's household successfully developed an ovenbrick-making industry.

The commuters' acceptance of their fathers' authority was equalled by their fear of the rural sarauta. Whereas the migrants criticized the sarauta and emphasized the freedom of urban life, most commuters accepted sarauta domination, illegal taxation (such as forced contributions to 'community development' projects) and the sarauta monopoly of power as the natural order of society. Some reported that officeholding was a gift of Allah, hence sarauta authority could not be questioned. Even when critical of the sarauta, the commuters despaired of altering their condition. From the commuters' perspective it was safer to avoid any conflict and to obey authority. (Again, as the PRP electoral successes indicate, the commuters' despair may have arisen from the absence of a possible alternative in

118

1972–5.) While one assumes that there is some self-selection, whereby the more politically independent commuters migrate to the cities, one suspects that part of the reason for the commuters' timidity may derive from prior servile or slave status which may continue to subject them to the authority of the sarauta. This explanation is speculative, but because many of the villages surrounding Kano were founded by officeholders as slave estate investments during the precapitalist period, this servile status may continue to exert influence on the commuters' perception of inequality and political authority.[21]

Nowhere is the backwardness of the commuters more apparent than in their perception of factory organization, in their occupational and material aspirations and in their perception of recent social changes. Commuters carry with them into the factory a patrimonial consciousness whereby they define themselves as clients, and the head of the household – i.e., the factory boss – determines authority relations according to his personal wishes. Accordingly, the most naive commuters believe that they have only the option of accepting these authority relations or leaving the factory. Unlike the migrants and the urbans, very few commuters possess a conscious sense of having definite rights sanctioned by the national state or by Islamic tradition. Similarly, while there are some learned mallams and Koranic students among them, the level of Islamic sophistication is lower among commuters than among migrants and urbans. For instance, few commuters translated Islamic ideology into beliefs that reinforced the legitimacy of working class activity. One commuting worker expressed his situation this way: 'We are peasants, so we are used to hard work, and we will endure here because we are accustomed to suffering.' The classic response to adversity and injustice, according to the typical commuter, is patience. One commuter justified his perspective in this manner, 'I started working here for 20 kwebo a day, and now I earn one naira. Did patience not bring this about? We rural people have no choice but to be patient because farming is not sufficient for our needs.'

Aspirations of the commuters contrast sharply with those of the urbans. While the latter aspire to build modern homes, visit Mecca and possibly open a modern company, commuters set their goals much lower. The commuters' typical aspirations are to have enough to eat and to clothe one's family, to build a house of sun-dried brick rather than straw, to purchase a bicycle, to pursue Koranic studies, to marry a new wife or to buy land in the peri-urban area. Of course, long-term employees tended to aspire to own modern consumer goods, such as a motor-bike, or to become a trader, so participation in an industrial labor process does exert its influence. One is struck by the poverty of the commuters. Some claimed to own only one suit of clothing and aspired to purchase a second. In many cases it appears that the more isolated commuters, that is, those who do not reside in villages where one finds networks of commuters to industrial work, resist becoming wage laborers until they are completely impoverished. Several mentioned

119

that life had changed for them when they accepted pay for laboring work, whereas, in contrast, their fathers resisted wage employment even if they were paid to take it. Again, like Weber's study of small-holding peasants, Kano's peasantry struggle to resist proletarianization and the loss of independent peasant landholding.[22]

Regarding how life had changed, the commuters' response contained some of the urbans' complaints about the commercialization of individual worth, but more concern was expressed about the lack of shame among youths, women and emigrants from the rural areas. Commuters denounced the freedom and individualism that attracted migrants to Kano and emphasized the decline in youthful respect for such traditional authorities as the head of the household and the traditional political authorities in general. Yet, unlike among urban residents, there was little criticism of materialism replacing traditional social relations such as friendship. In typically peasant fashion, and consistent with the high population of the peri-urban area, many commuters stressed the decline in fertility of the land, noting that harvests were smaller, rainfall was less than before and manure was necessary every year now. Just as in the case of the migrants and the urbans, commuters noted the technological and material advances in Kano but expressed little interest in mastering or participating in these advances. Finally, several mentioned that marriage costs had increased to such a degree that young men found it difficult to marry virgins, and older men found it difficult to marry a second time. Both reflect the rural concern for reproducing the household's labor supply as well as the value placed by Hausa-speakers on polygamy.

One of the oddities of the commuters is the high level of wage labor among friends, brothers and fathers as compared to urbans and migrants. Yet, because they view wage labor as a supplement to peasant household activities or else they choose to emigrate to Kano, the high level of wage labor involvement generates little change in the commuters' political or social identity. Though commuters may be a theoretical anomaly or a social category reflecting the transition to semi-industrial capitalism, they are unlikely to disappear from the industrial labor force of Kano. The expansion of the city, their natural fecundity and the creation of new industrial estates at Sharada and Challawa will reproduce the conditions that brought them into industrial employment at the Township and Bompai industrial estates.

Migrants: fully proletarianized seekers of urban opportunity

Whereas urbans and commuters are recruited from the same or similar communities, often retaining their residence from birth, migrants display none of the internal homogeneity of the latter two urban status groups. As an urban status group, therefore, migrants are extremly heterogeneous with regard to background, length of time in Kano, exposure to wage labor, education and commitment to urban residence. Their common experience, besides poverty, proletarianization and urban adjustment, arises from their dependence upon the urban market for food, housing, work and virtually all necessities. Unlike the urbans, most migrants have weak social networks and know little of urban lifestyles when they arrive in Kano. While they are similar in peasant background to the commuters, the migrants, unlike the latter, are forced to depend on the market for housing and do not possess the peasant household's resources to support them when they are in distress. For all of these reasons, the migrants experience the greatest amount of behavioral and attitudinal change through the urban social processes, not because they wish to do so, but because their involuntary conditions forces them to make adjustments, such as living in the same compound with previously unknown ethnic groups and Christians, or learning to develop multi-ethnic social networks that will enable them to secure employment.

Migrants vary enormously with regard to the length of time spent in urban centers, whether they originate from Kano State, whether they migrated early in their careers as Koranic students or seasonal workers, or whether they emigrated as youths with their families. Many have lived most of their adult lives in Kano and consider themselves members of Kano's urban talakawa. These migrants have taken on urban dress and lifestyles, such as abandoning the practice of shaving their heads in favour of modern haircuts. Further, many who migrated before the civil war and before the inflationary petroleum boom were fortunate enough to become supervisors or skilled laborers during the period when industrial wage labor expanded rapidly. It is of interest to note that most migrants intend to stay permanently in Kano, and while most continue to visit relatives, extensive kinship relations are not as common as they are among lineage-organized ethnic groups.[23] Instead, Hausa-speaking migrants tend to reaffiliate within urban networks and often utilize Islamic networks, developed either as Koranic students or after settling in Kano, for mutual aid during times of distress. Let us begin by describing the many reasons and conditions that brought the migrants to Kano.

Before settling in Kano, many migrants had spent one or more dry seasons there, or else they had wandered into Kano as Koranic students with their mallam. Hence, many had broken at least partially with village life before settling permanently in Kano. Workers from distant areas had heard stories about the wealth and opportunities of Kano before they arrived. Moreover, those living within the close-settled zone often had visited Kano with their parents or guardians before they emigrated permanently. Among younger workers, the death of their father occasioned conditions that encouraged their emigration, which often involved conflict with brothers over inheritance rights, especially with brothers of a different mother. Also, there were examples of sons selling their inheritance, usually land, for ill-fated commercial careers or a marriage that failed.

121

Whereas commuters tended to search for industrial labor because of poverty, migrants tended to emigrate at a young age in search of new occupational and economic opportunities and for the amenities of urban life that are denied by rural life. Again, these generalizations apply to the majority, for there were migrants who moved to Kano for reasons of poverty. Some emigrated as political exiles. One migrant was an organizer for NEPU in a rural district of Katsina; he was jailed by the Native Authority police and escaped to the NEPU offices, where he was hidden from the authorities by a previously unknown yet sympathetic tailor. Among migrants originating from the peri-urban area, most began as commuters to the factory or as casual laborers or even as labor service workers. Most decided to stay after securing a factory position. Others from the peri-urban area emigrated after their lands were confiscated by the state for urban expansion. Some migrants suggested that taxation and political domination by the sarauta were important reasons for emigrating to Kano. As factory workers, they reasoned, peasant possessions such as goats or sheep could not be confiscated for tax payments as was the case in rural areas. It would be difficult for a researcher to verify the reasons for individual migration in each case unless the research was undertaken in the village or settlement of origin. What is clear, however, is that urban capital investments, urban amenities, Muslim urban cultural institutions and the incomparable quality of urban life are the explanatory factors that attracted migrants and encourage them to stay. One worker expressed his delight with urban life by comparing it to life in his village: 'Here there are people like you. People that surpass me in everything. Every day I see those who surpass me in money, clothing, beautiful cars, beds and electric lights. Before, at home, we were all the same as the others. Even our gowns were all the same.' For recent migrants, the material advantages of urban amenities, such as clean water from a public tap, as well as hospital and educational facilities (i.e., the collective means of consumption) make a deep impression that encourages additional rural to urban migration.

Let us examine the data from workers' in-depth interviews (N=140) regarding migration. Out of fifty migrants, 72 percent stated that they intended to stay permanently in Kano. Among those under thirty, the figure rises to 77 percent. When one examines the migrants' first contact in Kano, the typical pattern indicates that most follow some known network: for example, 35 percent stayed with kin, 25 percent with friends from home, 25 percent with contacts developed from prior seasonal migrations and 12 percent with contacts originating from Koranic school networks. While the high level of kin contact reflects migration patterns among adults, many migrants reported being adopted as children by urban relatives upon the death of their father or to assist relatives who were without children and thus needed child labor in their household. Such a pattern is consistent with Hausa practices of exchanging and adopting children within kin groups. Almost all migrants knew someone in Kano or were immersed in a network that provided contacts before they entered urban Kano. Those without contacts or network connections managed to receive charity or mutual aid from strangers during their initial period of adjustment. Koranic school networks are important, as indicated earlier.

No feature of social participation in a peripheral capitalist urban center makes a greater impression on migrants than the impact of market relations and the commercialization of social status. Such impressions are individual experiences of commodity relations. While migrants valued the material amenities, occupational opportunities and freedom from the domination of the sarauta and their elders, they were less sanguine about the economic pressures and insecurities of the labor and housing markets. Moreover, in a period of rapid inflation they deplored and expressed bewilderment over the rising cost of food. When asked how life had changed for them, a number independently responded with the following slogan: 'What used to cost 2 pennies and fill my stomach, now costs 2 shillings and I am still hungry.' Even more than the urbans, the migrants described urban life as a situation where one was dependent upon one's money rather than upon one's moral character. Individualism and the pursuit of personal material advantage, according to most migrants, were the main differences between rural life and life in Kano. In summary, the migrants felt some ambivalance about urban life. On one hand, the benefits of occupational opportunities, material amenities, urban social life and the freedom of urban life were evaluated positively, while, on the other hand, their dependence upon the market for food, housing and work generated anxiety and uncertainty.

Unlike the urbans, who possessed a clear understanding of the alliance of wealth and political power in Kano as well as some organizational experience in opposing this bloc of power, only the most urbanized migrants understood the relationship between political authority and capitalist development. The most recent emigrants, as well as younger migrants who were too junior to have participated in the politics of the First Republic, tended to make no distinction between the federal governments and the sarauta, while more experienced migrants understood that the sarauta and the local government authorities were losing power to the federal and state government.

INDUSTRIAL LABOR WITHIN THE LABOR MARKET: OBJECTIVE EXPERIENCES AND SOCIAL TIES

Whatever their urban status, the leburori of Kano move frequently between the informal sector and the wage labor market. This section is intended to illustrate in empirical detail how workers move from occupations in distinct sectors and, at the same time, how urban status determines to a significant degree the employment and career opportunities available to each worker. Following the analysis of the objective experiences of industrial workers ($N=140$) in the urban labor market, I shall turn to their subjective

Table 3.6 *Industrial workers' careers: sector by urban status*

% with career history of:	Urbans (44)	Migrants (50)	Commuters (46)	Total (140)
Labor service	61.4	80.0	10.9	51.4
	(27)	(40)	(5)	(72)
Craft labor	36.4	10.0	0.0	15.0
	(16)	(5)	(0)	(21)
Commerce[a]	56.8	30.0	15.2	33.6
	(25)	(15)	(7)	(47)
Mallam or advanced Koranic studies	29.5	24.0	8.7	20.7
	(13)	(12)	(4)	(29)
Formal sector wage labor	52.3	54.0	45.7	50.7
	(23)	(27)	(21)	(71)

[a] Stationary, not hawking, with independent capital

evaluation of these experiences. Here the reader should bear in mind that my purpose is to provide empirical verification to more skeptical observers regarding the influence of *urban social processes* that unify independent commodity producers and wage workers into the populist class coalition known as the urban talakawa. Secondly, it will be shown how urban status structures the objective opportunities as well as the subjective evaluations of Kano's urban talakawa by examining the situation of industrial workers. Let us examine the occupational careers of those industrial workers selected for in-depth interviews.

After sifting through the quantitative and qualitative evidence, I concluded that the distinction between formal and informal sectors, while analytically valuable, obscured the intense interchange between sectors experienced by members of the urban talakawa. Thus, during the lifetime of an urban or a migrant, his career often involves casual wage labor, petty trading (hawking or peddling), craft production and several formal-sector, wage-earning occupations. Many industrial workers from the Birni have also been successful traders with sizeable amounts of capital. Indeed, it is a structural feature of industrial employment, with its periodic lay-offs and strikes that expel workers into the urban labor market and thus toward their networks within the informal sector, that integrates the informal sector and the formal sector in a city like Kano. Moreover, the turnover of factory workers is sufficiently high that many independent producers in the informal sector once worked in factories and thus maintain the social networks and some shared sentiment of industrial workers.

Let us examine the occupational careers of my sample of industrial workers as presented in Table 3.6. This table presents previous occupations of industrial workers by sector and occupation as well as by urban status. (Note that the category 'labor service' refers to casual wage labor, hawking,

Table 3.7 *Friend's occupation by urban status and sector*

Occupational sector of friend	Urbans	Migrants	Commuters	Total
Agriculture	4.5	8.2	23.9	12.2
	(2)	(4)	(11)	(17)
Formal-sector wage labor	31.8	36.7	41.3	36.7
	(14)	(18)	(19)	(51)
Craftsmen	18.2	16.3	6.5	13.7
	(8)	(8)	(3)	(19)
Commerce	31.8	12.2	8.7	17.3
	(14)	(6)	(4)	(24)
Labor service	13.6	24.5	15.2	18.0
	(6)	(12)	(7)	(25)
Religious – mallam or advanced Koranic student	0.0	2.0	4.3	2.2
	(0)	(1)	(2)	(3)
Total	100	100	100	100
	(44)	(49[a])	(46)	(139[a])

[a] One migrant reported 'no friends'

peddling, scavenging and irregular, impoverished occupations such as fingernail clipping or wood chopping.) One observes that over half the sample of industrial workers have worked in the informal sector as labor service workers. Migrants predominate, while commuters are underrepresented. Again, independent commerce and craft production are strongly represented in the careers of urbans. This is consistent with Tables 3.4 and 3.5 which presented the social and occupational origins of industrial workers (N=3075). Objectively, therefore, most industrial workers who are urbans are personally experiencing downward occupational mobility from independent commodity production to industrial proletarianization, a feature which is an important source of their political consciousness. Note that for most workers, regardless of urban status, the factory job held at the time of the interview was not their first formal-sector, wage-earning occupation and, further, that about one-fifth of the total sample and a higher proportion of urbans and migrants were full-time Koranic students or mallams prior to recruitment to their present job.

The particular influence of urban status as a source of unevenness within the urban talakawa and the industrial proletariat is even more apparent when one examines the first job undertaken by workers upon entering Kano's labor force. (This table is not presented due to space limitations.) As was suggested above, most urbans enter the urban labor force not as wage workers but as independent commodity producers: 25 percent of the urbans were employed in informal-sector commercial services; 4.5 percent were self-employed traders; and 35.3 percent were engaged in labor service,

Table 3.8 *Recruitment to factory by urban status*

Method of recruitment	Urbans	Migrants	Commuters	Total
Family	25.0	6.0	8.7	12.9
	(11)	(3)	(4)	(18)
Friends	45.5	40.0	47.8	44.3
	(20)	(20)	(22)	(62)
Bribe	13.6	32.0	32.6	26.4
	(6)	(16)	(15)	(37)
Personal	13.6	20.0	6.5	13.6
	(6)	(10)	(3)	(19)
Other	2.3	2.0	4.3	2.9
	(1)	(1)	(2)	(4)
Total	100	100	100	100
	(44)	(50)	(46)	(140)

almost exclusively as hawkers. The migrants' most common occupation of entry into the urban labor force, not surprisingly, is in labor service, both hawking and casual wage labor (62 percent). It is noteworthy that formal-sector wage labor is the first *urban* occupation for commuters: 78.3 percent of the commuters' first urban jobs were in formal-sector employment. To conclude, then, while urban status is correlated with sectoral entry into the urban labor market, the analysis of the careers of industrial workers indicates that there is a great deal of intersectoral mobility. Hence, the evidence from workers' careers illustrates how industrial workers are integrated with, rather than isolated from the independent producers of the informal sector.

In order to provide a second measure of social integration between industrial workers and other occupations of the informal sector, I have examined the friendships of industrial workers. Table 3.7 presents the sectoral location of the occupation held by the closest friend of each industrial worker, according to urban status. Though over one-third of the workers report primary friendships among formal-sector workers, the remaining two-thirds report friendships among craft, commercial and labor service workers. Again, migrants are more likely to have friends engaged in labor service and formal-sector wage labor, while urbans are more likely to have friends engaged in independent commerce and craft production. Note that commuters are the most likely to have their closest friends in formal-sector wage labor, a finding that I take to indicate the rapid rate of proletarianization ongoing in the peri-urban villages surrounding urban Kano. Since the finding regarding commuters' friends was unexpected, I checked the occupation of the mature brothers of workers as reported by respondents at the time of the interview. This data only confirms the high degree of formal-sector employment among the commuters and under-scores the intense social and economic integration of impoverished resi-dents of Kano's peri-urban area into the urban labor market. I found that among respondents with mature brothers (i.e., sixteen years and over), 54 percent of commuters, 39 percent of urbans and 24 percent of migrants had brothers engaged in formal-sector wage labor at the time of the interview. Note that the evidence underscores the intense integration of peri-urban villages into the urban economy, a fact that contradicts Polly Hill's interpretation of Dorayi village as rural.[24]

Migrant status is also an important determinant of the manner in which industrial workers are recruited into the factory. Table 3.8 presents modes of recruitment by urban status. Only one worker (i.e., 'other') reported being recruited through the Federal Government's labor office. While informal friendship linkages are the most important method of recruitment for all urban status groups, the family connections of urbans are much more important than those of commuters and migrants. And, of course, urbans are much less likely to be required to pay bribes for their jobs (i.e., less than half as likely as migrants and commuters). Given the fact that over a quarter of all workers and nearly one-third of the commuters and migrants admitted paying bribes in order to gain employment, one must reject any suggestions that African laborers are culturally unable to commit themselves and to adjust to modern industrial wage labor; if anything, they are overcommitted due to material circumstance.[25] Let us now examine the subjective evalu-ations voiced by industrial workers regarding their experiences within the urban labor market.

Industrial labor, clientage and occupational rank

Here we review the attitudes of industrial workers towards their occu-pational careers, as well as how urban status differentiates their subjective evaluation of industrial labor. Table 3.9 presents workers' evaluation of the best job in their career. As the table indicates, the longer one resides in urban Kano, the less likely one is to see industrial labor as one's best job. Since the difference between migrants and commuters is not statistically significant, it is the low value placed upon industrial labor by the urbans that requires comment. For the rural-born, i.e., migrants and commuters, industrial labor is better paying and more secure than labor service, declining craft production or peasant farming. But the urbans, perceiving themselves as independent 'sons of Kano', see industrial labor as downward mobility from their former position as independent commodity producers. Again, this is consistent with my interpretation of urban status and the role of urbans within the industrial proletariat.

The next question concerns workers' evaluation of clientage within a household organization as compared to wage labor. Much has been written about the high value placed upon informal clientage by the subordinate

Table 3.9 *Evaluation of best job[a] by urban status*

	Urbans	Migrants	Commuters	Total
Agriculture	0.0	4.4	4.2	2.8
	(0)	(2)	(1)	(3)
Manufacturing and modern construction	37.5	73.3	83.3	62.4
	(15)	(33)	(20)	(68)
Commerce	27.5	11.1	8.3	16.5
	(11)	(5)	(2)	(18)
Craft	10.0	0.0	0.0	3.7
	(4)	(0)	(0)	(4)
Labor service	12.5	6.7	0.0	7.3
	(5)	(3)	(0)	(8)
Other	12.5	4.4	4.2	7.3
	(5)	(2)	(1)	(8)
Total	100	100	100	100
	(40)	(45)	(24)	(109)

[a] For workers with two or more jobs in career history

Table 3.10 *Evaluation of clientage by wage labor*

	Urbans	Migrants	Commuters	Total
Prefers wage labor	74.4	83.7	87.0	81.9
	(32)	(41)	(40)	(113)
Prefers clientage	25.6	16.3	13.0	18.1
	(11)	(8)	(6)	(25)
Total	100	100	100	100
	(43[a])	(49[a])	(46)	(138[a])

[a] Two missing cases

members of a clientage relationship, i.e., *yara*.[26] In this instance, workers were asked to evaluate the benefits of wage labor as compared to clientage with a trader. Table 3.10 presents their responses by urban status. While urban residence is slightly correlated with a preference for clientage, over 80 percentage of the workers stated a preference for wage labor rather than clientage. As described in the previous section, clientage is viewed by workers as an institution undergoing rapid decline during the transition to semi-industrial capitalism. For, while clients formerly received some financial support from their patrons, workers now believe that clients are no longer advanced to the status of independent producer or trader, unless such clients are close family friends of the patron. In fact, many workers stated that clientage had become merely irregular and poorly paid wage

Table 3.11 *Workers' occupational ranking of 'self' and 'trusted people' by urban status*

	Urbans (43)	Migrants (49)	Commuters (44)
Total			
'Self'			
High	0.0	2.0	2.3
	(0)	(1)	(1)
Medium	20.9	16.3	15.9
	(9)	(8)	(7)
Low	79.1	81.6	81.8
	(34)	(40)	(36)
'Trusted people'			
High	9.3	2.1	4.5
	(4)	(1)	(2)
Medium	44.2	18.8	22.7
	(19)	(9)	(10)
Low	46.5	79.2	72.7
	(20)	(38)	(32)

labor, and for this reason they preferred the independence and certainty of formal-sector wage labor. Clearly, when faced with the choice between formal-sector wage labor and traditional clientage, industrial workers are extremely realistic about the constraints and insecurity of traditional household relations. Hence, they hold no brief for any romantic interpretations regarding the benefits of traditional social relations of the Hausa household. Finally, note that urbans hold a somewhat higher value for clientage, but this undoubtedly arises from their desire to regain their former occupational status as independent producers.

The issue of occupational status and workers' subjective ranking of occupations is a mainstay of industrial sociology. Although I collected occupational ranking data, using the three-tiered scale, the results are not surprising nor do they add in a significant way to the problems analyzed in this chapter. The results of the occupational status ranking are available to the reader in Table A.2. More germane to my argument are the self-rankings of the workers on the three-tiered scale. Table 3.11 presents the workers' self-rankings as well as responses to 'the people that you trust' category. Again, industrial workers, whatever their urban status, have no illusions concerning the social rank that they hold as industrial workers: there is no 'labor aristocratic' consciousness evident in Kano![27] Over 80 percent see themselves at the bottom of the occupational status hierarchy, along with cart pushers and casual laborers. Regarding the second question, i.e., social rank of 'people that you can trust', the social networks and the prior occupational status of the urbans distinguish them from the migrants and commuters. Hence, urbans remain subjectively as well as objectively integrated into the world of the independent commodity producers, a relationship that strengthens the populist class alliance between the latter and the leburori and, at the same time, contributes to the unevenness of Kano's first-generation industrial proletariat.

Summary: the social basis of the populist alliance

The argument has been made that independent commodity producers and the leburori form a conscious political stratum that is integrated by membership in the class-like precapitalist status group, the talakawa, and by the differentiating effects of semi-industrial capitalism. Just as these two social forces provide the social cohesion and energy for the urban talakawa political movement (i.e., PRP), urban status differences generate unevenness and differentiation within this politically conscious stratum. Furthermore, through qualitative and quantitative data we have attempted to show the movement of labor between the informal- and formal-sector labor markets, as well as how informal social ties integrate the independent commodity producers, the leburori and the urban poor into a common talakawa social identity. Again, urban status must be emphasized as a principal source of differentiation among the Hausa-speaking members of Kano's urban talakawa and among the industrial working class. For the concept of urban status offers researchers a crude measure of an individual's exposure to the micro-level urban social processes which, as I have argued earlier, are powerful determinants of urban working class formation.

Before moving on to a discussion of residence, religion and community, the key role played by the downwardly mobile independent commodity producers in the process of working class formation should be emphasized. Because these 'sons of Kano' claim a historic birthright and traditional political rights, the urbanized yet recently proletarianzed independent commodity producers play, in an informal manner, a role which guilds and similar corporate groups played more formally in the class struggles of nineteenth-century Europe. That is, European craft organizations, while disassociating themselves from unskilled rural emigrants, nevertheless provided leadership and models of organizations for the working class movement as a whole. But, after incorporation into the capitalist world economy as a colony, Kano's craft organizations and craft producers declined under imperial domination so as to be denied any analogous role in the leadership of the contemporary working class movement. Yet the urban producers are not without influence; rather, the influence of the urbanized, independent commodity producers is felt through more informal means: resistance by their mallams, who act as the intelligentsia of the urban talakawa, and by the urban-born 'sons of Kano', who refuse to accept without struggle the alienating and undignified experience of proletarianization. Let us now examine the process of class formation within a Muslim working class community.

4

Tudun Wada: Islam, class and community in a laborers' town

RESIDENCE AND THE SOCIAL REPRODUCTION OF LABOR

In order for the leburori to exist as a class they must form a community and a way of life that separates them from others.[1] Residence, therefore, is defined as the site where the leburori are reproduced socially as a class: where micro-level and macro-level processes of semi-industrial capitalism structure social life, where urban social processes outside the workplace socialize labor and where men and women draw upon precapitalist traditions in order to create supportive institutions that nurture family and community life. Therefore, it is not enough to specify the structural processes of change, nor to statistically analyze the social origins and social relations of an emerging proletariat. Rather, a researcher must attempt to convey the processes that structure everyday life from the perspective of the participants so as to provide an empathetic understanding of the consciousness and behavior of working class actors. To do so, one must present detailed descriptions of individual lives, with all their personal contradictions, achievements and failures. In this way it is intended to show just how talakawa and leburori actively create communities while struggling to act in a historical situation marked by relative powerlessness.

The study of the working class community necessarily introduces the problem of housing as a commodity and the effect of market forces on the ownership, distribution and use of this necessary wage good. Further, one must attempt to specify the visible effect, if any, that the intensification of rentier capitalism exerts on ethnic segregation patterns introduced during the colonial period. After examining the social areas of Kano, the focus of attention will be on the community of Tudun Wada, the city's oldest working community. Of interest here are: changes in ownership and residence patterns; the working class and talakawa political traditions; the role of Islam in structuring everyday community life; and the manner in which Islam articulates with semi-industrial capitalist processes such as daily discipline and timing, community control over resources, and the emergence of working class institutions. Important here is the problem of how Islam, a precapitalist force, articulates with market forces associated with capitalism so as to provide a trans-ethnic communal, or Islamic national, identity for members of the urban talakawa and the leburori. Above all, my

131

objective is to show how Muslim Hausa-speaking workers draw upon inherited traditions and institutions in order to resist the destructive and alienating aspects of semi-industrial capitalism. In doing so they create both working class institutions and historically specific popular traditions that support a regional Islamic national identity, which is, paradoxically, strengthened by contact with urban capitalism.

Most of this chapter is concerned with the migrants who are streaming into Kano at an unprecedented rate. As we have already seen, compared to others the migrants are the most proletarianized, the most uprooted and the most dependent upon the market for the means of subsistence. For this reason, migrants are the ideal subject for grasping empirically how pre-capitalist and capitalist structures articulate with each other within a first-generation urban proletariat; migrants must alter their behavior, if not their consciousness, in order to survive in a semi-industrial capitalist city. At the same time, migrants do not voluntarily or easily embrace their new identity as wage laborers; rather, the conditions of social and material existence compel them to act collectively, to alter their attitudes toward class-determined, inter-ethnic residential patterns and to create institutions that remain under working class control.

Finally, examination of a community like Tudun Wada enables one to observe the social bonds and the ecological conditions that integrate the independent producers and the wage laboring class. Here it will be demonstrated under the same conditions of social existence, how talakawa independent producers and wage earners interact, intermarry and participate in community life as members of the same politically conscious stratum, united as much by the opposition to absentee, rentier capitalism and corrupt state officials as by their common talakawa heritage.

SOCIAL AREAS OF KANO: CLASS AND ETHNIC RESIDENTIAL PATTERNS

It will be recalled from Chapter One that the colonial authorities created residential areas segregated according to class and ethnicity in the Waje area, while maintaining for the most part the traditional residential patterns of the Birni. Before analyzing the working class community of Tudun Wada, it is valuable to compare the latter's social, ethnic and material characteristics with other major residential areas of urban Kano. Table 4.1 presents the social and residential characteristics of industrial workers by urban social area. As previously indicated, Sabon Gari was intended to house migrants, usually Christian, from the southern states of Nigeria, while Gwagwarwa was designed as a residential area for non-Muslim yet northern migrants. Table 4.1 presents the distribution of ethnic groups among industrial workers interviewed across the four residential areas. (Note that this table is not a census but a sample of industrial workers.) Hence, Tudun Wada appears as the most Muslim area, after the Birni, with a majority of the population identifying as either Hausa or Fulani. Further,

Table 4.1 *Social characteristics and living standards by urban social area (1971)*

	Dimension	Birni	Sabon Gari	Gwagwarwa Gama	Tudun Wada
1.	% Muslim	98.7	18.4	43.4	76.2
		(518)	(99)	(383)	(218)
2.	% Hausa–Fulani	87.8	2.8	17.5	51.7
		(461)	(15)	(155)	(149)
3.	% Plateau–Tiv cluster	2.1	10.8	19.2	11.5
		(11)	(58)	(170)	(33)
4.	%Yoruba	1.7	21.9	5.5	1.7
		(9)	(118)	(49)	(5)
5.	% Babur–Bura	1.3	0.7	19.6	16.7
		(7)	(4)	(173)	(48)
6.	% Idoma–Nupe cluster	2.9	24.7	17.1	1.4
		(15)	(133)	(151)	(4)
7.	% Edo related	0.8	18.7	3.5	0.0
		(4)	(101)	(31)	0.0
8.	% Kanuri related	2.3	0.7	1.8	3.8
		(12)	(4)	(16)	(11)
9.	% Kilba related	0.0	0.6	12.4	9.4
		0.0	(3)	(110)	(27)
10.	% migrant	51.8	99.3	96.3	92.7
		(272)	(535)	(850)	(265)
11.	Migrants' years at Kano – mean	9.1	3.4	4.6	7.5
12.	% literate (western)	12.2	77.1	35.6	16.8
		(64)	(415)	(314)	(48)
13.	Amenities – none	68.8	36.5	56.9	81.9
		(349)	(196)	(500)	(235)
14.	Electricity	16.2	27.9	28.1	10.8
		(82)	(150)	(247)	(31)
15.	Electricity and water	11.0	31.8	13.0	5.2
		(56)	(171)	(114)	(15)
16.	% homeowners	13.1	0.9	2.5	4.5
		(68)	(5)	(22)	(13)
17.	% renters	53.1	96.5	94.2	92.4
		(276)	(518)	(833)	(266)
18.	Rent – mean (naira)	2.16	4.00	2.96	2.12
19.	Rent – median (naira)	1.98	4.00	2.97	2.00
20.	Daily pay (naira) – mean	0.83	0.97	0.87	0.91
21.	Daily pay (naira) – median	0.73	0.84	0.76	0.78

the Birni remains essentially unchanged; Sabon Gari remains a Christian community with increased numbers of migrants from the northern but non-Muslim states; and Gwagwarwa has become increasingly Muslim though still dominated by non-Hausa/Fulani ethnic groups originating from

Table 4.2 *Household residential characteristics by urban status*

% of respondents with cohabitant being . . .	Urbans	Migrants	Total
Total	(27)	(45)	(72)
1. a relative	51.9	13.3	27.8
	(14)	(6)	(20)
2. from the same factory	3.7	13.3	9.7
	(1)	(6)	(7)
3. a wage laborer	29.6	66.7	52.8
	(8)	(30)	(38)
4. a shop owner	14.8	2.2	6.9
	(4)	(1)	(5)
5. in labor service	44.4	60.0	54.2
	(12)	(27)	(39)
6. a craftsman	33.3	28.9	30.6
	(9)	(13)	(22)
7. a mallam or advanced Koranic student	18.5	8.9	12.5
	(5)	(4)	(9)
8. a Christian	0.0	15.6[a]	9.7
	(0)	(7)	(7)

[a] All are located in Waje rather than in the Birni

the northern states. Tudun Wada is overwhelmingly a migrant community as compared to the Birni but with a slightly more permanent community of working class residents than is the case for Gwagwarwa and Sabon Gari. Similarly, among migrants, the mean length of residence of Tudun Wada residents is closer to that in the Birni than in the latter two social areas. To summarize, therefore, Tudun Wada appears as a largely Hausa-Fulani and Muslim migrant community with migrant-residents having resided there for an average of 7.5 years.

Let us examine the remaining data presented in Table 4.1 pertaining to the skill and material status of residents in the four social areas. Predictably, the proportion literate is a correlate of the proportion of Muslim residents in each area. Just as in the case of the Birni, literacy in western script is low among Tudun Wada residents. Moreover, material not presented here shows that Tudun Wada residents hold the least skilled positions in the skill hierarchy of the factories, a fact that underscores the proletarian nature of this community. Materially, Tudun Wada's residents are the most deprived, for over four-fifths are without piped water or electricity, as compared to just over one-third of Sabon Gari residents. Note that the comparatively longer duration of residence and the particular nature of plot allocation during the colonial era mean that a slightly larger proportion of Tudun Wada's workers own their own homes. But here the figure is a trivial 4.5 percent. Even among residents of the Birni, only 13.1 percent of workers are homeworkers. Finally, the slightly higher than average pay for residents of Tudun Wada arises not from their skill levels but from the length of employment, since workers receive a mandatory raise of 2 kwebo per day for each year of loyal service.

In an effort to corroborate my findings with existing official statistics, I compared the incidence of PAYE taxpayers across the social areas of Waje. The reader will recall that wage workers pay their tax at the workplace while independent commodity producers and others pay the community tax. And, just as in the case of the commuters, the proportion of PAYE taxpayers served as a crude indicator of the degree of proletarianization within each social area. The tax data are presented in Table A.3. Not surprisingly, the PAYE tax data show that the proportion of wage earners has grown in all social areas. For example, the proportion of wage-earning males in Tudun Wada increased from 58.8 percent in 1967/68 to 80.1 percent in 1974/75. By this year Tudun Wada registered the largest proportion of wage earners on its tax rolls of any social area of Kano. Hence the official tax data, which is surely an undercount of the actual population, confirm the findings of the industrial survey regarding the degree of proletarianization found in Tudun Wada.

Before moving to the social history of Tudan Wada, some evidence is presented to support my contention that migrants and migrant residential areas are the spatial sites of social change and working class formation. To understand how market forces affect patterns of cohabitation among industrial workers, respondents in the depth interviews (N = 140) were asked to list the occupation, relationship and religion of co-residents. Table 4.2 presents social characteristics of cohabitants of industrial workers by urban status, among those living in multiple family compounds. Again, one observes how industrial workers are integrated residentially into social relations with labor service workers, craftsmen and even shopowners among urbans. More interesting on the subject of migrants and social change are the differences between urban and migrants. For migrants are much more likely than urbans to live with workers from the same factory, with wage workers and even with Christians. And migrants, as one would expect, are less likely than urbans to live with relatives, Islamic clerics and shopowners. The finding that migrants are twice as likely to live with wage workers as are urbans confirms my interpretation that migrant areas are the incubators of class formation. But the surprising finding concerns the willingness of Muslim Hausa-Fulani workers to cohabit with Christians, with all seven of the cases residing in the Waje rather than the Birni areas. I emphasize the significance of Muslim-Christian cohabitation in migrant communities because it provides evidence for the way in which the tight housing market forces Muslim workers to abandon Muslim norms of seclusion for their wives.[2] Hence, migrant areas provide the ideal situation for observing the complex and contradictory process of class formation. Moreover, Tudun Wada's long history as a working class residential area and its high proportion of experience, unskilled proletarians suggest that it is the ideal site for the qualitative analysis of class formation among Muslim Hausa-speaking workers. Let us examine the historical origins of this *garin leburori* (laborer's town).

TUDUN WADA: HISTORICAL ORIGINS AND THE COLONIAL STATE

When Kano was conquered, Bompai became the first British settlement area. Later, however, Nasarawa became the largest and most important European residential area. In order for the colonial state to provide minimum administrative services, wage laborers were employed for the unskilled and the burdensome tasks such as head-porterage, public order enforcement and night soil collection. Earlier the colonial state had formed an army and a police force. With Bompai as the British residential and administrative center as well as the settlement area for the colonial army and the police, a camp of casual laborers grew up nearby around the present site of Tudun Wada. It was originally called 'Gunna', a name which my informants assume was taken from the English term 'gunner'. Gunna became a settlement of seasonal and permanent laborers who sold their labor to the colonial state. Apart from rare permanent employment as unskilled laborers, most workers were employed for short term tasks: that is, to act as headporters for touring visits to rural areas by the colonial administrators, to supply administrative outpost areas with supplies or to work on construction projects when the colonial state required large amounts of labor for short periods. While the exact date of Gunna's founding escapes the memories of my informants, it probably was settled as early as 1910, and it continued to grow as a laborers' town spatially separated from Sabon Gari and the Birni for the next two decades.

It is important to emphasize that because the colonial state introduced wage labor after a violent conquest of a Muslim society, the demand for wage labor was determined from its inception by the needs of the colonial state rather than exclusively by the unfettered needs of capitalist production as had been the case in Western Europe. Rather than emerging from the internal logic of a precapitalist society, wage labor was inserted into Kano society by alien administrators of a colonial state which was allied with a Muslim aristocracy. Moreover, support of the latter required that the colonial state constrain the full development of capitalist social relations. Thus, the colonial state and its creation, the Native Authority Administration, became the major employers of wage labor during the colonial period. This point is made empirically in the industrial survey discussed in the previous chapter: among workers whose fathers were wage workers, 65 percent were located in the state sector.

At the level of Muslim nationalism and the relationship of Kano to the capitalist world economy, the particular way in which wage labor was introduced into Kano society shaped the perception of wage labor by indigenous Kanawa. Because wage labor was inserted by conquering Christian aliens, it came to be labeled as *aikin bature* (work for Europeans) by the Muslims of northern Nigeria. Among Muslim nationalists who were independent producers residing in the Birni, there developed a tendency to resist *aikin bature* because it involved an invidious and servile relationship to Christian conquerors. It also required the acceptance of an alien system wherein social relations were based upon the wage relationship, which of course contradicted a Muslim's normative expectations of relations between master and client. To reside in a 'garin leburori' such as Tudun Wada, then, was associated with deviance and servile social origins, for the area was considered *bariki* (barracks) by inhabitants of the Birni.

Towards the end of the 1930s, Gunna had grown to such an extent that the colonial government initiated a plan to survey the area and to allocate plots to former government employees: retired cooks and servants, soldiers, police and night soil collectors. Resident Carrow is remembered locally as the official who organized the official survey and the original allocation of housing plots. At that time, a village head was appointed in the person of Mahman Yelwa, who was both a Hausa and a former soldier from the district of Minjibir. Earlier he had become the 'headman' for the colonial authority charged with recruiting temporary laborers from Gunna. At the same time, a ward head was appointed for the Babur-Bura peoples, most of whom came from an area east of Kano called Biu; and another was designated for the peoples from the French colony of Niger, known locally by the pejorative term *Buzu*. Though the latter term refers to the slaves or clients of the Tuareg, in fact, the peoples that the *Sarkin Buzu* represented were mostly Hausa-speaking Adarawa people from an area north of Sokoto. Both Adarawa- and Tuareg-related peoples are perceived as more backward than Nigerians but not as alien, for the region was allied with the Sokoto Caliphate during the nineteenth century. Finally, the Tauregs and their subject peoples drew upon their reputation as fierce warriors by specializing as night watchmen for European residences and businesses. Together with tea-selling, security continues to be their principal occupation in Kano.

Thus, through direct initiation by a paternalistic colonial state on behalf of their employees, Tudun Wada was organized and named in 1940. The ward heads continued to collect taxes in their assigned areas, irrespective of the ethnicity of the residents and under the authority of the village head of Tudun Wada. Recipients of plots were responsible for erecting buildings, but in practice many sub-divided their plots and sold half in order to raise funds for building materials and labor. Once plots were surveyed and allocated to owners, Tudun Wada's spatial form was characterized by rectangular blocks of carefully measured plots with wide streets and a village center with a spacious open area facing the home of the village head. The first village head died in 1945 and was succeeded by a man originating from the French colony of Chad, Mahman Fort Lamy, who was also a headman for the colonial state. After the Second World War, African soldiers who served in Burma were settled in Tudun Wada. Until the creation of the Bompai industrial estate during the mid 1950s, the area grew slowly and remained a colonial-sponsored laborers' town with a paternalistic relationship to the colonial officials and the colonial state.

The establishment of the Bompai industrial estate and the nationalist political movement occurred during the latter half of the 1950s. Both were important in the shaping of Tudun Wada's working class character. In 1955 colonial authorities approved the establishment of a 160-acre industrial estate and an expansion of the existing township industrial estate.[3] Soon agricultural processing and consumer-oriented industries began to produce for the local market and to employ large numbers of unskilled and semi-skilled workers at both the Bompai and the Township industrial estates. Tudun Wada, together with the adjacent communities of Gamar Tudu and Gwagwarwa, expanded to house the new industrial employees. Yet the industrial estates, however important, were not the only source of growth. Nationalist politics had begun earlier, and a communal riot had occurred in 1953 when a prominent southern Nigerian politician spoke to his supporters at Sabon Gari. After the disturbance, colonial authorities decided to move from Sabon Gari all residents originating from the Northern Region, who were then relocated in the northern areas such as Tudun Wada.[4] Driven by these two forces, Tudun Wada expanded beyond the original settlement, creating new wards, until by 1970 the area was contiguous with the expanded area of Gwagwarwa and Gama. At the same time the population became younger, more transient and more likely to be unmarried, as well as directly and indirectly involved in wage labor for the formal, informal and state sectors.

At this point it is important to emphasize how each phase of capitalist development in Kano created a need for distinct kinds of wage labor, a need that shaped the physical and social character of Tudun Wada in such a way that one may distinguish distinct strata of labor corresponding to each phase. Initially, casual labor for porterage required only temporary buildings and no permanent settlement of any consequence. After the establishment of the colonial state with its necessary functions of sanitation, public order and the overseeing of seasonal exportation of groundnuts, Tudun Wada emerged from Gunna. Thus the second phase corresponded to the labor needs of a comparatively paternalistic colonial state that mediated between Muslim mercantile capitalist elements and the international firms that linked the region to the capitalist world economy. Import-substitution and industrialization initiated a third phase in the history of Tudun Wada, one marked by the emergence of an industrial proletariat which lacks any paternalistic relationship to the state and is more directly subordinated to the market for shelter. This phase reached its zenith during the decade of the seventies when, as described below, rentier capitalism's thirst for land and for building sites close to the centers of economic and administrative activity initiated the process of 'gentrification'. This fourth phase, if allowed to continue, promises to destroy the working class character of Tudun Wada, for the existing housing stock is gradually being replaced by housing that is affordable only to middle and upper class income groups.[5]

NEPU: the origins of populist politics

While I have not conducted a thorough history of Tudun Wada's role in the party politics of the nationalistic period, several important political experiences underscore Tudun Wada's commitment to leburori and tala-kawa political interests. Of course, given a population of laborers, the settlement was strongly behind NEPU during the nationalist period. Both the NPC and NEPU had party branches in Tudun Wada. Furthermore, while conducting a housing survey, I learned from informants that several large houses owned by mallams, which were also used as schools, were funded by the NPC in order to draw local opinion leaders away from NEPU. But an incident involving the struggle for control over the village headship (*dagaci*) reflects the strength of populist politics and NEPU. This incident occurred when the second village head had died and the Native Authority attempted to impose a *dagaci* upon the community. In response to the Native Authority, which was an organ of the NPC, local NEPU organizers demanded a public meeting and a public discussion of the candidates for *dagaci*. The issue was resolved when nearly all community members at the meeting walked to the side of the NEPU candidate, who was the son of the first village head and then a laborer at the airport. Faced with virtually no support for their candidate, the NPC supporters and the Native Authority officials were forced to accept the community's choice. The meeting is remembered as a great victory by NEPU supporters in the area.

Tudun Wada's reputation as a NEPU stronghold did not come easily or without cost. After a visit by the leader of NEPU, Aminu Kano, who called for the talakawa to organize in order to relieve themselves of sarauta exploitation, a NEPU committee was formed to secure a meeting place. At first, all homeowners refused, fearing attacks by thugs or similar reprisals from the authorities. Finally, three women who owned houses in Tudun Wada, one of whom was a factory worker, rented three rooms to the organizing committee. At this time the NEPU committee consisted of a bicycle repairer, a peddler of perfume, a laborer for the groundnut marketing board, two casual laborers and the son of the first village head, who became the successful NEPU candidate for the village headship. Later the NEPU committee was led by a butcher, whom we shall encounter again below, who was supported informally by a prestigious mallam affiliated with the Tijaniyya. As the election of the airport laborer to the village headship illustrates, NEPU was able to mobilize talakawa and laborers' consciousness to such a degree that they were willing to confront the repressive legal and police forces of the Native Authority.

From an independent source, that is, a factory worker selected at random for structured interviews, I obtained a graphic account of the repression inflicted upon Tudun Wada's NEPU organizers during this period. This is the account of a store laborer, uneducated, with only one eye, who resided in Tudun Wada during his first dry-season labor migration to Kano. Note that he is opposed to political activity on the part of workers:

> Before, when I was working as a cart pusher during the dry season, when I had not moved permanently to Kano yet [from rural Birnin Kudu], I lived in Tudun Wada. It was during the time of politics. I did not know it but the ward was considered by the Native Authorities to be a NEPU ward. One night the Native Authority police came and took the NEPU people away, including me because I was living in a NEPU ward. They put us in jail in the Birni for two months. For the first three days we had no food; we never went before a judge and there was no law applied to us. I thought I was going to die in jail.

Such experiences were common for the talakawa during the First Nigerian Republic. And, of course, repression served to integrate wage workers, independent commodity producers and the urban poor, creating a common populist class alliance that has gone on to control Kano State under the PRP.

By the time of the political crisis of 1966, therefore, Tudun Wada had grown from a settlement of wage laborers with a paternalistic relationship to the colonial state into a genuine working class community with distinct political and community institutions, one inhabited by former or actual wage laborers. Tudun Wada's strong support for NEPU, with its ideology of class struggle and Islamic populism, follows from the community's concrete social experiences as talakawa and as wage workers – colonial porters, night soil collectors and industrial workers. In retrospect, the significance of NEPU for the community of Tudun Wada was not in its electoral achievements, but rather in its successful mobilization of talakawa and leburori grievances into a conscious political movement directed against an authoritarian state and the extra-economic methods of coercion that were necessary to suppress the popular classes. This experience endowed Tudan Wada residents with organizational experience, leadership and, to some degree, familiarity with electoral and political processes; this created a foundation for NEPU's successor, the People's Redemption Party, which won the 1979 election in Kano State.

HOUSING AS A COMMODITY: THE RISE OF RENTIER CAPITALISM

When we compared urban groups in Chapter Three, migrants were distinguished from urbans by their dependence upon the market for housing. Indeed, for the migrants housing is a major expense over which they exert little control, and they possess even less chance of receiving or purchasing a housing plot. Dependence on the market for housing and the new social relationships that migrants encounter when they rent rooms in multiple family compounds are concrete examples of what is meant by urban social processes that integrate the leburori into a working class identity. To be sure, the migrants' response to market forces that require the sharing of housing with Christians and unfamiliar ethnic groups is not voluntary, nor, from the perspective of Muslim Hausa-speakers, is it an ideal living situation; rather, the choice to live in a community like Tudun Wada is determined by market forces and the class position of wage workers who must live in proximity to the industrial estate. Such community and residential relationships, while indirectly determined by their position as industrial and wage workers, are reinforced by the propinquity and social ecology of densely settled working class communities. Hence, as compared to urbans, who often possess or have access to family-owned homes, and as compared to commuters, who continue to live outside the urban housing market in peasant households, the migrants are involuntarily dependent upon the urban housing market. As a result, they enter into new social relationships that are determined by residence and by their class position as members of the leburori. In order to measure the degree to which capitalist social relationships have increased between landlords and renters in Tudun Wada, a housing survey was conducted in 1972. The survey was based upon a 20 percent random survey of houses in the first and oldest ward of Tudun Wada, founded in 1940, and a complete (100 percent) sample of the newest ward, which was begun in the 1960s and was still expanding at the time of the survey.

My purpose in examining housing ownership patterns is to illustrate the changes in housing ownership that underlie the rise of rentier capitalism and the importance of wage goods for the accumulation of capital by the upper classes of Kano. In comparing the oldest ward with the newest ward, it is not to be inferred that there has been a change in the same unit of analysis over time. Rather, housing ownership patterns in the oldest ward reflect an earlier form of colonial mercantile capitalism, while the patterns of the newest ward reflect the transition to semi-industrial capitalism marked by an urban proletariat whose subsistence needs create an opportunity for rentier capitalists to accumulate capital. And in doing so, rentier capitalism reproduces in the residential unit (the site of social reproduction), the commodity relationships experienced by workers at the workplace.

Let us examine Table 4.3 which presents differences between housing ownership patterns in the oldest as compared to the newest ward. In the old ward, wage laborers represent 48.5 percent of the landlords and own 45.2 percent of the housing stock; landlords with commercial occupations, representing 24.2 percent of the landlords, own 31 per cent of the housing stock. Each occupational group owns approximately the proportion of the housing that the number of homeowners would predict, and wage workers own the largest share of the housing stock. Let us examine the same figures

Table 4.3 *Tudun Wada: home ownership and landlord's residence by ward*

Landlord's occupation	Old ward				New ward			
	Number of landlords[a]	Total number of houses owned	Median number of houses per landlord	Median number of rooms per housing unit	Number of landlords	Total number of houses owned	Median number of houses per landlord	Median number of rooms per housing unit
Prostitute	0.0	0.0	0.0	0.0	18.5 (23)	17.8 (91)	2.1	6.1
Merchant/trader	24.2 (8)	31.0 (13)	1.2	5.0	36.3 (45)	53.6 (274)	2.6	6.1
Wage laborer	48.5 (16)	45.2 (19)	1.1	4.5	22.6 (28)	16.2 (83)	1.3	5.8
White collar worker	12.1 (4)	9.5 (4)	1.0	5.5	7.3 (9)	4.5 (23)	2.3	6.5
Craftsman	6.1 (2)	4.8 (2)	1.0	3.0	12.1 (15)	6.7 (34)	2.7	5.9
Others	9.1 (3)	9.5 (4)	1.3	2.0	3.2 (4)	1.2 (6)	1.3	5.0
Residence of Landlord								
Family or same house	67.4 (31)	55.7 (34)	1.1	4.1	44.9 (57)	14.5 (75)	1.1	5.8
Tudun Wada	6.5 (3)	8.2 (5)	1.8	3.0	24.4 (31)	27.9 (144)	3.3	5.9
Metro-Kano and absentee	26.1 (12)	36.1 (22)	1.7	6.5	30.7 (39)	57.6 (297)	3.0	6.3

[a] Due to missing data on the landlord's occupation, the total number of landlords and the total number of houses they own is less than the total reported for the 'Residence' category.

for the new ward, a ward that was built since the creation of the Bompai industrial estate. In the new ward, wage workers represent 22.6 percent of the landlords and own 16.2 percent of the housing stock; landlords with commercial occupations represent 36.2 percent of the landlords and own 53.6 percent of the housing stock. Furthermore, the trend toward increased absentee ownership in the new ward as compared to the old ward corresponds to the pattern exhibited in ownership of housing in the two wards; i.e., 36.1 percent of the houses are absentee-owned in the old ward as compared to 57.6 percent in the new ward. Note that 80 percent (210 out of 274) of new ward landlords with commercial occupations live outside Tudun Wada. Again, these data do not present a comparison of the same unit of analysis (e.g. a ward) over time, so one can not infer a change in housing patterns in a single ward. But one can conclude that the pattern of ownership of housing and the personal relationship of landlord to tenant is increasingly commoditized in the new wards as compared to the old ward. Clearly, this change corresponds to the allocation of housing during the colonial era as compared to the semi-industrial capitalist period when rentier capitalism penetrated Tudun Wada.

Some additional changes in housing patterns should be mentioned. Craftsmen have increased their ownership of houses from the old to the new ward. In fact, the change is due to the increasing economic power and wealth of butchers. All houses owned by craftsmen in both wards are owned by butchers. Prostitutes have increased their share of houses from zero in the old ward to 17.8 percent in the new ward. Most of these women are not active prostitutes but rather are older women who have invested their savings in housing. The trend toward concentration, that is, more houses per landlord in the new ward as compared to the old ward, should be noted: for example, among landlords with commercial occupations, the median number of houses per landlord more than doubled from 1.2 to 2.6. Further, the size of houses, as measured by the median number of rooms per house, increased for all ocupational groups across the two wards, and the absentee landlords appear to have the largest houses of all. Again, note how the ecological factors of congestion and propinquity contribute to working class communication.

Before leaving the topic of housing, I shall add a postscript concerning changes in housing at Tudun Wada observed during a short research visit during December 1978. Since the housing survey was completed in 1972, Nigeria has undergone an unprecedented petroleum boom, which has created a demand for secure investment opportunities on the part of beneficiaries of the boom, i.e., merchants, state contractors, civil servants and local capitalists of all species. Further, as the population of urban Kano has increased, the urban boundaries of the city and the number of plots in new areas of Tudun Wada have expanded to meet the demand for housing and secure investments. How have these economic forces altered the patterns described in Table 4.3? In general, the trends that we described above have intensified: now there are more larger and more densely populated houses because homeowners have built an additional story onto their original one-story houses; rents and the number of absentee landlords both are reported to have increased; and, most importantly, while most houses in Tudun Wada have formerly been constructed of sun-dried mud bricks, with the more affluent having cement plastering and tin roofs, many of the new houses are constructed completely with international-quality cement blocks and steel materials in European styles that formerly had been limited to middle- and upper-class housing areas of urban Kano. In some cases, plots formerly having houses constructed of sun-dried bricks have been purchased by merchants or upper-level civil servants, and modern international-styled housing has been erected in their place.

Part of the explanation for this change comes from the search by rentier capitalists and affluent civil servants for secure investments. But there is an additional explanation for this tendency toward the 'gentrification' of a working class neighborhood into a more middle-class residential area. The expansion of the urban perimeter since 1972 has created peripheral areas such as Dakata and Tudun Murtala where cheap, yet more distant housing is available for low-paid workers and recent emigrants. The expansion of the total urban perimeter means that areas like Tudun Wada, which were peripheral to the urban economy when created during the 1930s, have now become more valuable because of their proximity to the core sites of the urban economy: industrial estates, offices, markets and communications centers. By 1979, therefore, capitalist social relations and rentier capitalism had increased to such a degree that workers no longer aspired to own a house in Tudun Wada; rather, they questioned whether they could even afford to continue renting rooms there if gentrification continued unabated. As we shall observe below, the community responded defensively to the pressures of absentee ownership of land and housing and sanctioned those whom they believed were responsible.

Despite the recent pressures exerted by rentier capitalists for lucrative and secure investments, the majority of housing in Tudun Wada is oriented toward wage laborers. Most workers live in one or two small rooms, composed of sun-dried brick, perhaps with a zinc roof, a cement floor or cement plastering. Virtually all residents cook over open fires in the courtyard of the compound. Public sanitation remains backward, consisting of pit-latrines. Surface water from compounds runs into the street, where it forms stagnant puddles. The goal of the community development association is to construct open, cement gutters on the sides of the street so that surface and rain water will drain from the streets. Garbage and waste materials are not collected by public authorities and pile up in the streets. In short, public investment in sanitation is negligible, so that the community environment is filthy, unhealthy and declining.

TUDUN WADA: THE IMPACT OF INDUSTRIAL CAPITAL ON EVERYDAY
LIFE

Thus far, it has been shown how rentier capitalism and market forces
contribute to the process of working class formation in the community of
Tudun Wada. The argument has been made that the history and origins of
the community, the tendency for migrants to compete with each other for
housing as a commodity which is owned increasingly by absentee rentier
capitalists, the reported number of wage-labor taxpayers and the new social
residential relationships required of migrants who rent rooms in multiple
unit compounds are all objective indicators of working class formation at
the community level. In this section I intend to analyse the observable effect
of industrial capital on the rhythms and cycles that govern community life in
Tudun Wada. The objective is to show how industrial capital's production
requirements structure social relations and community interaction.

To move beyond the statistical measures of working class formation, one
must illustrate how a laborers' community differs from any other urban,
Muslim, Hausa-speaking community of northern Nigeria. Of course, as we
shall develop in the next section, change is slow and the fundamental
ideological patterns and behaviors of a Muslim Hausa community continue
to influence daily life. But in a community where the majority of males are
industrial workers and where many of the others are labor service workers
or those who service the needs of wage workers, the discipline and
organizational requirements of industrial production and bureaucratically
organized state services do influence Tudun Wada's daily rhythms and
seasonal cycles of social activity.

If one were to follow a factory worker living in Tudun Wada through a
typical day, one would first have to know which shift he was working:
typically the shifts extend from 7 a.m. to 3 p.m., from 3 p.m. to 11 p.m. and
from 11 p.m. to 7 a.m. Depending on market demand, most factories
operate only one or two shifts, while some work two twelve-hour shifts.
Most important for factory workers' daily lives is the requirement that
nearly all workers are obliged to accept rotating shifts that change weekly or
bi-monthly. The changing shift patterns mean that, from week to week or
from month to month, factory workers are not able to maintain continuous
participation in any after-work social, intellectual or political activity that
requires continuous participation during definite hours. For example,
changing shifts each week would not allow workers to attend night school in
order to gain literacy in Hausa or English. Nothing is more evident in Tudun
Wada than the impact of factory shifts – as workers dressed in factory
uniforms leave and return at precise and predictable hours – for structuring
everyday life. Besides isolating workers from continuous participation in
community life and, at the same time, reinforcing the solidarity of factory
workers on the same shift, research from industrial societies has found that
the rotating shift system is unhealthy.[6]

145

To return to the typical factory worker in Tudun Wada, after arising for prayer at sunrise, workers begin to leave for their factories after 6 a.m., stopping along the route to purchase breakfast in the form of fried bean cakes or porridge, sold by women who are usually unmarried or beyond the age of child-bearing. As the workers pass through Tudun Wada in groups that increase in size as they approach the main route, greetings are exchanged with the residents and beggars (the latter afflicted with paralyzing diseases, blindness, birth defects or leprosy) who congregate on corners to chant for alms during the passing of shifts. Uniforms with distinct colors, styles and insignias, supplied only by major employers, differentiate workers from others who are applicants, day laborers or petty traders. Around 2:30 p.m. the scene is repeated as the second shift of workers leaves for work.

By 3:30 workers from the first shift have returned to their homes; many have changed clothing and are running errands such as marketing if their wives are in seclusion or if they do not have an older child in their household. Peddlers are everywhere, bargaining with workers over the price of such necessities as a donkey-load of firewood, clothing, food and jewelry. Snacks such as cooked and spiced food, a gruel of grain and milk sold by Fulani women or kola nuts peddled by girls are consumed by factory workers sitting on mats with their friends, usually in front of their homes or in the entryrooms of large compounds.

Based on observations by a female observer, it is evident that the shift structure also affects the relationship between wives and their factory-worker husbands.[7] Factory workers' wives, who are in seclusion, rest for an hour or so after noon and put on clean clothing and cosmetics just prior to the return of their husbands from the first shift. Thus the shift structure and the demands of industrial capitalist production penetrate even the secluded compounds and structure male and female interaction. Similarly, preparation of the evening meals, family life and even sexual relations depend upon the shift of the husband.

During the evening, when factory workers return from the 3 p.m. shift, the afternoon cycle repeats itself as greetings are exchanged and tables serving tea, dried fish, soft drinks and all varieties of cooked food are found on street corners and on main routes. Workers may stop to talk, to drink tea or to have an evening meal if they are unmarried. By 11 p.m., however, few residents are still awake, with the exception of illegal gin shops and houses of prostitution where peddlers congregate to sell tobacco, kola nuts and snacks. The effect of the cycles and rhythms of factory production on community life is most evident on holidays and Sundays when the street population increases to several times the number expected during a normal weekday.

Rotating shifts are the most visible and formalized example of the manner in which capitalist social relations of the workplace are reproduced at the levels of community and family. But at the informal level, industrial capital

146

and the urban labor market are no less present in the social life of Tudun Wada. Workers in small groups regularly discuss working conditions, pay rates, recent strikes, the success of a particular trade union or the opportunities offered to employees by a new firm. Ensconced within the outward form of a Muslim Hausa community, a working class culture has emerged, wherein topics for discussion include information on the cost of a bribe for gaining employment in a new factory or even the consequences for workers of using a violent or non-violent method of striking. To participate in these discussions leaves one with the definite impression that the objective conditions described above have a counterpart at the level of ideology and culture that is shared by those who must sell their labor in order to live. The demands of the supervisors for bribes, the actions of the management to extend the working day, the short work-weeks due to a weak market or the failure of raw material inputs to arrive, and the grievances and fears of unorganized workers all punctuate the informal conversations of workers. Meetings are held in workers' homes to discuss tactics for receiving pay increases, back-dated increases that management refuses to grant, or strategies for organizing trade unions. News of industrial actions is exchanged during these informal discussions, which are usually accompanied by a radio whose news reports in Hausa stimulate discussion of national topics that are of concern to workers: e.g., industrial actions in other cities, wage-review commission reports, new industries in Kano, trade union reforms and the progress and programs of political candidates and parties. Again, industrial workers and wage laborers possess many interests and aspirations beyond the boundaries of industrial work, interests that they share with the talakawa in general; yet the requirements of industrial production and the communities' dependence upon the wages paid to workers for sales and services imprint an indelible working class character on the community.

URBAN ETHNICITY: THE IMPACT OF ISLAMIC NATIONALISM

So far the emphasis has been on how urban social processes contribute to the formation of the *urban leburori* while at the same time integrating them socially into the urban talakawa. Yet, while it is stressed that the primary determinant of class formation is located in the material forces associated with semi-industrial capitalism, it is also true that precapitalist elements contribute to the structure, consciousness and political activity of this first-generation proletariat. To be sure, talakawa consciousness is an important element contained within the actual (as opposed to an idealized) form of class consciousness expressed by urban workers. And, of course, talakawa consciousness provides a clear example of how precapitalist elements may articulate within a class created by semi-industrial capitalism in ways that both advance and retard the political development of that class. Nevertheless, a first-generation urban proletariat composed largely of

147

migrants possesses needs for community identity, social ritual and a system of meaning that link them to their rural and precapitalist origins. Islam fulfills this institutional need among Muslim, Hausa-speaking workers of Tudun Wada.

What then is the effect of this precapitalist force on the urban *leburori*? How do Islamic elements articulate with those created by semi-industrial capitalism? True, there is a process of conservation and dissolution, but this interpretation lacks the specificity of concrete, living individuals who form a class and a community during a particular conjuncture. My objective in this and the following section is to describe empirically what the articulation of Islamic and capitalist elements actually looks like, how these elements structure a working class community and to what degree Islamic elements – i.e., institutions and ideologies – are interpreted by community members to serve their class-determined needs.

It was argued in Chapter One that the particular history of Kano and the manner in which this Islamic social formation was incorporated into the capitalist world economy determined that Islamic nationalism would emerge as an anti-imperialist force and as a regional nationalist ideology. Islamic nationalism makes a claim on all Muslims of the region, but each class interprets doctrine in the light of its own needs and situations. Thus in Kano, for example, one witnesses working class and talakawa interpretations demanding social justice; the lumpen proletarians follow a millenarian leader to suicidal self-destruction; the bourgeoisie build mosques and call for social discipline; and the declining aristocracy struggle to retain their dominant position by manipulating modern and traditional cultural institutions while calling for a return to the norms of an earlier era, when their own interpretation of Islam was hegemonic.[8]

For most of the workers and independent producers of Tudun Wada, virtually all of whom are migrants, Islam provides the cultural and institutional basis of community and the means of bridging the differences among members of a common class, or among classes in the populist alliance, presented by distinct ethnic origins. Hence, while workers are socially integrated into a new urban ethnicity, one defined as membership in a regionally bounded Islamic nation, they also maintain ethnic and sub-ethnic identities, each of which is expressed in the appropriate situation.[9] At the same time, their interpretation of the meaning and appropriate behavior arising from membership in this Islamic nation is determined to a significant degree by their class situation.

Let us consider the fundamental question of ethnicity in Tudun Wada. Unlike lineage- and clan-organized societies found elswhere in Nigeria, among the Hausa talakawa anyone who speaks Hausa, practices Islam and maintains a Hausa lifestyle with respect to dress and social etiquette is accepted as a Hausa in Tudun Wada. To be sure, one's social origins and the status of one's community of origin are used to rank distinct Hausa communities and to differentiate more or less prestigious social pedigrees

148

from one another. For example, the son of a Fulani, sarauta-origin, village head is respected for that origin, and a Katsina-origin Hausa-speaker is considered a 'purer' Hausa than a southern Zaria Hausa-speaker whose father may have been a Gwari convert to Islam. Nevertheless, all status distinctions based upon membership in a corporate group (i.e., an ethnic group) are mediated by occupation, accumulated wealth or access to political power. Ethnicity is not a platonic essence; it is a historically created social identity. To treat ethnicity among the urban Hausa talakawa as primordial and immutable is an idealistic error that only obfuscates the dynamics of ethnic change in a peripheral capitalist city. Rather, in opposition to essentialism, ethnic identity should be seen as situational, as conditioned by materialist forces and, at times, as a social resource to be manipulated in order to serve concrete occupational and class interests.

Further evidence supports this view. During an interview a worker commented that, although he considers himself Hausa, when he visits his mother's relatives he is considered to be and acts as if he were a Fulani. Similarly, when I asked a Muslim Barbur worker whose children were speaking Hausa if his children would grow up as Babur or Kanawa Hausa, he replied that they would probably become Kanawa. He added that it was more important that they grew up as Muslims than as Barburs. Again, to cite an interesting example, while conducting an interview on the history of trade unions, I asked my informant to recall the ethnic origin of a worker who organized a union in his factory. Before responding to my question, he turned to a fellow worker and asked him, 'Does he pray?' When the fellow worker responded affirmatively, he responded: 'Yes, he is a Hausa, like us'. What is important in Tudun Wada's working class environment is not the purity of one's Hausa origins, but rather the degree to which one participates in and is integrated into the accepted forms of Muslim Hausa institutions. For, unless one is in the social position to 'market' status-honor in a capitalist city (e.g., sarauta), 'primordial' ethnic identities are rather useless, and unknown to most of one's social contacts. In urban centers like Tudun Wada, therefore, Islam provides a new social identity and a communal boundary which encourages heterogeneous ethnic groups sharing the same class situation to form a community, to live together in densely settled compounds and to trust fellow workers in a situation of class homogeneity. Empirical evidence to verify this assertion will be presented in Chapter Seven but for the moment it must be taken as an assumption.

My analysis of Kano's ethnic segregation patterns indicates that Islam has not integrated all Muslim ethnic groups evenly.[10] But, if one examines Muslim ethnic groups originating from the former Northern Region, there is a great degree of ethnic integration around Muslim institutions that has created a *regionally* defined Islamic *national* identity. Part of the reason for this degree of integration arises from Islamic ideology itself. Because Islamic law is formally opposed to ethnic or racial discrimination within the Muslim community, anyone slighted by a more powerful ethnic group may

149

accuse the other of practicing tribalism (*kabilanci*). In such a situation the slighted party is appealing to the higher Islamic principle (i.e., *Shari'a*) that calls for equality among male members of the Islamic community. If such a person is a devoted and publicly practicing Muslim, he has a strong moral argument for becoming assimilated into the Hausa. For example, even during the aftermath of the civil war, Ibo converts to Islam in Tudun Wada were treated as members of the Muslim community, and unless one was researching their ethnic origin, they remained indistinguishable from other members of the Muslim Hausa community.

The term used in Tudun Wada to infer acceptance into the Muslim community is *dan uwa* (literally: son of my mother). After interviewing in Socratic fashion about the application of this term to residents of Tudun Wada, and especially the attribution of the term to someone who was not born a Hausa, my informants agreed that a *dan uwa* in this context was someone to whom they had become accustomed, whose character was known to them and, most importantly, who practiced Islam.

Class formation in Kano, therefore, is accompanied by a new form of urban ethnicity, one that is based upon membership in an Islamic nation. For Muslims, the process of assimilation into this national identity corresponds harmoniously with the process of urban working class formation, though class formation and nation formation are distinct social processes, they articulate with and condition each other in unpredictable ways. And, as I shall argue in Chapter Seven under certain conditions Islamic national consciousness may reinforce class consciousness among Muslim workers who labor in a dependent capitalist situation.

ISLAM AND THE MAKING OF A WORKING CLASS COMMUNITY

The housing market is only one of the social forces that migrants must adjust to in order to survive in a peripheral capitalist city. To become proletarianized, to be labelled as a *lebura* and to accept this class identity personally is not a process that Muslim Hausa workers willingly undergo. Rather, the decision to migrate in search of work is forced upon them by historically developed forces that are beyond their control and whose consequences, in most cases, lie beyond their immediate comprehension. Even when migrants are forced to follow the dictates of the housing market, the labor market or the labor processes of capitalist industrial production, they carry with them a set of cultural values, institutional expectations and emotional needs which are fulfilled at the level of community which they create from precapitalist ideals. No one sets out with the intention of creating a 'working class community'. Initially, at least, these values and expectations are rooted in the precapitalist social relations of the countryside; yet the process of class formation and the necessity to survive, as well as the aspiration to prosper, induce migrants to alter their expectations in order to adjust to the competition for means of consumption. For most

migrants living in Tudun Wada, therefore, Islam provides the institutionalized expression of community, one with which they are familiar upon
arrival yet, at the same time, one that reflects the religious and community
needs of a migrant and laboring people. Let us examine how Islam creates
and structures community life and then probe how Islam responds and
adjusts to the particular needs of a migrant working class community.

Mallams: the intelligentsia of the talakawa

It is impossible to conceive of a Muslim Hausa community without allowing
for the prominent role played by mallams in officiating over life-cycle
events, in performing daily rituals, in organizing Islamic schooling and
scholarship and in protecting the community against injustice and tyranny.[11] Since most talakawa mallams pursue secular ocupations as well, they
and their mature students, the *gardi*, are numerous and interwoven within
the urban working class and the talakawa. Given the ubiquity of mallams in
the occupational structure, they cannot collectively form a class because
they are members of virtually all of Kano's classes and strata. Instead,
mallams are a classic status-honor group in the Weberian sense. The
diffusion of mallams and their students among all occupations allows a large
measure of autonomy from any hierarchically organized authority, such as
is encountered in many Christian sects. Further, the absence of hierarchical
or bureaucratic organization means that every mallam may produce succes-
sors among his students without reference to certification by centralized
authority. All of these structural factors allow mallamic leadership to
emerge through scholarly achievement or through charismatic qualities that
are recognized by the community. More importantly, because successful or
influential mallams are legitimated by the communities that they serve,
mallams closely experience and usually reflect the occupations, social
inequalities and social consciousness of their communities. For these
reasons, mallams are respected, looked to for interpretation of social
events, sometimes loved and always supported materially by their communities without regard to external legitimation by the dominant classes. For
these reasons also the popular classes have, historically, looked to mallams
for leadership against tyranny and social injustice.

In a community that is composed largely of migrants and leburori it is not
surprising to discover that all of Tudun Wada's seventy-seven mallams
(1975) who actively taught the Koran or other Islamic texts were migrants to
the city. Some had lived in Tudun Wada for over twenty-five years, while
others were more recent settlers. Several mallams worked as factory
workers, nightwatchmen or local government authority laborers while at
the same time maintaining modest Koranic schools. Thus laboring mallams
are common. Even the *imam* of the Friday Mosque, who inherited the office
from his father, is a retired railway laborer. Besides mature and settled
mallams, there are a number of *gardi*, that is, young men and youths who

may not have completed the memorization of the Koran. Many continue their Islamic studies by affiliating as a student with a mallam who specializes in the subject in which they wish to acquire proficiency: e.g., the life of Mohammed, commentaries on Islamic law, Arabic, Hadiths, rational theologies and mysticism (sufism).

The *gardi* exist in an ambiguous position between mallams and the community. They lack the independence and prestige of mallams, but are called upon by the community for ritual practices, such as the making of charms or the reading of the Koran for a supplicant's intentions. Many never complete the Koran and so are forced by economic circumstances to take up a craft or a wage-laboring position. Yet, should this occur, the *gardi* continues to identify as a student of a mallam by remaining in his network, even though he has ceased to seriously study the Koran with him. Those that complete the Koran, however, usually attempt to teach school and leave wage labor if possible. Unfortunately, many just continue to work in wage labor even after they have finished the Koran, for this informally organized system produces far more teachers and mallams than most communities can support. Hence, there is a continual movement of mallams as they search for a secure position, and a continual absorption of *gardi* into the urban leburori.

The mallams and *gardi* rank themselves by their achievements in the field of Islamic scholarship, by the number of students that are attached to a mallam and by the reputation of a mallam for successful intercession with Allah on behalf of a mallam's client. For example, the most respected mallam of Tudun Wada, Mallam Musa, taught the Koran and claimed to have over eighty-nine students. But few informants felt that he would be their first choice if they required someone to appeal to Allah on their behalf. Thus, while scholarship is praised, charismatic criteria and personal mysticism are important criteria for success as a ritual or personal mallam. Furthermore, in ministering to the ritual and emotional needs of their communities, mallams express in their style of life most of the classic ideals of Hausa society: patience, impeccable courtesy, proper verbal and gesticulatory greetings, generosity, modesty, wisdom and honesty.[12] A mallam's success depends on his ability to express these qualities in everyday life in full view of his community. Mallams determine community ideals not only in their formalized roles as scholars and priests but also in their informal roles as community members who maintain a mallamic style of life.

Mallams mediate all events in an individual's life cycle: birth and naming, early schooling and education, marriage, personal crises and death. If a man is not studying as his student, he probably consults with a mallam over important decisions, such as the astrologically correct day to perform a task or ritual event, or the correct marriage for himself or his child, or in order to improve his material life, such as through a trading venture or a new job. Mallams may be consulted to perform rituals to purge individuals of spirits or to remove curses on individuals that prevent them from remarrying,

152

becoming pregnant or giving birth to a son. Further, mallams may be commissioned by both wealthy and modest traders to read the Koran for a day or two or for a certain number of times in order to change their economic or social fortune. A few successful mallams, then, are able to accumulate wealth directly through investments and school fees and also through a patron's gifts in the form of houses, mosques and even marriages; the latter practice occurs when someone gives in the name of Islam his or her daughter to a mallam without requiring the fees and expenses normally associated with a marriage. While indicators such as a reputation for learning and piety are important for choosing a mallam, great emphasis is also placed upon the perceived personal ability of the mallam to mediate personally with Allah on behalf of the supplicant. Charismatic mallams who have a reputation for mystical rituals and direct communication with the divine are especially sought after by people whose problems could not be solved by ordinary means.

It should be emphasized that all social groups have mallams. Even deviants such as Tudun Wada's prostitutes maintain a mallam in their service. In order to increase their popularity with laborers, older prostitutes are reported to pay a poorly trained, peripatetic mallam of Tiv origin to write Koranic verses for them on a slate; the verses are then washed off and the liquid drunk. (This ritual is termed *rubutun sha* or 'writing and drinking'.) To be sure, the mallamic community did not recognize the prostitutes' mallam as legitimate, but the prostitutes believed that the use of *rubutun sha* would make them more popular with the laborers and single men who frequented them. Space does not permit more examples; this example illustrates that in Tudun Wada any ailment or source of anxiety is mediated by the ritual practices of the local mallams. Let us examine the role of Islamic institutions in reproducing a Muslim Hausa community in Tudun Wada.

Koranic schools: the cultural reproduction of the Islamic nation

Islam rationalizes daily time and seasons by its prayers and yearly festivals according to a lunar calendar. As we shall discover in forthcoming chapters, the demands of industrial rationality and the norms associated with Islamic timing and ritual discipline may articulate with industrial capitalism so as to increase class conflict and intensify working class solidarity against management. Within the community, however, the daily discipline and cultural sense of time is marked according to the logic of Islamic prayer times. Among Muslims, meetings and business arrangements, for example, are set according to the hour of a certain prayer. Muslim festivals are national holidays. And all residents of Kano, whether Muslim or not, must alter their schedules or their expectations of productivity during the month of Ramadan when Muslims abstain from taking food or drink from sunrise to sunset. Ramadan is a period when the social cohesion of the Islamic nation

153

is most visible. Islamic timing then articulates in complex ways with the shift structure of the factories in a workers' community like Tudun Wada.

In the life cycle of Muslims born and growing up in Tudun Wada, individuals enter Koranic school at the age of four or five years. Here they are initiated socially into the Muslim community. During late afternoon, one may observe fathers accompanying their children, who are scrubbed and neatly clothed for the occasion, to their first Koranic school class. More often than not, an advanced Koranic student of a Koranic mallam (a *gardi*) teaches the young children the basic elements of the Islamic faith: prayer, the first verses of the Koran, ablutions and the pillars of the faith. If compared to the discipline of formal western schooling, a Koranic school situated under a tree, in an entryway or simply in the street appears disorderly and confused because the children are eating, chanting, memorizing and moving about individually. But this appearance of disorder overlooks the social processes that children are experiencing for the first time. Though they may originate from diverse ethnic groups or sub-ethnic units of the Hausa, at Koranic school they are undergoing the process of socialization into urban Muslim society. Friendships and social bonds are formed at Koranic schools which individuals maintain throughout their lives; these relationships form important trans-ethnic networks within the Islamic nation. Whatever formal knowledge is imparted as Islamic learning, the social experience of Koranic schooling creates an urban Muslim identity which integrates the children into the wider Muslim community and inculcates in them at an early age an Islamic world view. Some of the older male children may be sent to rural areas with a peripatetic mallam, but as primary school becomes increasingly available and valued by workers in Tudun Wada, both primary and Koranic schooling are accomplished in the urban community.

Neighborhood mosques: ritual, social interaction and ideological hegemony

One way to comprehend the social organization and social interaction patterns of a Muslim Hausa community like Tudun Wada would be to locate and map the neighborhood mosques, the class position of their patrons and the social relationships of those men who attend each mosque. Mapping the prayer patterns around mosques should illustrate how Islamic discipline generates distinct spatial and personal interaction patterns. Virtually any space bounded by some physical material – a building, a cement wall or a series of stones – constitutes a mosque and thus is an appropriate place for the performance of the five daily prayers. Within Hausa and Muslim society in general, great social esteem is bestowed upon a benefactor who builds or endows a mosque. And the bourgeoisie are actively building both local and Friday mosques throughout Kano. Tudun Wada mosques vary from a recently constructed modern cement mosque, which serves as the Friday mosque, to nearly invisible cement platforms that are wedged between houses and stagnant gutters. Initially many mosques originate as a circle of stones pointed eastwards, as Islamic custom requires, but through voluntary contributions of community members and the endowments of the wealthy, walls and roofs are added until an edifice emerges. Of course, one method by which merchants pursue status-honor in Kano is, with great public ostentation, to endow the community with a mosque and with an *imam* of their ideological persuasion. And of course, given the political sensitivity of preaching, the bourgeoisie exhort the faithful to follow 'correct' mallams.

Neighborhood or ward mosques, then, are primary sources of interaction among males in a Muslim city. Men meet together, sometimes holding hands or their prayer beads, walk to their mosques and discuss personal business or even commercial transactions. After prayer, men return home and eat their evening meal from a common pot, as do the men who pray in front of their homes. Because this ritual may occur several times a day, up to six times during Ramadan, social relationships are constantly being reinforced by the social interaction required by Muslim ritual observance. Prior to prayer, water is passed from one to another, usually in tea kettles, for the performance of ritual ablutions, and conversation on all topics continues until they take a position for prayer. After prayer it is common for each man to clasp hands with the men to his right and left, thus symbolizing the unity of the Muslim community in a public manner. Clearly, Islamic ritual requires distinct timing and physical interaction that reinforces social relationships. When a community is overwhelmingly Muslim and leburori, as is the case in Tudun Wada, Islamic rituals reinforce the social relationships whose origins derive from production, market relations and the struggle over the means of consumption.

Social relationships and mosque affiliations in Tudun Wada generally are determined by the social ecology of the neighborhood. But individuals studying with a particular mallam or affiliated with an Islamic brotherhood, such as the Tijaniyya, may choose to pray with their mallam or brotherhood leader at symbolically significant events. As Paden has shown for the pre-civil-war period, political protest against existing authorities is often expressed in the form of Islamic ritual. For example, the followers of Ibrahim Niasse of Koalack, a major Tijaniyya leader of northern Nigeria and West Africa, pray with their hands crossed over their stomachs. During the intense political competition between the NPC and NEPU, this unusual ritual form came to be interpreted as public symbolism of support for NEPU, even though this was never formally acknowledged by either organization.

Prayer among friends also occurs in the privacy of a courtyard where someone leads the group in prayers. From my own observations of this ritual, it is clear that the chosen leader is endowed with esteem by his peers. And, as Tahir documents among the merchant-industrial class, the ritualized expression of trust and leadership acts to control social and economic transactions between members of the prayer group in their secular activities, such as credit relations and corporation formation. Similarly, to refuse to follow the leadership of someone acting as prayer leader or *imam* is often a successful method of exerting leverage against a group or an individual. Again, since all of these acts are public, this conflict is immediately known to the community, and the affected leader of prayer suffers embarrassment and public scrutiny. Public ritual performed at community and neighborhood mosques may be a source of community solidarity; in rare instances, however, deeper social cleavages may be publicly displayed in order to gain an advantage, to punish a moral transgressor or, as I shall describe below, to punish a member who has violated the trust of the community.

Hence, for a number of historical and pragmatic reasons, Islamic institutions are thriving among Kano's laboring classes, who show virtually no tendency toward secularism. Indeed, despite the association of capitalism with secularism and individualism and the virtually endless opportunities for deviance, mallams and Islamic institutions form the organizational and cultural basis for working class communities among Hausa-speakers and other Muslims. Because Islam has always been an urban-biased religion, migrants perceive migration to urban areas as an opportunity to improve their Islamic learning and status. For the leburori, therefore, Islamic institutions are attractive and are supported because Koranic schools, mosques and other institutions represent community-controlled institutions that respond to the social, emotional and ritual needs of migrants and laborers. Since Koranic schools are based upon neighborhoods, they also generate cohesion among the diverse occupational groups that make up the popular classes, who are forced by the housing market to reside together. Most importantly, Islamic institutions represent one of the few instances where leburori exert control over an esteemed institution. Finally, as bearers of Islamic ideology, mallams and *gardi* are interwoven within the social fabric of the urban talakawa and the leburori.

In order to locate my generalizations in concrete human experience and to humanize my treatment of mallams and Islamic institutions, I shall describe the life-history of one of Tudun Wada's more successful mallams.

The life and perspective of Mallam Ibrahim

Ibrahim was born in Bagawaye, a village in Bici District, located approximately 43 kilometers from Kano City. Both he and his brother, who also lives in Tudun Wada, were taught the first verses of the Koran by their father, who was a wandering mallam. (In 1972, Ibrahim estimated his age to be about 35.) His family owned and farmed land. Upon reaching the age of 12, the sons followed their father during the dry season to rural and urban centers of Koranic scholarship. When Ibraham was fourteen years old, his father rented a room in Makera ward in the city of Hadejia, which lies about 208 kilometers east of Kano, where Ibrahim taught Koranic school with his father. After several years of living in Hadejia, Ibrahim went out into the countryside in order to establish his own school. Meanwhile he married at home, a family

156

marriage in the Hausa custom, and visited his wife regularly as she did not accompany him to rural Hadejia.[13]

While living in rural Hadejia, Ibraham continued to pursue more advanced subjects of Islamic scholarship with a mallam from Katsina. He supported himself through school fees, gifts from patrons who asked him to pray for their intentions, and from the harvests of lands lent to him and tilled by his students. It was during this time that Ibrahim became a local organizer for 'mallam' Aminu Kano and NEPU. His reasons for supporting NEPU follow from his membership in the talakawa: the tyranny of the sarauta, the violation of Islamic principles of justice, sarakuna humiliation of the talakawa, illegitimate taxation and forced labor. When he completed the Koran and decided to migrate to Kano for more advanced studies, Ibraham left political activity behind in Hadejia.

Before Ibrahim moved permanently to Kano, he had visited and studied with talakawa mallams living near the Kurmi market. During the first two months at Kano, he stayed in Yakasai ward of the Birni with a mallam who was a friend of his teacher at Hadejia. The latter sent a letter of introduction with Ibrahim. After living on alms for two months in the Birni, 'resting,' Ibrahim searched for an area of the city that needed and could support a Koranic school. He chose Tudun Wada because there were not enough Koranic schools and because it was a relatively quiet and, for Waje, relatively respectable area, a necessary requirement for advanced Islamic studies. When he rented a room in Tudun Wada, he brought his two wives from rural Bici to live with him. Subsequently, Ibrahim moved into two rooms owned by one of his Koranic students, an older man who gave the rooms as *sadaka* (alms) and who, as many mature men do, aspired to finish the Koran before he died. In June of 1972 Ibrahim was teaching seven older students and four children. Most of the older students were studying the Koran; one was studying the *Risala* of the Ibn Abi Zayd al-Qayrawani, which is a commentary on Islamic (Maliki) law; and one was studying to be a *tafsir* mallam. Ibrahim is active as a public commentator on the Koran, that is, a *tafsir* mallam. It is common for *tafsir* mallams to preach in Tudun Wada during the month of Ramadan after the fast has been broken. (Traditionally, commentators on the Koran have focussed on social and political grievances to such a degree that the state government has attempted to administer an examination in order to certify *tafsir* mallams.) For Ibrahim to achieve mastery over these subjects before the age of forty is valued as a great achievement by the mallams and *gardi* of Tudun Wada. It is noteworthy that his mature students include a primary school teacher, a grain trader, a public works laborer, a small shopowner, a goat seller and two factory workers. The mixture of occupations illustrates the manner in which Islamic institutions integrate distinct occupations of the urban talakawa and the leburori.

By 1972 Ibrahim had accumulated enough savings from gifts and school fees to invest in the purchase of two shops in the local market, which he rented out for ₦5 a month. By 1975, he had purchased a plot in the expansion area of Tudun Wada, and was building a house and a Koranic school. Thus he has prospered with the growth of Tudun Wada in his eleven years of residence. Ibrahim was initiated into the Tijaniyya brotherhood when he lived at Yakasai ward in the Birni. His objection to joining the rival brotherhood, the Qadiriyya, derives from their use of drums during their rituals. Note also that the Tijaniyya is associated with opposition to Sokoto and with support for NEPU among Kano's urban talakawa. During the month of Ramadan,

157

Ibrahim preaches by commenting on the Koran (*tafsir*) during the evenings in front of the house of a trader wealthy enough to have electric lighting.

Compared to other mallams living in Tudun Wada, Ibrahim is unusually successful. By combining Koranic, legal and advanced Islamic studies he has established a reputation both as a learned mallam, and as one whose intermediations on behalf of the wishes of his supplicants are esteemed by the community. Of course, he makes no certain promises to his supplicants; rather he promises only to ask Allah to consider the requests of his client. No exact fee is demanded by Ibrahim. Instead, the supplicant pays according to the seriousness of his or her request. But it is also understood that the more generous one is to the mallam interceding on one's behalf, the more likely that one's request will be fulfilled. Most of Ibrahim's income comes from interceding on behalf of his supplicants rather than from school fees or gifts from his students. Below are some examples of the requests from Ibrahim's applicants. The examples provide us with insight into the emotional life of recent urban migrants as well as the therapeutic and emotionally supportive role played by mallams in a rapidly changing semi-industrial urban center.

Ibrahim received ₦20 from a western-trained nurse working at the Birni hospital for saying the Koran on behalf of the man's requests. The nurse feared that he was to be fired by a new supervisor. (Ibrahim assured me that the man was still employed at the hospital.) A second man asked that the Koran be said for him as he wanted to become a truck driver for the new Top Beer company factory. The man was not a Hausa but a Muslim who originated from Jos. According to Ibrahim, the supplicant was able to move from store worker to truck driver. Further, Ibrahim cites several examples where unemployed workers paid him two or three naira to pray that they would receive positions at a kitchen utensil factory. The outcome is unknown.

Ibrahim's ritual practice is not limited to men. During the time of the inter-view, Ibrahim had received a woman accompanied by her daughter for twenty consecutive days. A Birni resident, the woman was concerned about her daugh-ter's inability to remarry after two years as a divorcee. She believed that her daughter's former husband had cursed her, thus preventing marriage. Ibrahim reports that the woman paid him twenty naira in order that he would say the Koran for the intention of removing the curse. The daughter has remarried. Other common examples where Ibrahim intervenes on behalf of women's requests include situations where women fear that their husbands will divorce them when they marry a younger woman. Ritual intervention during the weaning of children is a common request because Hausa custom forbids inter-course while the mother is nursing. For weaning, as in ritual solutions, Ibrahim writes a specific verse of the Koran on a wooden slate and, after washing the verse into a bowl, the ink is administered to the child. Given the number of children and the desire of women to end breast-feeding so as to become pregnant again, this was a common request in Tudun Wada. The standard fee was twenty kwebo in 1972. The drinking of Koranic verses is a widespread cure for physical or emotional problems. My own observations indicate that people with physical problems invest in all types of medicine – western, traditional Hausa and Islamic – and attribute the 'cure' to the kind in which they have most confidence.

How does one interpret these examples? The list of problems that are brought to Ibrahim for his mediation reflects tensions in a rapidly growing city: i.e., advancement of sons into secondary school, the opportunity to purchase a housing plot, career or commercial advancement. Also included are more traditional problems of aging and family life, infertility, tensions between sons and fathers, and endless marriage and divorce cases. Clearly, mallams like Ibrahim not only teach Islamic studies but provide emotional therapy for Tudun Wada's residents. The assumptions of both parties to this arrangement ascribe all effects to divine intervention or divine determination. According to Mallam Ibrahim: 'Allah gives you everything. I may know the correct verses to write for *rubutun sha*, and I may go between someone and Allah, but I can do nothing by myself.' To conclude, if anything positive should occur in the life of the supplicant, then the success is attributed to the intermediation of Ibrahim. Failures, on the other hand, are attributed to the will of Allah, and thus malpractice is eliminated as an outcome by both parties.

Before we leave the example of Ibrahim, we should contrast his success with that of his non-uterine brother Shehu, who, like Ibrahim, began as a wandering Koranic student. Shehu is married and continues to describe himself as an *almajiri* or *gardi*. His marriage and three children have forced him to seek wage labor. He has been a factory worker, a mason's assistant and a peddler of used clothing. In 1978, he was a washerman for the students' dormitory at Bayero University, a secure position in the highly desirable state sector. Despite this long career of wage labor, he still considers himself a Koranic student and close follower of the most learned Koranic mallam in Tudun Wada, Mallam Musa. The careers of Shehu and Ibrahim illustrate how two migrants from the same family may achieve radically different levels of success, and how *gardi* and Koranic students who enter the leburori maintain their linkages to the mallamic community throughout their adult lives.

Islam and class in a laborer's community

So far we have examined the institutions of Muslim Hausa society as they structure social life and function to create a sense of community in a migrant *garin leburori* such as Tudun Wada. Before leaving this topic, we should confront the question regarding the particular role of Islam in a working class community and perhaps ask if what has been described above could not apply to any community in Kano. Here I want to show, through example and interpretation, how class position articulates with Islamic institutional ideals to generate a class-based Islamic identity in Tudun Wada.

For most residents of Tudun Wada, scarce material resources and the limitations rising from their class position constrain them from the complete realization of Islamic ideals. In the case of industrial workers, for example, the rotating shift system, the refusal by many factory managers to allow prayer at the proper hours and the inability to attend Friday prayers at either of the Friday mosques act to constrain full participation in Muslim community life.

Similarly, casual workers who unload trucks or push carts in the streets are treated as *yan iska*, or hooligans, by the middle and upper classes and thus are not able to participate in many Muslim rituals such as Friday Mosque. The income of wage workers and labor service workers prevents them from making the pilgrimage to Mecca which, besides being obligatory for all Muslims, has become a religious and cultural event of enormous ostentation and corruption in Kano. While wealthy merchants attend annually and return with consumer goods worth more than the annual income of a wage worker, only the more affluent residents of Tudun Wada are able to make the *hajj* once during their later years. During the *hajj* season, when tens of thousands of pilgrims depart for Mecca from Kano's airport, a mini-industry emerges to service and care for the pilgrims, thus providing a highly visible reminder to workers that their material resources are inadequate for them to fulfill the ideals of Islam. Not only are workers frustrated by their inability to fulfill the Muslim ideal of the pilgrimage, but the visible corruption, where the wealthy and powerful make annual pilgrimages – often for obviously commercial purposes, often accompanied by their mistresses, generates a sense of moral outrage among those too poor to make even a single pilgrimage.[14]

The question of laboring sects

All of these factors create a shared sense of deprivation among many residents of Tudun Wada, one that finds expression in the belief that even though they are poor they are living a purer life, closer to the Muslim ideal, than are the wealthy and powerful who have forgotten the obligations of wealth. Given the Islamic emphasis on the unity of the Muslim community, there is not yet a working class sectarian movement. Nevertheless, there is a shared sense of belonging to the talakawa and of having 'our' religion, which does not violate puritanical Islamic principles, as opposed to the internationalized consumption styles practiced by many of the wealthy and powerful.

The question of sectarian movements among urban workers and the urban talakawa, however, remains germane because of the recent interest and the growth of the Ahmadiyya movement in Tudun Wada. When the survey of Tudun Wada's mallams was conducted in 1975, several described themselves as converts to the Ahmadiyya movement, which is widespread in the southern states of Nigeria and is respected by the residents of Tudun Wada for its education and a quality medical clinic. Theologically, the sect is heretical because it acknowledges a prophet after Mohammed and because it does not follow the *Shari'a*. For these reasons, religious authorities attempted to ban Ahmadiyya followers from participating in the state-sponsored pilgrimages to Mecca. Of seventy-seven mallams enumerated in the Tudun Wada survey, five and possibly six were identified with the Ahmadiyya. Furthermore, several of the mallams who converted to Ahmadiyya are alleged to have received houses, cars and monthly donations from the Ahmadiyya movement. Hence, the movement has gained a significant amount of influence in a short time, even in the face of active opposition by the religious authorities. Yet, while there is interest in the movement among workers and residents, it has not generated mass conversions and remains a minority sect.

Nevertheless, some innovative aspects of the sect and its relationship to urban workers and the urban talakawa require mention. In 1975, the local Ahmadiyya group met on Sunday evenings near Tudun Wada, at Gama. The leader was a Hausa man who had been active in NEPU and had organized trade unions in Kano during the fifties and sixties. While I had never met him before 1975, I knew of his trade union-organizing efforts from completely independent sources who described him as a founder of a lorry (truck) drivers' union at Kano. It is of interest that this man should become the local leader and that he should lead a multi-ethnic religious sect advocating western scientific knowledge – a sect, further, that would relieve talakawa workers from the burden of satisfying a standard of ideological hegemony established by the sarauta and the dominant classes.

However interesting the Ahmadiyya example may be, Sunni orthodoxy remains dominant among the leburori and the talakawa. Tendencies toward class-based sectarianism will probably take the form of reformist associations within Sunni orthodoxy or will appear through heterodox movements such as the *Yan Tatsini*, a millenarian movement that attempted to seize power in December, 1980, resulting in thousands of deaths and a complete breakdown of public order. Since I have analyzed the social basis of this movement and the movement itself elsewhere, there is no need to discuss it here. Suffice to say that there is no evidence linking wage laborers and industrial workers to this movement. But the strength and the violence associated with this movement informs us that the political potential of lower class movements inspired by Islamic ideology is enormously explosive and is perceived as a major threat by the dominant classes.

Islam, rentier capitalism and class struggle

I shall conclude this topic with an incident that exemplifies the capability of mallamic authority to defend the legitimate interests of this talakawa and laboring community against rentier capitalism. It will be recalled that by 1978 new building plots had been allocated in Tudun Wada's ward. Prior to the allocation of plots, however, a wealthy and politically prominent individual, residing adjacent to Tudun Wada, campaigned for the community's support in the local government elections that preceded the national elections of 1979. He was elected to represent the area in the local government council. During the campaign, the question of the allocation of the new plots arose, and Tudun Wada residents were told that they would receive their fair share of the new plots. Nevertheless, when the plots were allocated, the official obtained several plots upon which he built a villa-like modern house surrounded by a green lawn and an ornamental cement block wall. Furthermore, the majority of the plots were allocated to wealthy Birni residents, most of whom were his political allies. Very few plots were allocated to residents of Tudun Wada. Upon learning of their exclusion from the distribution of the plots, community members lodged their protests and consulted with the official, but to no avail. The reader will recall from the housing survey that housing in the new ward, even before the allocation of new plots, was increasingly owned by merchants who lived outside the community. Thus, without a share of the new plots on which low-cost housing could be constructed, many community members were forced to relocate in distant and more peripheral areas where rents were cheaper and where housing was not of internationalized middle-class standards.

Earlier, the same official had built a mosque that was frequented by residents of Tudun Wada, and as was often done for a patron, the Koran was read there for the official's benefit by the students of Mallam Musa, one of the most learned and respected mallams in Tudun Wada. When the plots were allocated and the protests of the community were ignored by the officials, Mallam Musa instructed all of his eighty-nine students to cease attending the official's mosque for daily prayers and to cease reading the Koran for his benefit. Despite the official's request that the ban on attending his mosque be removed, Mallam Musa refused, and his students as well as other sympathizers refused to pray at the official's mosque. Therefore, though the community failed to alter the allocation of plots in favor of working class and talakawa housing needs, they were able to deny the official the social esteem that normally accompanies both a mosque and a public official. Moreover, the banning of his mosque by the community's most prestigious mallam subjected the official to public humiliation and personal shame which, in the context of Muslim Hausa society, was a severe and onerous punishment. Predictably, the official who violated community trust was defeated in the local government election of 1979.

Though Mallam Musa and the community were not able to reverse the corrupt allocation of building plots, they used the only weapons available to them to struggle against rentier capitalism and the process of gentrification that threatens to eliminate working class and talakawa control of Tudun Wada. While cynics may argue that the gain for the official was surely worth the sanction imposed by the community, the humiliating stigma imposed by Mallam Musa will certainly undermine the official's trustworthiness and reputation. To conclude, the example illustrates how mallams interwoven within the talakawa and leburori use Islamic institutions to resist rentier capitalism. Though unsuccessful in this instance, the experience contributes to the creation of a popular tradition of class awareness and class struggle which, like NEPU, will generate solidarity in future struggles.

PORTRAITS AND PERSONALITIES IN A GARIN LEBURORI

One may argue that in Tudun Wada semi-industrial capitalism articulates with Islamic institutions in complex and contradictory ways, but at the empirical level personalities give the community its human character. In the following section, detailed descriptions are presented of individuals who reflect the contradictions and social processes which hitherto have only been described in more general terms. Initially, I shall examine the lives and families of three prominent, long-term residents of Tudun Wada, who would be considered notables by the community. The first personality exemplifies the historical origin of Tudun Wada as a camp for low-status state-sector workers. Tsoho's life is of interest because his origins as a slave of the Emir illustrate the continuity of personalities who traverse the precapitalist and capitalist periods. Although he lived most of his life as an employee of the Native Authority Police and as a slave of the Emir, he administered a ward largely composed of industrial wage laborers.

Tsoho

Tsoho is a prominent personality in one section of Tudun Wada, where he had been a ward head until he contracted a crippling illness. Like most of Tudun Wada's officials, he was a wage worker with a close association with the colonial state. Tsoho's relationship to the state derives from his origins as a royal slave (*bawan sarki*) and his service as a Native Authority policeman and as a 'volunteer' for the colonial division that fought in the Burma campaign of the Second World War. Though impoverished during a period of inflation and capitalist growth, he holds and cherishes his status as a servile dependent of the Emir's household. And he has married a woman from the Emir of Zaria's household, presumably having the same royal slave origins. Tsoho's social origins and his paternalistic relationship to the colonial state are typical of Tudun Wada's original settlers. Yet his background and his military service to the state did not end with colonial rule, for his eldest son now serves with the Nigerian Army and his younger sons spend a portion of the year living with their elder brother in the Nigerian Army barracks. Thus, Tsoho's family has served the state in a military or police role across three generations, and while the organization, ideology and form of the state has changed radically, there is remarkable occupational continuity of service in his family.[15]

In a community of industrial wage earners who are integrated into Kano's most advanced sector of capitalist production, the unevenness and layering of change is reflected in Tsoho's role as ward head. Aside from collecting community taxes from those not employed in the formal sector, whom the tax records show to be a minority, Tsoho took his role of ward head very seriously. Despite his poverty, Tsoho considered himself to be a *mai sarauta*, a minor office holder, and one who once held a close association with the royal household and the officials of the former Native Authority. His claim to this 'prestigious' status was often publicly announced in the street when he was

163

engaged in one of his frequent verbal disputes. In attempting to overwhelm his unfortunate opponent, Tsoho would announce to the neighborhood, 'You know I am not a talaka. I am a royal slave of the Emir.' At the same time, despite his irascible temper, Tsoho endeavored to maintain a moral order in his ward. Through his knowledge and use of Hausa greetings and idioms he directed street life and greeted those who passed by his home, where he sat on a woven mat in the afternoon. Mediation of marital disputes, usually marked by husbands threatening divorce and threats by wives to return to their fathers' houses, was Tsoho's specialty. He counseled both parties in the traditional Hausa virtues of patience, avoidance of shameful behavior and the extension of generosity, often achieving the respect and appreciation of his community.

Public disorder by unmarried youths and prostitutes or their clients took much of his attention. Tsoho had the misfortune to live directly across the street from one of the largest and most dilapidated brothels in Tudun Wada. The brothel was built and owned by a local resident who migrated to Kano as a seasonal worker, but who now owned several houses in Tudun Wada which he maintained by himself. His dedication to hard work, saving and frugality fulfills the Weberian ideal of the abstemious protestant businessman. But in Islamic Tudun Wada, he was despised by the community for his miserly ways and for not hiring laborers to repair his houses. For it was reasoned that a prosperous man should have pity on unemployed workers and create opportunities for them to earn a living. The mud-brick brothels that he built were near collapse and always needed major repairs during the dry season. Furthermore, because older prostitutes, drug addicts and illegitimate children lived there, respectable Muslims considered the owner immoral for profiting from prostitution and forbidden practices.

The brothel was a center of commercial and social activity. In front of its door congregated prostitutes, unemployed workers and peddlers of meat, kola, tobacco, drugs and foods of all variety. Saturday nights were especially active, because workers were paid on that day and Sunday was a holiday. Oftentimes music, laughter and occasional disputes produced loud noise until the early hours of the morning. This usually brought Tsoho to the scene to denounce the shamelessness and hooliganism of the prostitutes and their following. Oftentimes, after Tsoho threatened to call the police and to charge the crowd with disorder, some weeks of relative peace would follow.

To sit with Tsoho on his mat exposes the contradictions of those who try to maintain a Muslim Hausa lifestyle in a working class community. Next to the brothel, mallams and Koranic students may be reading and teaching. Children of devout and correct Muslims may congregate in front of the brothel because of the opportunity to sell cakes and food prepared by their mothers to the crowds of single men. The density and requirements of daily interaction inherent in Hausa society require that the two groups come to terms with each other, irrespective of the contradictions between their ideals and everyday life. One observes prostitutes moving in and out of the building and occasionally crossing the street to greet or talk with Tsoho. He responds warmly as they genuflect to his age and official status as ward head. Workers, having returned from work, earn a few shillings by selling perfume to prostitutes during breaks in front of the brothel. At the same time, peasants collecting household sweepings and manure from deposits in the street, where women's sheep and goats are tethered during the night, greet Tsoho and exchange information and news about mutual friends. Together with other permanent residents and the mallams. Tsoho attempts to maintain a Muslim hausa sense of moral order in a community composed of renters, migrants and transients.

Butchering as an affluent craft: a portrait of Abdu

As we have already observed, butchering was a craft accorded very low status in the 'traditional' or precapitalist occupational hierarchy, but because of increased demand for butchering services, caused in turn by the rise in the urban population and a higher standard of living for many, it has become a lucrative talakawa occupation for the more successful butchers. Earlier we saw that the urbans, as opposed to the migrants and commuters, ranked butchers higher on the status ladders than the traditional Hausa system would justify. Further, according to the housing survey, butchers were the only craftsmen wealthy enough to purchase houses in Tudun Wada. These facts serve to introduce Abdu as a successful community notable, for he has prospered as an entrepreneur in a dirty craft during a time when many migrants are more impressed with the earnings of an occupation than with the prestige it holds according to traditional criteria.

Abdu was born in the peri-urban area at Mairiri in Kumbotso District around 1930. During his childhood he visited urban Kano regularly, and when he was about 15, he came to live in Kofar Mata ward of the Birni with his father's brother who rented a room there. He continued to return home to help his family with farming for four consecutive years. His uncle died in a cinema fire during the early 1950s. Because his father had taught him the crafts of butchering, Abdu made and sold roasted meats, *Tsire*, as a peddler in order to support himself. When he was about 24 years old, he met Kane, a senior butcher, who taught him how to trade and prepare cows for the urban market. Abdu already knew how to butcher and prepare the meat of cows, camels, sheep and goats, but Kane took him in as a client and taught him how to purchase cows from herdsmen. Abdu also learned about credit relations and the procedure for shipping cattle by rail to Lagos and Ibadan, where they fetched greater profits. When Kane's business collapsed and after Kane migrated to Ghana, Abdu became the client of a man from Dakata (Waje) for about four years. When the man died, Abdu butchered and traded animals on his own.

Abdu continues to trade and to butcher cows regularly. From his account, the intricate credit system described by Cohen for Ibadan butchers used to operate in Kano before the civil war, but since the war and the petroleum boom many butchers possess enough cash to purchase cattle directly. As a consequence, those without cash or superior credit relations could not trade and profit in cattle. According to Abdu, in Kano a butcher used to arrange for credit for a cow on Monday, butcher and sell the cow meat on Tuesday and repay his *maigida* or creditor on Wednesday. But since there are now more people with money than cattle available, the butchers are increasingly forced to accept payment in kind for slaughtering, or a fixed wage per cow, and thus gradually give up marketing the meat. Abdu's arrangement for slaughtering a cow calls for him and his assistants to work for about three hours. It begins by tying up the cow; a mallam is then paid four kwebo (1975) to slaughter the cow according to proper Muslim ritual; and certain parts of the animal – kidney, liver, neck meat and other parts – are allocated to Abdu by the owner. The owner then sells the meat for roasting and peddling by apprentice butchers or street peddlers. On a long day Abdu may complete four cows. When Abdu has enough cash or when he may be fortunate enough to arrange a credit transaction, he buys and slaughters a cow and sells the meat to retail butchers at the market. Occasionally he speculates by purchasing a sick cow and then nurses the animal back to health in his compound, where he is assisted by his wives. In return for caring for the cow, however, his wives are entitled to sell the manure produced by the cow to farmers.

Abdu came to Tudun Wada in the late 1950s. He met a goat trader and animal broker, Yusufu, who had purchased a large plot in Tudun Wada. Such plots are usually divided in two plots, and Yusufu allowed Abdu to buy half of his plot on credit, so that Abdu now owns his house. After becoming more prosperous, partially through political advancement in the Kano State Butchers' Union, Abdu was able to purchase a second housing plot upon which he constructed a house for rental income. By 1975, however, he had sold the house in order to make the pilgrimage to Mecca. In the competitive market of the cattle trade, Abdu believes that he has little opportunity to become a large trader, and because such large traders are responsible for a larger share of the market each year, opportunities for small butcher-traders like Abdu are scarce. Despite this limitation, he owns a motorcycle and is considered prosperous by local standards.

Abdu has been married six times, but in 1975 he had only two wives. Four marriages ended in divorce. His eldest son is a secondary school student and has learned the butchering trade from his father. As was customary among the Hausa, Abdu's first marriage was a family marriage: he married his father's sister's daughter. Three of his wives originate from butchering families: one is the daughter of a praise singer, a status even lower than butchering, and two are the daughters of mallams. His present wives keep comparatively strict seclusion and neither one works in factories.

Abdu spends most of the daylight hours at the market or at the slaughter-house. Nevertheless, he is a pivotal figure among the senior notables of Tudun Wada. This status derives from his political networks which originated with activities in the Kano State Butchers' Union as well as organizing sporting events in Kano. By 1978, when Nigeria was preparing for elections to return to civilian rule, Abdu was a member of the local branch of the successor party to NEPU, the PRP.

If Tsoho's role in Tudun Wada is to provide a proper moral order according to traditional Muslim Hausa standards, then Abdu represents the local political representative who links the community to the local and national political organizations. Rather than denouncing transgressions as Tsoho does, Abdu receives petitioners who ask him to intervene on their behalf. Hence the community considers Abdu a resource that links them to a political structure and a process that they may not fully comprehend, yet, at the same time, they know that they will probably need his advice or intervention in the future.

Yusufu and his family: a note on women's roles

In our third example of Tudun Wada's notables, I shall discuss Yusufu's family and their experiences as well as his own.

166

Yusufu was born around the year 1924 in Wudil, a town about 43 kilometers southeast of Kano City. After attending Koranic school at home and wandering with his mallam during several dry seasons as a child, Yusufu migrated to the tin mining area of Burkutu which lies near the city of Jos (Plateau State). There he became a tin miner, venturing into mines up to fifty feet in depth and often working in cold water for long periods. Yusufu worked as a tin miner for 15 to 20 years, advancing to the position of headman. He left mining because he feared illness caused by the effects of the cold water. At that time he earned nine shillings for a seven day week (around 1958). When Yusufu decided to leave mining, he made his way directly from Jos to Tudun Wada, because he had heard from miners that it was a laborers' town. Thus he assumed that he could settle comfortably there without feeling shame on account of his laboring status. By 1978 he had lived in Tudun Wada for around 20 years. Initially he lived in the older ward of Tudun Wada, where he met a butcher who taught him how to be a goat and sheep broker at the market. Before he became a broker, he worked as a casual laborer, unloading trucks and stacking bags of groundnuts near the railhead during the dry season. When the new ward was being surveyed, Yusufu invested his savings in a housing plot for ₦120; similar plots now sell for over ₦7,000. Over time, using traditional materials, he built a large house and compound (by local standards) so that he is able to lease several rooms to tenants. Yusufu continues to buy and sell goats and sheep at the new Gwagwarwa market and has prospered with the increase in the price of food during the 1970s. Together with a relative, he has invested in two passenger vans, which are driven and repaired by his son-in-law and his nephew. By 1980 both vans were broken down. As always, Yusufu studies the Koran with a mallam, even though he had developed a reputation for evening gambling in the neighborhood. Recently, shame felt by his son encouraged him to quit gambling.

Yusufu's career moved from peasant to wage worker to commission-broker and finally to self-sufficient entrepreneur at the end of his active life. While he is a shrewd broker and trader, his success is largely due to the unprecedented expansion of economic opportunity created by the petroleum boom. Yusufu possesses the urban networks and resources that have enabled him to respond to the opportunities created by capitalist growth in Kano. For a short period, his vans prospered, because Kano State provides no intraurban transportation system and because the local government, in an effort to rationalize transport patterns, has banned hand carts from main streets. Both of these factors insure prosperity for small van owners who are profiting from the transition from human power to motor transport. Yusufu is prominent in Tudun Wada, in part because of his family networks and the size of his household. Let us examine his family networks in order to illustrate how community cohesion is maintained through the cyclical patterns of the Muslim Hausa family system which, in practice if not in theory, allows for considerable female economic independence marked by a high rate of divorce.

While Yusufu has been married at least six times, in 1972 he had three wives. His senior wife was an active household entrepreneur who cooked meat and fried yams in front of their home in the evenings for her customers. The latter were mostly single workers without families. She was assisted by her daughter who, in 1972, was between marriages and was actively seeking to remarry one of the single men in Tudun Wada. The senior wife has no children by Yusufu.

The second wife of Yusufu was the mother of Yusufu's only living son, Mohammedu, who had entered secondary school by 1978. Of course, given the Hausa preference for sons, Mohammedu was the joy of Yusufu's life, and for this reason the second wife was especially loved by Yusufu. In 1972, as many older men do, Yusufu married for a third time. His choice was a daughter of a local carpenter who originated from the Adarawa Hausa area of Niger. Then she was about 16 years old and had grown up on the same street as Yusufu. It was an arranged marriage, her first, and she accepted it willingly as it promised her economic security.

It was customary for Hausa men to give their wives money to feed them and their families for a few days to a week. Women then purchase and prepare food, usually on the night that they spend with their husband. Custom allows them to keep any savings after meeting household expenses for their own enterprises. Enterprises include food preparation, tying cloth for merchants producing tie-dyed cloth, sewing hats, knitting babies' clothing or weaving cloth, leather or straw products. Female household production indicates the historical layering of production processes that are subordinated to semi-industrial capitalism. What women save from food preparation becomes their working capital. Hence, men often complain about the quality of the food served to them and often joke about the price that they pay for their wives' economic ventures. Thus, to maximize their own labor, most Muslim women in Tudun Wada wish to practice seclusion, at least during the day, for husbands must provide labor for water, firewood or marketing. Relatives or adopted children fulfill this function within the compound if the household is without children. Further, both the supply of raw materials and the distribution of production from a secluded woman's household is carried out by children who may be close relatives, adopted for this purpose, or the children of co-wives or co-residents. Streets are filled with young girls and adolescents marketing the products of their household, usually to men who flirt with them. Thus the economic function of distributing household production also exposes young women to the marriage market, where men, sometimes twice or three times the age of the girls, discuss and select candidates for marriage.

With this comment on the household and women's economic roles, let us return to the marriages of Yusufu.

Tensions developed when the second wife felt that she needed more economic resources and decided to work in a candy factory that was owned by Sudanese Muslims, one that employed large numbers of women. She walked to the factory with other married women, all of whom veiled their heads, and returned each day after the first shift, around 3:15 p.m. From that time, she assumed a secluded role in Yusufu's household and ignored the contradiction inherent in her role as a factory worker and her role as a secluded Hausa woman. Of course, Yusufu was embarrassed by this contradiction, but because of his affection for her, and especially out of love for Mohammedu, he refrained from forcing her to quit factory work or from divorcing her. By 1978, Yusufu's new affluence enabled him to satisfy her economic needs and she terminated factory employment.

A second incident illustrates that though divorce is frequent among the Muslim Hausa of Tudun Wada, bonds of affection continue between household members even after divorce.

> When the youngest wife, acting in anger over a trivial household matter, cursed the young Mohammedu and refused to repent, Yusufu declared, 'Anyone who curses my son Mohammedu also curses me.' And then he divorced his youngest wife. When the senior wife complained to Yusufu about the conduct of Mohammedu and the severity of divorce for the youngest wife, since she was also carrying his child, Yusufu responded in anger by divorcing the senior wife also. Saddened by the consequences of his impulsive actions, Yusufu then discussed his situation with intermediaries, including Tsoho and his sister Binta, a female notable who loaned money at usurious rates. They negotiated upon his behalf. After Yusufu sent gifts to the family of the youngest wife, they agreed to allow her to return to him. The senior wife, however, refused to return, regardless of the gifts sent by Yusufu. Yet, despite her rupture with Yusufu, when she made the *hajj* to Mecca in 1978, she brought gifts and sacred water from Mecca for Yusufu to drink. While they avoid direct communication when possible, the two keep in contact with each other because of their mutual household and family networks.

Because they integrate independent producers and wage workers, marriage and household networks are major sources of community integration in Tudun Wada. Let us examine the tragic life of Yusufu's daughter Amarya.

> Born in Jos when Yusufu was a tin miner, by the time she was 22 Amarya had been married five times and had several children who lived with their fathers, as is the custom among the Muslim Hausa. When I knew her, she was married to Idi, a Muslim Bolewa man from Potiskum (Borno State), who owned and often pushed several large, four-wheeled carts made from auto frames. Her co-wife was a young Fulani woman who was born and raised in Tudun Wada. In an unusual relationship, Idi's senior wife lived apart from them in Gwagwarwa where she owned a house and a restaurant. Even in the context of a working class community, where ideal Muslim Hausa standards are not possible to maintain, Amarya was considered a powerful and independent personality. Given the opportunity, she smoked tobacco with her co-wife, and she was immensely popular with the women of Tudun Wada. Her main occupation was knitting and selling children's garments made from synthetic yarn. Amarya's popularity and her social networks immersed her in a complex network of gift-giving relationships (*biki*) with other women, where each successive gift between friends was superseded by the giving of an even larger or more cherished gift. Over time, these relationships appear to provide credit and social security for women whose insecure marital situations encourage them to accumulate economic resources, through the development of such female networks, that can be drawn upon should divorce threaten them.
>
> Amarya's life with Idi was tranquil, and her relationship to her co-wife was an ideal one. They shared child rearing, loaned each other money, secretly

169

smoked cigarettes together and prepared food for each other without conflict. While Amarya was very experienced and, after four previous marriages, was wise to the ways of married life, her co-wife was shy, inexperienced and extremely anxious that her newborn son survive. Idi tolerated Amarya's activities, often quoting Hausa proverbs that exhort men to be patient and saying one should be tolerant of any act as long as it did not bring public shame to him or his household. The neighborhood, in turn, respected him for his gentle ways and for the manner in which he treated the clients who pushed his carts. So trusted was Idi that the owner of the house in which he rented rooms entrusted him with collecting rents and minding the house, mostly because her husband's addiction to pills (amphetamines) rendered him too unreliable to be trusted with the rent collection.

During the winter of 1974, Idi and several other household members became ill with deep coughing and soon died of tuberculosis. Amarya, at the same time, had given birth twice, but each time the child had died within the first year, leaving her extremely weak. Upon the death of Idi, Amarya and her young co-wife separated; she remarried a carpenter and the co-wife remarried a truck driver. Both continued to live in Tudun Wada and to maintain their friendship during weddings and night visits, when women are permitted to leave seclusion, and also during visits to the hospital where women bring their children, ostensibly for health reasons but also for obvious social purposes. The tragedy of Amarya's life is that she contracted tuberculosis from Idi and that continual childbirth had weakened her to the point that medical authorities at the hospital told her that if she continued to bear children, she would die from the strain. Instead, she was instructed to rest and avoid pregnancy. For Amarya, the choices were cruel: to return to her husband and her desired social role as a married woman and thus risk death, or to return to Yusufu's household as an unmarried daughter – an awkward role considered useless in Hausa society. Unfortunately, rather than remain a barren woman in the household of her father, Amarya chose to marry again and to give birth twice. She died of tuberculosis in the winter of 1979.

Yusufu's household provides the reader with a glimpse into the social processes associated with family life in Tudun Wada. Marriage, remarriage, divorce and the marriage of children occupy people's social lives to a degree unimaginable in western industrialized societies. Virtually no woman remains unmarried during her lifetime; all have careers and many become wealthier than their husbands. While in theory Muslim women have few rights and remain under the domination of their husbands, in practice more experienced and stronger women make material demands upon their husbands and subject them to ridicule if they cannot provide for them in the material style required. While it is true that a man may divorce his wife at any moment, to exercise this prerogative means that, in order to remarry, he must expend large sums of money, introduce strain into the relationship with his children and arrange for his household services during the interim. Women, on the other hand, have few legal rights, as they are treated as minors under Islamic law, but they exercise great leverage on their husbands by fleeing to the household of their senior male kinsmen or guardians when they are involved in a domestic dispute with their husbands.

In order for his wife to return, the husband must renegotiate the terms of her return with her kinsman or guardian. This practice is quite common in Tudun Wada among the urban talakawa and the working class.

Community portraits: residents and transients

Most of the inhabitants of Tudun Wada are neither homeowners nor relatively prosperous men like Yusufu and Abdu. Rather they are younger men who work for a wage or who maintain clientage relationships with their patrons. Some, like Idi or Shehu, the brother of Mallam Ibrahim, consider themselves permanent residents of Tudun Wada. Others lack this sense of commitment to the community, though I encountered many cases where seasonal migrants return each dry season for many years, and several have done so for over twenty years. One finds them packed into small rooms, engaged in marginal activity and saving every kwebo. Our first resident has lived in Tudun Wada for many decades and, though committed to the community, would not be considered a notable but rather only a poor bicycle repairer. As a member of the laboring poor and the founder of NEPU, his life bridges the many historical phases of Tudun Wada.

Mudi Mai Keke: a life of urban poverty

Mudi was born at Yan Danko in Kumbotso District. His father was a farmer who irrigated a small plot during the dry season. While his ethnic origin is Fulani, he has been completely assimilated into the Hausa. After several years of Koranic school with a mallam in rural Kano, he migrated to Tudun Wada in 1936. At first he worked as a houseboy for an African sergeant in the West African Frontier Force, which was stationed at Tudun Wada (or Gunna, as it was formerly called). At that time, Tudun Wada had a reputation for illicit practices such as gin-making, prostitution and gambling. As a houseboy, Mudi received two shillings per month, plus food and shelter. When the war broke out, he worked at the Birni hospital as a cleaner for four years for 15 shillings a month. From the Birni hospital, he moved to the eye hospital run by the Sudan Interior Mission, where he worked until independence was announced (1960). A few years after independence, Mudi took his savings and purchased some bicycles for hire and opened a repair shop under a tree in the open area of Tudun Wada across from the dagaci's house and the Friday mosque.

Mudi was a founding member of the NEPU committee which elected the present village head of Tudun Wada. He felt a strong personal attachment to Aminu Kano, referring to him as 'Mallam Aminu' and thus emphasizing the mallamic attributes of Kano's foremost populist politician. In advancing the cause of NEPU, Mudi has been jailed, evicted from his living quarters by a landlord who feared reprisals from the Native Authority policemen, and, of course, subjected to personal abuse. By 1978, however, he believed that seven out of ten aspects of the tallakawa's former suffering had been ameliorated by subsequent reforms. For example, 'Now we do not have to take our shoes off in front of the sarakuna', and the talakawa are now allowed to speak in their own defense at court and are no longer required to prostrate themselves in front of the judge. Forced labor and illegal taxation have also been elimi-

171

nated, in Mudi's opinion, but the talakawa remain impoverished and blocked from effective participation in the new wealth by the wealthy and the powerful. Thus Mudi sees economic advancement as the talakawa's goal in the future.

Mudi's perspective on the talakawa and their relationship to the leburori is worth reporting. In his view, those who do 'the work of poor people' are brothers and should help each other, and when asked for a definition of a talakawa now, he responded, 'A talakawa is someone who comes when he is called'. When asked, Mudi listed the following occupations as the work of poor people: head porters, factory workers, bicycle hirers, blacksmiths, indigo dyers, tin can collectors, washermen, used-clothing peddlers, tanners and peddlers of inexpensive things. Mudi believes that striking factory workers are his brothers (i.e., *dan uwa*) and sympathizes with them when they are beaten by the police. Regarding workers' pay increases such as 'Adebo' and 'Udoji', he commented, 'Since they live in Tudun Wada with us, if they receive more money, they will spend part of it on new bicycles or in renting my bicycles. So we shall all prosper together.'

Mudi enjoys his trade as a repairer and renter of bicycles. He has lost any hope of ever owning a house in Tudun Wada and believes that his children will take care of him in his old age. He believed that he was about 60 years old in 1978. Recently Mudi was elected chairman of Tudun Wada's PRP committee, NEPU's successor party. Other committee members include Abdu the butcher, a cloth trader, a truck driver and a small cooking oil trader. Despite his poverty and an occupation that is associated with urban marginality, Mudi's election as chairman of the local PRP branch pleased him enormously.

Portrait of an industrial worker: Ahmadu's life and struggles

Ahmadu has been a factory worker since I met him in 1970. His story and his career are more varied than most, and his involvement in workers' struggles is more extensive than the average worker's. For this reason, I intend to review his life and work history in detail.

Ahmadu was born in 1949 at the village of Makouda, Dambatta District, which lies about 60 kilometers north of Kano City. His father was a prosperous farmer who traded in animals during the dry season. At the age of 16, Ahmadu came to Kano for the first time in order to study the Koran with a mallam in Yakasai ward (Birni). At this time he married his paternal cousin, but the marriage ended quickly in divorce. After returning each successive dry season to study the Koran, on his fourth seasonal migration he paid a foreman in order to be employed as a thread winder at the blanket factory. In order to live near his job, he moved from the Birni to Tudun Wada, where he rented a room in a compound of single men. One of the co-residents was a mallam who studied with Mallam Ibrahim during the day and worked as a night watchman at a private residence during the evenings. (Known as a notorious pill taker, the mallam left Ahmadu's compound when he married Azumi, a woman who had been abandoned in Tudun Wada by her husband, on the condition that she quit her job at the candy factory and stop smoking cigarettes.)

After working at the blanket factory for nine months, Ahmadu was laid off and at the same time involved in a wildcat strike by workers to obtain their back pay according to the terms of the Adebo Commission. (We shall analyze the commission and the strike in Chapter Six.) When he received his Adebo arrears pay, ₦30, he invested it in candy, kola nuts and cigarettes, which he peddled in Tudun Wada during the day and at the local cinemas during the evening. Gradually Ahmadu's living expenses exceeded his profits from petty trading, so that after three months he had insufficient capital to purchase new supplies. Since it was the dry season, he became a laborer for a traditional mud-brick mason, receiving 6 to 7 shillings per day when the minimum factory wage was 7/1d per day. When he was unable to obtain work as a traditional mason's helper, he unloaded trucks and, for a short time, became a cart pusher. He despised the latter occupation because cart pushers wore only short pants, cursed anyone in their way and had a reputation for taking pills (as do many laborers engaged in arduous work, in order to maintain their physical strength). Shame prevented him from continuing as a cart pusher even though the average daily wage usually exceeded that of a beginning factory worker.

After several months of varied casual labor, Ahmadu paid ₦4 to the headman at a tannery, where he worked for four months and ten days before being laid off. During that time Ahmadu participated in a strike against a new manager who began to harass workers in order to speed up production and attempted to fire two older and popular supervisors who had worked there for 22 and 15 years respectively. In response, the workers went out on strike and stoned the factory, a move which brought the riot police to the factory. During the negotiations, workers called for the removal of the new European manager and the reinstatement of the two supervisors. When asked if and why he participated in the rock-throwing, Ahmadu responded, 'Yes, I did it because I knew that some day the manager would fire me without a fair reason, and then what would I do?' The strike was settled by the police when the assistant manager became the factory manager and when he agreed to reinstate the supervisors and to pay workers for the days lost due to the strike. Earlier Ahmadu had refused to join a company union that was corruptly administered by an accountant.

After several months of casual labor, mostly unloading trucks for a labor contractor at the Sabon Gari market, Ahmadu's friend arranged a job for him at a groundnut crushing mill that was owned by one of Kano's most prominent merchant-industrial capitalists. His friend was a Muslim Tera from Borno State who worked at the Kano Club as a waiter, where he had the opportunity to arrange for the job with an Arab manager of the factory. Ahmadu paid the waiter ₦4 with the understanding that the factory supervisor would receive ₦3.50 and the waiter 50 kwebo as a commission (*lada*). At this time (1972/73), when the minimum factory wage for an eight-hour day was between 8/9d and 9 shillings, Ahmadu was paid 5 shillings for a ten-hour day, 7 a.m. to 5 p.m., with breaks for lunch and prayers at 1:30 and 4 p.m. He was one of ten male laborers who carried bags of groundnuts to a machine that dispensed the nuts to a moving conveyor belt where older women picked out the premium quality nuts from those that were to be crushed for groundnut oil. Most employees were women who worked for 4 shillings a day plus commission. In general, the workers were poor peasants from the peri-urban villages or former prostitutes whose age forced them to accept factory labor.

After working there for a month, Ahmadu discussed the pay with a fellow worker, Isa, a commuter from the peri-urban area who had also been involved in several strikes at other factories. Drawing upon his experience in a strike (see Factory A, Chapter Six), Isa suggested forming a strike committee. Together with three other workers – two commuters and a literate urban –

they formed a committee and asked the factory manager to pay the legally correct daily wage rate. After the manager's initial statement of 'take it or leave work', the workers appealed for him to take the matter up with the owner. Two weeks passed without a reply from the owner. When they asked the manager again, he told them to speak with the owner, and because it was Saturday, they decided to visit him at his home in Nasarawa. When they met the owner at his home, they greeted him with the traditional Hausa greeting that an inferior uses to greet someone of superior status (i.e., *Ranka ya dade*, or 'May your life be a long one') and then explained their pay request to him. After the owner had agreed to raise their pay, they returned to work the following day only to discover that the factory manager intended to dismiss all of them, saying that he had been ordered to do so by the owner. At this stage, the workers became angry and demanded severance pay (*kudin notis*) before they would sign the pay form. The manager responded by threatening to take them to court, and they responded affirmatively, saying that they would tell the judge about the factory's pay scale and thus expose the local industrialists for failing to pay the minimum wage.

Later that afternoon, Ahmadu and Isa went to the labor office maintained by the Federal Ministry of Labor to explain their case. The labor officer agreed to go with Isa to discuss the matter with the owner. After some negotiations, the owner offered to rehire the workers at a higher pay rate, but they had already agreed to quit the firm. The commuter, Isa, reprimanded the owner, saying 'he was shameless in his treatment of workers'. Finally, the owner agreed to pay them severance pay, and each received ₦4. The experience of confronting the owner was a significant event for Ahmadu because he was forced to admit to himself that the owner, a Muslim Hausa, was not being misinformed by his factory manager and that he knowingly intended to exploit a fellow Muslim Hausa worker. Later Ahmadu commented that there did not appear to be any difference between Hausa and foreign factory owners, except that the former allowed breaks for prayer.

Following this dispute, Ahmadu returned to the tannery where he worked for two years. He was fired when he returned home for three days without permission in order to visit his mother, who was ill. After several months of casual labor, mostly unloading trucks in front of factories, his friend at the Kano Club arranged for him to work as an electrician's helper in a large textile factory. He was the single Hausa among 29 workers; the remaining workers were Yorubas, as they predominate in the skilled trades. Unfortunately, Ahmadu's opportunity for a skilled job ended after four months, when the manager accused the electricians of stealing tools and fired nearly all of the work group. Subsequently, he obtained daily paid work for a Hausa industrialist who made cement bricks and who also owned a modern construction company. He was paid 6 shillings a day for making bricks and up to 12 shillings a day for working as an apprentice mason. When construction work declined due to the rainy season, Ahmadu returned to his original industrial job at the blanket factory. There he moved from winder to a higher paying position as weaver. After working as a weaver for eight months, Ahmadu became involved in a strike over arrears payments that had been announced by the Udoji Commission in 1975. He was also involved in the struggle by rank-and-file workers to rid themselves of a corrupt trade union that supervisors controlled in order to sell jobs to new workers (see Chapter Six). He was laid off at the blanket factory shortly thereafter, when a trade recession forced them to eliminate a shift. Again he searched for work but found only casual labor unloading trucks at a furniture factory, where the labor contractor demanded thirty percent of all fees paid to workers. With inflation from the petroleum boom increasing the cost of food and housing, Ahmadu decided to search for work elsewhere.

At this time, 1975-7, Nigeria had imported millions of tons of cement along with other capital and consumer goods. The cement imports caused an unprecedented scandal and left hundreds of ships waiting to discharge their cargos at Lagos port. Ahmadu had a friend who had worked at the docks unloading cement, so he decided to take a van 800 miles to look for work at Lagos port. Traveling by van directly to Lagos, the trip took 24 hours and cost ₦10 per passenger. When he arrived at the docks of Apapa, his friend introduced him to a Beriberi (i.e., Kanuri) labor recruiter, and the next day he began unloading cement. Ahmadu received ₦10 per day for a nine-hour shift beginning at 7 a.m. and ending at 4 p.m. During the five months that he unloaded cement, he worked every day except for seven days when ships were unable to dock due to the congestion caused by over 800 ships in the harbor. From the remains of packing cases, he and nine others constructed huts on the dock to provide shelter. Here Ahmadu squatted for five months with other northern Muslim laborers; Hausa, Fulani, Nupe, Shuwa Arabs, Adarawa and Kanuri-speakers. Just as one would expect, the Muslim workers constructed a mosque from packing crates and appointed as imam a laboring mallam from Gumel (Kano State) to lead them in prayer. The mallam had finished the Koran and was the most learned among them. During his five months in Lagos, Ahmadu never left the port area, for fear of robbery and violent attacks that are notorious in the Lagos area, especially at night. In order to provide for his wife, a divorcee whom he married in 1974, he sent part of his wages north with trusted friends to Tudun Wada. He arranged for an Ibo woman to bring him food twice daily for ₦2 a day. After five months he was laid off, but he had managed to save ₦450, most of which was spent on clothing for his wife, household goods and a radio.

When Ahmadu returned to Tudun Wada, he rested for a week and then began unloading trucks as a casual laborer at a furniture factory. From there he was able to purchase a worker's time card at a German-managed candy factory. Here he worked as a store laborer under another's name for three months, but left because the weekly wage of ₦10.50 was insufficient to pay for food and housing for his family. Furthermore, rising rents caused by gentrification in Tudun Wada forced him to seek cheaper housing in the new expansion area behind the Bompai industrial estate, called Tudun Murtala. He was fortunate to find work at the tannery again, as he now had many contacts with the company's workers. The tannery was considered a dirty and dangerous place to work because of the chemicals used to remove animal hair from the skins. Nevertheless, it paid much better than the candy factory and there were many opportunities to work overtime. His weekly pay averaged ₦15 at the end of 1978.

Inflated costs of housing and food in the face of great inequities of income and wealth generated a movement among the tannery workers to demand an increase in their daily pay rate. Earlier, in 1977, Ahmadu had joined other experienced workers in attempting to organize a trade union, but the rural resident commuters feared for their jobs and refused to support the organizing drive. So the movement to organize a trade union failed at the tannery. As a measure of Ahmadu's socialization into the urban leburori, note that he referred to the commuters as 'ignorant peasants who take food from our mouths', even though he had been urbanized for only nine years.

175

Despite their inability to form a union, the militants at the tannery were able to organize several wildcat strikes that were designed to increase the pressure on management for higher wages. In November 1978, the headmen met with the militant workers, including Ahmadu, and agreed to walk out of the factory after a new batch of valuable skins had been placed in the vats containing chemicals. They reasoned that if the skins stayed in the vats too long, they would be destroyed, and the management would be held responsible. (The firm had recently been purchased by Lonrho, a diversified multinational corporation.) Further, the militants demanded that any pay increase be backdated for several months. Using this tactic, the strike was successful, and the workers received both some back pay and a wage increase. Ahmadu continues to advocate trade unionism at the factory.

As a document, Ahmadu's career history gives the reader an insider's view of the urban labor market, the continual circulation of labor between the formal and informal sectors and the way in which proletarianization socializes Muslim Hausa workers into active participation in class struggle. Throughout, Ahmadu remains a devout Muslim and a dignified member of Tudun Wada's laboring residents. His knowledge of English terms that organize his life – 'overtime', 'arrears pay', 'notice', and mechanical terms – has increased several fold since I first met him in 1970. The number of strikes and union organizing drives in which he has personally participated is exceptional but not unheard of. Yet, despite the inequities of urban working class life, he plans to remain, for according to him, conditions of rural life are worse still, and life in Kano offers opportunities and some promise of a better life for him and his new son.

Lawal's career and marriage: the vicissitudes of merchant clientage

Our last portrait of a Tudun Wada resident focuses on the life of a petty trader, his relationship with his patron (*maigida*) and his preparations for marriage. Lawal's life reflects the circulation of labor between the informal and formal sectors and offers a grounded example of why industrial workers reported a preference for wage labor over clientage.

Lawal was born in 1950 in Sabon Birni, Sokoto State. His father was a cattle trader who once held a minor office at the district level of the Native Authority. Thus, Lawal may be seen as downwardly mobile from a minor office-holding family, which is not uncommon given the fecundity of office holders' households. When Lawal was 13, he traveled widely as a Koranic student visiting urban and rural centers of Koranic studies. After spending several months in the Birni as a Koranic student, he was offered the opportunity to work as a laborer for a kola nut trader who operated from Lagos. Lawal took the offer and worked in the kola producing areas of southern Nigeria until he decided to visit his father's brother, who resided in Tudun Wada. Without any visible opportunity to advance in independence in the kola trade, Lawal decided to stay in Kano. Initially he worked as a laborer for a Hausa-owned construction company. After being laid off during the rainy season, he worked as a laborer at a bed and furniture factory. After he was laid off there, he traveled back to southern Nigeria and worked for three months in a cement factory at Ibadan.

While Lawal was working in the furniture factory, he became acquainted with one of the major landlords of Tudun Wada, who was a trader in foodstuffs and lived in Bakin Zuo ward of the Birni. When he lost his job at the cement plant, Lawal returned to Tudun Wada and encountered the landlord, who was looking for someone to act as his rent collector. Lawal agreed to collect the rents, and the landlord agreed to help him become a trader in the unspecified future. Soon an opportunity appeared, when a kiosk that sold everyday commodities – food, coffee, tea, aspirin and soft drinks – was offered to Lawal for ₦40. He went to the landlord to ask for a loan and the landlord agreed. To be exact, Lawal never asked for the ₦40 loan; rather he went to greet the landlord and described his needs. Thus the landlord could reject or accept his request, but the tension between parties is reduced when the landlord or the patron can appear spontaneous in his generosity. Lawal had already proven to be trustworthy by faithfully collecting rents from the landlord's tenants. The relationship of client to patron allows the patron to exert control over the client in a wide variety of situations. From the perspective of the landlord, the initial loan need not be repaid as long as the client continues to pay him loyally in diffuse labor services. To purchase reliable and honest labor services in Nigeria would be expensive, but integrated within the patron-client relationship, labor services that are unmediated through a market on a fixed wage continue as long as the relationship of trust exists. Furthermore, the patron always has the leverage of calling in the loan. Since the landlord was also a wholesaler and retailer of imported and locally manufactured foodstuffs, accepting Lawal as his client enabled him to increase his volume of wholesale sales. At the same time, he could take advantage of Lawal's diffuse obligation to pay labor services to him.

In order to stock his kiosk, Lawal invested his savings of ₦15 and received an additional credit in stock from his patron. To save money and to protect his investment against theft, he gave up his rented room and slept on the floor of his kiosk at night. After a year of petty trading, his stock was worth over ₦100, but he profited little from the sales since he could only sell products that his patron distributed and also because it was necessary to give credit to Tudun Wada's wage workers. Given the precarious state of a wage laborer's finances, Lawal was often unable to collect past debts. Because there were several petty traders selling the same commodities within the same city block, largely through personal networks, the extension of credit was necessary in order to compete against other petty traders.

By acting as rent collector and overseeing his patron's interests in Tudun Wada, Lawal hoped that his patron would finance him in a larger venture such as a market stall at the Sabon Gari market. Meanwhile, his responsibilities for his patron increased as he became responsible for collecting the rent in 33 compounds owned by his patron, an increase of 23 over his original 10. Moreover, Lawal was unmarried at the age of 26, and after residing in Kano for 10 years, he was anxious to marry.

Marriage is a ubiquitous and consuming activity in Tudun Wada. Because there is a surplus of eligible men, especially during the dry season, recently divorced women appear regularly in the household of their kin, usually their senior brothers, and within a year many have remarried local men. On Sundays, factory workers and other laborers may be seen with their gowns draped over their bicycles courting eligible and carefully groomed divorcees who maintain proper decorum by staying close to the household of their kin while, at the same time, carrying out some public yet accepted activity such as selling oranges or sewing hats. Because they do not take on the recognizable lifestyle or the dress of prostitutes and because they do not cover their heads with a shawl, men know that they are neither prostitutes nor married women. If a factory worker or a laborer does not marry from the rural areas, usually his village, he probably cannot afford to pay the enormous expenses required in order to marry a maiden from the city. Instead, many lower their ideal expectations and search for an eligible young divorcee, in which case the marital expenses demanded by her family will be much lower. Still others, usually recent migrants to the city, discover that maidens raised in the city are too independent and too demanding to qualify for marriage. Hence they prefer to return to their village to marry local women who do not 'lack shame'. At the same time, examples abound of young girls who, when forced to marry older men of their parents' choice, soon abandon their new spouse in favor of a life as a 'free woman', where they are usually kept by a wealthy man as a mistress rather than becoming a bordello-style prostitute. Thus older men who risk a forced marriage with a maiden also risk public ridicule when they are rejected by increasingly independent urban-born maidens. For western readers, it is important to remember that in a society where men may have up to four wives, where divorce and remarriage are normal and where young women marry at fourteen or fifteen years of age, the sheer quantity of time devoted to arrangement, reunions and negotiating divorces by all parties is enormous. Let us examine Lawal's marriage to a working class maiden.

> Though most young men in Lawal's economic situation were forced to marry a girl from their village or an urban divorcee, Lawal continued to aspire to marry the ideal, an urban-born maiden. The following is his account of the courtship and negotiations that preceded his marriage to Amina. She was the daughter of an unskilled Fulani tannery worker who migrated to Tudun Wada from the close-settled zone about 15 years earlier. Lawal had observed Amina as she peddled the household products distributed by her mother to women in secluded compounds and also as she sold food as snacks to men relaxing in the streets of her ward. According to Lawal: 'One evening I was sitting here without kerosene for my lamp. It was when I first began collecting rents for Alhaji. Amina was moving from compound to compound selling her mother's kerosene in small bottles. I said, "Maiden, could you bring me some kerosene, but I have no money," Amina responded, "It does not matter, but I shall give you some anyway." Then I said that I liked her and wanted to marry her. And she agreed.'

At this time Amina was around thirteen years old, so that it would be normal in Tudun Wada for her to begin thinking of marriage. In practice, however, many courtships are aborted by the maiden's family or by the inability of the prospective groom to provide economic security for the maiden as evidenced by the quality of the gifts he presents to the maiden and her family. In theory, the gifts and expenses of bride-price are supposed to guarantee financial security for the maiden. Like all other expenses in Kano, however, both inflation and income inequality have increased the bride-price significantly and thus allow older and wealthy men to marry several maidens, much to the chagrin of younger and poorer men. While forced and family-arranged marriages are very common, there appears to be a growing awareness by the parents of Tudun Wada's daughters that family-arranged marriages are unstable and painful for all parties involved. Most fathers, for example, agree that the daughter or the son should be consulted before arranging a marriage, but consent is often achieved through familial persuasion and pressures that make it difficult for a fourteen-year-old to refuse overtly to follow her parents' wishes.

> After Amina reciprocated and agreed to marriage, Lawal felt shame about directly confronting her father, and instead asked a factory worker, Mallam Yahaya, to intervene on his behalf, as he was both a mallam and a friend of Amina's father. When Amina's father was informed of the proposed marriage, he told Lawal, 'Only death will prevent you from marrying each other since you both wish to marry'. Although not a modern man, he recognized the value of a love marriage. At this stage, Lawal, through a woman acting as an intermediary, gave Amina's family ₦40 as bride-price. It is understood that bride-price will be used to pay for outfitting a household. Lawal believed that the bride's family would pay for a bed, mattress, six bags of grain, one bag of rice, one bag of wheat and assorted household utensils. During the next festival of Id-el-Kabir, Lawal gave Amina jewelry, cosmetics, dishes, shoes, cloth and perfume, worth over ₦30. Furthermore, cash gifts had to be given to Amina's senior brothers and sisters as well as to her parents. Just prior to their marriage, at the festival of Id el-Fitr, Lawal gave Amina a watch, more household utensils, six yards of expensive lace cloth and assorted cosmetics. He expected to pay over ₦100 for marriage expenses, including a ram to be slaughtered by a mallam as part of the marriage ritual. Given Lawal's financial situation, the costs of the marriage caused him great anxiety and forced him to borrow funds from all of his friends and relatives. Moreover, he considers himself fortunate, as he reported that a similar marriage to the daughter of a wealthy trader costs over ₦600. Nevertheless, Amina and Lawal were married, and by 1978 Amina had borne a son and was expecting a second child at the age of 17.
>
> By 1978, Lawal's life had changed because he had sold his kiosk, ended his clientage with Alhaji and found work as a laborer for a small-scale industry, a woodshop owned by an Igbo entrepreneur. His relationship with Alhaji ended when the landlord accused him of spending rent collections to pay for the costs of his marriage. While Lawal denied the accusation, the landlord refused to stock his kiosk until he could account for his marriage payments.

Thus Lawal was forced to end trading and search for wage labor. Lawal's inability to move upward from petty trading to stall owner at the Sabon Gari market is typical of clients who lack capital or a close family relationship with their patron. By 1978, his family responsibilities required that he maintain a stable income from wage labor, so his aspiration for trading was more muted and instead he hoped to learn a skill from the woodworking business.

179

Summary

Space limitations do not allow additional ethnographic material to be presented. There are infinite variations in the way capitalist social relations articulate with precapitalist Islamic institutions, ideologies and practices, as seen in deviant practices such as spirit mediums (*bori*), the local drug culture, and the complexity of family life and the changing status of women. For example, the head of the local *bori* cult (pre-Islamic) announced that he was sending his daughter on *hajji*, yet no one felt any contradiction. Several examples exist of situations where women refuse to continue taking birth control pills procured by wage-laboring husbands because they need children to engage in petty commodity production. To be sure, there is an infinite number of empirical oucomes possible in a situation where semi-industrial capitalism articulates with a Muslim Hausa social formation. Class and nation are forming and shaping each other's mutual development in migrant areas such as Tudun Wada. And a new urban-born Muslim working class is being reproduced in this situation, one that is not descended from independent commodity producers but that has matured in the timing and discipline of the shift system of capitalist production. Let us examine the response of Muslim workers to participation in industrial capitalist production.

5

Industrial labor and the labor process: alienation, resistance and social mobility

WHY THE INDUSTRIAL PROLETARIAT?

If, as I have argued, Kano is in transition from mercantile to semi-industrial capitalism, then it is crucial to examine the structure, consciousness and action of the industrial proletariat. For, more than any other social category, the industrial proletariat is the unique product of industrial capitalism. And more than any other class fraction of the urban *leburori*, industrial workers are subordinated to the discipline and the production requirements of industrial capital. If one accepts the notion that industrial capitalist production undermines mercantile and precapitalist forms of production, exchange and consumption through the expansion of commodity relations, then the consciousness and behavior of the class fraction most subordinated to industrial capital should reflect the effect of these structural changes. For this reason, industrial workers merit serious analysis by scholars concerned with the capitalist transformation of peripheral capitalist societies.

It would be helpful to outline the questions and issues that form the subjects of this chapter. Initially, the abstract concept of industrial capital must be defined, delimited and described in its proper historical context. Questions here concern the origins of industrial capital, the role of state and foreign capital and the management style implemented by the owners of industrial capital. To be sure, my focus is on the structure, consciousness and action of industrial workers. But this raises questions about workers' adjustment and response to the conditions and activities required by industrial production. What are the expectations and moral standards held by Muslim Hausa-speaking workers when they enter the industrial labor process for the first time? How do these expectations condition their attitudes toward industrial wage labor, supervisors and management? To understand how workers develop a particular form of class consciousness and how they engage in class struggle, the actual *labor process* of each factory's production system must be described in detail. Only after comprehending the actual situation in the factory will workers' consciousness toward management, job security and social mobility be meaningful to the reader. And finally, what of questions regarding the permanence of this class fraction? How do opportunities for upward mobility for themselves or

181

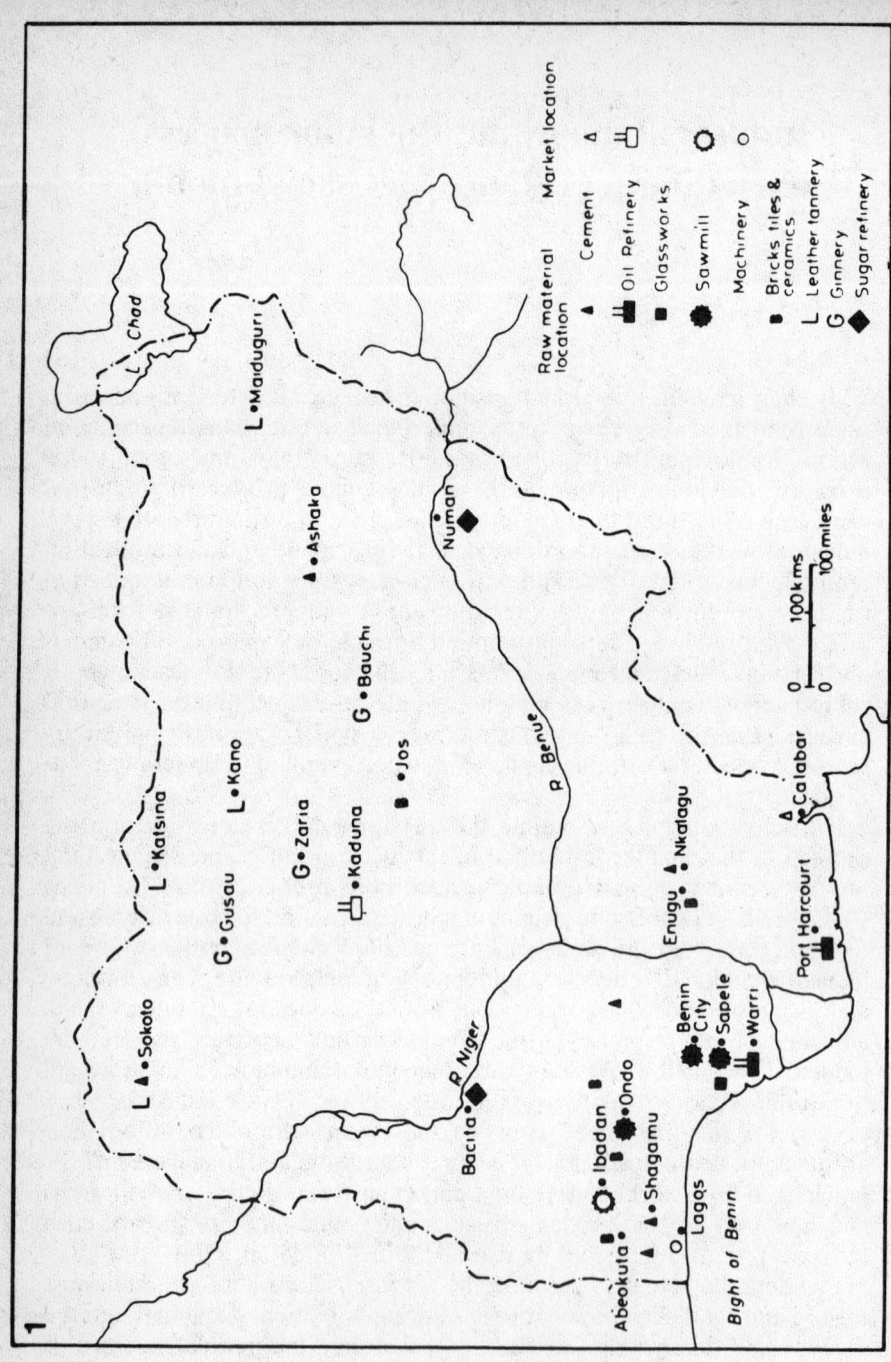

4. Location of plants

182

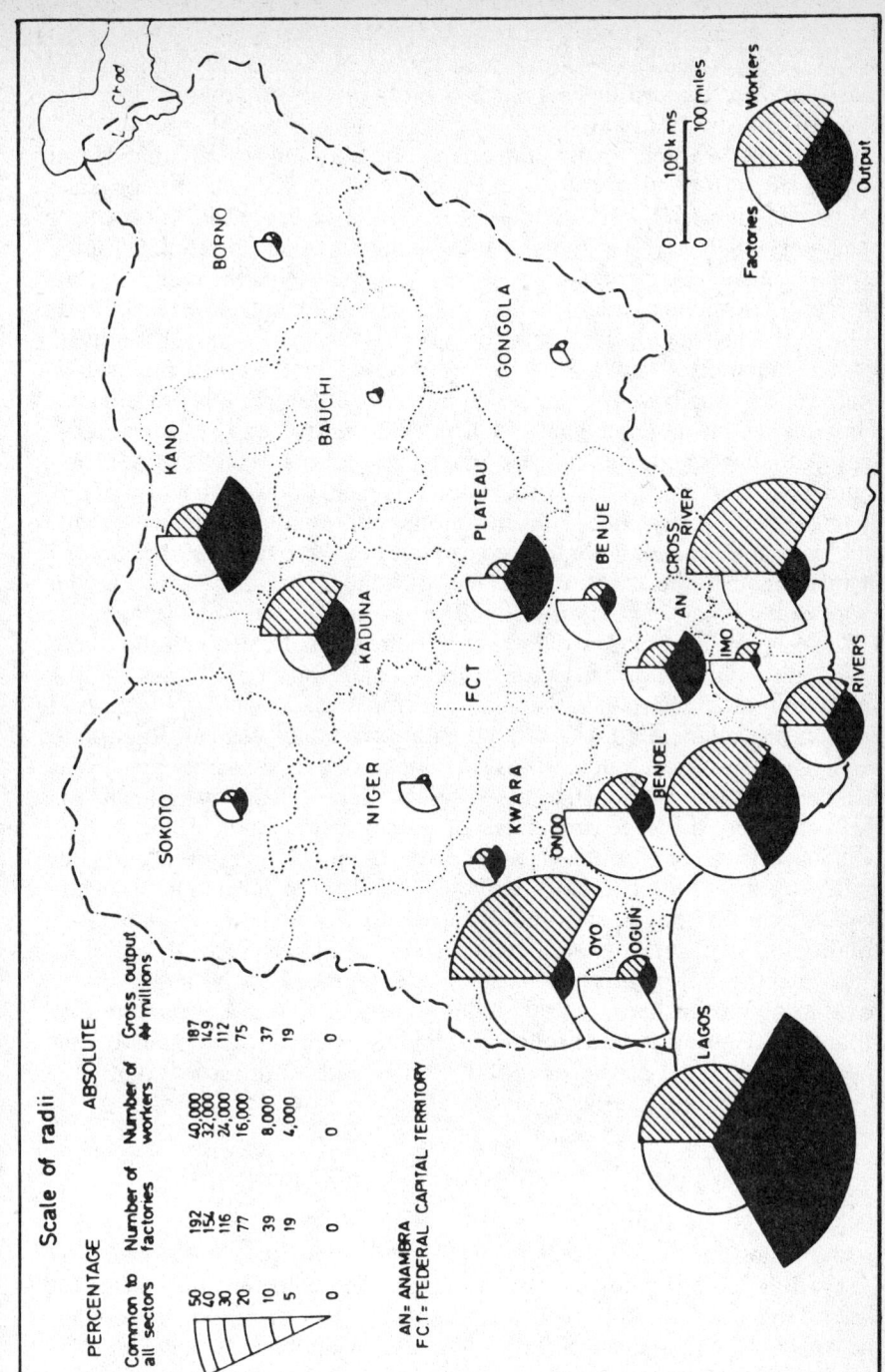

Scale of radii

	PERCENTAGE		ABSOLUTE	
	Common to all sectors	Number of factories	Number of workers	Gross output ₦ millions
50		192	40,000	187
40		154	32,000	149
30		116	24,000	112
20		77	16,000	75
10		39	8,000	37
5		19	4,000	19
0		0	0	0

AN= ANAMBRA
FCT= FEDERAL CAPITAL TERRITORY

5. Spatial pattern of industrial structure. Factories, workers and output

mobility through education for their sons affect their behavior and solidarity as a cohesive class fraction? Indeed, these are the classical questions that Marxist theorists and industrial sociologists have debated since the onset of industrialization.

As I argued earlier, industrial workers possess an autonomy that distinguishes them from other wage workers of the leburori. In order to produce for profit, industrial workers must relate to fixed capital in the form of machinery and raw materials, while remaining concentrated within a production site. Fixed capital must be automated by labor under a management-determined discipline that is designed to maximize the profitability of investment. Structurally, labor is always in an antagonistic relationship to fixed capital, for the cost of production or a new threat from competition usually results in the elimination of labor for more efficient labor-saving machinery. Thus, in order to survive and to accumulate capital, management must view labor as a cost of production, for labor costs stand in an inverse relation to profits. Hence, industrial workers are distinguished by discipline, concentration, subordination to management, and the relationship of labor to fixed capital. For these reasons, the concern of this chapter is to explain the effect of factors that are *internal* to the factory on workers' consciousness and behavior.

The relationship of industrial workers to the state also distinguishes them from state- and informal-sector workers and thus contributes to the autonomy of industrial workers as a distinct class fraction. Industrial workers are enumerated, taxed and regulated by state agencies. Rights and privileges of workers, such as pay, working conditions, safety provisions and pensions, are legally guaranteed by the state, a feature that contrasts them with less privileged members of the leburori. And, of course, the political activity of workers through trade unions is monitored and controlled by the state. Therefore, any analysis of class formation and class consciousness among Kano's industrial workers must take account of the conditions established by the state as well as the manner in which the state intervenes in the relationship of labor and capital. Finally, although the relationship of the state, capital and labor during a period of intense class struggle is the subject of the following chapter, it should be noted here that the legal rights and privileges of industrial workers are rarely granted to them without intense struggle on the part of the workers.

EXPLAINING WORKERS' CONSCIOUSNESS: ALIENATION AND THE
INDUSTRIAL LABOR PROCESS

In the following pages I shall take the reader into the world of a first-generation Muslim industrial proletariat as they labor in three factories. Accordingly, the concepts of *alienation* and the *labor process* are seminal to the analysis that is advanced here. The use of the concept *labor process* refers to the mental and physical activities performed by workers, activities undertaken under the concrete conditions of social life through which workers use their creative powers to act upon nature in order to create objects of value.[1] The concept of labor process involves *practical* and *relational* aspects. Thus, in the context of industrial capitalist production, the labor process refers to a worker's practical activity and his use of tools and machinery to produce commodities for sale in a market. The relational aspect refers to the social relations entered into necessarily by a worker in order to perform a practical activity. Social relations are *horizontal* if they involve interaction and cooperation with other wage-laboring proletarians, or alternatively, social relations may be *vertical* if they involve interaction with representatives of capital, who are usually supervisors and managers. Simply stated, class solidarity is generated by horizontal social relations among workers who share common activities and a common vertical relationship to representatives of industrial capital. Just as horizontal relations generate class solidarity, vertical relations generate class conflict which takes expression as class struggle between capital and labor.

Why, a skeptic might ask, does the vertical aspect of the labor process of industrial capitalist production usually lead to class conflict? Herein lies the unique feature of industrial capitalist production as compared to historically prior forms of production such as handicraft or peasant production. As contrasted to the latter two forms of production, where the direct producer controls his own labor process and owns the means of production (e.g., tools, raw materials and building), the labor process of industrial capitalist production is one where the representative of capital directly intervenes in the production process so as to organize, monitor and reorganize the activities of workers, who do not own the means of production. Unlike earlier forms of production, such as household handicraft production, no mutually recognized moral relationship exists between management and labor, for the manager merely purchases the laborer's creative potential to produce commodities for a fixed period of time. Labor is a commodity, one that is managed and reorganized by management in a manner similar to other commodities in order to reduce costs and thereby maximize profits. Hence, since the laborer does not own the means by which he produces commodities, even the most naive worker soon recognizes the insecurity of his situation, which often leads to class conflict as representatives of capital and wage laborers struggle both subtly and overtly to gain advantage at the work site. Finally, it is important to realize that the struggle between capital and labor cannot be successfully mediated by extraordinary personal or moral attributes on the part of management. To avoid reducing labor or to postpone introducing labor-saving machinery only risks the future viability of the enterprise in the face of competition from producers who do manipulate labor in order to maximize production for profit. In this sense, owners of capital are not free from the pressure to grow and to accumulate, a factor Marx notes as an expression of alienation.

In addition to direct management control, intensified commodity rela-

185

tions and subordination to the demands of capitalist efficiency, industrial wage laborers are required to perform fragmented tasks that not only allow the employment of cheaper, unskilled labor but also eliminate the potential power of artisans and other skilled laborers to exert any political control over their working lives. Unskilled, routinized, fragmented tasks under the strict control of management are typical of industrial workers' activities during the initial stages of industrialization. What effect does participation in such a labor process have on the worker? Here it will be argued that the Marxian concept of alienation has great explanatory power, but only if it is applied to the historically specific social formation in which Muslim, Hausa-speaking workers are located.[2]

Marx assumes that human nature is inherently creative. In the production of material life and in the sexual reproduction of the human species, human beings realize their creative potential. For Marx, purposive human activity (e.g., labor) and the social relations involved in a historically specific form of creative activity structure the consciousness and behavior of humans in a manner that directly reflects the degree of free, creative expression permissible in the performance of that activity. Simply stated, consciousness is determined to a significant degree by activity and social relations. When the free, creative activity of human beings is thwarted, subordinated or otherwise estranged from the control of the individual, through slavery, patriarchy, serfdom or wage labor, an individual becomes *alienated* from his/her creative potential and from communal relations with other human beings.

For workers engaged in the activity of industrial capitalist production, therefore, alienation is a subjective state that occurs when workers are: estranged from fulfilling the potential of their natural creative powers; separated from the final product of their labor; denied the intrinsic creative pleasure of organizing and completing a product; forced into hostile relations with fellow workers who compete for limited employment opportunities; and driven to antagonistic relations with supervisors and representatives of capital with whom they must cooperate while, at the same time, recognizing the opposition of their interests. The conditions whereby free producers voluntarily agree to submit to proletarianization do not come easily. Therefore, through a multiplicity of methods (enclosures, debt peonage, market forces or enormous material imbalance between regions), a supply of labor emerges that is separated from the means of production or, alternatively, is unable to fulfill a historically relative moral standard of material existence. Under this condition a worker must sell to a capitalist his/her creative ability, which takes the commodity form of labor power. In such a situation, one observes the ultimate alienation of a person's creative potential and human essence. For, once proletarianized, an individual worker's labor is useful and valued *only* if that worker is successful in finding a capitalist who is willing to purchase his/her labor power. Without a willing purchaser, an individual's creative potential is essentially worthless.

Alienation with an 'alien' system of production

So far, the concepts of alienation and the labor process have been discussed in an abstract and generalized sense so as to emphasize the necessary, universal structural features of capitalist production. But all instances of capitalist production occur within a particular historical situation, marked by cultural expectations and practices which shape workers' perceptions of industrial wage labor. What then are the expectations that Muslim Hausa-speaking workers bring into the factory when they accept industrial wage labor? Does it matter that, in contrast to the experience of Western Europe, where capitalist production evolved from the internal dissolution of feudal social relations, capitalist production was introduced into Kano from outside, by aliens who earlier had violently conquered a Muslim society?

To address the latter question first, one must emphasize that Hausa workers perceive the discipline and labor process of capitalist production as inherently alien and associated with European political and economic domination of their society. This is not to say that workers necessarily perceive employment by Hausa capitalists as preferable to work in European firms. Rather, the social organization of production, the relationship between superordinate and subordinate, the timing of daily activity and the relationship between workers from diverse ethnic origins are perceived and labeled as *aikin bature* or 'European work'. For example, a worker employed by a Hausa farmer and who works according to a Muslim daily time concept and receives food in addition to wages is called *aikin kodago*. Hence, unlike in Western Europe, where representatives of capital and labor usually but not always believed in the same Christian religion, shared the same ethnicity and language and employed a technology that emerged from the internal processes of a common society, Muslim Hausa-speaking workers are thrust into a set of social relations where the technologies employed are externally 'inserted' and the language spoken (English) is one they associate with alien rather than indigenous institutions.

Given a situation of dependent industrialization, where most raw material inputs, all capital goods and machinery and most of the management personnel are imported from the world economy, one encounters a situation where the world division of labor merges with and reinforces the social division of labor in the labor process of capitalist production. If the units of analysis in the world division of labor are nation-states and regions, and the corresponding units of analysis in the division of labor of capitalist production are classes, then it is possible to speak of a conjunctural situation where nation overlaps and reinforces class and where national consciousness reinforces class consciousness. As Chapter Four illustrated, for the Muslim Hausa-speaking workers of Kano, Islamic national consciousness is the broadest and most effective ethno-national identity. Thus, though rooted in the communal identity of a precapitalist social formation, Islamic national consciousness is stimulated and strengthened by reaction to the dependent position of the Islamic region of northern Nigeria within the world division of labor. Hence, unlike the corresponding situation of Western Europe, religious and national bonds of solidarity reinforce class cohesion among Kano's Muslim Hausa-speaking workers. And this difference creates the possibility that Islamic nationalist consciousness may be mobilized as a weapon by conscious workers to struggle against the alienation and exploitation experienced at the workplace.

Let us consider now the moral standards employed by workers to evaluate industrial labor. The first standard draws upon norms governing the relationship between household head (*maigida*) and client (*yaro*), a relationship that involves mutually understood rights and duties for both parties. The household is a ubiquitous form of elementary social organization governing production and consumption in Hausa society.[3] The term *gida* (house), for example, is commonly used to describe factories or European work in factories, e.g., *gidan bature* (European houses). Obligations of the client to the head of the household are diffuse: loyalty and respect for the household head are assumed, and interpersonal relations are conducted without violence, insults or public humiliation of the client. In return, the client expects to have his minimal material needs provided for and, if blessed with success, to share in the good fortune of the household. After an initial period when trust is established, a client may aspire to and receive capital and training from his patron, to enable him to trade or to produce on behalf of the patron. Above all, the client expects to be treated with respect and dignity and to receive his minimum material necessities, provided he maintains the dependent posture of a client. To be sure, this is an idealized description of a clientage relationship, yet one that workers not only carry with them into the factory but, initially at least, use as a standard against which to evaluate treatment from supervisors and management.

Islam demands that clients faithfully and honestly serve their masters and that masters provide for and justly treat their clients. Patrons are expected to encourage their clients to practice Islam and to allow time for the performance of ritual prayer and for family obligations associated with birth, marriage, death and mourning. All this conforms to the Hausa notion of household relations, and indeed, the two have influenced each other for centuries.

Yet when injustice is perceived to be inflicted on a client, the solutions prescribed by the two standards are radically different. The norms of the household relationship counsel the client to be patient, to withdraw, or to ask his patron to arrange for a new position, sometimes with a new patron. Islam, by contrast, encourages collective solidarity among Muslims in order to correct injustices and to introduce reforms according to Muslim practice. In fact, a believer has an obligation to rebel against un-Islamic practices when peaceful methods fail. True, urban and educated workers are more likely to interpret Islam in a militant fashion, but within rural communities mallams and *gardawa* also provide leadership against injustice.

188

When one refers to alienated labor and when one interprets workers' subjective evaluations of industrial labor, it is important to bear in mind the household and Islamic standards of evaluation that are consciously or unconsciously employed by a first-generation industrial proletariat. Moreover, because the industrial system of production is perceived as alien as well as alienating, one should look for workers to employ Islamic concepts as tools to wage class struggle against representatives of capital. Again, such standards are external to the labor process of capitalist production. Yet, if one pursues a dogmatic analysis of class formation, relying solely on the labor process in order to explain class formation and class consciousness, one obscures the reality of the working class experience and the way in which precapitalist standards continue to articulate within the consciousness of that class fraction that is the sole creation of industrial capitalism. Let us examine the nature, origins and management style of industrial capital that controls Kano's industrial working class.

INDUSTRIAL CAPITAL: OWNERSHIP PATTERNS, TECHNICAL LEVEL AND MANAGEMENT STYLE

As discussed in Chapter One, Kano's industrial sector emerged after the Second World War and evolved from the investment of merchants' capital, both Hausa and alien. The transition to industrialization occurred as merchant capitalists sought to supply their market with locally produced consumer goods. Until recently, most state capital was invested in enterprises managed by entrepreneurial, as distinct from bureaucratically-organized, capitalists. Again, for the reasons outlined in Chapter Two, the petroleum boom brought a dramatic increase in the role of multinational corporate capital in the manufacturing sector, especially after 1975. Yet, with some exceptions, such as the Fiat assembly plant, Kano's commercial origins have left their mark on the structure and orientation of Kano's industrial sector. Most manufacturing enterprises process raw materials, such as leather, groundnuts, foodstuffs and textiles, or produce light consumer goods for sale in the regional market. Hence, Kano's industrial sector lacks intermediate or heavy industries and the skilled working class that is associated with such industries, as well as a significant state capitalist presence.

The technical backwardness of the industrial base complements the low educational levels achieved by the indigenous members of the labor force. Predictably, this situation creates a shortage of skilled and managerial personnel, who in turn are recruited from the southern states or from overseas. Compared to other industrial centers like Kaduna or Lagos, Kano's industries are labor-intensive, and the value added at Kano is less than one encounters in more capital-intensive centers such as Kaduna.[4] Most of the industrial inputs and all of the capital goods in the form of machinery are imported, though once the petroleum-product pipelines

Table 5.1 *Distribution of equity capital in Nigerian industries (1975)*[a]

State	Private Nigerian	Private non-Nigerian	State government	Federal government	Total
Lagos	40,674,229	112,909,660	11,489,594	31,303,000	196,376,483
	20.7%	57.5%	5.9%	15.9%	100.0%
	[49.8%]	[65.5%]	[19.1%]	[31.0%]	[47.3%]
Kaduna	6,549,521	20,291,198	7,724,068	8,189,844	42,754,631
	15.3%	47.5%	18.1%	19.2%	100.0%
	[8.0%]	[11.8%]	[12.8%]	[8.1%]	[10.3%]
Bendel	5,885,260	4,522,878	7,569,352	20,398,825	38,376,315
	15.3%	11.8%	19.7%	53.2%	100.0%
	[7.2%]	[2.6%]	[12.6%]	[20.2%]	[9.2%]
Kano	9,976,613	15,243,225	2,882,719	3,877,323	31,979,880
	31.2%	47.7%	9.0%	12.1%	100.0%
	[12.2%]	[8.8%]	[4.8%]	[3.8%]	[7.7%]
Total	81,727,541	172,481,970	60,196,341	101,089,971	415,518,023
Nigeria	19.7%	41.5%	14.5%	24.3%	100.0%
	[100.0%]	[100.0%]	[100.0%]	[100.0%]	[100.0%]

[a] Source: World Bank and Federal Office of Statistics

reach Kano and once the Nigerian steel industry begins operation, it is likely that the patterns of dependence upon imported inputs will change.

From this perspective, Kano appears as a classic entrepreneurial capitalist manufacturing center where the Asian, Levantine and indigenous industrial bourgeoisie first accumulated capital in the commercial sector and then invested in industrial production. Most indigenous investors remain merchant-industrialists with extensive investments in wholesale trade, construction, real estate and transportation, rather than becoming specialized solely in industrial manufacturing. Notwithstanding these limitations, it is important to emphasize that the growth potential for industry and for indigenous capital accumulation is enormous, due to the size of the regional market, the control exerted over this market by Kano businessmen, and the potential of Kano as a food processing and agricultural service center.

The distinctive entrepreneurial capitalist character of Kano's industries (1975) becomes apparent when one examines the distribution of equity capital in manufacturing industry across selected states of Nigeria. Table 5.1 presents manufacturing equity by state and by origins of capital. Each cell in the table contains three descriptive statistics regarding a source of industrial capital for each state. The first statistic (in descending order) reports the absolute amount of capital (e.g., Kano – ₦9,976,613). The next statistic reports the proportion of an individual state's equity that is controlled by a particular branch or national origin of capital: for example, in the case of Kano, 31.2 percent of all capital is controlled by private Nigerian investors. The last statistic, presented in brackets, reflects the column percentage, that is, the proportion of a particular sector or origin of capital found in a state against the column total for all states of Nigeria. In the case of Kano, for example, the aforementioned absolute amount of capital invested by private Nigerians represents 12.2 percent of all private capital held by Nigerians in Nigeria's manufacturing industries.

The data from Table 5.1 indicate that the largest share of all Nigerian equity is held by private foreign investors, i.e., 41.5 per cent, followed by federal government and private Nigerian investors. Note that most foreign capital is not represented by international firms but rather by Levantine and Asian owners. Lagos State, a congested center of import substitution, possesses over 47 percent of all Nigerian investment, a disproportionate share that reflects its external dependence and political centrality. Within Lagos, private foreign capital surpasses the national average in that over 57 percent of capital investment is controlled by foreign investors. When one compares the statistical profile of Kaduna with that of Kano, the relative weight of the Nigerian state versus Nigerian private capital in Kaduna is apparent. Not surprisingly, since Kaduna lacked a precolonial bourgeoisie and since it was founded as an administrative center for the Northern Region, state rather than private capital is predominant in Kaduna's industries.

Consistent with the relative strength of both alien and indigenous mercantile capital, Kano possesses the largest amount of private Nigerian capital invested in manufacturing industries after Lagos. This figure is half again as large as the amount invested by private Nigerians at Kaduna. Furthermore, the relative proportion of indigenous private capital is greater at Kano than in any other state, i.e., 31.2 percent as against 20.7 percent for Lagos State. And finally, while Kano represents only 7.7 percent of all equity invested in Nigeria, it represents 12.2 percent of all private Nigerian equity. (Here it is assumed that 'fronting' for foreign investors by Nigerian businessmen is distributed equally across all states.) Bendel State has been included for comparison because, as the center of the state-dominated petroleum industry, it illustrates the overwhelming importance of federal capital investment in the petroleum industry.

To continue with the analysis of Kano, one is struck by the strength of private capitalist investment, both Nigerian and foreign (together reaching nearly 79 percent), and the relative absence of state capitalist investments. The statistical data illustrate the competitive and entrepreneurial character of industrial production in Kano. It will be recalled from Chapter One that Hausa merchant-industrialists first invested their capital, together with state capital, in a textile firm as early as 1952. Accordingly, one should bear these statistics in mind when the description of the labor process of industrial production in three selected firms is made, for managerial orientation toward labor reflects the entrepreneurial capitalist ideology implied by these statistics. Entrepreneurial capitalism, whether Asian, Levantine or Hausa, is paternalistic at best and highly exploitative at worst.

191

The number of industrial workers employed in Kano State was estimated to be 50,000 in 1980, of which approximately 40,000 were employed in urban Kano. The increase is considerable from 1966 when the figure was only 7,659.[5] According to official records, during 1978 there were 1,069 manufacturing industries in Kano State employing five or more employees, of which 470 were located in urban Kano.[6] When one examines the breakdown of firms by number of employees, one learns that 529 of the 1,069 firms enumerated employ less than ten workers; 143 employ between fifty and one hundred workers; 85 employ over one hundred; and, within the latter figure, 5 firms employ 1,000 workers or more. All evidence suggests that the larger firms are located in urban Kano and, further, that many of the smaller employers of labor are workshops rather than modern large-scale industries.

Before moving to an analysis of micro-level processes of urban capitalist development, mention should be made of Kano's industrial sector as I have observed its evolution for over a decade. Empirically, as Hoogvelt and others have pointed out, Kano's industrial sector contains many of the features of a dependent industrial sector: reliance on imported capital goods and inputs; dependence upon foreign personnel for skilled and managerial positions; and a preference on the part of many, but certainly not all, industrial capitalists for 'fronting' and portfolio investment rather than active management of the production process.[7] Nevertheless, over the decade both the level of technique and the scale of production have become increasingly sophisticated, such that it is clear that the transfer of modern, productive technology has occurred as compared to earlier periods. Even if one accepts the 'underdevelopment' hypothesis, Nigerian capitalists have increased their financial control to a degree that is unrivaled by any comparable African state. While the indigenous bourgeoisie may favor state subsidies, an increasing proportion of merchant capitalists are investing in industry or are actively considering such investments. Regarding the technical underdevelopment of Kano's merchant-industrialists, it is expected that this situation will be remedied somewhat by their investment in modern technical and managerial education, a vocation which was observed to be widespread among their sons.

THE LABOR PROCESS OF CAPITALIST PRODUCTION IN THREE FACTORIES

With the concepts of alienation, the labor process and the structure of industrial capital in mind, let us now turn to the micro-level processes within the three firms from which the sample (N=140) was drawn. Each firm's production process and management style will be described in sufficient detail so that the subjective responses of workers to the labor process will be recognizable and meaningful to the reader. Note that in the following chapter, which focuses on class struggle, these same firms will remain the site of analysis. After describing the labor process of production in each firm, the subjective evaluations of industrial labor by workers employed in the firm will be presented. Throughout this analysis the intention is to focus on the unique effect exerted on workers' consciousness by participation in the labor process of capitalist production. Nevertheless, despite the focus on industrial workers within the labor process, secondary factors such as Islamic affiliation or urban social processes will be integrated into the analysis whenever appropriate.

Though space does not permit a detailed discussion of management styles, the origins of industrial capital and the economic history of Kano determined that the managerial style of industrialists and their managers be entrepreneurial rather than bureaucratically rational.[8] Rather than seeking to cope with the motivation of workers and to eliminate non-productive and sometimes costly abuses of labor, especially by supervisors, the entrepreneurial style of management treats labor as an undifferentiated, unskilled mass, one in which supply exceeds demand and which is deemed unworthy of investment in skill acquisition. Further, as opposed to the bureaucratically rational style, where management assumes direct control, Kano's entrepreneurial style allows supervisors great latitude toward workers. Of course, the entrepreneurial style also allows supervisors to exercise arbitrary power over dismissals, to extract bribes from naive rural-born workers and to undermine workers' attempts to form trade unions. While entrepreneurial styles of management accept supervisory control, and although individual managers may intervene against a supervisor's decision on behalf of a worker in a paternalistic and idiosyncratic fashion, most of the discipline and abuses practiced by supervisors neither increase labor productivity nor accelerate the accumulation of capital. Hence, from the perspective of bureaucratically rational management, much of the supervisory abuse of labor is non-productive and thus irrational from the point of view of increasing the efficiency of labor. But since the majority of Kano's industrialists – Asian, Levantine and Hausa – have no experience in bureaucratically rational production organizations, instead having entered manufacturing from the commercial sector where entrepreneurial styles of management prevailed, they have little interest or sympathy for the industrial relations policies currently introduced by international firms. Kano's class structure and the character of class struggle in the industrial sector therefore reflect the entrepreneurial origins of its industrialists. Let us now turn to the first of three firms selected for in-depth interviewing from the original sample of the five largest employers of labor during 1972.

Factory A: the production of household utensils

Though equity ownership in this factory is divided between the state and a Levantine entrepreneur, management is determined solely by the entrepreneur. Supervisory personnel are Asian and maintain a close personal

193

relationship with the factory manager. Production began in 1958. The production process calls for imported scrap metal to be punched by machines into various utensil shapes in a machine shed. After being dipped in a chemical solution, they are baked in ovens located in a second building. Finished products are taken from the decorating section to warehouses whence they are marketed. Technology is simple: the factory uses second-hand machinery for punching metal; ovens for baking on the enamel finish are constructed on-site from available materials. Inputs in the form of scrap metal, chemical coatings and paint are imported, though these can easily be produced within Nigeria by steel and petrochemical industries currently under construction.

Utensils are produced first by a machine-tending labor process whereby a worker guides a sheet of rolled steel under an automatic punching machine. Then the pieces of flat metal, which vary in size according to the utensil to be produced, are molded into a particular utensil's shape by a second worker operating a molding machine. A third worker grinds an edge around the punched-out utensil, and after dipping, it is sent to the firing section. Porters carry the semi-finished products from one machine operator to another. For workers in the machine shed, the labor process is determined solely by the machine. Labor is paced by the machine. The noise prohibits communication between workers, and the labor process isolates a worker from any other worker performing the same task. Workers relate to the machine, not to each other. Throughout the 1970s, workers wore no protective glasses, and the machines had no safety devices. Consequently, workers frequently were disfigured, often losing fingers or sustaining eye injuries.

Class integration through the labor process

Most of the 500 to 900 workers employed at the utensil factory work in the fire and decorating sections. In the fire section, a locally constructed petroleum furnace with an open hearth is central to the process of production. A work group of approximately eight workers takes the utensils from the machine section and processes them. The utensils are dipped in several chemical and paint mixtures, then dried for a minute or more on racks resting on masonry extensions of the furnace. Depending on the demand for products, one or two workers perform each task. Finally, the pans are brought from the furnace extension to a 'U'-shaped rack near the open hearth which lies in reach of the fireman. The fireman stands in front of the open hearth with a ten-foot-long, two-pronged fork, which he uses to lift the dried utensils from the waiting rack and insert them into the furnace. After dipping the fork in a container of water and pausing for a minute, he reaches into the mouth of the furnace, placing his face within inches of the furnace opening, to remove the baked utensils, which have turned white. These he places on a metal table to his left, where a worker using two forks cools them, inspects them for flaws and stacks them in an adjacent area.

194

From there, porters take them to the decoration section or, in some instances, directly to the warehouse. Demand for utensils determines the number of furnaces and firework groups employed.

In contrast to the machine section, the labor process of the fire section requires constant cooperation between workers as they move utensils through the dipping, drying and baking stages of production. Communication among workers is intense and meaningful because conversation is possible and because the speed and intensity of the production process is controlled by the workers themselves. In Kano's arid climate, where temperatures reach 120°F in the shade during the hot season, the heat generated by the furnace makes working in the fire section bearable only for short periods. Accordingly, the fireman changes every hour and the remainder of the crew every two or three hours. Bonds of solidarity generated by the cooperation of the labor process, moreover, are reinforced by rest periods when teams of workers rest and socialize together. The physical deprivation of working in the fire section, without gloves, masks or protection of any type (at least during the first years of the decade) resulted in severe burns and alleged stomach illnesses. Taken together, the cooperative labor process, the collective rest breaks and the physical deprivation of the fire section created cohesive work groups and a subjective identity as 'fireworkers'. The distinctiveness of the 'fireworkers' was sharpened further by a rotating twelve-hour work shift, which isolated workers from other factory workers on the eight-hour shift, as well as from non-industrial employees. The fire section represents a clear example of a labor process that creates horizontal social solidarity among members.

In the decoration section the labor process was individualized and controlled by the worker. Here workers stencilled recently baked utensils with colorful designs. Each product was completed by a single worker, so that the division of labor was limited, but communication between workers was relatively easy. The only disadvantage came from the fumes emitted from the paint spray guns. Compared to the machine and fire sections, few workers were employed in decoration.

Labor and capital: relations with management

Among the workers of Kano, the management of the utensil factory developed a reputation for labor exploitation: verbally abusing workers, using daily paid workers in order to avoid paying minimum wage rates, and neglecting safety precautions. More than in any other factory, there was a strict demarcation between the Asian supervisors and the Nigerian supervisors. The former were personal clients of the factory management, so Nigerians never rose above the rank held by Asian supervisors. Unlike the Levantine supervisors and managers, the Asians never learned to speak Hausa with any degree of fluency. When these supervisors corrected or disciplined Nigerian workers, therefore, they used abusive and humiliating

195

language, in part because they were unfamiliar with the meaning of the Hausa curses used to correct workers.[9] Hence industrial work that was objectively dangerous, exhausting and poorly paid was exacerbated further by abusive and insensitive supervisors.

To be sure, the backwardness of managerial style was not constant throughout the decade, but reforms were short-lived. The problem was that the management had a short time perspective without any commitment to training Nigerian labor. Unfortunately, Nigerian directors who represented state capital were not involved in actual management of production. As long as it was more profitable in the short run to employ alien supervisors and to exploit indigenous labor, reforms could be postponed indefinitely. One of the ironies of this firm was that state capital was accumulated from marketing board funds, which represent forced savings of peasant producers. Hence, the surplus extracted from peasants during one phase of capital accumulation confronted and exploited the same peasants, or their sons, as a hostile force in the form of industrial capital during a subsequent period. This factory has remained under the same ownership and management throughout the 1970s.

Factory B: a modern textile factory

The textile firm was founded during the same period as the utensil factory. Its equity was shared by state, Levantine and international interests, but the controlling interest and the management were entrepreneurial, at least until the latter half of the 1970s when the firm was purchased by a French multinational. In 1972, it employed 1,000 to 2,000 workers. The technology and division of labor were significantly more advanced than in the utensil factory. But here too, technical and highly skilled work was still, after more than a decade, in the hands of foreign technicians. Supervisory positions, however, were completely Nigerianized, and some skilled positions, such as loom repairers, were also filled by Nigerians. Foreign technicians were Asians whose services were contracted from the supplier of industrial equipment and who rotated with others in six-month shifts.

The labor process of production is typical of a weaving mill. (By the end of the decade a spinning mill was added by the French multinational.) Thread is taken from spools and rewound for weaving in a winding section, where workers tend winding machines. The winding section acts as the training place for raw recruits because the task requires no skill. Workers are able to communicate in this section. A tiny section prepares the beams of thread through which weavers weave designs. Most of the factory's labor is employed in the weaving section. Here hundreds of workers are concentrated in one shed, where each tends one loom. Technique varies according to the specifications of the product. In 1972, since most workers were illiterate, beads were used to count the number of lines of thread used to create a given design. Porters carry the rolls of woven cloth to the inspection section, where several teams of workers inspect the product for flaws. Inspected and approved cloth is then processed in a raising section. Finally, cloth is either printed with designs or sent directly to the finishing section, where it is cut, edged and labelled for shipping to customers.

Weaving is the section where most workers are employed and where the strictest supervision of labor occurs. Excluding the managers, there are five supervisory levels here: the standard three – shift foreman, section supervisor, and headman – plus two additional levels. If a weaver fails to meet his quota, or continues to make errors, he is dismissed; and, by the same measure, experienced workers who surpass their quota receive a bonus. Workers view the weaving section with some ambivalence: on the one hand, with a properly functioning loom, it is possible to increase earnings significantly by surpassing the quota; on the other hand, it is a position involving great insecurity because any error affords supervisors and foremen the opportunity to dismiss a worker in order to 'sell' the position to a new recruit. While each worker tends his loom, the noise and intensity of production do not allow for extensive communication between workers, though it is possible for brief conversations to occur.

The remaining sections are not as intensely monitored as the weaving section. The laboring activity is not as isolated nor as intense, nor are the opportunities for rewards and dismissal so dependent upon production. Winding, for example, only requires that a worker monitor a thread-winding machine, during which time he may converse with other workers. The task is so simple that error is easily avoided. Inspection has a system in which workers inspect in teams and then work individually to repair the flaws found in the cloth. They are allowed to talk as long as production continues at an average rate. Unlike in weaving, no machine paces their activity. Moreover, the section is small, so that workers may develop a personal relationship with their supervisor, who also weighs and records production. In the raising section, the cloth is processed by machines in order to create an attractive finish. Workers tend and monitor continuously operating machines under a headman who sometimes fills in for workers during breaks. A foreign technician acts as the section supervisor and is responsible for repairing the machines, though minor repairs are made by the headman. Despite the dust and lint which workers are forced to breathe in this section, the absence of harsh supervisors and the opportunity for workers to feed cloth into the machine at their own pace creates a comparatively attractive work site for unskilled workers. Since the headmen are involved in the labor process, close affective ties develop, and a rotating credit association (*adashi*) among members of this section has endured for several years.

The finishing section offers neither bonuses nor the opportunity to learn skilled work. And yet it was selected as an ideal place to work by many workers. Why? The labor process is very diversified: some workers cut cloth, others operate sewing machines that edge the final product, and still others pack and prepare the product for marketing. Ecologically, the section is physically isolated from the shift supervisor, the personnel manager and the factory manager. Moreover, workers are able to sit down on benches and converse while performing their tasks. All of these conditions allow workers to develop a sense of solidarity among themselves and to negotiate a personal relationship with the section supervisor without fear of intervention by the shift supervisor. Hence, these factors allow workers to exert some control over their environment and to negotiate conditions with the supervisor. If one views factory work as a closed mobility system, as most do, then finishing offers a secure haven in an insecure occupation, one that is comparatively unalienated.

Management: the absence of bureaucratic rationality

During the period in which the labor process was observed and the workers interviewed, prior to the firm's purchase by the French multinational in 1974, the high level of technical organization in the factory constrasted sharply with the backward management style. On one hand, the firm possessed one of Kano's most modern physical plants, as well as the outward symbols of bureaucratic rationality: distinctly colored uniforms for each supervisory rank; posted warnings and precautions against fire; facilities for workers' dining; and the strictest regard for bureaucratic details such as shift scheduling, overtime and time cards. But the technical and bureaucratic features of production were not applied to the management of labor. For example, the factory manager intervened personally into the duties of his subordinates, often using abusive language. The latter usually responded obsequiously to his personal demands. Further, when workers were laid off without regard for seniority, they appealed to him personally, and some were reinstated. A rigid system of discipline prevailed: workers were punished by not being allowed to work if they arrived a minute or two late; they were required to stand by the machines waiting to receive a metal pass from their group supervisor before they could go to the toilet. Workers despised this last practice because there were not enough passes in large sections such as weaving and, most importantly, because they bitterly resented the indignity associated with asking permission for the opportunity to perform a natural function. The management also refused to allow workers to pray at 2 p.m., and instead forced them to wait until the end of their 3 p.m. shift. Nigerian supervisors and the Nigerian personnel manager verbally abused workers by publicly humiliating them and by demanding bribes for employment. More than any other firm, workers at this factory reported paying bribes to their supervisors, both to obtain work and to retain jobs during downturns in the business cycle. Trade unions were repressed until 1975. Worse still, the supervisors intimidated workers, especially commuters and other naive rural recruits, by making themselves leaders of a defunct union without a proper election and demanding bogus payments from workers as union dues. These extortions continued even with the knowledge of the management. When asked about the practice, the factory manager said it could not be stopped and that it was 'traditional' for supervisors to demand bribes for jobs.[10] The problem, of course, is that tolerance of this practice created an incentive for supervisors to dismiss workers without reason, so they could then enrich themselves by selling the jobs to new recruits.[11] This is a costly and irrational use of labor. Thus the entrepreneurial style of management at Factory B dominated, exploited and abused labor in so many instances that production suffered in the long run from unnecessary dismissal of workers and the failure to encourage workers to learn more productive skills.

Factory C: a Nigerian textile factory

The final subject of the sample is an indigenously owned and managed factory located in the Fagge-Birni industrial area. Like the two previous firms, state capital was important in founding the firm (1952), but ownership and control was exercised by indigenous Hausa capitalists.[12] European management, however, organized production within the firm, and through the period of the Adebo strikes (1971) the technical management of the factory was under the authority of an Englishman. The firm exhibited signs of gross mismanagement. During the first years of the 1970s, a major expansion was undertaken without regard for market conditions, the availability of spare parts or the financing of debt. By 1972, machinery from the new section was scavenged for spare parts for the older sections. This firm was unable to compete with new firms and instead depended upon government contracts or institutional orders for its products.[13] It was also smaller than the two other firms in the sample, employing around 600 people during peak periods and about 200 during slack periods.

The organization of production and the labor process is similar to that of the modern textile mill. There is a small winding section; most labor is engaged in weaving; and there are a small number of workers engaged in beaming, dyeing, bleaching and finishing the final products. Weaving, however, differs in that here workers compete with each other in order to obtain the maximum number of looms. The greater the number of looms, the larger is the potential bonus for weavers. The bleaching and dyeing section employs under ten workers, and, unlike Factory B, it lacks strict discipline or close supervision by the foremen. After winding thread onto spools, the beams are prepared and placed upon looms. Woven cloth is taken for bleaching and dyeing before it is inspected and packaged for sale in the finishing section. There are about a dozen service workers, including watchmen, porters and storeworkers. The hierarchy of supervisors is relatively simple: aside from the managing director and the factory manager, there is a foreman and a section supervisor. In the weaving section the supervisor is assisted by a headman. In general, the division of labor is less differentiated, the technology less complex, the pace of production much less intense and the supervision more lax and personalized than in the first textile firm.

Management: indigenous capitalism

As one might expect, the managerial style reflects indigenous ownership and the orientation of production for consumption by state agencies. The intense alienation and exploitation of workers that characterized the two previous case studies is generally absent from Factory C. Workers, for example, are allowed to attend Friday prayer, an important source of community solidarity in Kano. Few report paying bribes in order to be hired. Whereas at the two other firms workers were dismissed or punished for being late or absent upon a death in their family, employees at Factory C were allowed unpaid leave time to fulfill family obligations. Furthermore, a moderate amount of lateness went undisciplined, and workers were observed wandering around the factory occasionally without apparent purpose. Workers commonly sold used clothing to other employees or engaged in other forms of petty trading during work hours. And, most importantly, all workers were allowed to pray collectively for the 2 p.m. prayer under the leadership of their chosen worker-*imam*. Discipline was enforced as much by a client of the owner-manager, a former Native Authority policeman who acted as doorman, as it was by the shift foreman. Hence, in contrast to the two other firms, the management style was *paternalistic* rather than aggressively entrepreneurial or rationally bureaucratic. And so, despite the obvious problems of efficiency, the firm continued in production under the same ownership until losses finally shut it down completely.

It should be emphasized that the relaxed working conditions and paternalistic management style involved a cost to the worker. Wages were below the national minimum standard in most cases. State-initiated wage arrears payments often went unpaid or were paid only in substandard amounts. Experienced workers, moreover, reported that former benefits, in the form of health benefits, loans and other valued services, had been reduced gradually, and the length of each working day had been extended by a half-hour.[14]

The fact that this firm was paternalistic in dealing with employees, that the management respected shared local cultural traditions and that workers felt some subjective identification with indigenous capitalism should not be generalized to include all examples of indigenously owned firms. In fact, during the Udoji strikes of 1975, more recently established firms engaged in bitter and violent forms of class struggle with their employees. Hence, under Hausa ownership and management, the degree to which relations between management and labor may be defined as paternalistic should be established in each instance.

200

EVALUATING INDUSTRIAL LABOR: ALIENATION IN AN ALIEN SYSTEM

To accept wage labor or, as Hausa workers put it, '*aikin bature*' or *leburanci* is to give up the independence and freedom that workers formerly enjoyed as craftsmen, traders, peasant farmers or mallams. Accepting clientage involves some sense of lost independence, but the loss is immeasurably greater in factories, where the labor process is determined by the need of capitalist production. Workers, of course, vary in their response according to their pre-recruitment experience and the degree of rationalization and supervision involved in the labor process. Thus, a neophyte rural-born worker was observed greeting supervisors by genuflecting with his right arm raised in the traditional greeting given to authority. In contrast, experienced urban workers are less terrified initially and merely express nominal greetings to supervisors.

Following standard procedures used in studies of worker satisfaction, I asked workers to discuss their likes and dislikes associated with their work. Oddly, many workers found the question 'What is it that you like about your job?' to be incomprehensible. But the parallel question regarding 'dislikes' met with no such difficulty. Nevertheless, when workers were asked to state the feature of their jobs that they liked most, 46.5 percent responded with an instrumental (i.e., alienated) economic response such as 'only the money', 'it allows me to feed my family and to avoid suffering' or 'it's steady work, every day, not like casual labor'. The next most frequent response, accounting for 19.4 percent, was 'Nothing, there is nothing about this work that I like.' And the third most frequent response, accounting for 8.5 percent, was 'No one bothers me', or 'Usually I am left alone to do my job'; that is to say, the worker was not abused or intimidated by his supervisor. If one interprets these responses as expressions of alienated labor, as I do, then 74.4 percent find nothing meaningful in their work. (At the same time, however, it should be noted that a minority of workers gave responses such as 'I enjoy being around machines and I hope that I can learn to become a skilled worker' or, more commonly, 'I enjoy being with my friends here at the factory.')

Expressions of dislike, not surprisingly, were easily articulated. To summarize briefly, 35.7 percent noted working conditions (dust, unsafe machines, poor lighting, pressure from supervisors, physical exhaustion, no time to rest and no freedom to move) as their most important dislike. Several workers complained about not being allowed to pray at the correct hour. And finally, 21.2 percent responded with 'Nothing'.

Many responses were firm-specific. For example, a worker employed in the machine section of the utensil firm (Factory A) responded to the 'job likes' question by stating, 'I am fortunate. I have never lost any fingers. Others have lost three, two or one fingers.' Fire section workers mentioned injuries suffered from burns. From the perspective of industrial workers, disfigurement is a common result of industrial labor. Regarding the pass system at Factory B, one weaver responded, 'If one wants to go outside for water or to urinate, we must ask the supervisor for a pass. For us, this is suffering.' A second worker from the same factory questioned the usefulness of deductions for the National Provident Fund, which allegedly serves as a retirement fund for workers: 'I do not believe that I shall ever receive the money. If I wait until I am fifty years old, I shall be dead. If I leave work before I am fifty, how shall I receive the money that I have saved?'

The subordination of labor: relations with supervisors

When the labor process and managerial style of the three firms were described, the supervisors of Factories A and B were observed to enforce strict discipline, to demand bribes for jobs and to humiliate workers. Bearing in mind the moral expectations and standards held by clients and patrons in Islamic Hausa society, let us examine how workers respond to questions regarding relations with supervisors at Factory A. Regarding relations between supervisors, a rural-born but experienced migrant responded with this comment:

> The manager and the Asian supervisors? Well, they curse us when they tell us to to do something. They call us *shege* (bastard), *dan iska* (hooligans), and scream *ubanka* (father-fucker). Everyone is *banza* (worthless) to them. They do not give human dignity and self-respect to human beings, not even to each other.

A second worker described work at the same factory in this way:

> Workers here are treated like domestic animals. If you want them, you keep them. If you do not want them you chase them out and bring in new ones. It's their house, thus it's not necessary for them to keep their workers.

Workers at the utensil factory expressed the greatest distrust of their supervisors. Many were bitter over the ethnic ties between the factory manager and the supervisors, which many ambitious workers felt unfairly blocked their legitimate advancement.

If we turn to Factory B, where all supervisors were Nigerian, the relationship between supervisors and workers is equally tense, though for different reasons. A mallam-worker who paid ₦6 for his job presented this evaluation of supervisors at the modern textile factory:

> In our opinion, we the laborers, we believe that foremen dismiss workers in order to take bribes from new applicants for the same jobs. Supervisors do not criticize workers in order to correct their work, only to dismiss people.

An experienced headman who was involved in the labor process of the raising section brought up the question of justice:

> Supervisors do not want justice. They send you home for the whole day if you are three minutes late. They punish you for small errors by not allowing you to work.

An experienced worker expressed the workers' feelings about supervisors eloquently, attributing abuse to the alien character of the industrial system:

> Everyone fears that they will be dismissed here. At *gidan bature* [European house], all are dismissed eventually and new laborers are brought in to work. You see, the new workers fear everyone and everything. But the experienced workers have less fear of the supervisors' orders.

Finally, because the above responses are clearly militant, I want to include a response from an oppressed worker who only wished to survive:

> Supervisors? I fear them. Because, if you do not flatter them and greet them with prestige, they will take your way of earning a living away from you. If you do not humble yourself and show shame before them, they will search for some little thing that you are doing wrong and dismiss you for it.

Clearly, many workers believed that the supervisors at Factories A and B were arbitrary and exploitative in their treatment of workers. Many workers tried, especially at the textile factory, to curry favor with their supervisors in the manner of clients to aristocrats. However, for the supervisors, jobs were a commodity to be sold for profit, a fact that rendered the workers' efforts totally ineffective. A second point, which a comparison between the two factories makes apparent, is that Nigerian supervisors were considered almost as exploitative as Asian ones. This point will be pursued below when we observe workers' evaluations of Nigerian managers.

Alienation and job security under industrial capitalism

Industrial production for a competitive market under entrepreneurial capitalist management that is directed by exploitative supervisors offers labor none of the job security afforded by international firms which exert oligopolistic or even monopolistic control over the market. Dependent upon the whims of supervisors, nothing more starkly characterizes the condition of an industrial worker's sense of alienation than his deep fear of losing his job. The appropriate questions, then, are how do workers subjectively respond to these conditions and how does insecurity shape a worker's consciousness? Table 5.2 presents workers' responses to my question concerning job security and dismissals. Just as one would expect, though 80 per cent acknowledge fear of dismissal, the degree to which workers acknowledge worrying intensely over dismissal (i.e., every day) varies according to the labor process of each factory. Not surprisingly, nearly three-quarters of workers at Factory B and 60 percent at Factory A reported that they worried every day about being dismissed. But only 51 percent of those employed in the indigenously owned firm, Factory C, reported worrying every day about job security. Yet, however stark these

Table 5.2 *Job security by factory*

Amount of concern over job security	'A'	'B'	'C'	Total
Worries often	60.0	74.7	51.9	66.9
	(18)	(59)	(14)	(91)
Worries a little	16.7	12.7	14.8	14.0
	(5)	(10)	(4)	(19)
Not worried	23.3	12.7	33.3	19.1
	(7)	(10)	(9)	(26)
Total	100	100	100	100
	(30)	(79)	(27)	(136)[a]

[a] Missing cases = 4

data on job security may be, they do not convey the subjective terror experienced by workers daily as they attempt to survive doing alienated labor in an alien system of factory production. For the Muslim Hausa-speaking workers the alienation is intensified further because all decisions are carried out in an alien language (English) that very few understand. Let us move beyond the statistics now and introduce empathetic understanding by looking at workers' descriptions of job insecurity and how it affects them.

The first statement comes from a worker at Factory A. For him, the uncertainty and the absence of a visible reason for dismissals generated despair:

> Laboring is like death. One never knows when one will be dismissed without reason. Tomorrow, for example, I might be dismissed without knowing it now or without any reason. One cannot plan for anything.

A second worker, at Factory B, has come to an understanding of what is meant by the expression 'labor as a commodity'. Given his lack of formal education, this insight into the workings of the capitalist labor market is truly remarkable:

> Working in a factory is like being in a market. Everyone does what they have to do and then leaves. Since no one knows if or when they will be dismissed, work becomes like a market and it depends on demand for them at the market. For example, if there are sales, the manager and the supervisors will not dismiss you for a small fault. But now, because of the lack of sales, they will dismiss someone for a small fault.

The daily repetitive fear of dismissal appears as a ritual of daily life and a source of personal anxiety for this rural-born worker at Factory B:

> Every day when I come to work I pick up my time card and then I look to see if I received a dismissal paper. I think about dismissal every day because I do not

know if I will have work or if I will be able to continue working at my loom without making a mistake.

Obviously, these conditions do not inculcate a strong sense of commitment to industrial labor nor the expectation of endurance for a lifetime. This view is expressed by a young fireworker at Factory A:

> Because I am a small boy I do not ask for a reason why people are dismissed. When my time has come, I shall return to Koranic studies with my mallam. Truly, I never thought that I would remain employed for this length of time.

Finally, the absence of seniority rules designed to protect older, experienced workers from dismissal in order for management to recruit younger, more docile and lower-paid recruits generates bitterly contested struggles for job security. An experienced worker offered this view on job security and the high turnover rate:

> I do not want to work here until my strength is gone. I want to obtain a craft where I can earn a living when I am an older man. Because, if I remain here until I am old, and my physical strength is gone, I will be dismissed for a younger worker.

To conclude, workers experience factory labor in large firms as an intensely insecure occupation. Moreover, any evidence drawn from high turnover rates purporting to show a lack of commitment to industrial labor or a culturally induced inability to adjust should be treated with skepticism. The evidence presented here argues that problems of labor turnover during early industrialization under entrepreneurial management are, to a significant degree, *induced* by management themselves. Arguments that place the blame for high turnover on the cultural attributes of labor merely blame the *victims* of ruthless exploitation and irrational methods of labor management.

Alienation and insecurity: the Nigerianization-of-management solution

Let us ponder the following question: Are the problems of insecurity, exploitation and alienation that exist objectively and subjectively among Kano's factory workers universal and structural features of industrial capitalist production, or could the situation of workers, and labor/management relations in general, be significantly ameliorated by the recruitment of Nigerian managers? That is to say, is the problem a structural one, or a national-cultural one? A nationalist view, for example, might argue that Nigerianization of managerial personnel would reduce racism, insensitivity, alienation and other forms of conflict between capital and labor. In fact, though the demand for Nigerian managers exceeds the supply of qualified candidates, the federal government has pursued a policy of Nigerianization of management by controlling the issuance of visas for foreign management personnel. One way to test the validity of these

Table 5.3 *Effect of Hausa managers on workers' welfare, by factory*

Perceived effect of Hausa managers	Factory			
	'A'	'B'	'C'	Total
Increases welfare	44.4	58.1	46.2	52.2
	(12)	(36)	(12)	(60)
Decreases welfare	48.1	33.9	53.8	41.7
	(13)	(21)	(14)	(48)
No difference	7.4	8.1	0.0	6.1
	(2)	(5)	(0)	(7)
Total	100	100	100	100
	(27)	(62)	(26)	(115)[a]

[a] Missing cases = 25

competing explanations of poor labor/management relations, which for convenience I shall label *structural* and *national*, would be to inquire whether workers believe that their welfare would improve if Nigerian managers were appointed to their factory. In order to reduce distortion and ambiguity that might arise from competition between ethnic groups in Nigeria, I labelled the proposed managers Hausa managers rather than merely Nigerian managers.

Table 5.3 presents the results of this survey by factory. Only slightly more than 50 percent of the total sample believed that workers' welfare would improve under Hausa managers. This is a surprising finding given the significance that the Nigerian bourgeoisie and popular Nigerian media have attached to the Nigerianization program. Even more surprising is the fact that only a minority of workers in two out of three firms believe that their welfare will increase under Nigerian management. Note that in the Nigerian-owned and -managed firm, whose workers were ideally placed to evaluate Nigerian management, a majority of workers believe that their welfare will actually *decrease* under continued Nigerian management. While the data is too evenly distributed to interpret in unambiguous terms, it is clear that nearly half of the workers believe that Nigerianization will not improve their welfare. Moreover, those workers with the greatest exposure to Nigerian management are the least optimistic about the potential value of this 'reform' for their well-being. All of these findings suggest that workers perceive the conflict between capital and labor to be structural rather than national in origin.

Since this finding was unexpected, the question was pursued with a probe asking the 'structural response' workers to describe their reasoning as to why they believed their welfare would decrease or remain constant if Hausa management were introduced throughout Kano's factories. An urban worker offered this reflection:

I live in a ward of the Birni with people who own companies. Earlier, I thought that we would be happy with Hausa-owned companies. But now, after they have entered into company ownership, I see that we shall suffer. The talakawa, they will suffer. You know, the owners of the companies only wish to love and take care of themselves.

A migrant employed at Factory B appears to have formed his opinion on this question by generalizing from his relationship with Nigerian supervisors:

The Hausa managers will only help themselves. They will not help us. They are educated. And they will not be patient if you make a small error. They will fire you. Look at the Nigerian supervisors here in this factory. They are hypocrites. If you make a small error they will dismiss you, and the manager does not even know about it. Why? The supervisors take our jobs and sell them to new workers.

Many workers are cynical regarding the reliability of the Nigerian managerial class to improve the welfare of workers. The following statement comes from an experienced but downwardly mobile worker from the Birni who worked at Factory B:

Well you see, for example, here if twenty workers are dismissed without a fair reason, the workers can go to the government and demand an explanation. But, when the Hausa managers take over, they will say to the government, 'you sent us here to be managers. We know our work. You tell your leaders that we, the managers, are the brothers of the workers and that we would not cheat them.' You see, that is why I think that this change will be worse for us.

Finally, an experienced worker from the Nigerian-owned textile firm and a resident of a prestigious ward of the Birni, who was also unusually well informed about contemporary politics in Kano and the relationship of state and capital, offered this explanation as to why he believed workers' welfare will decrease under Hausa managers:

Why do I think our welfare will decrease? Take strikes for example, there is a difference between useful and non-useful strikes. If you, a foreigner, start a company, the government will force you to pay wage increases like Adebo. Then in this case strikes are useful. But in the example of companies owned by Nigerians, it is useless to strike because the people who own the company are, at the same time, the government.

From his perspective, Nigerianization of management and ownership will reduce the tendency for state power to intervene on behalf of workers because the Nigerian bourgeoisie is integrated into and shares interests with the administrators of the state. This is a class response, from one who comprehends the political implications of Nigerianization.

So far, the data on worker evaluation of industrial labor is unambiguous: workers find themselves in competition with each other for a limited number of unskilled jobs, which leaves them at the mercy of supervisors. Most workers feel profoundly insecure about their jobs. Due to the

207

historical development of peripheral capitalist industrialization, workers lack a craft or guild tradition which European workers used to resist the domination of capital and the destruction of a subjectively meaningful labor process. Racism, capricious supervisors, lack of safety devices and dependence upon the vagaries of the market all force workers to submit to commodity relations instead of traditionally legitimated relations between master and client. The system is perceived, at least in Factories A and B, as fundamentally alienating and anomic, because work norms are determined to a significant degree by supervisors' caprice or market demand for products. Nor, as Nigerian nationalists assume, are all workers sanguine over their future when Hausa managers assume control over factory production. Despite the fact that workers are at the periphery, their location in production for a competitive market with unlimited supplies of labor subjects them to forms of exploitation which, while not identical, are similar to those of early industrialization in what are now advanced capitalist states. Furthermore, from the texture and content of the quotes expressing the individual worker's consciousness, the process of proletarianization is one that forces experienced workers to abandon the standards and expectations that were learned in the Hausa household and in Islamic social organizations such as Koranic schools. Having examined how workers evaluate industrial wage labor, supervisors, job security and changes for improvement under Hausa management, let us now look at workers' aspirations for mobility within the firms' skill hierarchy.

Occupational aspirations within the firm: the question of achievement

If, as apologists for managerial capitalism such as Inkeles and Smith would have us believe, participation in industrial organizations predisposes workers to accept the alleged achievement-oriented norms of industrial capitalism, then one should expect experienced workers to aspire to achieve more skilled positions within the firm.[15] The logic here is that workers most exposed to industrial capitalism will be most likely to aspire to fulfill their achievement goals within the firm. In order to test this hypothesis, I asked each respondent to name the occupation that he aspired to achieve in his factory. When asked to name the job of their choice, 52.6 percent of the respondents chose their present job, and 10.3 percent named a different though equally unskilled position; that is to say, nearly two-thirds of the unskilled workers interviewed had no aspiration to move upward in their firm's skill hierarchy. Among the remainder, 11.9 percent aspired to become headmen, and an equal number aspired to become skilled workers (i.e., mechanics, loom repairers or craftsmen). Note that only 5.9 percent aspired to become supervisors or foremen. Significantly, the greater a worker's exposure to wage labor, the more likely he was *not* to aspire toward greater upward mobility within the firm. Among those workers with less than five years' experience, only 39.1 percent preferred their present job, but among those with five years or more, the percentage rose to 64.8. This suggests that factory work socializes workers to lower their original aspirations for achieving upward mobility within the firm. Rather than inspiring commitment to achievement within the firm, industrial experience lowers workers' aspirations to move upward in the skill hierarchy.

To comprehend the reasoning behind these responses, one must remember that the factory is perceived as a closed mobility system where those without technical education or a marketable skill are locked into their present insecure positions. Modern education, rather than hard work and achievement motivation, now determines access to skilled positions. Moreover, in many factories there is little opportunity for advancement and great risk of dismissal if one takes on a new, unfamiliar position. Hence, workers' lack of education, their fear of dismissal and their distaste for foremen combine to encourage them to stay in their present positions. Risks are great and incentives are absent.

SOCIAL MOBILITY: OBSTACLE TO CLASS FORMATION?

In order for an emerging working class to form and to achieve its potential, members of this class must perceive their objective class position as relatively permanent. For, as Marx correctly observed in the American case, if there is a high degree of exchange between classes, workers will tend not to identify with or commit themselves to the interests and organizations of the wage-earning class.[16] Indeed, if a majority of workers aspired to achieved class mobility, usually from the working class to the petty bourgeoisie or to the salaried middle class, then the political and social potential of the urban working class would be dramatically reduced. In the case of Kano, it should be borne in mind that there is no objective possibility that a majority, or even a sizeable minority, of the wage-earning class will achieve upward class mobility and enter the petty bourgeoisie. Rather, the process of capitalist development in Kano is an asymmetric one that concentrates economic power in the hands of those with linkages to state patronage. Yet, as illustrated earlier for former craftsmen and traders, commercial, financial and industrial capital becomes concentrated in the hands of a comparatively small number of entrepreneurs. Competition between the remaining small capitalists, traders and craftsmen constantly expels members of this intermediate class into the wage-earning class. True, some wage workers and petty traders are successful enough to enter the petty bourgeoisie, but for the majority of independent commodity producers the openness of the informal sector means that any effort to accumulate capital is constrained by the ruthless competition among craftsmen and traders in that sector. Nevertheless, both the values of the precapitalist society and the demonstration effect exhibited by unusually successful capitalists create an aspiration on the part of wage workers to enter commerce. Let us examine this aspiration among the sample of

Table 5.4 *Ideal lifetime occupation by urban status*

Occupation	Urbans	Migrants	Commuters	Total
Trader	88.6	85.7	65.2	79.9
	(39)	(42)	(30)	(111)
Factory laborer	2.3	4.1	15.2	7.2
	(1)	(2)	(7)	(10)
Technician	4.5	2.0	4.3	3.6
	(2)	(1)	(2)	(5)
Other	4.5	˙8.2	15.2	9.4
	(2)	(4)	(7)	(13)
Total	100	100	100	100
	(44)	(49)	(46)	(139)

Missing case = 1

industrial workers in order to discover if, as critics suggest, upward mobility promises to undermine class stability and thus class formation itself.

Entrepreneurial aspirations and working-class solidarity

Table 5.4 presents responses of workers to the open-ended question: What is the occupation that you would like to hold if you were able to choose? The reader will recall that, in contrast to workers' aspirations within the firm, which were static in that nearly all preferred their present or a similar unskilled job, nearly 80 percent wish to leave the factory for independent trading or commercial occupations in the informal sector. Note also that exposure to the urban social processes of a semi-industrial capitalist city, as measured by urban status, discourages workers from remaining industrial workers and increases their preference for trading. Hence, it is impossible to argue from the empirical evidence provided here that the lack of *commitment* to industrial labor voiced relentlessly by industrial sociologists derives from the workers' backwardness or unfamiliarity with industrial culture, or from the absence of consumption needs. Rather, the opposite is true: those least urbanized, the commuters, express the greatest interest in factory employment and the least interest in moving into the informal sector; and the converse is true in the case of the urbans. This finding suggests that the aspiration to leave factory work in favor of commerce is part of the subjective process of proletarianization, whereby those most exposed to urban capitalism are the first to realize that wage labor offers alienation, little opportunity for skill acquisition, and great insecurity. But before offering an explanation for this consciousness, let us examine the response of these same workers to the equally important question regarding the likelihood of achieving this aspiration.

210

Table 5.5 *Workers' evaluation of chances of becoming a trader by urban status*

Chances of becoming a trader	Urbans	Migrants	Commuters	Total
Little or no chance	61.5	73.8	63.0	66.7
	(24)	(31)	(17)	(72)
Good chance	38.5	26.2	37.0	33.3
	(15)	(11)	(10)	(36)
Total	100	100	100	100
	(39)	(42)	(27)	(108)

Missing cases = 3

Questions that elicit workers' ideal occupations tell us very little about behavioral aspects of class formation or class solidarity, because the 'dream' of trading does not negate the objective deprivation experienced in the labor process. Nor, of course, does aspiring to enter trading create objective material and social relations that are separate from the reality of being a wage-earning proletarian. One way to evaluate how significant a trading aspiration may be for predicting either an individual worker's behavior or the permanence of Kano's industrial proletariat as a class fragment is to ask workers if they believe they will actually *achieve* their stated ideal occupation. Here it is assumed that workers who believe that there is little or no chance of their realizing an independent entrepreneurial occupation are likely to identify with the material interest of workers and, conversely, that they are unlikely to identify with the interests of the commercial bourgeoisie.

Table 5.5 presents workers' evaluations of their chances of becoming independent traders (among those workers who voiced the aspiration to enter trade). Note that two-thirds of those with such aspirations believe that they have little or no chance of successful upward mobility. Hence, if two-thirds of those aspiring to become traders do not even expect to realize their ambition, then it is exceedingly unlikely that entrepreneurial aspirations will be a salient factor in reducing working-class cohesion or collective class action. True, some may achieve their aspirations, but by their own estimate an overwhelming majority are locked into their present class position.

How do workers explain this occupational preference? Most repeat points made earlier: insecurity, abuse from supervisors, working conditions and lack of safety precautions at their present jobs. Another common reason given for this aspiration is that factory work denies them the 'freedom' to participate in community social life (a privilege characteristic of independent commodity producers), such as rituals surrounding birth, marriage, the greeting of friends and communal prayer. But 'freedom' also means freedom from the discipline and abuse associated with the labor process of industrial production. Still others emphasized the lack of physical mobility demanded by factory work as compared to the geographical mobility and social freedom involved in commercial occupations. Others repeatedly pointed to the low income of factory work as compared to petty commerce. A common comment was, 'What I would earn in a day as a market trader is more than my weekly earnings here'. More importantly, whereas factory work is correctly perceived as a closed mobility system, commerce is perceived as promising at least the possibility of unlimited social mobility and wealth. Expressed in the language of Muslim culture, several workers offered this comparison: commerce opens one up to unlimited and unknown opportunities to be rewarded through Allah's generosity, but the rigid pay structure of the factory eliminates even the possibility of receiving good fortune from Allah.

Aside from these reasons, a major factor that encourages workers to aspire to enter commerce is explained by the insecurity and exploitation involved in the factory labor process itself. As was explained earlier, the absence of seniority rules under competitive capitalism forces workers to aspire to petty commerce in order to plan for their later working years. According to a migrant textile worker from Factory B:

> When I am old they will dismiss me from this factory. What do they want with an old man working for them? Trading will allow me to earn a living when I am old, when my strength is gone. You see, factory work is the work of strength and when I am old I will not be able to do heavy, difficult work.

Thus in most cases the desire to enter commerce, while clearly reinforced by Muslim (i.e., precapitalist) cultural standards, is induced by the insecurity and irrationality contained in the exploitative practices of competitive industrial capitalism. The unlimited supplies of unskilled labor, the lack of seniority rules, and declining real wages all combine to encourage supervisors and management to turn over labor very recklessly, because the management is not penalized by such practices. Quite logically, after observing these management practices for a number of years, experienced laborers conclude that they must prepare for an uncertain future by searching for entrepreneurial occupations as informal-sector traders who, nonetheless, remain members of the urban talakawa and the populist class alliance.

To return to the original question posed in this section, the evidence indicates that, indeed, Kano's industrial workers do aspire to enter commerce in the informal sector. Yet two-thirds see little or no chance that they will achieve this aspiration. Since the 'dream' of becoming a trader cannot create the objective opportunity to enter commerce, and since most aspirants are pessimistic about achieving upward mobility, a high rate of upward mobility among industrial workers poses no threat to the ongoing process of class formation in urban Kano. Nevertheless, critics of class analysis have argued that workers' petty entrepreneurial aspirations contradict the argument that working class formation is a structurally transforming process in West African cities. Let us examine one such critique.

Entrepreneurial aspirations: petty bourgeois consciousness or resistance to proletarianization?

Critics begin with a consistent finding of empirical studies of West African workers, which is that a high proportion aspire to enter commerce not as the bourgeoisie but usually as petty traders in the informal sector. In a review article, the anthropologist Peter Lloyd seizes upon this fact in order to suggest that class consciousness itself is an 'ethnocentric question'. Furthermore, he argues that 'the African working class differs from western counterparts' because 'its members are not fully committed to wage employment'. Regarding entrepreneurial aspirations, Lloyd notes the existence of 'apparent paradoxes [such] as the juxtaposition of militant strike action and petit bourgeois aspiration for success as small entrepreneurs'.[17] Lloyd raises some reasonable questions that deserve answers.

Let us begin with the alleged lack of *commitment* by African workers to wage employment. After viewing the conditions of work, service and security that exist today in Kano's factories, one must wonder why anyone would expect any sensible human being to be 'committed' to industrial wage labor.[18] Clearly it is not in a worker's rational self-interest to be committed to an employer who does not acknowledge reciprocal obligations or to a position for which the wages decline in real terms (see Table 2.1). The concept of commitment, moreover, is a purely managerial ideology. It assumes that proletarianization is a completely voluntary act and not a choice conditioned by political decisions and market forces which leave the potential proletarian little other opportunity to earn a livelihood at a historically acceptable level. Although it is true that Muslim culture places a high value on commerce, the conditions of labor and the real value of industrial wages offer no incentive even from the perspective of neoclassical economics for anyone to remain a wage-earning factory worker. Furthermore, no known proletariat has ever been committed to the conditions of employment that I have shown to exist in Kano's factories. Workers in advanced capitalist societies, to use Lloyd's reference group, have struggled successfully against such conditions.

But this is not the most serious methodological error contained in Lloyd's critique. By treating the preference for commerce as a cultural (precapitalist) value orientation, and avoiding any discussion of the objective conditions of factory labor which must exert at least some influence on this aspiration, Lloyd ignores the possibility that the aspiration to leave industrial work arises from the labor process itself. That is to say, this aspiration is managerially induced by exploitative conditions. Indeed, the conditions and attitudes that have been described are not designed to commit workers to wage employment. Rather, management policies, arising from both neglect and intention, are designed to generate high profits in the short term; this is possible only because social and economic conditions guarantee unlimited supplies of unskilled labor.

What of Lloyd's allegation that the African working class differs from its western counterpart with regard to a commitment to wage employment? When one examines the literature on comparative industrialization, one discovers that it is common for both experienced and recently proletarianized workers to aspire to enter the competitive sector as small businessmen, as in, for example, Chinoy's study of American automobile workers and Taira's study of Japanese workers.[19] Elsewhere, Touraine and Rangazzi's research on French industrial workers of agrarian origin indicates that they, too, consider industrial employment a 'defeat' and wish to escape factory employment, albeit through the route of higher education.[20] And finally, Stearns's survey of German workers, circa 1900, confirms this same aspiration: 'Young skilled German workers talked often of wanting "to run a small business on my own", in the interests of independence. This was the most common single goal of Berlin mechanics interviewed.'[21] Hence, because the data are in fact very ambiguous, if not contrary to Lloyd's assertions regarding any first-generation working class's commitment to wage labor, it should not be presumed that African workers are *deviant* from western workers at a comparable historical phase of proletarianization. Indeed, I would argue that commercial aspirations reflect the resistance of independent commodity producers (e.g., petty traders, craftsmen and small holders) to the loss of control over their working lives that proletarianization entails. In the conclusion of his classic study of the English working class, Thompson underscores the same pattern of *resistance*, where independent producers refused to become committed to wage employment:[22]

> It is easy enough to say that this culture was backward-looking or conservative. True enough, one direction of the great agitations of the artisans and outworkers, continued over fifty years, was to *resist* being turned into a proletariat . . . During this time they were, as a class, repressed and segregated in their own communities . . . . Whenever the pressure of the rulers relaxed, men came from the petty workshops and weavers' hamlets and asserted new claims. They were told that they had no rights, but they knew that they were born free. (Emphasis Thompson's)

As Thompson suggests, the deprivation that workers undergo in order to resist proletarianization is both extraordinary and nearly universal. In this regard one notes that Max Weber's early empirical research attempted to answer this very question: that is, why would small-holding agricultural producers endure extreme poverty in order to avoid becoming proletarianized rural wage workers?[23] In Kano, therefore, it is not surprising that resistance to proletarianization takes the form of aspiring to enter the informal or competitive sector. Remember that this aspiration does not separate them from the urban lower class that shares a talakawa political identity. There are few wealthy traders within this sector: all are members of the urban talakawa; all are threatened by the concentration of foreign and local large-scale merchant-industrial capital; and, as illustrated earlier, many are socially integrated with wage and labor service workers by residence and social ties, as well as by the shared political consciousness of the urban lower stratum. Hence, entrepreneurial aspirations do not necessarily indicate 'petit bourgeois' aspirations, but rather merely a return to independent commodity production, a class that is in alliance with wage workers.

Let us conclude our discussion of occupation aspirations and of Lloyd's critique of Marxist class analysis. The process of proletarianization for independent producers is not voluntary, desirable nor socially valued in any known society. No conscious, self-interested human being would wish to be subjected, let alone 'committed', to the discipline, abuse, insecurity and low wages which exist in Kano's factories. Given the ubiquitous idealization of commerce in precapitalist West Africa, as well as the Muslim preference for commerce, it is logical that workers' resistance to proletarianization should take the form of an idealized aspiration to enter the commercial sector as a petty commodity producer. Yet, the data indicate that workers are also starkly realistic about the actual opportunities for achieving their ideal.

In a situation of transition to industrial capitalism, where elements of capitalist and precapitalist society articulate and influence each other, it follows that first-generation industrial workers, like their European and Japanese counterparts during the transition to semi-industrial capitalism, should aspire to become self-employed. Rather than viewing this typical form of resistance to proletarianization as a 'paradox', to use Lloyd's phrase, I would argue that such an aspiration, in combination with militant expressions of class consciousness, is the prototypical consciousness of an industrial proletariat in the process of formation; that is to say, it is the consciousness appropriate to a class recruited from peasants and independent producers and formed in a situation marked by the articulation of precapitalist and capitalist elements.

Class formation is a historical process, one that requires several generations, at the least, to erase memories of independent commodity production. Moreover, since the conjunctural features of the period in which industrialization is occurring in the contemporary Third World do not destroy independent commodity production located in the informal sector but may actually expand this sector, entrepreneurial aspirations are unlikely to disappear with the deepening of the industrialization process.[24] To conclude, Lloyd's 'paradox' is misguided and based upon an erroneous reading of Western European labor history. His error is to compare an actual historical process (i.e., proletarianization in West Africa) to an ideal-typical image of the 'committed' western industrial worker, whom the historical record shows to have been equally as uncommitted to proletarian-

215

Table 5.6 *Value of western education by urban status*

	Urbans			Migrants			Commuters		
	Self	*Son*	*Daughter*	*Self*	*Son*	*Daughter*	*Self*	*Son*	*Daughter*
None	2.3	2.3	44.2	4.1	8.3	41.7	8.9	9.1	65.9
	(1)	(1)	(19)	(2)	(4)	(20)	(4)	(4)	(29)
Low[a]	48.8	18.6	39.5	49.0	16.7	41.7	44.4	22.7	15.9
	(21)	(8)	(17)	(24)	(8)	(20)	(20)	(10)	(7)
High[b]	48.8	79.1	16.3	46.9	75.0	16.7	46.7	68.2	18.2
	(21)	(34)	(7)	(23)	(36)	(8)	(21)	(30)	(8)
Total	100	100	100	100	100	100	100	100	100
	(43)	(43)	(43)	(49)	(48)	(48)	(45)	(44)	(44)

[a] Low = primary school or basic literacy
[b] High = secondary school or as much as possible

ization as his West African counterpart at a comparable stage of industrialization.

INTERGENERATIONAL MOBILITY: THE QUESTION OF EQUITY FOR
WORKERS' SONS

A second aspect of social mobility which might mitigate against the formation of class solidarity and consciousness among industrial workers arises from possible upward mobility on the part of workers' sons through the modern educational system. A critic, for example, might argue that workers' sons are ideally situated to take advantage of urban educational investments such as Universal Primary Education (UPE) and, further, that such education opportunities could motivate workers to identify with the careers of their children rather than with their objective class position as urban workers. In order for this hypothesis to be valid, workers would first have to favor western education for their sons, and equally important, workers must believe that their sons possess the opportunity to take advantage of western education. If both of these conditions were met, then it would be plausible to argue that class formation is situational and transitional for industrial workers. Why? Because, if this were true, the sons of industrial workers would be likely to move upward in the occupational hierarchy and become integrated into the new middle class. And thus working class formation would be constrained by the absence of second-generation workers, i.e., those born and raised in an urban working-class environment, who often provide leadership for a working-class movement. Thus, while an industrial working class would still effectively exist, its political development and level of class consciousness would be retarded both by the absence of second-generation industrial workers who could socialize raw recruits into the industrial proletariat and by the relative lack of class permanence and cohesion. Let us empirically investigate the likelihood of such an outcome.

In order to test this hypothesis, the attitude of industrial workers toward western education should be examined. Accordingly, Table 5.6 presents workers' evaluations of western education for self, son and daughter by urban status. When one examines workers' educational aspirations 'for self' it is noteworthy that urban status makes virtually no difference. The evidence indicates that less than half the workers in each urban status group favor high levels of education for themselves, yet nearly three-quarters of the sample favor high education for their sons. Why? The answer is that industrial workers perceive themselves as too old to obtain the education necessary for upward mobility in the factory. Instead, they aspire to enter the informal sector as traders, where high levels of western education are considered unnecessary for success. Not surprisingly, given the content of fundamentalist Islamic beliefs regarding the social position of women, educational aspirations for daughters are significantly lower than for sons. To answer the first question then, it is certain that most workers favor high levels of western education for their sons.

Now, the second aspect of the 'upward mobility through sons' mobility' hypothesis requires not only that fathers want their sons to achieve higher education, but also that fathers believe that there is sufficient social equity operating in Nigerian society to allow a worker's son to achieve the desired high standard of western education. Furthermore, in order for workers to identify with the actual or potential class position of their sons, and thus avoid identifying with their own class situation, workers must believe that their sons have the opportunity to obtain an education sufficient to enter the salaried middle class or the managerial bourgeoisie. Given the social context in Kano during the present conjuncture, secondary school or above is the minimum standard of education necessary to enter the salaried middle class. Moreover, because the federally sponsored Universal Primary Education has and will increase primary school enrollments several-fold in the immediate future, competition to enter secondary school will be intensified as primary school leavers struggle to obtain limited secondary school places. Just as is currently the case in the southern states of Nigeria, primary school leavers who are unable to enter secondary school will probably migrate to cities like Kano in order to obtain wage employment. For these reasons, entry into secondary school is a crucial transition for workers' sons, one which, in all likelihood, will determine their opportunities to enter the salaried middle class. Let us examine Table 5.7 which presents responses from Kano's industrial workers to the question of whether workers' sons have the same opportunity as others to enter secondary school.

As one examines Table 5.7 it is important to realize that even the existence of secondary schools or the fact that secondary school follows

217

Table 5.7 *Perception of educational opportunity by urban status*[a]

Opportunity for worker's son to enter secondary school[a]	Urbans	Migrants	Commuters	Total
Equal opportunity	22.6	36.7	53.3	34.2
	(7)	(11)	(8)	(26)
Less than equal opportunity	77.4	63.3	46.7	65.8
	(24)	(19)	(7)	(50)
Total	100	100	100	100
	(31)	(30)	(15)	(76)

[a] Among workers familiar with secondary school

primary school is not known by many rural-born factory workers. There-fore, workers who were unfamiliar with secondary schools are not included in Table 5.7. Of course, compared to rural-born migrants and commuters, the urbans were more familiar with secondary school because many had friends or relatives who had attended or, more frequently, who had applied but were not admitted. When one examines workers' perceptions of educational opportunity as measured by equality of opportunity for workers' sons, one discovers that a linear relationship exists between 'familiarity with secondary schools' and the perception that workers' sons do not have equality of opportunity. For, while the urbans are most familiar with secondary school, over three-quarters believe that workers' sons have a less-than-equal opportunity to enter secondary school. But among those least familiar with secondary school, i.e., the commuters, more than half believe that workers' sons have an equal opportunity to enter secondary school. It appears that the more workers become integrated into the urban social processes of a semi-industrial capitalist urban center, the more they become aware of class discrimination in the distribution of what Castells calls the means of social consumption. As will be shown in Chapter Seven, urban-industrial experience is correlated with increasing awareness of class discrimination and the recognition of social inequity.

Finally, because it is important to understand, with empathy, the consciousness of workers who perceive that workers' sons will be denied equal access to secondary school, I offer two workers' statements given in response to this question. The first is from an urban worker from Factory C:

> They do many bad things at the schools. If a laborer's son passes the exam, they will take his exam and give the score to a rich man's son or to the son of an aristocrat (sarauta) because they will pay bribes in order to place their son in secondary school.

A second urban worker generalizes from his brother's experience:

> Even if the son of a laborer passes the exam, he must pay a bribe to enter secondary school. For example, I have a younger brother who passed the

exam but he had to pay a bribe in order to enter secondary school. Now he works as an assistant manager at Gashash's groundnut mill.

The evidence is unambiguous with regard to workers' perceptions of the educational opportunities available to their sons. Of those familiar with secondary school, nearly two-thirds believe that their sons will not have an equal opportunity to enter secondary school. Moreover, those most familiar with secondary school, the urbans, are most likely to perceive inequality of opportunity. To conclude, just as in the example of entrepreneurial aspirations, there is no evidence that workers' aspirations for their sons' upward mobility through western education are capable of reducing class solidarity or of deflecting such workers' political loyalties to the intended class position of their sons. Indeed, the evidence strongly suggests that access to educational opportunity for industrial workers' sons only reinforces existing class inequities in urban Kano.

Summary

During the period of interest, Kano's industrial labor force expanded in number yet remained predominantly under entrepreneurial rather than bureaucratic capitalist forms of control. In turn, the entrepreneurial forms of control over the labor process allowed particularistic and corrupt supervisors to abuse labor such that most workers expressed alienation, fear of supervisory injustice, little aspiration for mobility within the firm and profound levels of job insecurity. In response to these conditions – which were much less exploitative and more paternalistic in the indigenous-owned textile mill – workers aspired to leave the industrial labor force in order to gain freedom and security in their mature years. Contrary to critics of the class formation and resistance thesis, workers were pessimistic about the possibility of achieving their aspiration to return to independent commodity production. Furthermore, it has been argued that the prototypical consciousness of a first-generation industrial proletariat is not 'labor commitment' in the managerial sense of the term, but rather resistance to proletarianization. Nor were the industrial workers of the sample sanguine about upward mobility for their sons through the achievement route offered by modern secondary education. At the level of consciousness, industrial workers expressed awareness of increasing commodification of labor (e.g., the market) and expressed some frustration that the normative expectations associated with Islamic tradition and household relations went unfulfilled. Let us now examine the same workers in the same three firms under the conditions of class struggle when workers became mobilized as an active class with clear political and economic goals.

6

The process of class struggle: state intervention and trade union formation, 1970–9

CLASS STRUGGLE UNDER SEMI-INDUSTRIAL CAPITALISM

Throughout the decade of the seventies, Kano's industrial working class expanded in number and matured in terms of industrial experience, class consciousness and class organization. With the maturation process in mind, my primary objectives in this chapter are to describe the formation of a first-generation industrial proletariat, to present a detailed description of the uneven and contradictory forms of consciousness expressed by workers as they engaged in class struggle, and to analyze their awkward efforts to form effective workers' organizations. In Chapter Five, which described the labor process of capitalist production in three firms, workers expressed the tension between capital and labor rather passively, in the form of alienation, resistance and escape. Here the focus is on the active component of this tension, which centers on overt expressions of class struggle between labor and capital. Just as in the preceding chapters, attention will be paid to the complex texture and contradictory meanings of working class struggle from the perspective of the participants. Finally, I shall analyze workers' efforts to form legitimate trade union organizations from the Adebo strikes of 1971 to the return of civilian rule in 1979.

Initially, the problem is to apply the concept of class struggle to the situation of Kano's industrial working class. Given the emergent nature of the industrial proletariat, with its relative backwardness in terms of industrial experience and education, as well as its diverse social and ethnic origins, one must define and analyze expressions of class struggle that are appropriate to both the level of development of the productive forces (i.e., depth of semi-industrial capitalism) and to the level of social development of the industrial proletariat as reflected in its precapitalist and capitalist social relations. When analyzing class struggle, moreover, one must be historically grounded and objectively realistic about the political and social potential of a first-generation proletariat that only recently has become differentiated from the precapitalist talakawa stratum and, by extension, from subordination to authoritarian and extra-economic forms of coercion.

As applied to the activity of Kano's industrial proletariat, therefore, class struggle occurs when this class fraction takes direct collective action against the interests of capital and, at the same time, pursues the material, social or

220

political interests of the industrial working class. Accordingly, the appropriate situation in which one may analyze direct collective action on the part of Kano's industrial workers occurred during two national strikes and during local efforts to form trade unions in the face of opposition from entrepreneurial capital. To be sure, in a situation marked by the transition to semi-industrial capitalism, one should not expect to discover revolutionary consciousness where class action is directed toward the realization of an alternative social vision, such as socialist society. Rather, the appropriate objective is to assess the class component of workers' subjectivity and activity, as expressed in the transition from independent or peasant producer to first-generation industrial proletarian. Of course, the semi-industrial, transitional nature of urban Kano necessitates that one recognize the unpredictable positive and negative effects that precapitalist elements (i.e., articulations) exert on the process of class struggle.

Just as in the analysis of the labor process, one must distinguish between the *internal* and *external* determinants of class struggle, as well as the combined effect of both acting simultaneously in a given situation of industrial class struggle. Internal factors include: the solidarity of work groups formed by a particular labor process; the physical and ecological conditions of a factory; management style with respect to managerial or supervisory control; the recent history of the firm regarding relations with workers; the social rank, status and social relations of factory owners within a particular community; and the unique preconditions and/or processes required in the production of a particular commodity such as leather, textiles or utensils. External factors that may determine the timing, intensity and trajectory of class struggle include: state policy toward labor and workers' organizations; the effect of precapitalist-origin customs, rituals and material exchanges that are usually governed by religious and ethnic membership; international factors such as war, historical patterns of aggression or economic competition; consumption patterns of both the product produced and the commodities consumed by labor; and general socio-economic factors such as competition for the means of subsistence, especially housing, the degree of inequality in income distribution and the rate of inflation. Again, it is the dialectical combination of factors both internal and external to the labor process that energizes an instance of class struggle and determines any particular outcome.

After discussing the role of the Nigerian state in structuring the process of industrial class struggle, the Adebo strikes of 1971 are described in detail; first, by analyzing the active process of class struggle in three factories; and second, by describing in the workers' own words the motivation of those who, willingly or unwillingly, had been involved in the Adebo struggles. I emphasize that 1970–2 was a period of rapid industrial growth and capital accumulation, e.g., the value added in manufacturing industries grew at an annual rate of over 15 percent. My contention is that the Adebo strikes represent the first collective act of class struggle undertaken by the

221

predominantly northern, Muslim industrial proletariat since the onset of the civil war and military rule. It was argued earlier that the latter two events mark Kano's transition from Muslim mercantile to semi-industrial capitalism. For this reason, it is important to establish a baseline from which to measure the maturation of Kano's industrial proletariat during the latter years of the decade prior to the return of civilian rule. Furthermore, since trade unions did not function in Kano's factories during the Adebo strikes, this episode offers a glimpse of rank and file class struggle without any contamination from outside organizers or trade unionists.[1] For most of Kano's workers, the Adebo strikes marked their first act of collective class struggle levied against the classes that dominate them economically, politically and socially. For this historical reason alone, the class struggles over the payment of Adebo arrears merit a detailed analysis.

With the Adebo strikes serving as a historical benchmark for the emergence of industrial class struggle in Kano, the maturation of class struggle during the Udoji strikes of 1975 will be traced by comparing the Udoji and Adebo strikes. Finally, the chapter concludes with an assessment of trade union formation at the national and local levels. To begin, let us examine the role of the Nigerian state in industrial class struggle.

THE ROLE OF THE STATE IN INDUSTRIAL CLASS STRUGGLE

The Nigerian state has always played a critical role in the definition of economic and social relations, in the shaping of economic development programs and in the legal definition of workers' benefits, rights and conditions of employment. Like all capitalist states during the contemporary period, the Nigerian state is expected to foster and to nurture economic growth through economic development planning. At the same time, the state is expected to provide social, political, legal and other institutional support for the maintenance of public welfare. How do these two purposes relate to each other? O'Connor offers some insight into the problem of the capitalist state:[2]

> Our first premise is that the capitalistic state must try to fulfill two basic and often mutually contradictory functions – *accumulation* and *legitimization*. This means that the state must try to maintain or create the conditions in which profitable capital accumulation is possible. However, the state also must try to maintain or create the conditions for social harmony. A capitalist state that openly uses its coercive forces to help one class to accumulate capital at the expense of other classes loses its legitimacy and hence undermines the basis of its loyalty and support. But a state that ignores the necessity of assisting the process of capital accumulation risks drying up the source of its own power, the economy's surplus production capacity and the taxes drawn from this surplus .... The state must involve itself in the accumulation process, but it must either mystify its policies by calling them something that they are not, or it must try to conceal them (e.g., by making them administrative, not political issues).

If applied to Kano, then, access to marketing board surpluses, tax privileges and subsidized infrastructure in the form of land, railway lines, roads and industrial estates illustrate how the Nigerian state has aided capital accumulation in the interest of capitalist classes. But it would be an error to see the state as simply a one-sided instrument of the Nigerian and international bourgeoisie, precisely because the systematic needs of capitalist development require that the capitalist state avoid serving one class's interest at the expense of systemic stability. The process is much more complex and the outcome more uncertain. Wage review commissions like Morgan (1964), Adebo (1971) and Udoji (1974) are instances of state intervention on behalf of workers' interests which reflect the *legitimization* function of the capitalist state. Hence, the need for the state to legitimize itself beyond those classes which directly benefit from its accumulation activity creates a role for the state in the process of industrial class struggle.

Clearly, the tension between accumulation and legitimization applies most appropriately to advanced capitalist states that are formally democratic if not socially democratic in political structure. But some modification of the concepts is necessary in order to apply them to a peripheral capitalist state which only recently has undergone centralization and is still in the process of developing into a regional capitalist or sub-imperial (i.e., semi-peripheral) state.[3] Regarding workers' rights in this context, Touraine and others have pointed out that in many peripheral capitalist states formal workers' rights, which in the case of Europe were guaranteed through prolonged class struggle by the European working class, are gratuitously granted to workers by the post-colonial state.[4] However, given the observable deficiencies inherent in the operation of the Nigerian state – described as corrupt, inefficient and undisciplined by virtually all commentators – the question arises as to whether Nigerian workers *actually* enjoy the protection and benefits that the state is formally and legally obligated to provide them. To be sure, the answer to this question is no. Instead, I would like to suggest that the real process of receiving 'rights' is one where the Nigerian state, responding to class-based and other interest groups, defines a set of legal benefits and rights for subordinate classes. But it remains for workers themselves to engage in class struggle in order to obtain the rights they theoretically possess. Without class struggle, these rights would remain mere legal rights, notwithstanding the need for the state to legitimize itself to non-accumulating classes.

Though precipitated by the centralized state's need for legitimacy, class struggles surrounding national wage review commissions create traditions and trigger processes that, in an uneven and contradictory manner, usually advance and give expression to working class formation and working class institutions. To participate in the process of class struggle marked by direct class conflict with employers is a transforming social experience for first-generation factory workers. During this process, which may endure for hours or weeks, neophyte workers learn that they must plan to take

223

collective class action; that they must create ideological positions and tactical methods of justifying their claims for an increased share in the socially produced surplus; that they must develop strategies for both conflict and negotiation with management; and that they must produce reliable leaders from their ranks who are capable of directing the self-confidence expressed during a strike toward the formation of disciplined working class organizations.

State intervention: the Adebo commission and class struggle

At the conclusion of the Nigerian civil war, the Gowon government appointed a wage and salary review commission under Chief Simon Adebo which was charged with reviewing the conditions of public-sector workers. Such commissions of review are rooted in the wage determination process of the colonial and post-colonial state. Historically, they have defined the area in which industrial class struggle is waged. Though technically limited to making recommendations for the public sector, the commission's recommendations become the medium through which representatives of labor and capital struggle for the determination of the wage rate. In 1964, for instance, the failure of the Balewa government to implement the Morgan Commission's recommendations resulted in a national general strike.[5] By 1970, forced contributions to the civil war by wage laborers, coupled with a rapid rate of inflation caused by the war and war-related economic growth, pressured the Gowon government to appoint the Adebo Commission. The latter body took evidence both from the representatives of management, led by the Nigerian Employers Consultative Association (NECA), and from representatives of labor, led by Lagos-based central trade union organizations under a common negotiating committee called UCCLO. Representatives of labor pursued the tactic of demanding an interim cost-of-living allowance (COLA) in order to compensate workers for loss of earnings due to war-related inflation. The interim COLA award gained widespread popularity in the media, and upon pressure from labor, in December 1970 the Adebo Commission announced an interim award amounting to approximately ₦4 per month or 17 kwebo per day, which was to be backdated nine months so that a wage worker was promised one lump sum payment as COLA. The commission's concern with establishing the state's legitimization function was evident in the language of its interim report. After estimating that the inflation in food prices since the previous wage increase in 1964 varied between 25 and 165 percent (for an average of 50 percent), the commission explicitly questioned the legitimacy of recent accumulations of wealth during the civil war by the Nigerian bourgeoisie and the inequalities generated by war-induced growth:

> Such sacrifice would be easier to bear, however, if it was seen to fall equitably on all sections of the population, such that the least sacrifice was made by those in the lowest income group. From some of the representations made to us, it is clear not only that there is intolerable suffering at the bottom of the

income scale, because of the rise in the cost of living, but also that *the suffering is made more intolerable by manifestations of affluence and wasteful expenditure which cannot be explained on the basis of visible and legitimate means of income.*[6] (Emphasis theirs.)

While the commission recommended that the interim COLA award be paid to both private- and public-sector employees earning less than ₦1,048 per annum, sufficient ambiguity existed to encourage NECA and other employers to lobby the Gowon government to limit implementation solely to the public sector. The Commissioner for Labor, Enahoro, partially acceded to the demands of private employers by qualifying the award in such a way that he exempted those companies who had made wage adjustments since 1964 from paying the COLA award. In practice, if a firm's wage increases were not up to the Adebo standard, or if they had made no cost-of-living increases since 1964, as was the case in most of Kano's factories, then the company was obligated to pay COLA to its employees. But Enahoro's qualification allowed employers to define any wage increase since 1964, whatever its original purpose (e.g., seniority, productivity or skill), as a cost-of-living payment, thus avoiding the arrears payment. Peace's description of class conflict at Ikeja (Lagos) informs us that while national union leaders apparently accepted the qualification, militant workers denounced the government for selling out the workers. Neither the military government's banning of industrial strikes (Decree No. 53) nor timid union leadership prevented workers in all of Nigeria's industrial centers from striking until they had forced the government to cancel the Enahoro qualification.[7] By the end of February 1971, the military government published the following announcement in all major Nigerian newspapers:

> After careful consideration of the problems involved, the Federal Military Government has decided that in view of the general situation regarding the cost of living, employers in the private sector will be required to pay the Adebo award in full to their employees in the affected categories, notwithstanding any wage or salary increases or adjustments which they might have granted since 1964.[8]

Between December 1970 and the publication of this announcement in February, Nigerian wage workers, by heightening and intensifying the level of class struggle, had forced nearly all employers to disregard the Enahoro qualification and to pay COLA. In this sense, it is true that the wage rate was determined by the level of class struggle, for without exercising their collective class power against owners and managers of capitalist enterprises, industrial workers would not have received the recommended COLA payment.

THE RESPONSE TO ADEBO IN KANO: UNEVEN DEVELOPMENT AMONG UNORGANIZED WORKERS

To comprehend the impact of the Adebo Commission's recommended COLA payment in Kano, the circumstances which surrounded the announcement must be borne in mind. Unlike in Lagos, there were no

225

functioning trade unions in any of Kano's factories during the period of 1970–2; thus workers lacked trade union leadership or information from trade union representatives of UCCLO. The situation in Kano was much more provincial than that in Lagos: workers and management alike were uncertain about government policy. Most workers learned of the Adebo Commission's interim award from a radio broadcast, which they interpreted as a statement from the military government obligating employers to pay COLA.

Upon hearing of the award, Kano's industrial workers cared little about the 17 kwebo-per-day increase but were elated over the interim COLA, which was to be retroactive for nine months. For the typical industrial worker (i.e., unskilled and paid daily), the COLA award amounted to eleven times his weekly wage in one lump sum. Immersed in a situation where saving an equivalent amount from their meager wages would take years or would be impossible, workers discussed little else but their plans for spending the COLA payment during the first months of 1971. It did not matter that the payment was unexpected, nor that Enahoro had pronounced a qualification. From the perspective of most workers, the award was justified by their past labors. Moreover, since the military government announced the award, support for immediate payment increased even among timid workers, who interpreted government support as adding legitimacy to their pay claims. Finally, the amount of the award is also important because such a comparatively large sum would allow workers to finance a second occupation, through the purchase of a bicycle for peddlers, a sewing machine for tailors, or raw materials for leatherworkers; for others, COLA would allow them to pay the expenses of marrying a virgin or to acquire the luxury goods, such as a radio, a watch or clothing, which they had long sought. To be sure, the size of the payment crystallized workers and management into two hostile yet interdependent classes, as an urban-born worker's statement indicates: 'What caused the strike? Love of self caused it. The managers wanted their money and the workers wanted their Adebo money.'

The articulation of precapitalist institutions: Muslim festivals

Clear as the material interest of each class appeared to be, other factors, *external* to the labor process, shaped the intensity of the conflict which alternately flashed and simmered throughout the months of January and February. For Kano's Muslim workers, the timing of the announcement in late December came on the eve of the most lavish and materially demanding Muslim festival, *Id el-Fitr*, an event which is accompanied ideally by slaughtering a ram, feasting, exchanging presents and offering customary gifts of new clothing to a worker's wives and children. Failure to clothe one's wives properly during the days of the festival is considered shameful and often a cause for divorce. In this instance, therefore, pressures for consumption generated by precapitalist institutions articulated with a

226

classical situation of industrial class conflict to intensify the participation and the solidarity of Muslim workers. Interestingly, workers felt the contradiction expressed in this articulation. In the following quote, a worker-mallam expressed the ambivalence he felt about striking before the festival by chiding himself for his inadequate manifestation of the Hausa virtue of patience:

> The company said it needed time to figure up Adebo, but the workers said that they must have the money before the festival. If there were no festival there would not have been any strike . . . . Me, I agreed [with the strike] but it was a lack of patience that brought it. I wanted the money like everyone else.

The combination of festival pressures, inflation and the workers' generalized perception that the military government ordered employers to pay COLA created a wave of strikes and negotiations throughout the months of January and February, with several types of resolution. Among smaller firms which employed many casual but few permanent employees, representatives of labor and capital negotiated a date for COLA payment without conflict. But the majority of firms, especially those with large payrolls (i.e., over 100 workers), resisted payment by stating that COLA only applied to the public sector; these firms experienced long, sometimes violent strikes before a date for payment was set. Finally, a minority of firms, usually owned by Hausa industrial capitalists, experienced long and bitter strikes but never paid any COLA. Of our three sample factories from Chapter Five, Factories A and B fall into the second category of resolution, as both experienced bitter, violent strikes; Factory C falls into the last category, having undergone a long strike without payment by the Hausa owners. Again, while state intervention set the stage for collective class struggle, both the outcome and the forms of struggle depended on the relations of labor and capital at the factory. Let us return now to Factory A.

THE ADEBO SETTLEMENT AT FACTORY A: NEGOTIATION AND STRUGGLE

The Adebo Commission's announcement of COLA came on the heels of a wildcat strike at the utensil factory by workers who protested the prolongation of their casual labor status. This status meant they could be paid for only eight hours of work instead of for the twelve-hour shift they actually worked. Interestingly, most strikers were commuters from the villages, and their leader was an experienced commuter who had worked at the firm earlier as a permanent worker. By combining oppressive fire work, dangerous safety conditions, abusive supervisors and the underpayment of casual workers, the utensil factory had earned a reputation as the most exploitative industrial employer at the Bompai industrial estate. Attempts at forming a trade union had collapsed under pressure from political parties prior to the civil war, and during the war, union leaders were lost to military service.

After waiting patiently until mid-January for an announcement by

227

management regarding COLA payment, workers delegated several senior workers and trusted headmen to ask the Asian manager to set a date for receiving their 'Adebo'. At first, the manager informed the workers that permission must be obtained from Lagos in order to pay them and that 'if any other firm paid in Kano, then the utensil firm would be second in paying Adebo arrears'. Though not satisfied with the manager's statement, workers accepted it until the following pay-day. But at that time, when the manager repeated his statement that they would be the second to pay, he added that a poor groundnut harvest had reduced the market for their products, so that it was unlikely that the company could easily meet the cost of Adebo arrears for a labor force of 900 workers. That same day a second meeting was held between representatives of labor and management. The manager again repeated his earlier statements and added that it was unlikely that the military government would require payment or that the firm could afford to make such an arrears payment. The meeting concluded with a statement from the manager that workers had best forget about ever receiving a COLA payment.

When the manager's statement was carried to the production workers by their representatives, production discipline declined rapidly as workers met in small groups to discuss their situation. *Id el-Fitr* was approaching, and COLA remained unpaid. Most importantly, rumors circulated that a groundnut crushing mill with few permanent employees had paid COLA in full. During the afternoon, headmen, experienced workers and most fireworkers met to discuss a course of action. Soon it was agreed that the night-shift workers should be informed of the manager's refusal to pay COLA, that both the night-shift workers and the day-shift workers should meet at the manager's office the following morning during the changing of the shifts, and that workers from both shifts should collectively demonstrate their support for their representatives while they were negotiating within the manager's office.

The next morning, while both shifts demonstrated outside, workers' representatives met with the manager and informed him that the groundnut mill had paid COLA and that, according to the manager's earlier statement, the utensil factory thus was obligated to pay COLA to its workers. When confronted with this information, however, the manager is said to have countered that he was referring to the major employers on the Bompai industrial estate and not to small groundnut crushing mills in the township area. After arguing for payment, the workers returned to work, but with a more cynical opinion of their opponent, as a workers' representative recounts: 'The other companies [mentioned by the manager] told their workers the same thing he is telling us: "They were all planning to pay us." They were "playing" with us, we laborers. But they were playing with eggs on top of rocks.'

Again, on the following morning, the negotiation ritual was repeated with both factory shifts present in the factory yard, but in this instance the leaders declared that they would refuse to leave the factory until a date was set for payment. By now, a number of Kano's factories had announced a date for payment. Responding to the workers' demands, the manager pointed out that those firms having paid already were much smaller than the utensil factory and that for large employers of labor it was more difficult to find the cash for the unexpected Adebo payments. As the negotiations continued, workers became restless and irritated over the failure to reach an agreement. But when the manager stated that the workers could not be paid because the Nigerian paymaster (who was intensely disliked by the workers) was not present, the workers' representatives left the office in disgust. They knew the paymaster merely followed the manager's orders.

Before the older workers and headmen could meet and agree on a new negotiating strategy, workers whom informants described as 'younger and less patient' began throwing rocks and hardened chemicals taken from the factory stores at the manager's office, breaking the windows of the factory, the office and the company vehicles. The workers' representatives claim that they did not join the younger workers, but instead were told by them to await the arrival of the police and then to announce their opposition to violence, while continuing to press for the Adebo arrears for all workers. After nearly two hours of siege, the manager was able to contact the police. When the police did arrive, the frightened and mildly injured manager immediately capitulated by agreeing to pay the Adebo arrears and to negotiate with the workers' committee. Before leaving the factory, the representatives demanded and received assurances that half of the Adebo money would be paid before the festival of *Id el-Fitr*, that no punishment would be given to striking workers and that meetings would be scheduled to discuss and correct the factory's hazardous working conditions.

Efforts to form working class organizations

Whereas few other factory strike committees survived beyond the payment of Adebo arrears, the committee at the utensil factory struggled for several months to transform itself into a viable workers' organization. Initially at least, the committee enjoyed the support of a majority of workers, most probably because the leadership advocated broad improvements in pay and working conditions for the rank and file. Democratic and open meetings were held, and workers proposed concrete reforms to management. The most important recommendations made were: (1) Economic benefits – demands for wage parity with laborers in the public sector, incentive bonuses, loans for workers with seniority, increased pay for seniority and overtime, and loans for transport (i.e., for bicycles and motorbikes); (2) Health and safety – correction of existing safety and health hazards, including guards for pressing machines, helmets, gloves and vests for fireworkers, salt tablets and other 'medicines against fire' for fireworkers, ready transport to the hospital for injured workers, the establishment of a factory dispensary, and fans for circulating noxious gases and heat from the fire section; (3) Conditions of service – daily paid workers should receive legal rates for a twelve-hour day and a permanent factory number; (4) General – demands for uniforms, vacations with pay, and regular meetings between management and workers' representatives in order to air griev-ances. Finally, supervisors were exhorted to treat workers with respect and dignity rather than with humiliation and curses.

With these demands as a platform, the committee held several meetings with management and initially did succeed in achieving some reforms. For example, casual labor was temporarily paid equal rates, and cotton gloves and some salt tablets were provided to fireworkers for a short time. But within five months of the strike, the achievements of the workers' commit-tee were dramatically undercut by management. In a cynical but neverthe-less cunning maneuver, the management created a new level of supervisors located between alien supervisors and headmen. These new supervisory positions were offered to and accepted by prominent members of the strike committee at a wage approximately three times that of an ordinary wage laborer. When the new supervisors were installed, the factory's rank and file and the remaining strike committee members refused to participate in the committee's deliberations. The new supervisors, ignoring the antipathy shown to them by rank-and-file workers, still wished to represent the workers. The following dialogue reflects the tension between workers and 'supervisors' over the latter's hypocrisy toward fellow workers. The dia-logue was paraphrased to me by a fireworker, Y.B., who was active in the strike; his former friend, S.H., had just accepted a new supervisory position:

Y.B.: We chose you to be one of our leaders and now you have become a big man, but not with our agreement nor with our advice. Now you must be a friend of the manager but you must go and tell the manager that you represent us and are a friend of the laborers. How can you do this?

S.H.: No! Allah has given us our new position. I want the new job and it is a victory [advancement] so I want it.

Y.B.: Since you have achieved victory do you think we small laborers will tell you what is bothering us now that you are friends with the manager and will tell him?

S.H.: No, no it is not like that. Do not tell the others what I told you. Whatever bothers you small laborers I will go and tell the manager, but the manager has not done anything about them. I will not tell the manager anything laborers tell me secretly.

The demise of the strike committee reaffirms the difficulty first-generation workers encounter when attempting to form working class organizations in an atmosphere of rapid economic growth, growing inequality and the attraction of upward mobility. Yet, despite this setback, workers at the utensil factory continued to maintain a high level of militancy, especially those in the fire section, who were much more likely than others to support the Adebo strike. Several months later, when a popular timekeeper was fired by a corrupt Nigerian paymaster, workers engaged in violent wildcat strikes which were repressed only by police intervention and the imprisonment of many workers. For their part, management continued to exploit workers by laying off older and experienced workers during a trade recession and then hiring temporary commuters from the village who, unknowingly, worked a twelve-hour shift for eight hours' pay.

Adebo at Factory A: consciousness and class struggle

The process of securing COLA was neither orderly nor disciplined but rather an example of what Hobsbawm calls 'collective bargaining by riot'.[9] Even though workers were sold out by most of their leaders, and though many of the abuses were reintroduced by management during a trade recession when class solidarity was at a low ebb, workers participated in, or at least were part of, a typical form of early class struggle between capital and labor. How did this unique experience affect their perception of themselves, fellow workers and management? To answer this question, we must move from an abstract level of class consciousness to the texture and actual content of workers' consciousness as expressed in their own words. The following quotes were taken from workers after the strike. The purpose of their inclusion here is to provide an understanding of the range of possible interpretations of the strike and the variety of motives for men to support class struggle or, alternatively, to reject it.

To begin, let us examine the perspective of two militants from the fire section who were firemen from the Birni. Of interest here is their critical perception of how the benefits of the social division of labor are distributed between direct producers and owner-managers:

> Here there is five times more work than pay we receive. They [management] have cars and money, but they have no mercy and do not help us. If you are old they will chase you from the factory.

The second worker also emphasizes the insecurity of factory labor at the utensil factory:

> The company gets a big profit from our work, this is not fair. They do not do anything for us . . . I have worked here a long time but we have no seniority benefits: we are all paid the same.

From these comments and others, one can surmise that fire-section workers born in the Birni had developed the most advanced level of working class consciousness of all the workers I encountered. It is obvious that their perspective goes beyond the moralistic interpretation of workers who are offended by insulting language or the failure of management to respect the mutual obligations assured in the master-servant relationship. Rather, the militants interpret the conflict as arising from inequality that is rooted in the social division of labor and distribution of surplus. Hence, for them, the conflict is not moral but structural, in that they both recognize that they produce more value than the amount they receive.

Class cohesion: the creation of fictive kinship

One may distinguish a second motive for supporting class struggle among workers at the utensil factory: that originating from the labor process and the social bonds which join men together to form fictive kinship relations. Below are two statements expressed by rural resident commuters that reflect elements of class consciousness. While not as articulate nor as militant as the prior examples, they do express the subjective feeling of class solidarity between workers who recently participated in class struggle:

> The manager said he would pay a long time in the future but the fireworkers said that they would not want to wait for a long time. It is obligatory to strike for they are my brothers and I will receive money with them.

The second commuter expressed a deep ambivalence regarding this class conflict. But, in spite of his peasant instinct to avoid conflict with authority, he reluctantly supported the strike:

> The company said that they would pay later ... Me, I am against it [striking], but because of my brothers, the laborers, I cannot say I am against it ... I prefer resting peacefully.

Finally, a migrant uses the language of kinship to express class solidarity even beyond the individual factory where he is employed:

> All laborers are brothers, we must help each other because the company did not give us what was ours.

As we shall see in Chapter Seven, not all workers supported the strike. Yet their reasoning for not supporting the strike is complex and worthy of analysis. One urban worker at the utensil factory supported class struggle in principle but was dismayed by the violent tactics used by workers to gain their COLA:

> The company did not pay early and the workers wanted money for *Salah* [*Id el-Fitr*]. I did not agree with the strike because of the violence, the destroying of property and the unreasonable waste. It is not fair to destroy the company's property. If there were no violence I would agree with the strike.

Others, however, believed that they would be paid if they remained patient. This man worked in the machine section where the labor process isolated workers from each other. Apparently the fireworkers forced recalcitrant workers to respect the strike:

> The fire workers forced us to strike. I prefer patience. Violence is not good. How can this [violence] agree with Islamic teachings?

232

To conclude, factors internal to the labor process, such as dangerous working conditions, racist and humiliating treatment from Asian supervisors and the class solidarity generated by the labor process, best explain the intensity of class struggle at the utensil factory during the Adebo strikes.

THE ADEBO SETTLEMENT AT FACTORY B

At the time of the Adebo negotiations, this textile factory was the largest employer of industrial labor in Kano (with about 1500 workers), operating at full capacity with three shifts. Under management pressure, earlier efforts at trade union organization had degenerated into a supervisor-dominated extortion agency which extracted 'union dues' from naive workers, especially commuters (who accounted for a significant minority of the labor force). Yet, despite the strict factory discipline and management's repression of workers' organizations, workers possessed a collective memory in the form of working class oral tradition, the ability to learn from management's past deceptions and the willingness to consult with experienced workers who, though not employed at Factory B, shared a common territorial community with the textile workers. Past conflicts shaped the Adebo struggles at Factory B.

In a deliberative process similar to that used by the Adebo Commission, the Morgan Wage Review Commission had issued a report in 1964 recommending a wage increase and an arrears payment. But these recommendations were not implemented immediately in the private sector, and organized labor declared a general strike in order to make the Morgan Commission's recommendations binding on the private sector. The management at Factory B, however, instead of paying all workers the recommended arrears payment, paid only the supervisors, and then instructed them to inform union leaders, gathered at a general strike center, that Factory B had paid the Morgan arrears to all workers in full. In response to the management's chicanery, a minority of workers attempted an industrial action, but they were unsuccessful. The following quote comes from an experienced worker, a prominent leader in the Adebo conflict, who reflected upon the Morgan settlement:

> We were patient, because we had no power nor anyone to carry our complaints to . . . . Beside, we knew we would not be successful. The workers were not together in their agreement, they were afraid of losing their jobs. When we heard on the radio that this company had paid, we were very sad because we did not receive anything.

Once Adebo was announced, the older and experienced workers, having been cheated during the Morgan settlement, quickly made the analogy between the two and informed the younger and inexperienced workers of company tactics in 1964. Just as in the case of Factory A, management refused to set a date for payment, offering only a vaguely worded statement

233

about possible payment in the future. But, unlike at Factory A, it appears that the driving force propelling suspicion toward management's intentions was rooted in the historical lesson of the Morgan Commission. Meanwhile, as December passed into January without payment, it became known that the management was finalizing plans to lay off an entire shift, numbering around 400 workers. Therefore, in addition to *Id el-Fitr*, retrenchment added more pressure to the already boiling cauldron. This created two distinct yet mutually reinforcing industrial actions over the Adebo payment.

The strike by retrenched workers

The shift designated to be laid off was composed of the most recently employed workers, many of whom were also recent migrants to the city.[10] Although they were illiterate, they recognized the significance of a red line beneath their names on their time cards, and they demanded an explanation from the timekeeper. Though claiming to be uncertain, he confirmed the forthcoming retrenchment. Industrial discipline broke down: those workers affected either stopped work completely or merely worked at a fraction of the normal pace. All discussion centered on how retrenchment would affect their Adebo payment.

Fortunately, one of the activists, a young Hausa worker who had lived in Kano less than a year and had worked in the factory for a few months, was available for interviewing during the first industrial action. In recounting the shift's preparation for the industrial action, he informed us that before going to the factory he sought advice from his experienced neighbors who resided in the working class area of Tudun Wada. Here one observes how social ecology structures communication within an emerging yet unorganized working class. For, in the absence of formally organized communication through trade unions, the homogeneous, densely packed communities adjacent to the industrial estate provided the medium for informal class communication and the formulation of strategies with which the workers hoped to obtain their COLA. Our informant offered this account of his consultation with his Tudun Wada neighbor, an experienced industrial worker:

> He told us that he had struck once before at the utensil factory [Factory A] because the company attempted to decrease wages . . . he advised us to strike as it would be profitable; he said that we should go to the gate and force everyone to keep away from work.

After discussing strike tactics and the Adebo situation with experienced workers from other factories, the activists decided to explain what they had learned to all workers on their shift, and to meet the following day in front of the factory immediately prior to the 3:00–11:00 p.m. shift:

> We met the next day, Tuesday, before we entered, at the tables in front of the factory where we ate [bread and tea]. We decided that if they pay us, we will take it and then leave. We decided that we needed at least five pounds [₦10]

234

... We thought that they did not want us and were going to dismiss us without any reason; we felt very bad about this because we would not see the other workers again.

Through the agitation of the activists, most of the remaining workers on the shift also recognized their plight, and factory discipline broke down until the shift foreman called a meeting around seven in the evening. He confirmed that most of the shift was to be terminated. Furthermore, because of their lack of discipline, he told workers not to return again until pay-day, which fell on the following Saturday. Informants differ over precisely what the foreman said regarding Adebo payment. Some believe he told the workers that the Adebo arrears would not be paid to the retrenched workers. Others disagree. Regardless of the content of the actual statement, it is important to understand that scores of workers *believed* that the supervisor, in anger over their rejection of his authority, told the retrenched workers that they would not be paid their Adebo arrears. Moreover, when coupled with the knowledge of the company's chicanery over the Morgan payments in 1964, the foreman's statement left little doubt in the minds of most workers on that shift that conflict was imminent. (Subsequently the foreman was attacked by striking workers, an action described as retribution for accumulated abuses and extortions.) Accordingly, when the shift was let out at eleven o'clock, a group of workers met to discuss their situation and to develop a strategic understanding among themselves. Here is our informant's account:

> First, we listened to A.B., who said that they were being dismissed without a fair reason and would not be paid, and that they all should return the following morning and stop people from entering work .... Then, he said, 'those who agree to come back should come back tomorrow morning around 8:00. The company wants to cheat us; we should not allow them to do this.' We said, 'yes we agree', and then we agreed to come back.

The following morning, after first obtaining an agreement from the security guards and gatemen not to interfere with their industrial action, approximately 300 workers who were to be dismissed waited outside the gate. When the factory manager arrived, he agreed to speak to the workers in the yard but was unable to satisfy their demands for payment immediately. (Some informants state he refused outright to commit the management to payment, while the manager states he fully intended to pay all workers.) Within minutes of entering the factory yard, the dismissed workers began attacking and screaming at the manager and throwing stones at the company's office, breaking windows and damaging parked vehicles. Meanwhile, the supervisors closed the doors from the factory to the yard in order to block sympathetic friends working on the first shift from joining and aiding their fellow workers. According to a militant leader of the second strike who was working inside, 'The doors were closed down so the finishers and weavers could not join the striking workers. We wanted to join them.'

235

By 9:00 a.m. the police arrived, only to discover that tear gas was necessary to force the striking workers from the factory yard. Then, because the police demanded a solution to the civil disturbance, the management agreed to pay Adebo arrears to the striking workers of the retrenched shift on the following Saturday. Interestingly, informants report that after being taunted by the workers the police confided their support for the claim for COLA payment.

Strikes under democratic leadership

Following this conflict, production was erratic. Each shift demanded to be paid, but the company procrastinated, stating that they must undertake the proper accounting in order to pay the dismissed workers correctly. When Saturday arrived and the striking workers were being paid their Adebo arrears, the morning shift was informed by the manager that the remaining two shifts would be paid in April of that year, over three months later and long after the Muslim festival of *Id el-Fitr*. This statement provoked a distressing memory among the first shift's workers, according to a weaving instructor (headman) and strike leader:

> We were inside the factory watching those workers being paid outside. We thought about the last time [1964], during the time of Morgan. We were patient then, but now we feared that we would not be paid, just like before. And after that, where could we carry our cries [grievances]? When we saw the other shift being paid, we thought that we did not agree with this.

During the noon lunch break, the COLA payment was discussed among workers of the first shift, but neither an organization nor a strategy was developed, and at the end of the break, all returned to work without incident.

Finally, while most workers returned to their machines, three experienced workers, who were weaving instructors or headmen in the weaving and beaming sections, met to initiate a strategy for work stoppage. One should note that the noon break was an opportune moment, for it was known that the factory manager was usually absent from noon until approximately 2:00 p.m. After agreeing on the necessity of a strike action, each of these three men went to one of the remaining sections (i.e., winding, raising and finishing) and made the proposal to their work groups to strike for an immediate Adebo payment. Soon the production workers had left their machines and were milling in the factory yard. Although resistant at first, the better paid and more prestigious loom mechanics eventually responded to the urging of striking weavers and followed the production workers out to the factory yard. The process of calling out workers for the strike did not follow ethnic, religious or community networks; instead, both leadership and tactics were derived from the skill hierarchy and the social organization of the factory, that is, from the labor

236

process. The determinants of class struggle at Factory B, therefore, were *internal* rather than *external* to the industrial labor process. Leadership emerged from the headmen who worked alongside unskilled laborers. By 1:00 p.m. production had stopped, and the shift foremen telephoned the factory manager at his home. When the manager returned, he demanded to know what the workers wanted. The weaving instructor informs us of the strikers' response:

> We said that, 'we wanted our Adebo'. Then the manager came closer and some workers came forward to beat him, but he was protected by the foreman and the supervisors.

It is important to note that there was no stone-throwing or violence during this episode, perhaps because these 'second strikers', unlike the dismissed workers, knew that they would continue to work at the factory. As at Factory A, there was a tactical division between the pro-violence and anti-violence factions, but in this instance the non-violent workers prevailed. They exercised class discipline by threatening and cursing the violence-prone workers, labelling them *yan iska* or hooligans. To some degree, older and senior workers exercised class discipline by cautioning younger and more impulsive workers against attacking the manager and his supervisors or throwing stones at the vehicles and the factory windows. According to an experienced urban worker:

> When we heard about the strike we said: 'Just refuse to work. Do not throw rocks or do anything violent. It is better this way; we will get our money this way.'

A second experienced worker, a migrant, defined the problem of class discipline as one of restraining the peasants and recent rural emigrants from engaging in violence:

> We told those peasants: 'If you throw stones and destroy company property then we will be at fault. It is a crazy thing to do. It is better if you sit down and refuse to work. Then the police will not hit you. But if you hurt someone with stones, then the laborers will be at fault.'

Soon after the manager returned from lunch, a tired and harried detachment of police arrived, under the authority of an inspector. When the latter asked the workers what had caused the walkout, their leaders responded:

> We want to be paid our Adebo. We remember when you, the police, came and beat us and drove us away during the time of Morgan. We did not receive our Morgan money then.

The inspector informed the workers that they should form a strike committee with a spokesman to negotiate with management over the date of payment. The workers chose T.R., a weaving instructor who lived in the new workers' residential area of Dakata. (Interestingly, his family had once

237

cultivated land which was confiscated by the state for the Bompai industrial estate. During the interview, his father described in graphic detail the trauma of being driven off their land during the mid-1950s by mounted police who cleared the future industrial area of resistant villagers.) Ironically, T.R.'s first wage-laboring experience was as a day laborer for the construction of the present textile mill.

After forming a committee, all parties agreed to return to the manager's office with the police inspector in order to negotiate a settlement. Acutely aware of probable accusations of being 'paid off' by management, T.R. first announced in front of management as well as the assembled workers that any agreement must be democratically ratified by the assembled workers. Then the management made an initial offer of ₦10, to be paid immediately, with the remainder to be paid in April. According to T.R., he took the ₦10 offer and returned to the assembled workers:

> There I mounted a bench that was brought over from the food vendors' area and I told the laborers what the manager had offered. When the workers heard the offer, they said 'no, we do not agree'.

T.R. presented a workers' counter-demand for ₦20 now and the remainder in April. It was rejected. Finally, after more discussions and pressure from the police inspector for a resolution, both parties agreed to accept ₦15 immediately and the remainder in April. In finalizing the agreement, T.R. gives this account:

> We signed a paper with the manager and the police on our agreement. Then we demanded to be paid ₦15 that day. Those workers who were to be dismissed received all of their money at that time.

Just as most experienced workers feared, the price for leadership was heavy, for within four months T.R. and the other activists were dismissed for disrespectfulness to a supervisor. T.R. gave this account of his dismissal:

> It was the month of May following the strike. Sule, the shift foreman, accused me of sleeping during work. He punished me by ordering three days without work. After three days, I returned to pick up my pay and I received a termination notice. I left the money with the accountant and went to Sule to ask him why I was terminated: '*Ranka ya dade* [may your life be long – a traditional greeting given by commoners to the aristocracy]. Why did you terminate me?' Sule responded: 'You are a *dan iska* [hooligan]. You show me that you have no shame.' I returned the insult with '*Ubanka*' [father-fucker]. Then I wanted to beat him, but the other workers stopped me. Me, I knew I would be dismissed because I was the leader of the strike.

The last time I interviewed T.R., he was hiring out and repairing bicycles at the entrance to Dakata. Most of his clients were laborers or the laboring poor. Thus, in this instance, a working class leader's militancy channeled him into Kano's self-employed, informal sector. Again, T.R.'s experience illustrates the circulation of labor and class experiences between wage workers of the leburori and the independent producers of the informal sector.

Class struggle at Factory B: some perspectives

Following the format used in presenting workers' interpretations of the strike at Factory A, I want to present some quotes from workers who participated in the strike at the textile factory. Just as in the case of Factory A, factors internal to the labor process determined the outcome of the strike. Weavers took leadership roles, a fact that arises from their concentration, close supervision by management and their understanding that production depended on their output. Yet differences also exist between the two situations. Here workers attacked violently exploitative African supervisors, the labor process did not create solidarity like that among 'fireworkers', and rural workers (commuters) seemed to be less involved.

Many workers supported the strike because they distrusted the management. An experienced migrant described the situation:

> The company would not say when they were going to pay and the workers feared that the company was planning something in order to cheat the workers .... If you are supposed to get something and it's yours, and they said it was yours, and then they say wait, then you have to do something yourself to get it.

For most militants, therefore, the experience of Morgan and the distrust of management brought a succinct and straightforward response:

> They cheated us by refusing to give us our money. If you talk to the manager, they will fire you.

But for a large number of workers, it was the timing of the payment which moved them to support the strike, for they felt the pressure from the expenses involved in *Id el-Fitr*:

> The company did not tell us the date when we were to be paid, and the *Salah* [*Id el-Fitr*] was coming closer; and we and the other workers had many people to feed like wives and children.

Finally, a rural-resident commuter who supported the strike only as a last resort commented:

> If someone says that they will pay you today, then tomorrow, then again and then again, people like me who do not have anything, will think that we will not be paid.

Most workers who did not support the strike accepted management's promise to pay in April, but more importantly, they were appalled by the violence of the first strike. According to an urban worker:

> The company said that they would pay later, but some workers have no patience. You see patience brings rewards ... I did not come to work that day because of the strike. I do not like violence and cursing.

239

A commuter offered a conservative interpretation of Islam regarding the strike:

> They broke windows. This is not good. Allah brought the Adebo money, the strike did not bring it.

Precapitalist structures: the patrimonial consciousness of the household

While a significant proportion of workers did not support the strike for reasons of timing, tactics, or simply because they maintained consensus with management, a small number of workers did not recognize the situation as one of class conflict or even that they were employed in a capitalist industrial organization. For this minority, the process of class struggle was *iskanci* (hooliganism) because they applied the relationship and consciousness of the precapitalist household to their dealings with management. Thus, for this minority, household norms apply: gifts are not obligations, and public attacks on the household head are forbidden. Their statements are evidence not only for the unevenly developed nature of a first-generation industrial proletariat but also for the constraining influence exerted by the articulation of precapitalist structures on class solidarity within an emerging urban proletariat. Hence it should be emphasized that elements of precapitalist institutions may articulate with capitalist elements to strengthen working class consciousness, as in the example of the talakawa or certain features of Islamic institutions, but at the same time, these elements may dilute the cohesion of an emergent urban working class, even during the intense class struggles surrounding Adebo payments.

Such forms of consciousness, which I have labeled household or patrimonial consciousness, were expressed by workers of all urban statuses and from all three factories. Here an urban worker from Factory B offers his perception of the strike:

> The workers feared that they would not be paid, like the Morgan money when the government said pay and the company did not pay ... I did not know Adebo was coming; the government gave it to me. I cannot strike about something that is not mine, that does not come from my efforts.

A migrant from the same factory expressed a similar view:

> If you are a laborer, and they say that they will give you something, and then they do not give it to you well, then it is not yours, is it? Because of this, you cannot complain or strike over it.

A third worker states the ideology of household relations overtly:

> Adebo was a gift; therefore we should not cause trouble because it is not my family nor my house.

Patrimonial consciousness illustrates how social experiences within a precapitalist household retain a grip on the consciousness of workers subordinated to the labor process of capitalist production. Though some

240

workers expressing patrimonial forms of consciousness toward the Adebo strikes are found among urbans and migrants, most were commuters. Thus patrimonialism among commuters suggests how factors external to the labor process, such as residence and ongoing social relations, mediate and constrain the impact of the labor process on the formation of class consciousness. Unlike the rural-born but urban-resident migrants, commuters were divorced from the urban social processes that structured the cultural and social life of the leburori and the urban talakawa. Impoverished, dominated by authoritarian rural aristocracy, threatened by urban expansion and their own demographic fertility, the majority of commuters at this factory were not only caught between two radically different systems of production, they often thought of themselves as too poor to participate in working class struggles and therefore unable to take advantage of the relative freedom of urban life. As one commuter expressed his perspective on class struggle:

> We rural people have a great fear of suffering. The strike was not good because if there is no work, there is no food.

A second commuter is both pragmatic regarding his work and hostile to the strike:

> The strike prevented me from working and earning a living . . . . It wasted our time . . . . It is useless; what I want to do is rest peacefully.

To conclude, Factory B presents a paradox. Although it was the largest and most organizationally complex factory and, at least superficially, had the most formally rationalized management structure, class struggle here took the most disorganized form yet found in any firm: two strikes, widespread violence, and great resistance on the part of commuters to support class struggle. Unlike Factory A, no strike committee attempting to evolve into a trade union was formed during the Adebo strike. Yet, by 1978, this same textile firm had undergone a profound transition. A militant, worker-supported trade union emerged to overthrow the 'broker'-organized union that had been formed by trade union professionals from Kaduna.

Finally, let us examine class struggle at an indigenously owned firm, Factory C, with attention focused on the question of whether 'national' capital can successfully mediate the tension between capital and labor.

THE ADEBO SETTLEMENT AT FACTORY C: COMMUNITY CLEAVAGES AND CLASS STRUGGLE

Workers at the Hausa-owned textile factory struggled for months to receive their COLA. Despite their disciplined and virtually non-violent strategy, their struggle produced nothing in terms of benefits, only the loss of several weeks' wages. Nevertheless, this case study is an extremely valuable one,

241

for it provides insight into the process of class struggle under Nigerian capital. Here Kano's merchant-industrial bourgeoisie used capital siphoned off from groundnut marketing board surpluses to make the transition to industrial production. Yet it retained many of the institutional features characteristic of mercantile capitalist production. For instance, the ideology of management was overtly paternalistic; and workers felt some communal pride in working for the first indigenous textile firm to be established in Nigeria. Because local merchant capitalists founded the firm, workers initially felt a tinge of communal loyalty that mediated their class differences with management. It is noteworthy that during the first decade of operation, and even until mismanagement, embezzlement, and competition from more efficient firms reduced profits, the evidence indicates that the owners made an effort to define laborers as subordinate members of a Muslim urban community. The observance of Muslim obligations toward dependents – Friday prayer, a factory imam, time off for bereavement, family visits – reflects the Hausa industrialists' immature understanding of the necessity to control and subordinate labor under industrial capitalism. Nevertheless, though Hausa industrialists soon overcame this immaturity, Factory C represents a sincere effort to introduce industrial paternalism on the Muslim model.

If one analyzed the period prior to the Adebo strikes, it is not the case that class conflict was absent, but rather that the resolution of the conflict between workers and the managing director took on the paternalism so typical of household relations under mercantile capitalism. To take an illuminating incident, a dispute arose during the late 1960s over the abolition of paid leave periods and the half-hour extension of the working day with no pay increase. The weavers led the strike, and the managing director fired all the strike leaders. But after the dismissed workers visited his office, begging his forgiveness, expressing sorrow for their action and appealing to his sense of mercy, all were reinstated, provided they promised never to strike again. Furthermore, the workers' belief that a personal relationship existed between the managing director and certain workers, mostly experienced residents of the Birni, persisted well beyond the conclusion of the Adebo strike. An older, downwardly mobile worker from a trading family, with a marriage link to the managing director, felt it was still possible for him to intervene personally: 'I know the director. If anyone is dismissed, I can go and talk with him, and he will bring them back. I have done it twice already.'

Paternalism, Islam and class struggle

Paternalism, however, did not eliminate class tensions and the emergence of class struggle. This is clear when one examines the origins of the first trade union at this factory. In 1961, a British factory manager punished a worker-mallam found praying without permission by imposing a seven-day

242

suspension from work. In response, the worker-mallam organized a strike over the prayer issue. When I interviewed the latter in 1972, he had left the factory to earn his livelihood as a Koranic school teacher in the Birni. According to his account:

> It began when I went outside the factory to pray. The European manager caught me and sent me home for seven days. The laborers held a meeting in Garanya ward, behind the Palace Cinema. There I told them that we should not agree to this ruining of our religion by this company. We should do something about it. I told them that the Koran and the *Hadith* of Bukari instructed us to come together in order to help each other. Then all the laborers went to Sarkin Sanusi (Emir of Kano) with our complaint. Sanusi called the managing director but he ran away. Then he called the European manager and told him 'You cannot stop our people from praying at the correct time.' Then we were given permission to pray at the proper time at the factory.

Of interest here is the manner in which workers responded to the alienation emanating from the labor process of capitalist production. The observance of exact prayer time is fundamental to Hausa interpretations of Islam. By mobilizing workers around this issue, the worker-mallam transformed a class issue into an Islamic national issue. The outcome of this struggle was the formation of a trade union that went on to pursue mainstream working class issues such as pay, paid leaves, benefits and trade union recognition. Here class and national consciousness converged in the face of a ruling by a European manager representing the interest of a Hausa industrialist. In contrast to situations where factors internal to the labor process determined class struggle, in this instance precapitalist ideological and organizational elements articulated with capitalist social relations to strengthen the power and solidarity of an emerging industrial proletariat. What this example suggests is that, whenever appropriate, workers will draw upon precapitalist resources in order to struggle against the demands of capitalist production, regardless of the apparent contradictions imposed by the internal logic of both systems.

At the time of the Adebo Commission's announcement of COLA, the firm was undergoing a new process of capitalist rationalization whereby paternalistic privileges were reduced in order to lower the cost of labor. Not only had the working day been extended by one half-hour (i.e., absolute surplus value), but paid vacations, paid leave for family deaths (three days), medical services at the factory and company-sponsored loans had been eliminated. It is important to remember that the Adebo announcement coincided with a period of increased competition in the Nigerian textile industry, declining profits and a movement on the part of the local bourgeoisie toward investment in modern industrial production at the new industrial estates (i.e., the transition to semi-industrial capitalism). Thus, in order to accumulate capital in the face of competition with larger, more modern and internationalized capitalists, the paternalistic ethic so char-

243

acteristic of an earlier, mercantile phase of national capital was giving way to more efficient and more exploitative forms of production. Lest these changes on the part of Hausa industrialists be interpreted as morally invidious, it must be emphasized that the *only* advantage available to Hausa industrialists, relative to foreign capitalists, rested on lowering the cost of labor power. All evidence indicates that Hausa industrialists pursue this advantage whenever the labor market allows, thus creating a tendency toward a segmented labor market.

Class struggle under paternalism

After Factories A and B had gone out on strike to receive their COLA, and after February began without a confirmation of payment from the managing director at Factory C, workers there met and sent delegations to the managing director to inquire about payment. After receiving obscure statements which workers interpreted as procrastination, a group of weavers on the night shift (11 p.m. to 7 a.m.) called a meeting during their dinner break to discuss a plan for an industrial action. Those favoring an immediate strike prevailed over those favoring patience and continued negotiation.

By midnight, the shift had abandoned the factory and demanded that the manager agree to the Adebo Commission's recommendations. The following morning the first shift's workers were informed of the night shift's strike action and an informal picket line developed around the factory gates. According to informants, one of the purposes of the picket line was to prevent frustrated workers from destroying factory property. Soon several police officers were sent to guard the factory, but no conflict erupted as negotiations had begun indirectly with the managing director. In this instance, community ties with factory owners encouraged workers to conduct a disciplined, non-violent strike.

During the first day of the strike, workers asked the office personnel to intervene on their behalf and to encourage the company to pay them. Approximately one week later discussions with the federal labor officer brought the management response that, if the workers returned to work, the company would try to pay them at some future, though unspecified, date. Meanwhile, workers had selected negotiating representatives, including supervisors, headmen and rank-and-file workers, and after some discussion with the managing director, the chief representative advised returning to work. But militant workers meeting in a democratic assembly rejected his advice. The managing director repeated his position: the firm was losing money and thus was unable to pay COLA. After two weeks of striking and after the festival of *Id el-Fitr* had passed without arrears or even a weekly income, the workers of Factory C met again. During the debate the supervisors argued that the manager was too powerful to be resisted successfully, and the workers decided to return to work. Despite the absence of strike violence, however, there appears to have been some dissent among militant workers. Immediately following the return to work, an unknown group of workers sabotaged the looms by cutting the rolled beams of thread while they were attached to the looms, thus destroying both the labor involved in the preparation of the beam and the material itself. When this was discovered, the managing director responded angrily by locking out the workers for several more weeks, thus compounding their loss of income during an inflationary period and successfully intimidating them into following company directives. As in several other indigenously owned factories, the owner's position as a state commissioner afforded him the political clout necessary to avoid paying COLA. Thus, unlike in Factories A and B, class struggle here failed, and the workers lost the strike.

For readers interested in the articulation of Islamic institutions to capitalist organizations of production, it is noteworthy that the spokesman for the faction counseling patience was an extraordinary and immensely popular young mallam. Though he worked as a weaver, he was descended from a line of respected scholars who normally hold the office of *imam* in a respectable talakawa ward of the Birni. Earlier in his youth, he was the ward secretary of his ward's NEPU branch. Deprived of the opportunity to attend western school, he acquired literacy in Hausa at night school, and through a London school of correspondence he learned to read, write and speak English. In fact, he was the only worker in my sample of 140 who was literate in English. Not only was he *imam* of the factory, leading prayer each day during the day shift, but when workers were asked during the structured interview to select a leader for a trade union at this factory, this mallam was the person usually chosen. The typical explanation for their choice was: 'He is our *limam (imam)*. He has achieved both western and Islamic learning. And we know and have confidence in his character.' It is rare, indeed, when one discovers the idealization of western and Islamic leadership models articulated within one personality. Even though he disagreed with the strike tactics, he supported the decision of his fellow workers and later participated as a member of the strike committee in the negotiations with the managing director.

In retrospect, the workers at Factory C were caught in a dilemma: they knew that the firm was antiquated and uncompetitive in comparison to the new firms at the Bompai industrial estate, and that the firm had lost money due to mismanagement and competition. Further, any violence against an indigenously owned firm with a paternalistic reputation would only alienate their natural allies in the community. Given this situation, many of the experienced and skilled workers resigned to seek employment in the Kaduna textile industry or elsewhere in Kano. Of the remaining workers, most returned with the hope that traditional community pressure might prevail, as expressed by a weaver: 'Perhaps they will feel shame and pay us.'

In fact, however, owners never paid COLA or the new Adebo wage rate to all workers. Nor was the refusal of Kano's indigenous industrialists to pay legal rates limited to this firm or solely to the Adebo Commission's recommendations. Rather, the process of class differentiation whereby a merchant industrial bourgeoisie differentiated itself from the urban tala-kawa had reached a critical stage. For although a largely merchant bourgeoisie introduced paternalistic forms of industrial relations in its first industrial venture during the decade of the 1950s and early '60s, by the early 1970s a merchant-industrial class had matured with a clearer sense of its own class interest. Competition from other firms, increased class differentiation and closer ties with the state (which brought war-related profits and a share of political power) created an industrial bourgeoisie that cared little about community opinion and surely was not likely to alter its rate of capital accumulation because of shared feelings of 'shame'. Thus paternalism ceased as a policy of industrial relations during the transition to semi-industrial capitalism.

Interestingly, a shared sense that class relations were changing, that shame and paternalism were over and that the emerging industrial bour-geoisie cared little about their communities of origin became widespread among urban workers. An urban worker from the Birni employed at Factory A expressed this sense:

> Everyone paid but them. You know he [the managing director] is a Hausa and comes from the same ward as us, but he closed the factory when the workers went on strike [for their Adebo]. The workers had families, but they were forced to return to work. He has no mercy for his brothers.

I find this quote especially valuable because working class formation and class consciousness reach some minimal level of maturity only when wage workers begin to perceive that household relations are no longer operative, that honest, dedicated work will not receive certain reward or job security, and that waiting patiently for their master to be merciful or communally responsible only yields frustration, disappointment and more exploitation. Again, the experience of workers under indigenous capital and manage-ment explains why workers express skepticism regarding improved welfare under Hausa management (see Table 5.3).

Class struggle at Factory C: workers' perspectives

The role of Islamic institutions, ideologies and personalities, and the shared sense of community involvement in the factory, meant that external factors were as important as internal ones in determining the outcome of class struggle at Factory C. Not only was there little antagonism between workers and supervisors and an absence of violent tactics, but the belief that workers could win the strike by appealing to community norms of social solidarity and Islamic values of social justice brought the struggle out of the factory and into the wider community of the Birni. Yet this did not bring victory to the workers. Unlike Factories A and B, where Adebo arrears and wage rates were achieved through class struggle, Factory C presents a case where workers were defeated during a critical phase when the paternalism associated with mercantile capitalism was being replaced gradually by more alienating and exploitative forms of industrial relations appropriate to semi-industrial capitalism.

The consciousness of workers at Factory C, therefore, reflects their defeat during the Adebo affair. No one maintained any consensual trust with management, as was encountered earlier; nearly all workers believed that their demands were just. Factory C is of interest because the consciousness of workers with regard to class struggle, even one ending in defeat, provides a valuable perspective on the process of class formation during the transition to semi-industrial capitalism. Again, while most felt their cause was just, several workers disagreed with leaders over tactics and the very wisdom of striking against a politically powerful managing director. The first example comes from a Birni-born militant whose reference group is the urban working class and not merely the factory:

> All companies paid except here [sic]. It was necessary to strike in order to get our money and to halt the cheating of the workers. The government [F.M.G.] listened and saw that laborers were suffering.

A second militant, who was a long-term migrant to Kano, describes his perception of conflicting class interests in personal terms:

> Other companies paid Adebo. Here the managing director refused. According to us he is cheating us. With him it is not cheating; he just prefers to help himself.

Just as in the case of Factory A, where the bonds of social solidarity among laborers pushed timid workers into supporting the strike, an urban-born storehouse worker from a declining leather-working family described his motivation for supporting the strike as follows:

> People said that the company would pay when the others [companies] did. Then the company did not pay and the workers refused to work, but when we returned, we still did not receive anything. I agree with the strike because they are my friends at work. If they say they will not work, I feel their opinion also.

It would be romantic to believe that defeat does not, in fact, demoralize workers and reduce working class solidarity. A depressed strike supporter offers his views after the defeat:

> I agreed with it then as it was fair for us to receive our Adebo, just as everyone else did. But now we lost over two weeks' pay and still no increase in daily wages. I do not think strikes have value .... The next strike, if three men return to work, I will be the fourth.

The necessity of wage labor and the recognition of bourgeois hegemony appear to have left a profound impression on a store laborer:

> Workers did not receive Adebo and then they went out on strike. Before I thought it was correct, but now I do not think it was correct, because they exceeded our strength .... I need the work; I am against trouble. We did not

247

get any Adebo [arrears] nor did we get two weeks' pay, we lost both ways. If it gets too much for me, I should just leave work.

Still others were critical of the strike leadership. A young, literate weaver rejected the particular organization and tactics used in the strike, but called for more effective working class organization and tactics in the future:

It was a fair strike, but I am against the way the strike was run. Those in the third shift pushed others without meetings and without putting our heads together [i.e., organizing them]. It is useless to do this without getting the workers together first. I knew that we would not be successful, so I am against it because we lost two weeks of pay.

Finally, I want to present two worker observations which, like those from Factory A, do not recognize the class nature of capitalist production and instead interpret the situation as a household relationship. Here, even among the urban-born, precapitalist-origin household relations articulate in industrial organization. To be sure, these are uncommon attitudes for members of the labor force from Factory C; nonetheless, their consciousness underscores how uneven the process of class formation is among first-generation factory workers, and how urban birth and life-time urban residence in a peripheral capitalist city like Kano may yield only negligible changes in social consciousness. Note that the next speaker originates from an impoverished group of tanners from the Birni who hold an extremely low rank in the Hausa hierarchy of status honor:

I was sick at the time of the strike, but when I returned people told me that there was no work because of Adebo .... Was this not a gift? If the father of the house gives a gift, this is fine; but if he does not, the children of the house cannot say anything because it did not come from our work like a weekly salary .... A man who has a way of earning his food should not spoil his work .... I do not know about this Adebo; they [the strike leaders] asked me. I have to feed and take care of my family.

A second urban worker indicates both patrimonial consciousness and the acceptance of defeat:

Other companies paid, the managing director refused. The head of the house exceeds everyone else in strength. What he wants, he has the freedom to do. I was against it [striking] when someone exceeds our strength, it is best to go ahead and work. It [Adebo] was like a gift to laborers ... to make them work harder. It was not ours .... They [laborers] did not ask me before they struck. And they were cursing the company, this is not good.

To conclude, thus far it has been shown how the experience of class struggle is reflected in workers' consciousness. Many workers have developed an elementary form of class consciousness, while others remain passive or even unaware of their class situation, despite extensive exposure to the labor process of industrial wage labor. Given the relatively limited duration of industrialization in Kano and, more importantly, the backward development of the forces of production in the urban society at large, it is not surprising that this emerging class is unevenly developed in consciousness and in organization.

While no trade union emerged as a direct result of the Adebo strikes, the events and the actions that have been described are crucial for understanding the consequent evolution of class relations and the trade union movement in Kano's industrial sector. From the Adebo experience, workers learned a great deal about state intervention into industrial relations, about their legal rights and viable tactics and about the difficulty of organizing workers' organizations when, after the strikes, militants were purged from many factories. As the Udoji strikes and subsequent trade union formation suggest, lessons were learned and implemented as the industrial working class matured and increased in number, once Nigeria's petroleum boom attracted more industrial investment.

After the Adebo strikes, the next example of industrial class struggle occurred during the petroleum boom when a weak regime triggered a national strike. Again, just as in the Adebo case, state intervention and inflation created the material conditions for a protracted struggle between capital and labor in Kano's factories.

THE UDOJI STRIKES: INFLATION AND CLASS STRUGGLE DURING THE PETROLEUM BOOM

The announcement of the Udoji Commission's recommendations (1974) for reform of the civil service and the subsequent strikes undertaken by workers to enforce payment of wage arrears must be considered against the background of the declining popularity of the Gowon government. Gowon's fall from power in July 1975 was due partially to his failure to curb the corruption of close associates and partially to the inability of his regime to conduct a competent national census and thus to make rational decisions regarding the creation of new states or the equitable distribution of petroleum revenues. But the primary cause of his removal, by bloodless coup, was his decision not to return to civilian rule in 1976 as promised.

Nigeria profited enormously by the OPEC price increases; but soaring revenues from oil exports led to massive corruption, financed an overabundance of imported luxury and wage goods, worsened the income distribution and stimulated a rise in the inflation rate in wage goods such as housing, food and other necessities. The Gowon government's acceptance of the high wage increases recommended by the Udoji Commission is understandable, given the regime's need to legitimate itself to non-accumulating classes by responding to declines in workers' real income and by making a symbolic gesture toward distributing new petroleum wealth more equitably. After two years of study, the Udoji Commission submitted its report in late 1974, and the Gowon government made its recommendation based upon that report in December of the same year. Much of the report was devoted to recommendations for reorganizing and rationalizing the Nigerian civil service. Our concern, however, is with the recommended wage and salary increases, which, as in the Adebo case, were retroactive for nine months (to April 1974). Though designed to reduce income disparities between private and public sectors, especially for skilled and managerial employees, the recommendations called for wage increases of up to 133 percent, with enormous absolute increases for the very senior ranks of the civil service. For formal-sector wage workers, the lowest paid worker's annual income increased from ₦132 to ₦720. In contrast, Nigeria's average per capita income in 1975 was approximately ₦172.[11]

It will be recalled from the commodity wage and price data presented in Table 2.1 that the cost of wage goods such as food increased at a much higher rate than corresponding wage increases throughout the decade of the 1970s. Hence the real wages of unskilled industrial workers probably declined or remained stagnant throughout the decade. That inflation would devour any increase in the daily wage rate was understood by experienced workers and urban dwellers when the Udoji Commission's recommendations were publicized. And this understanding only reinforced the workers' contention that the only real gain from the Udoji increase would come from the nine months' arrears payment, which was scheduled to be made in January 1975. Finally, because state-sector workers were paid immediately, both stimulating demand for available consumer goods and raising the local rate of inflation, industrial workers also understood that each day of delay would reduce the real value of their arrears payment.

For the second time in four years, therefore, class struggle among Kano's industrial workers took the form of state wage recommendations followed by negotiations with management, strikes and occasional violence. It is unnecessary to go into detailed descriptions of the process of class struggle at the factory level as I already did for the Adebo affair. Instead, comments will be confined to any changes in the tactics or organization of class struggle that occurred in the Udoji strikes as compared to the Adebo strikes. Overall, workers possessed greater confidence, had more experienced leaders and employed more advanced tactics of management intimidation in the Udoji negotiations. Moreover, workers exhibited a deeper understanding of the technical processes of industrial production and of management's communication linkages to the authorities. Two instances illustrate well the advances in workers' tactics. When negotiations in two separate firms failed to produce a written agreement signed by management to set a date for payment, and workers decided to strike, management's telephone links to the police were destroyed immediately. In both cases, this intimidation was successful. The second example shows how workers manipulated technical knowledge as a weapon of class struggle: workers in a tanning factory deposited raw skins into chemical vats and then walked out on strike; in order to save the valuable skins from being destroyed by the chemicals, management quickly agreed to set a date for paying Udoji arrears. Further, just as in the Adebo strikes, workers in several factories attacked factory property – office buildings, vans and stores – in order to intimidate management into setting a date for payment. Workers had learned something from the Adebo experience: this time they were more confident of their legal position, better organized, more disciplined and less prone to divisions between violent and non-violent workers. They were also more aware of their rights as workers to negotiate collectively through trade union representatives.

Indigenous capital and class struggle

When describing the forms of class struggle during the Adebo affair at the Hausa-owned and -managed firm, Factory C, it was noted that paternalism was in decline, that community ties to the factory, though weakened, still existed, and that, unlike those at many foreign-owned firms, the unsuccessful strike here was without violence. But the industrial conflict arising from the Udoji award confirms that one may not generalize from the case of Factory C. For one of the most violent incidents in the Udoji struggle occurred during a seven-day strike at a new textile factory at Bompai, a factory controlled and managed by one of Kano's most prominent industrial capitalists. The latter had accumulated a fortune from war contracts and was (is) linked to Rockefeller interests. Even though there was a weak trade union in the factory, the managing director refused to pay Udoji arrears. In response, the workers launched a violent demonstration against the firm, destroying the factory's windows, vans and trucks. After this demonstration, the managing director summoned laborers and trade union representatives to a public meeting in the factory yard, where he informed the assembled workers that arrears would not be paid and, further, that if the strike continued, all workers would be dismissed and new workers hired. In response to his threats, the workers showered him with the most abusive curses and bitter insults contained in the Hausa language. Finally this violent struggle was settled when the trade union brought pressure from the government to bear on the firm so that the managing director agreed to pay three months' arrears pay (not the recommended nine), amounting to about ₦45 per worker. Yet, as in the Adebo strikes, the leaders of the union were dismissed because most were lower-level supervisors or headmen and, therefore, the managing director demanded that they support his position rather than that of the striking workers.

Hence, in contrast to Factory C during Adebo negotiations, the Udoji strikes at the modern factory owned by indigenous capitalists exhibited some of the bitterest forms of class conflict recorded in Kano. Not only were workers outraged at the indigenous industrialist's treatment of strikers and their trade union leaders, but the prominent political position of the factory owner encouraged workers to make the link between industrial class struggle and society-wide forms of class struggle. Informal interviews of

251

workers in 1975 and again in 1978 confirmed that the Udoji strikes were much less isolated from society-wide political struggles, mostly because, with the increased indigenization of industry, the merchant industrial class had emerged in a more visible antagonistic relationship to Kano's leburori. Although a complete analysis of the link between class struggles at the point of production and society-wide struggles associated with the return to civilian rule lies beyond this study, it is clear that Kano's merchant industrial capitalists are a primary *bête noire* of the more leftist faction of the populist PRP.

More importantly, while the struggles at the workplace are poorly articulated by workers as society-wide struggles, it is significant that when the military government attempted to disqualify the PRP's presidential candidate, Mallam Aminu Kano, popular demonstrations protesting the disqualification attacked the residence of the same industrial capitalist who had threatened workers and dismissed trade union leaders during the Udoji strikes. Hence, there is some evidence for the recognition of a linkage between industrial and society-wide class struggles on the part of Kano's lower classes. But the full potential of this alliance and the power of industrial workers to exert leverage against both local and international capital remains latent due to poor organization, federal reorganization of trade unions, and weak integration of industrial workers into organizational and leadership roles within the PRP.

To conclude this comparison, the Udoji strikes did indeed register real advances in working class organization and tactics as compared to the earlier Adebo affair. But the most important change during the period from Adebo to Udoji was in the level of trade union representation in Kano's factories. By 1975/76 a sizeable minority of factories possessed legitimate trade unions. Two factors explain this trend toward trade union organization: the first was a pragmatic understanding between militant workers and professional trade unionists, and the second was state intervention into the organization, funding and political activities of Nigerian trade unions.

THE TRANSITION TO WORKING CLASS ORGANIZATION: TRADE UNIONS AMONG INDUSTRIAL WORKERS

So far, it has been argued that industrial workers form a distinct and self-conscious class fragment of the urban leburori. As a militant class fragment, they exercised their class power to gain economic benefits at the workplace and, to a limited degree, to improve working conditions for industrial labor under entrepreneurial capitalism. At the same time, the evidence indicates that their spontaneous and economistic forms of class consciousness, once exerted, have been insufficient to transform effective strike committees into disciplined yet autonomous working class organizations. Viewed from a historical perspective, there is a cyclical character to the process. Workers achieve class solidarity, usually over a single issue, then they take collective action to achieve their goal, and then management either co-opts the informal organization or dismisses its leadership.

Without disciplined and legitimate trade unions, the cyclical trap of angry protest and despair will continue unabated; workers will not exert even minimal control over the process of production that undermines their mental and physical health; and most importantly, workers will continue to live in perennial fear of losing their livelihood to avaricious supervisors, competition from younger and lower paid workers, or other forms of exploitation. Finally, since the Nigerian state will continue to mediate the relationship between capital and labor, disciplined trade union organization extending from the factory to the national level is obviously necessary in order for labor to exert influence on national policies outside the workplace that affect industrial workers and the laboring class in general. Yet serious obstacles have blocked trade union formation in Kano's factories.

In an article published in 1975, I described the difficulties of forming legitimate, worker-supported trade unions in Kano's factories during the First Nigerian Republic (1960–6) and in the period of military rule until 1972.[12] It was found that workers' experience with and attitudes toward industrial trade unions until 1972 were overwhelmingly negative for several reasons. In some cases workers were forced to join and to pay dues to undemocratic 'trade unions' which were subsidiaries of national political parties such as the Northern People's Congress. In other cases, once legitimate trade unions were weakened by management pressure, they became income sources for unscrupulous supervisors. And finally, in several cases the post-coup (1966) ban on political parties was interpreted by local authorities to include legitimate trade unions (e.g., at Factory C). My published survey data confirmed that in 1972 over three-fourths of the workers interviewed (N=140) were either unaware of the meaning and function of trade unions or else were familiar with but negative toward trade unions as they had experienced them. Nevertheless, workers were still very positive toward trade unions that could respond to their needs.

To be sure, part of the reason for the absence of active, legitimate trade unions during the Adebo strikes was the exodus from Kano of the trade union organizers from southern states during the political crisis and civil war. And of course, local entrepreneurial capital's close relationship with the military governor meant that the Kano State government did not enforce laws upholding the right of workers to organize. (Subsequent public commissions of inquiry confirmed persistent rumors that Governor Bako was a silent business partner of several factory owners). Furthermore, rivalries between the two major trade union congresses, the Nigerian Trade Union Congress (NTUC) and the United Labor Congress (ULC), also contributed to Kano's weak trade union movement. Moreover, because the NTUC was affiliated internationally with the eastern bloc, and the ULC with the western bloc, external funding by international sources contributed to the rivalry, thereby further dividing the energy of the labor movement

253

and creating a dependency relationship that undermined membership control of leadership. Such was the situation prior to the Udoji strikes of 1975. At this stage, the Nigerian state experienced a coup, the Murtala-Obasanjo government emerged, and the reorganization of trade unions was initiated within three years.

The Nigerian state and organized labor

After experiencing two major national strikes in less than five years, federal policymakers were concerned about the congresses' external affiliations, the fragmented organizational structure of trade unions and the difficulty of controlling the militancy of workers. The reorganization of the trade unions occurred as the Nigerian state was extending its involvement into the production and distribution of commodities such as petroleum, automobiles and steel. Clearly, part of the inspiration for state intervention was nationalism, and part was an unveiled attempt to bring trade unions under the control of a capitalist state apparatus.

Yet, at the same time, trade unionists also attempted to unify themselves. Though short-lived, a joint committee labeled UCCLO negotiated the Adebo settlement in 1971–2. The most important effort toward unity came at the death of a venerated trade union leader, whereupon the leadership of Nigeria's trade unions signed the Apena Cemetery Declaration (1974) and committed themselves to a unified trade union movement. Subsequently, in 1976, these same groups formed the first Nigerian Labor Congress, a meeting in which representatives of Kano's labor movement participated. But the FMG refused to recognize this voluntary effort at trade union unity, citing the leadership's past record of corrupt practices, the undemocratic methods of affirmation and the unrepresentativeness of NLC leadership *vis à vis* their members. However valid some of these points may be, observers in Nigeria argue that the dominant classes and the policymakers within the Nigerian state were threatened by a unified, autonomous and militant trade union movement that was not dependent upon state patronage.

Following the banning of the first NLC, the FMG dissolved the existing trade union central organizations, i.e., NTUC and ULC, and placed their assets and affairs under the responsibility of an appointed administrator. In February 1978, the FMG promulgated a decree that recognized a single central trade union organization, the Nigerian Labor Congress, reorganized the hundreds of fragmented and overlapping unions into forty-two industrial trade unions, and banned external affiliations with the east and west except for the International Labor Organization and the Organization of African Unity. Most importantly, the decree banned the participation of active trade union leaders in political parties and forbade the use of trade union funds to support political parties or candidates. To sweeten the arrangement and to co-opt the trade union bureaucrats, the decree formally recognized the workers' right to organize trade unions and the unions' right to receive compulsory 'check off' of union dues from their members' wages and salaries. Further, an initial monetary grant was allocated to the NLC during its first year.

Clearly, the FMG's rejection of the first NLC and the creation of the second NLC indicate a corporativist strategy designed to incorporate and subordinate organized labor to the capitalist state in a manner similar to Latin American states such as Brazil. On one hand, one can observe the rationalizing and legitimizing function of the capitalist state in this act: for the immediate and direct needs of capital, especially entrepreneurial capital, will not be served by the recognition and reorganization of a single central trade union organization. But, on the other hand, the reorganization of the NLC and the trade unions reduces the possibility that organized labor will join with a political party or a political movement oriented toward the radical reformation or the abolition of the Nigerian capitalist state. By depending on the state for recognition of a single NLC, for funding and for enforcement of the 'check off' system, the NLC has lost much of its real and potential political autonomy. At the same time, it should be recognized that trade union leaders did resist complete incorporation in that, by organizing committees for trade union freedom, the trade unions retained control over the appointment of general secretaries; thus, as the election results appeared, the Marxist and Marxist-oriented general secretaries, rather than American-trained business unionists, gained or maintained control over a significant share of Nigerian trade unions. Just as in the case of wage review commissions, therefore, state intervention generated contradictory outcomes that conflict with state policymakers' original intentions and that serve both the legitimization and the accumulation functions of the capitalist state.[13]

If one examines the impact of the reorganization of trade unions on Kano's industrial working class, several positive features are evident. Previously, Nigeria had over 900 'house' unions, which mitigated against formation of a common policy toward employers in any single industry. Furthermore, the elimination of foreign sponsors, from both the eastern and western blocs, could only enhance rank-and-file control over leaders, as well as reducing opportunities for corruption and indirect manipulation of trade unions by foreign interests. But most importantly, the reorganization of house unions into industrial unions and the establishment of local branches of the NLC in Nigeria's nineteen states brought greater organizational strength and trade union leverage to comparatively backward regions of Nigeria. In Kano, where state collusion with entrepreneurial capitalists effectively repressed autonomous trade unions in the factories, the reorganization of the NLC brought the legitimacy of the federal government to Kano's fledgling trade union movement. By 1979, it was too early to assess the concrete effects of the reorganization of trade unions and the NLC.

THE PROBLEM OF LEADERSHIP IN WORKING CLASS ORGANIZATIONS

To move beyond spontaneous forms of class struggle and toward disciplined working class organizations, a leadership cadre must emerge capable of directing working class energies toward solving the myriad problems facing industrial workers. But industrial workers in Kano have been and continue to be faced with a leadership dilemma: to date, only professional trade union organizers possess the knowledge and organizational skills necessary to form and register trade unions, to negotiate with management and to command sufficient respect from state officials so that the latter will enforce existing labor laws. The problem, of course, is that professional trade unionists are rarely recruited from the ranks of industrial workers and therefore tend to relate to industrial workers as would a 'broker' or lawyer, with little sympathy or understanding of the working class. In practice, many professional organizers maintain dual loyalties and follow a career path where trade union organizing is merely a stepping stone to a more secure and lucrative position in politics, labor/management relations or the civil service.

The other side of the industrial workers' dilemma concerns the difficulty that militant and competent leaders drawn from the rank and file have in retaining their jobs. Moreover, such men must not only be literate and competent leaders, they must also be personally capable of resisting management's offers of advancement or outright bribes. It was noted during the Adebo strikes that the leaders of the strike committee at Factory A became supervisors; in both the Adebo strike at Factory B and the Udoji strikes at the Hausa-owned textile factory at Bompai, leaders of successful strikes were dismissed after they led workers to victory; and in many other recorded examples, workers who tried to form trade unions were dismissed without legitimate cause. Furthermore, given the high incidence of corruption among politicians as well as among rank-and-file leaders, workers are understandably cynical about anyone negotiating with management on their behalf. One such rank-and-file union organizer who was a member of at least two strike committees described his situation well: 'It is difficult. If we organize ourselves and select leaders to go to the managers, no one will believe them, even if they tell the truth. It is very difficult to find a leader that they will follow.'

State intervention into the relationship between labor and capital has created the conditions for a militant and organized trade union movement. But obstacles remain in the form of corrupt leadership, timidity on the part of rank-and-file workers and management repression and co-optation of leaders. To date, two leadership tendencies are evident in the formation of working class organizations among Kano's industrial workers. Political brokers represent the first, and rank-and-file workers represent the second. Let us examine the strengths, limitations and achievements of each.

256

Political brokers as trade union organizers

In an earlier article investigating the absence of formal trade unions in Kano's factories during 1970–2, I concluded that since the conditions for the emergence of rank-and-file leaders were hostile, a 'marriage of convenience' between workers and professional trade union organizers, however opportunistic, was probably the best hope for workers during the period prior to the reorganization of the NLC by the FMG (1976). Apparently, such a marriage took place during the years 1973–6, under the leadership of a former NEPU and Action Group politican who organized trade unions in several of Kano's factories, including Factory A. It would be difficult to find a better stereotype of the opportunistic 'broker' trade unionist.

He was born in a talakawa trading ward of the Birni. At the same time as he claimed to represent the United Labor Congress in Kano, he also represented the indigenous contractors of Kano State, possessed a contractor's license himself and described himself as a former import-export merchant. Further, he identified himself as a follower of Ibrahim Niasse's branch of the Tijaniyya, as an avowed anti-communist and as a protector of 'northerner interests' in the Nigerian trade union movement. His personal style conveyed an aggressive, confident and verbally articulate personality that certainly would impress workers and intimidate management during negotiations. During an interview with him in 1975, after describing in detail the industrial trade unions that he had personally organized, as well as the countries that he had visited as a representative of Nigeria (Cuba, USA, UK and USSR), he confided that he was opposed to strikes as a weapon of negotiation with management. Since 1975, this professional organizer had emerged as a leader in the Kano State PRP and in 1979 was elected to the federal legislature. Moreover, when workers pointed out the modern cement rental units that had been built in Tudun Wada, they noted with chagrin that several of the units were owned by this former trade union organizer, in contradiction to working class needs for cheap housing. The broker is an absentee landlord who is gentrifying the oldest working class area of Kano. Yet, at the same time, workers are ambivalent in their evaluation of him: while they acknowledged that he was a self-interested opportunist and that they could not trust him completely, as compared to the trust invested in a personality like the mallam-strike leader in Factory C described earlier, he was the only labor leader they had in 1975. Hence, realism and pragmatism required that workers follow him until more reliable leaders emerged. From the workers' perspective, therefore, the broker trade unionist possessed critical resources such as extensive knowledge of the state apparatus and of the personal lives of the officials, and the capacity to intimidate management into accepting his proposals. Even allowing for the workers' pragmatic acceptance of his leadership, his speculative investments in their communities and his rapid mobility from trade unionist to federal legislator underscore the tension between the interests of broker trade unionists and industrial workers.

The transition to legitimate leadership: obstacles and strategies

Despite the shortcomings of broker trade unionists, the FMG's reorganization of trade unions will probably mean that rank-and-file trade unions will be organized in Kano's factories during the 1980s. But, again, this raises questions concerning the relationship of rank-and-file workers to their trade union and, more importantly, their ability to use the union to alter the abusive and exploitative conditions described earlier. To be sure, for most rural-born workers, who dare not forget the sanctions exercised by the rural aristocracy against expressions of political independence, the transition to full and confident participation in trade unions will be a slow and gradual process. In this regard, the situation in Kano is not significantly different from that described by Barrington Moore for recently proletarianized, nineteenth-century German workers who were recruited from authoritarian rural communities in eastern Germany: 'many workers had to be told what their rights were, and there had to be a fair chance that they would actually put them into practice, before they would believe in these rights and make them into their own standards of justice and injustice'.[14] Labor's rural origins and educational backwardness coupled with management resistance and corruption among broker trade unionists pose real yet not insurmountable obstacles to the formation of legitimate, democratic and militant trade unions in Kano's industries. Given the financial arrangement between the NLC and the federal government, broker trade union leaders in the mold of Kano's aforementioned federal legislative representative will, undoubtedly, appear in abundance. But the problem lies in the formation of rank-and-file leaders and in explaining the situations and issues that give rise to rank-and-file leaders with the capacity to lead trade unions.

If one examines the consciousness and action of Kano's industrial workers over the decade, no issue has been more important for rank-and-file workers than job security. Of course, job security in the face of threats from new technologies, arbitrary dismissals and competition from workers willing to accept lower wage rates has always been (and continues to be) an issue that has rallied workers around trade union organizations. The reader will recall that even Kano's most neophyte industrial workers bitterly resented paying bribes for work, expressed fear of dismissal without a fair reason by supervisors who sold jobs to new workers, and cited numerous examples where management lowered their wage bill by dismissing experienced workers in order to employ raw recruits at lower wage rates. Job security, therefore, is an issue that lies at the heart of industrial class struggle, for both the rate of capital accumulation and the welfare of labor are determined to a significant degree by the amount of security enjoyed by

258

workers. Moreover, not only is job security an issue that arises from the experience of wage workers in the industrial labor process, but precapitalist standards of dignity and mutual respect between master and servant also reinforce the tension felt by workers when labor is 'dismissed without a fair reason'.

If one searches for a seminal issue provoking industrial conflict since Adebo (1972), one discovers that many of the most violent and bitterly contested strikes occurred over the right of management to dismiss workers arbitrarily. Before describing these strikes, it is important to emphasize that since Adebo, rank-and-file workers have become much more aware of their rights: for example, workers routinely demand severance pay if dismissed arbitrarily or even if due to insufficient demand for a product. Yet, during the period 1970–2, few workers even mentioned knowing about severance pay. This change is an indication of maturing working class consciousness. Let us examine a strike over job security that occurred in a container-producing plant that employed about 500 workers at Bompai.

Management had paid Udoji arrears without resistance and did not interfere with the organization of a trade union. But in 1978, perhaps due to a trade recession, a new manager incited a major strike by dismissing several experienced workers without severance pay. Two were officials in the trade union. Workers raised two issues. First, by employing inexperienced and younger workers in lieu of older workers with seniority, the factory avoided paying the legally required annual wage increase, which was based on number of years of service. Dismissals, therefore, lowered the wage bill and intimidated the remaining workers. The second issue concerned control over the labor force and the labor process of production. One of the major ways workers are disciplined to accept the alienating and abusive conditions that are typical of life in Kano's factories is for management to threaten experienced workers with dismissal. In the case of the container plant, after a popular yet comparatively aged clerk was dismissed along with several senior employees, the workers walked out and demanded the reinstatement of the senior workers as well as their trade union leaders. In response to management's refusal to negotiate over arbitrary dismissals, the workers took direct action: they destroyed the telephone exchange, broke windows and overturned factory vehicles. In order to quell rebellious workers, management offered to re-employ the dismissed workers only if they accepted the wage rate of new workers. Outraged by this attack on their rudimentary yet legal seniority rights, the workers raised funds to send a delegation to Lagos where they could consult with the national trade union officials at the NLC. Soon NLC representatives returned to Kano with the striking workers and made a formal complaint to the military governor of Kano State; the dismissed workers returned to the factory with full seniority benefits. The strike lasted for sixty-five days, the longest known by my informants. The strike and negotiations were hailed as a major victory by the ordinary factory worker.

259

Evidence from Chapter Five confirmed that job security was a major source of worker discontent at Factories A and B. How did the reorganization of trade unions alter these conditions? Let us return to Factory B and examine rank-and-file actions over the issue of job security. In 1973 a trade union was organized by professional trade unionists from the Nigerian Textile, Garment and General Workers' Union. Gradually, fearful workers participated in and supported the factory's trade union, and some successful strike actions occurred. Udoji arrears were paid without a violent strike; a wildcat strike eliminated the despised 'pass' system used to control access to the toilet; and a second wildcat strike, one tacitly accepted by the trade union officials, directed the attention of the Kano State military government to management's refusal to allow prayer at the correct hour. The prayer issue was resolved by guaranteeing Muslim workers a break for prayer at the proper hour, and further, the management agreed to build a rudimentary mosque in the factory yard. Yet these externally and internally determined expressions of class struggle did not resolve workers' fears concerning job security arising from the arbitrary dismissals by supervisors and management.

At issue here is more than just job security, however, for here and in other factories, unskilled workers had developed an awareness of their right to participate in democratically run trade unions. Thus, internal struggles at Factory B provide an excellent example of the organizational advances in class consciousness since 1972. Just as had occurred in the past, when a trade union was organized in 1973 it quickly became a fief of the foremen and the supervisors. From the unskilled workers' perspective, the trade union could never be completely legitimate as long as foremen and supervisory personnel controlled access to jobs and possessed the prerogative to dismiss workers 'without a fair reason', usually in order to sell the jobs to new workers. It must be emphasized that even though the trade union had successfully negotiated the Udoji arrears payment, the right to pray at the correct hour and the elimination of the pass system, workers still feared and loathed the arbitrary dismissal powers of the supervisors.

The issue of job security took precedence when, in October 1975, non-supervisory workers, led by headmen and a mechanic, held a meeting at a popular workers' bar to plan for the removal of supervisors from the trade union, so as to enable the union to protect workers against arbitrary dismissals. Initially the leader of this group went to the European manager and informed him that the workers were discontented over the arbitrary dismissals of workers by supervisors who then took bribes from new workers. Later that week, when the supervisor and the inspector attempted to dismiss an older and popular worker for allegedly defective weaving, the insurgents declared a wildcat strike and brought a number of workers to the manager to testify that they had paid bribes to the supervisor in order to obtain work. The insurgents then refused to return to work until the manager showed them a paper dismissing the supervisor and the union leader. The strike was finally settled when the manager agreed to allow secret balloting for union officials instead of the open meetings during which supervisors easily intimidated workers into accepting their leadership. During the next two years, the manager also agreed to allow the new trade union president, a loom mechanic and insurgent leader, to visit the factory during all shifts to consult with all workers.

By 1978, then, the process of class struggle at Factory B had yielded major victories for workers: passes were abolished, breaks for prayer took precedence over production requirements, and, after a ten-year struggle, a democratic trade union was in place to resist arbitrary dismissals. Just as in the case of the container factory, rank-and-file workers collectively withdrew their labor in order to protect the job security of older and vulnerable workers. When contrasted with the organizational outcome of the Adebo strikes, these two examples underscore the degree to which rank-and-file industrial workers matured in their ability to transform their class solidarity into functioning working class organizations that actually increased job security. In the face of the weaknesses of the NLC and the failure of the populist PRP government to transform the material and political conditions of industrial workers, these were important organizational successes by labor against capital. For, despite major obstacles to legitimate trade unions, Kano's industrial workers have achieved significant victories if one compares their organizational situation on the eve of civilian rule (1979) to the first year of the decade.

Summary

Class struggle, though full of uneven and contradictory elements, was a constant force in Kano's factories during the 1970s. State intervention into the relationship between capital and labor acted both to advance and to contain working class political and organizational capacity. My analysis of the consciousness of workers during the Adebo and Udoji strikes confirms the advances made by a first-generation industrial proletariat in exercising control over their working lives. To be sure, by the onset of civilian rule a majority of industrial workers did not enjoy legitimate trade unions governed by rank-and-file leaders, but the formation of such trade unions to protect job security was high on the agenda of virtually all workers. Equally important, though nurtured by a bumbling state bourgeoisie whose interventions into the economy raised the cost of labor without necessarily increasing the working class standard of living, industrial workers created, virtually by their own efforts, a political tradition of industrial class struggle. This tradition was absent in 1970, but it emerged again in May 1981 when industrial workers responded positively to the NLC's call for a general strike.

7

Class consciousness, Islamic nationalism and class integration

EXPLAINING WORKERS' CONSCIOUSNESS: A METHODOLOGICAL NOTE

This chapter employs multivariate statistical methods in order to verify empirically the relationships between workers' structural experiences and particular forms of social consciousness. Methodologically, the unit of analysis shifts from the individual factory workplace to Kano's industrial working class as represented by the sample (N=140) drawn from the three factories. The objective is to examine many of the conclusions put forward in previous chapters through the use of multivariate techniques of statistical analysis. Again, my purpose is *not* to legitimize the conclusions reached by field methods and historical methods by showing that the same conclusions can be reached through statistical analysis, for many of the conclusions put forward already are not subject to verification by statistical methods. Rather, the objective is to examine the structural relationship between participation in capitalist social relations and the acquisition of theoretically appropriate forms of social consciousness. As argued elsewhere, one becomes more informed and confident of one's interpretative conclusions if the same outcome can be verified by multiple methods of data collection and analysis.[1]

The analysis of the structural sources of workers' consciousness offers the researcher an opportunity to summarize the three major determinants which, together, explain the process of social class formation among Kano's industrial working class. Let us review the three forms of social participation that are treated as variables in this chapter: (1) participation in the urban social processes of a semi-industrial capitalist city located at the periphery of the capitalist world economy; (2) participation in the labor process of industrial capitalist production located in a situation of dependent capitalist development; and (3) participation in *precapitalist Islamic organizations* and institutions through which precapitalist ideologies and practices are produced so as to articulate with capitalist elements within the urban working class. While the previous descriptive material and the analyses of urban class formation extend beyond these three factors, for the purposes of multivariate statistical analysis these factors neatly summarize

262

the arguments put forward to explain the structure, consciousness and actions of Kano's industrial working class.

Accordingly, the problem is to illustrate empirically how these three forms of participation structure industrial workers' consciousness toward management and toward fellow workers. Initially, two aspects of class consciousness – the vertical and the horizontal – are defined and the relevant dimensions and appropriate empirical indicators of the vertical aspect developed. Then the empirical relationship between definite forms of social participation is examined, represented by the three aforementioned factors, as well as working class support for distinct dimensions of the vertical aspect of class consciousness. Finally, the integrative or horizontal aspect of class consciousness, measured by the degree of tolerance expressed by Hausa-speaking workers toward alien ethnic groups, will be analyzed by examining the effect of the aforementioned factors on workers' ethnic tolerance.

The reader should bear in mind that this data represents a cross section of workers' consciousness during one moment in a long-term historical process of class formation. To repeat the analogy of photography, the data represents a snapshot of a working class in a particular moment of social development, while the ideal method of data collection would be a moving film in which class consciousness could be analyzed over the long term of historical time. Alas, one must be satisfied with this snapshot of working class consciousness as it was expressed during a critical transition to semi-industrial capitalism (1972). Finally, it should be emphasized to skeptical readers and advocates of qualitative methods that the advantage of multivariate statistics is that the assumptions and the ideological expectations of the researcher can either be subject to falsification or allow the theory to be refined even further. With this caveat in mind, let us examine the dimensions and indicators of class consciousness for Kano's industrial working class.

THE PROBLEM OF DEFINING CLASS CONSCIOUSNESS

Before one applies the concept of class consciousness to a class fraction of the urban leburori of Kano, it should be known that scholars distinguish several dimensions of class consciousness.[2] Generally, all accept the fact that, in a capitalist society, class consciousness refers to widely shared assumptions and beliefs among indivuduals who perform a similar and defined role in the social division of labor. For wage-earning proletarians, class consciousness involves two sets of social relations: first, between workers and capitalists or their representatives, and second, between fellow workers. The first set of social relations refers to the *vertical* aspect of class consciousness. It is marked by an increasing awareness on the part of workers that their interests are in conflict with those of capitalists and/or their representatives. The second set of relations refers to the *horizontal* aspect of class consciousness. Rather than involving conflict, it is marked by an increasing awareness that workers share common interests, regardless of differing status characteristics separating individual workers; in turn, this awareness leads to a sense of class solidarity that is manifested in the process of class integration and class action.

Virtually all commentators agree that, among industrial wage workers, the concentration of labor at the factory site, the cooperation required for commodity production, the discipline and abuse from supervisors and the continual dilution of skill as a result of the introduction of more productive machinery all act to create a subjective awareness among workers that a structural antagonism exists between workers and capitalists. In turn, this awareness generates a shared material and social interest among workers performing the same role in the social division of labor: i.e., an objective and subjective class interest. In his early writings, Marx suggested that class consciousness increases from awareness to conscious political action:

> Economic conditions had first transformed the mass of the people of the country into workers. The domination of capital has created for this mass a common situation, common interests. This mass is already a class against capital, but not yet for itself. In the struggle, of which we have noted only a few phases, this mass becomes united, and constitutes itself as a class for itself. The interests it defends become class interests. But the struggle of class against class is a political struggle.[3]

To apply the sequence suggested by Marx to the leburori of Kano, it is assumed that there is a progression from class awareness to recognition of common class interests, to collective action as class struggle and finally to the formation of political organizations to pursue the political interests of the working class against the interests of capital.

Scholars in the Marxist tradition differ, however, over the meaning of the movement of the proletariat from a class 'in itself' to a class 'for itself'. A central issue in the debate concerns whether the proletariat, in order to be a class *for* itself, must possess a revolutionary vision of an alternative society as a component of its class consciousness.[4] Whatever one's interpretation of this debate, this issue is inappropriate to the problem of class formation and class consciousness in Kano. Why? Because, in Kano, a first-generation proletariat is immersed in a society that is in transition to semi-industrial capitalism, where precapitalist elements continue to exert influence on workers' consciousness. That is, neither the social forces of production nor the social relations of production, distribution and consumption are sufficiently developed along capitalist lines for revolutionary consciousness to exist within a first-generation industrial proletariat. In my field research, moreover, I never encountered a worker with any alternative vision that could be considered revolutionary or one that sought to abolish 'class society'. Hence, in order to apply Marx's concept of class consciousness to Kano's industrial workers, one must accept the objective condition that, during the present conjuncture, the most advanced level of class consciousness attained by this class fraction is the political reformist rather than the revolutionary.

Measuring class consciousness: dimensions and indicators

In order to measure class consciousness, one must develop indicators for the distinct dimensions of class consciousness that are appropriate for a first-generation Muslim industrial proletariat. The most elementary dimension of class consciousness refers to an 'awareness' on the part of class members of their class position in relation to other classes. Through the use of occupational status rankings, evidence that this awareness exists for four-fifths of the sample was presented in Chapter Three (Table 3.2). At this time, it was noted that 80 percent of workers, irrespective of urban status, placed themselves at the bottom of Kano's occupational hierarchy. This finding is sufficient evidence for the interpretation that nearly all workers, or at least 80 percent, recognize their class position and thus possess at least an 'awareness' of belonging to the urban leburori. Hence, if 'awareness' of one's class position within a class hierarchy is accepted generally as the most elementary dimension of class consciousness, then 80 percent of the workers sampled have attained a minimum degree of class consciousness. Whereas one may conclude from the occupational ranking that nearly all workers possess an elementary awareness of their class position in the urban leburori, the remaining dimensions of class consciousness are not as widely recognized nor as easily measured.

Let us first examine expressions of class consciousness that arise from the wage relationship, where, historically, class struggle often erupts over the wage rate (e.g., Chapter Six). Although Marx supported workers' struggles to increase wages and recognized that initial expressions of class consciousness centered on the wage rate, he never held that mere improvement in the wage rate could, by itself, ameliorate the spiritual deprivation that he associated with alienated wage labor: e.g., 'in proportion as capital accumulates, the situation of the worker, be his payment high or low, must grow worse'.[5] Nor did Marx hold that the mere increase in wage rates under capitalist industrialization could ameliorate the tensions between capital and labor, precisely because the material needs of an urban proletariat are not fixed as a definite rate but rather are historically and socially determined. Thus wage rates, whatever their absolute levels, are evaluated by workers not in comparison to their previous wage rate or to those more impoverished, but in comparison to other social groups, such as management, who possess more. According to Marx:

> Rapid growth of productive capital calls forth just as rapid a growth of wealth, of luxury, of social needs and social pleasures. Therefore, although the pleasures of the laborer have increased, the social gratification which they afford has fallen in comparison with the increased pleasures of the capitalist, which are inaccessible to the worker in comparison with the general stage of

265

development of society in general. Our wants and pleasures have their origin in society; we therefore measure them in relation to society; we do not measure them in relation to the objects which serve for their gratification. Since they are of a social nature, they are of a relative nature.[6]

Employed as an indicator of class consciousness, attitudes towards wage rates reflect a worker's evaluation of the justice involved in the capital-labor relationship. Note that, just prior to being interviewed, the same workers had received both their second Adebo arrears payment and an increase in the minimum wage rate from ₦.54 to ₦.89 per day. Hence, by evaluating workers' attitudes toward the fairness of wages, one may evaluate Marx's prediction that increases in wage rates do not dampen militant class consciousness.

For these reasons, equity of pay provides a grounded indicator of the degree to which workers view their relationship to capital (management) as antagonistic. In order to measure this antagonism, workers were asked: 'When you consider the work that you do at the factory, do you consider your wages to be fair or not?' Workers who believed that their wages were not fair were coded as having achieved the second dimension of class consciousnes; that is, such workers are assumed to have advanced from mere awareness of their class position to the belief that the socially produced surplus was unfairly distributed between owner-managers and wage workers, and therefore their material interests were in opposition to those of the owners of capital.

Thus far, neither dimension of class consciousness, 'awareness' nor wage antagonism, necessarily involves any collective expression of class action against capital on the part of workers. Therefore, it is possible for workers to possess an elementary level of class consciousness, as reflected in these two dimensions, yet avoid any public manifestation of class struggle. The third dimension of class consciousness, therefore, refers to a willingness on the part of workers to engage publicly and collectively in class action that is designed to advance their class interest as they perceive it. One should view this third dimension of class consciousness as qualitatively more advanced than the two previous dimensions. In order to create an empirical indicator for this third dimension that would separate supporters of collective class action from non-supporters, workers were asked to comment on the Adebo strike. These same workers then were asked to state whether they supported or rejected the strike action. As an indicator of class consciousness at the level of a commitment to collective class struggle, the decision to focus on the strike event itself was advantageous because it was an unambiguous indicator in that all workers interviewed were employed during the period of the Adebo strikes. Therefore, workers who supported the Adebo strike were coded as having achieved the third dimension of class consciousness: a commitment to supporting collective class action against capital.

A commitment to class action, however, may not be measured by referring only to the Adebo strikes. In Chapter Six, it was observed that some workers disagreed over the tactics pursued by the striking workers. In order to adjust for the peculiarities of the Adebo strike, a second, more abstract indicator of this third dimension of class consciousness was created. Moreover, besides intending to develop a multiple indicator of this third dimension, I also wanted to discover if class conscious workers reinterpreted their precapitalist Islamic cultural values so as to justify supporting collective class struggle; or, alternatively, whether workers supported the Adebo strike, but believed that it contradicted the precepts of Islam; or, equally important, whether those who believed that Islam supported a strike for just reasons were the most or the least integrated into Muslim institutions. My own view is that the process of becoming class conscious requires workers to reinterpret precapitalist beliefs so as to apply them to new situations of injustice and inequality. For all of these reasons, workers were asked: 'Does Islam agree with striking for a fair reason or not?' Workers who believed that Islam agreed with striking for a fair reason were coded as having met, in an abstract manner, the third dimension of class consciousness. In summary, the indicators referring to the Adebo strikes and Islamic agreement are designed to measure workers' normative commitment to support collective class action as a means to realizing their collective class interests.

The description of class struggle in Chapter Six observed that collective class action in itself achieved little over the long term unless a legitimate workers' organization, usually a trade union, emerged to pursue workers' class interests. Accordingly, a fourth dimension of class consciousness, reflecting a more advanced level than the latter three, involves a conscious commitment on the part of workers to support a workers' organization that pursues in an organized manner their collective interests and needs at the factory level. In order to measure this dimension, workers were asked an open-ended question: 'What could workers do here in this factory to help themselves?' Respondents who favored forming workers' organizations to negotiate with management over pay and working conditions or over other collective interests were considered to have satisfied the fourth dimension of class consciousness.

The fifth dimension of class consciousness advances beyond the factory and locates class struggle in the wider society, i.e., at the political level. This fifth dimension refers to workers' political engagement at the wider societal level. Clearly, a commitment to form a workers' organization at the factory level reflects a more advanced dimension of class consciousness than the aforementioned dimensions. But a commitment to political struggle indicates an even deeper and more sophisticated consciousness toward workers' class interests, which are determined outside the factory and within the state apparatus (i.e., labor laws, education and housing, social rights and the public ownership of industry). In order to measure this dimension of class consciousness, workers were asked both positively and negatively phrased questions inquiring whether they believed that it was necessary for workers to engage in politics as workers in order to satisfy the needs of workers. Those responding affirmatively were coded as having satisfied the fifth and most advanced dimension of class consciousness.[7]

Having defined several dimensions and appropriate indicators of class consciousness, let us turn to the relationship between participation in capitalist social relations and the development of class consciousness.

DETERMINANTS OF CLASS CONSCIOUSNESS: CAPITALIST SOCIAL RELATIONS

For purposes of analytic clarity, the articulation of precapitalist elements within the leburori are ignored for the moment and attention is devoted instead to three indicators of participation in semi-industrial capitalist society that are germane to working class formation in Kano: (1) residence in large, peripheral capitalist urban centers; (2) wage employment in large-scale capitalist organizations of production; and (3) literacy in western script, which is an attribute rather than a form of participation in capitalist society.

Urban residential experience

Urban residential experience in a large, semi-industrial city such as Kano is assumed to indicate participation in increasingly capitalist kinds of social relations in a city which serves as an integrative link to a wider capitalist world economy. Chapter Two argued that to reside in Kano means that workers experience capitalism at the level of circulation, exchange and consumption. Even if they are not employed directly in a capitalist enterprise, they participate in the *urban social processes* of a semi-industrial capitalist city. Residential experience in a city like Kano exposes workers to great inequities of wealth, an increasingly impersonal and competitive labor market, the commoditization of housing, land and other wage goods, and increased class differentiation in the areas of housing segregation, education and other forms of consumption. Furthermore, the intervention of a capitalist state in regulating and policing the city introduces an element of bureaucratic capitalism that differentiates the experience of residents in the contemporary city from that of those in the countryside or a precapitalist city. Therefore, residence in Kano exposes the potential or actual proletarian to the dominant classes that control the economic and political power which determines to a significant degree a worker's life chances, opportunities for material and social advancement and standard of living. Urban residence in the centers of power allows the consumption patterns, the political activities and the class relations of the dominant classes to become visible to the worker, especially to the migrants from the more authoritarian countryside where many relations of exploitation are obscured by isolation, ignorance and fear.

268

Spatially, the dense, class-segregated residential patterns allow workers to communicate class perceptions to each other. It is in the semi-industrial city that the advancement of capitalist over precapitalist practices is most evident, a change which workers must adjust to in their daily lives. In the context of semi-industrial capitalism, then, the city is more than a large, dense and heterogeneous demographic mass; rather, it is a class-differentiated and market-determined environment regulated by semi-industrial organizations: the state administration, multinational firms and parastatal agencies. For most residents of Kano, capitalism is experienced as the substitution of commodity relations for human relations at the levels of consumption and exchange rather than at the level of production. Yet, as compared to social relations arising from residence in the countryside, to reside in Kano is to participate in the most advanced expression of capitalism that has emerged in the region; it is the effect of this experience on class consciousness that I wish to measure.

Let us compare the urban experience of urbans and migrants. For the urban-born workers, the advance of semi-industrial capitalism and greater integration of the city into the capitalist world economy reduce opportunities to become independent commodity producers, i.e., craftsmen and traders. Given the intense competition among themselves, most independent producers and traders must survive on relatively marginal incomes. Finally, for the urban-born workers, who view themselves as the 'sons of Kano', the rapid urban growth, the concentration of capital and power and the increasing class differentiation mean that their control over their own urban social and economic life is significantly reduced as they become downwardly mobile entrants into the urban working class.

For the migrants to Kano, on the other hand, urban residence means socialization into urban capitalist life and into the urban leburori. Most importantly, it means accepting commodity relations and nearly complete dependence upon the market for work, food and shelter. At the same time, the experience of rural to urban migration opens their eyes to the inequities of urban capitalist life. The revolutionary theorist Cabral, writing on changes in consciousness that accompanied migration to the city, put it succinctly: 'The importance of this urban experience lies in the fact that it allows comparison: this is the key stimulant required for the awakening of consciousness.'[8] Hence urban residence indicates participation in the urban social processes of semi-industrial capitalism at the level of consumption, exchange and exposure to the capitalist state.

Let us examine the relationship between urban status and the remaining four dimensions of class consciousness as presented in Table 7.1. The relationship is verified for each indicator of the four dimensions: participation in urban social processes of a semi-industrial capitalist city correlates with all dimensions of class consciousness. Note that though wage differentials are insignificant across the urban status groups, the proportion of workers who evaluate their pay as 'unfair' increases from 13 percent for

Table 7.1 *Class consciousness and urban status*

Dimension of consciousness	Variable: urban status	Positive or agree	Negative or disagree	N=	Statistics
Agrees that pay is unfair	Commuter	(6) 13.3%	(39) 86.7%	(45)	Gamma = .68 P < .00
	Migrant	(25) 53.2%	(22) 46.8%	(47)	Corrected x^2 = 30.14
	Urban	(30) 69.8%	(13) 30.2%	(43)	
		Total N 135 Missing Cases = 5			
Adebo strike support	Commuter	(16) 34.8%	(30) 65.2%	(46)	Gamma = .43 P<.01
	Migrant	(28) 56.0%	(22) 44.0%	(50)	Corrected x^2 = 10.38
	Urban	(30) 68.2%	(14) 31.8%	(44)	
		Total N 140			
Islamic approval of fair strike	Commuter	(12) 26.1%	(34) 73.9%	(46)	Gamma = .57 P<.00
	Migrant	(27) 55.1%	(22) 44.9%	(49)	Corrected x^2 = 20.07
	Urban	(32) 72.7%	(12) 27.3%	(44)	
		Total N 139 Missing Cases = 1			
Agreement with organizing at the factory level	Commuter	(10) 26.3%	(28) 73.7%	(38)	Gamma = .52 P<.00
	Migrant	(21) 44.7%	(26) 55.3%	(47)	Corrected x^2 = 14.54
	Urban	(30) 68.2%	(14) 31.8%	(44)	
		Total N 129 Missing Cases = 11			
Agreement with workers engaging in politics	Commuter	(6) 15.8%	(32) 84.2%	(38)	Gamma = .44 P<.01
	Migrant	(18) 38.3%	(29) 61.7%	(47)	Corrected x^2 = 9.54
	Urban	(21) 47.7%	(23) 52.3%	(44)	
		Total N = 129 Missing Cases = 11			

commuters to nearly 70 percent for urbans. Here is dramatic evidence that workers' material needs are socially created and that urban residence facilitates comparison and thus social dissatisfaction, as they compare their consumption levels to those of the dominant classes. Further, the commitment both to class action and to organizing at the factory is also determined by the degree of exposure to urban life. Not surprisingly, given the lack of opportunity for political participation during military rule, the percentage supporting workers' engagement in politics is lower, though the correlation between urban residence and political action remains almost the same as the other indicators. (Note that since both are highly interrelated, urban status and urban residential experience are used as surrogates for each other; see Table A.4 which presents 'Urban residential experience by class consciousness.') If, as has been argued, participation in the urban social processes of a semi-industrial capitalist city socializes workers into a class-conscious perspective, then the degree of urban residential experience should be correlated with the indicators of class consciousness.

Participation in the labor process of industrial capitalism

If urban residential experience exposes workers to semi-industrial capitalism at the level of consumption, exchange and state regulation, and if such experience generates class consciousness, what then is the independent effect of participation in the labor process of capitalist enterprises on class consciousness? Because the argument concerning the labor process and the development of class consciousness has been presented in Chapters Five and Six, it will not be repeated here. Since most industrial workers reside in cities, I am interested in the *independent* effect that participation in a capitalist labor process exerts on the development of class consciousness. Table 7.2 presents Class consciousness by wage labor experience. Again, in general, the evidence confirms the argument that participation in a capitalist labor process generates class consciousness. Yet there are important differences, if compared against Tables 7.1 or A.4. Whereas the degree of urban residential participation had an enormous effect upon workers' evaluation of the fairness of their wages, there is a weak relationship between this dimension of class consciousness and wage labor experience in capitalist enterprises. Further, there is virtually no relationship between class consciousness at the political level and the degree of exposure to wage labor. But both dimensions of class consciousness integral to the labor process, i.e., support for the strike and a commitment to organizing at the factory, are moderately correlated with wage labor experience. Hence, as Lenin once stated, working in capitalist enterprises predisposes workers to support class struggle and to organize trade unions within the factory, but by themselves, these experiences do not necessarily encourage workers to seek political solutions to society-wide problems.[9] Hence, political dimensions of class consciousness do not emerge spontaneously from the labor process but

Table 7.2 *Class consciousness and wage labor experience*

Dimension of consciousness	Variable: number of years in modern wage labor	Positive or agree	N=	Statistics
Agrees that pay is unfair	High number of years [a]	(36) 51.4%	(70)	Gamma = .26 P< .18 Corrected x^1 = 1.79
	Low number of years[b]	(25) 38.5%	(65)	
Adebo strike support	High number of years [a]	(47) 65.3%	(72)	Gamma = .48 P< .00 Corrected x^2 = 8.18
	Low number of years [b]	(27) 39.7%	(68)	
Islamic approval of fair strike	High number of years [a]	(43) 60.6%	(71)	Gamma = .37 P< .03 Corrected x^2 = 4.48
	Low number of years [b]	(28) 41.2%	(68)	
Agreement with organizing at the factory level	High number of years [a]	(37) 54.5%	(68)	Gamma = .30 P< .12 Corrected x^2 = 2.36
	Low number of years [b]	(24) 39.3%	(61)	
Agreement with workers engaging in politics	High number of years [a]	(25) 36.8%	(68)	Gamma = .09 P< .77 Corrected x^2 = .08
	Low number of years[b]	(20) 32.8%	(61)	

[a] High = 5 or more.
[b] Low = 4 or less.

instead appear to require exposure to ideologies and organizations that are located in the institutions and social processes of the semi-industrial capitalist city.

Since urban residential experience has a stronger and more consistent relationship to all dimensions of class consciousness, it raises the question of whether wage labor experience in capitalist enterprises has any independent effect on class consciousness that is not explained by urban residence. Clearly, the data indicate that the political engagement and fairness of pay

Table 7.3 *Strike support by wage labor experience controlled by urban residential experience*

		Adebo strike support	N=	Statistics
High urban residential experience (6 years or more)	High wage labor experience [a]	(35) 72.9%	(48)	Gamma = .43 P< .08 Corrected x^2 = 3.02
	Low wage labor experience [b]	(17) 51.5%	(33)	
Low urban residential experience (5 years or less)	High wage labor experience [a]	(12) 50.0%	(24)	Gamma = .43 P< .16 Corrected x^2 = 1.95
	Low wage labor experience [b]	(10) 26.6%	(35)	

[a] 5 years or more.
[b] 4 years or less.

dimensions of class consciousness are determined primarily by urban residential experience rather than by wage labor experience. But what of the relationship between wage labor experience and the two factory specific indicators, i.e., support for the Adebo strike and organizing at the factory? Does the experience of wage labor have an independent effect on these two dimensions of class consciousness? And further, do the effects of urban residential experience and wage labor reinforce each other so as to create an additive effect on these two dimensions of class consciousness?

To answer these questions, Table 7.3 presents support for the Adebo strike and wage labor experience, where the effect of urban residential experience is controlled for. The data confirm that wage labor experience has an *independent* effect on this dimension of class consciousness and that the combined effect is *additive* in that support for the Adebo strike increases as a result of either wage or urban residential experience. If one examines the relationship between support for the Adebo strike and wage labor experience within each category of *urban status* (not presented here), then the results are even clearer than those presented in Table 7.3. For example, when commuters with low and high wage labor experience are compared, support for the Adebo strike doubles from 24 percent among those with less experience to 48 percent among those with high wage labor experience. Among migrants, the equivalent difference increases from 45 percent to 71 percent respectively.[10] Hence, even without urban residence, participation in the labor process of capitalist production does indeed have a strong effect on that dimension of class consciousnes that pertains to workers' commitment to engage in collective class action. Furthermore, while the effect of

Table 7.4 *Class consciousness and literacy*

Dimension of consciousness	Variable: literacy	Positive or agree	N=	Statistics
Agrees that pay is unfair	Literacy	(16) 66.7%	(24)	Gamma = .50 P< .03 Corrected x^2 = 4.64
	No literacy	(44) 40.0%	(110)	
Adebo strike support	Literacy	(18) 75.0%	(24)	Gamma = .53 P< .03 Corrected x^2 = 4.84
	No literacy	(55) 47.8%	(115)	
Islamic approval of fair strike	Literacy	(18) 75.0%	(24)	Gamma = .56 P< .02 Corrected x^2 = 5.72
	No literacy	(52) 45.6%	(114)	
Agreement with organizing at the factory level	Literacy	(18) 75.0%	(24)	Gamma = .63 P< .00 Corrected x^2 = 8.04
	No literacy	(42) 40.4%	(104)	
Agreement with workers engaging in politics	Literacy	(15) 65.2%	(23)	Gamma = .66 P< .00 Corrected x^2 = 10.22
	No literacy	(29) 27.6%	(105)	

wage labor experience on organizing at the factory level within each urban status category is weaker than for Adebo strike support, the direction is the same and the combined effect is additive.

To conclude, participation in the labor process of capitalist production is correlated with all dimensions of class consciousness. But industrial wage labor experience exerts a strong effect that is *independent* of the effect exerted by urban residential experience only in the dimension referring to support for collective class action (e.g., Adebo support). Contrary to theoretical positions emphasizing the effect of participation in a capitalist labor process on the determination of class consciousness, the evidence suggests that the industrial workers of Kano acquire organizational and

Table 7.5 *Class consciousness and literacy among high urban residents*

Dimension of consciousness	Variable: literacy	Positive or agree	N=	Statistics
Agrees that pay is unfair	Literacy	(15) 71.4%	(21)	Gamma = .34 P < .31 Corrected x^2 = 1.04
	No literacy	(31) 55.4%	(56)	
Abedo strike support	Literacy	(17) 81.0%	(21)	Gamma = .52 P < .10 Corrected x^2 = 2.71
	No literacy	(34) 57.6%	(59)	
Islamic approval of fair strike	Literacy	(18) 85.7%	(21)	Gamma = .64 P < .04 Corrected x^2 = 4.41
	No literacy	(33) 56.9%	(58)	
Agreement with organizing at the factory level	Literacy	(16) 76.2%	(21)	Gamma = .51 P < .08 Corrected x^2 = 3.06
	No literacy	(29) 50.9%	(57)	
Agreement with workers engaging in politics	Literacy	(14) 70.0%	(20)	Gamma = .65 P < .01 Corrected x^2 = 6.70
	No literacy	(19) 33.3%	(57)	

political dimensions of class consciousness through participation in the urban social processes of a semi-industrial capitalist city. Therefore, it is this combination of long-term exposure to urban social processes and participation in a capitalist labor process which explains the development of all dimensions of class consciousness among Kano's industrial workers.

Literacy: a cultural attribute of semi-industrial capitalism

Literacy, the third measure of participation in capitalist social relations, is more an attribute of such participation than a form of organizational experience. In this sense, literacy in western script is treated as a measure of the degree to which an individual has acquired the tools of capitalist society which enable him to communicate with other workers and to cope with the capitalist organizations that dominate his relationship to work, community and the state. Literacy, moreover, allows workers to read newspaper accounts and other forms of literature that describe their legal rights as well as the condition of workers beyond their immediate personal networks. Literacy is defined here as the ability to read western script rather than Arabic script (precapitalist) and thus refers to a form of literacy that appeared only after Kano was incorporated into the capitalist world economy. Therefore, literacy is assumed to be an excellent indicator of the effect of participation in capitalist social relations. For these reasons, it was expected that literate workers would be more class conscious than others, especially with regard to the organizational and political dimensions of class consciousness. Table 7.4 presents 'Class consciousness and literacy'.

The data confirm my expectations: literacy is correlated with class consciousness, not only at the level of commitment to class action but also at the levels of commitment to organizing at the factory and to engaging in political action. Since most literates are long-term urban residents, in order to control for the effects of urban residence, one should examine the effects of literacy on those workers with high urban residential experience (Table 7.5). While the strength of association declines in the case of fair pay, the remaining dimensions show that literacy has an independent effect upon the formation of a class conscious perspective even after controlling for urban residence. More importantly, literate workers are significantly more likely to possess class consciousness at the more advanced levels pertaining to organizing at the factory and engaging in political action at the societal level. Nigeria has embarked upon a program of universal primary education, so the finding regarding the effect of literacy on class consciousness is crucial precisely because the proportion of literates in the industrial labor force will increase enormously as primary school leavers enter the industrial labor force and become integrated into the urban leburori. If this relationship holds for the future, and there is no certainty that it will, then one should expect a more organized and politically conscious working class to emerge as an immediate consequence of state educational policy.

Allow me to summarize the empirical findings of this section. *Urban residential experience*, indicated either by urban status or the number of years of urban residence, is the strongest and most consistent single determinant of all dimensions of class consciousness. *Industrial wage laboring experience*, acting in combination with urban residential experience, is additive and increases the absolute levels attained by all dimensions of class consciousness. Taken by itself, participation in the labor process of capitalist production is strongly correlated only with that dimension of class consciousness that refers to a willingness to support collective class action at the factory level. Here it is important to remember that for most workers,

276

except the commuters, wage labor experience in a factory accompanies residence in a large peripheral capitalist city, so that in actual social practice the two determinants of class consciousness exert their influence jointly. Finally, *literacy* exerts an independent effect on all dimensions of class consciousness. Most important for the future of working class politics in Kano, the political dimension of class consciousness is where literacy exerts its strongest influence, even when controlling for urban residential experience.[11] It should be emphasized that each of the three indicators of participation in capitalist social relations has an additive effect on class consciousness such that support for any single dimension of class consciousness increases as each indicator of participation in capitalist social relations is accounted for.

Thus far, for the purposes of empirical analysis, only the determinants of class consciousness that are indisputably identified with the extension and deepening of capitalist social relations in Kano have been dealt with. It has been shown empirically that participation in capitalist social relations or the acquisition of attributes integral to capitalist development generates class consciousness *appropriate* to the degree of capitalist development attained in Kano. Now I shall turn to questions regarding the influence, if any, that precapitalist elements exert on working class consciousness.

THE ARTICULATION OF PRECAPITALIST ELEMENTS WITHIN SEMI-INDUSTRIAL CAPITALISM

To speak of the articulation of precapitalist elements to capitalist elements and, in this case, within an emerging class fraction of the urban leburori requires that one bear in mind several points made earlier. The present conjuncture is marked by the transition of a peripheral capitalist economy that was dominated by merchant capital, under the control of international firms and local merchants, to one increasingly dominated by state expenditures and joint state-multinational industrial enterprises. Though entrepreneurial capital remains dominant in the industrial sector, demand for industrial products depends, directly or indirectly, on petroleum revenue rather than on groundnut exports. At the level of urban society, the *process* of transition is one from Muslim mercantile capitalism to semi-industrial capitalism. In turn, the international transition to semi-industrial capitalism is complemented in its *external* relationship (i.e., at the world systemic level) by reduced autonomy for the local ruling class, greater integration through the federal state apparatus into the national economy and, through the mediation of the state, far greater integration of the urban economy into the capitalist world economy. Yet precapitalist elements – ideologies, institutions and organizations – have not disappeared. Indeed, certain precapitalist elements may be strengthened and/or transformed by contact with the advance of semi-industrial capitalism. Within the social life of urban Kano, the range and depth to which capitalism has penetrated

277

precapitalist institutions, ideologies and practices is highly uneven. Clearly, both capitalist and precapitalist elements co-exist within the urban leburori. Insofar as precapitalist elements influence, constrain, reinforce or otherwise affect the logic of capitalist development toward the universalization of commodity relations and the accumulation of capital through the use of wage labor, one encounters a situation where precapitalist elements articulate within an emerging semi-industrial capitalist society.[12]

Earlier, when discussing the urban class structure and the social relations that integrated the urban lower classes, I emphasized that talakawa consciousness, though originating as a political class-status in the precapitalist society, acts as a material force that gives political meaning to economic forms of deprivation experienced by industrial workers. In this instance, membership in a class-like, yet precapitalist, political status group articulated in such a way as to reinforce and to give *political* expression to economistic forms of class consciousness among industrial workers.

Indeed, in any situation where peasants and independent commodity producers become proletarianized for the first time, forms of organization, ideologies and practices that originated in a precapitalist society, especially in one with a development market system like Kano, continue to articulate within the process of capitalist development. Often the combination of precapitalist and capitalist elements takes the form of worker resistance to accepting proletarianization. In other instances, privileges and rights derived from the precapitalist society, which are virtually unrecognized by the controllers of capitalist production, are consciously used by workers to resist proletarianization and/or to improve their working conditions. Thompson's argument that the 'rights of the freeborn Englishman' were consciously used by workers to resist proletarianization finds its complement among Kano's workers in Islamic nationalist consciousness, whereby workers use issues like 'correct prayer time' to instigate strikes so as to achieve sufficient collective solidarity to form a trade union.[13] In both cases, precapitalist ideologies and practices are used to advance the interests of a new class created by capitalism: a wage-earning industrial proletariat. And in each case elements of the precapitalist society continue to articulate with capitalist production, not passively, but actively, as workers seize upon precapitalist traditions as weapons in order to force managers of capitalist production to take account of their involvement in precapitalist traditions. In such a process, which can only be understood as a dialectical and contradictory one, certain elements of the precapitalist society may be transformed into new ideologies, identities and organizations, or they may wither and disappear as capitalism progresses. Again, only an empirical analysis of a given historical situation of articulation can explain the influence that precapitalist elements exert on new working classes created by a global form of capitalism.

It was demonstrated in Chapters Four and Six that Islam, acting within concrete arenas of community, class and nation, remains the most resilient element of the precapitalist social formation which articulates within semi-industrial capitalism in Kano. Even urban-born workers participate in Islamic institutions at the same time as they undergo the process of proletarianization. Membership in the urban working class does not eliminate participation in the rituals, practices and social relations of urban Muslim institutions. Not only do precapitalist and capitalist practices co-exist within Kano's industrial proletariat, but the effect of contact with semi-industrial capitalism may *strengthen* rather than dilute workers' commitment to Islamic organizations and ideologies. Of course, this interpretation raises the theoretical question, how does the articulation of Islamic organizations with capitalist ones affect the consciousness of a first-generation industrial proletariat which is integrated into the social relations of each mode of production? Empirically the problem asks: what effect does participation in Islamic organizations have on the development of class consciousness among first-generation Muslim industrial workers?

Class consciousness: The impact of Islamic participation

Without repeating the arguments made in Chapters One, Four and Six concerning the role of Islamic institutions, it should be clear that these institutions have been mobilized to resist the penetration of imperialism and to defend the interests of the urban talakawa during the nationalist period (e.g., NEPU). One of the contradictory outcomes of British imperialism was that it reinforced the organized practice of Islamic culture among the talakawa, which in turn expressed itself as a regionally bounded form of Islamic cultural nationalism. Throughout the precapitalist and the colonial periods, mallams, *gardi* and their students followed networks from Koranic schools located in both city and countryside in order to teach and to advance the quality of Islamic learning. As described in Chapter Four and elsewhere, these networks often unintentionally brought clerics and their students into the urban labor market and eventually into factory work. Most importantly, whatever their original intention, many such factory workers continue to teach and to pursue Koranic and Islamic studies. Since they are interwoven within the urban working class, the leburori, mallams and Koranic students form a classic status group in the Weberian sense of the term. Moreover, because they continue to maintain the subjective identity of a mallam or a Koranic student when they participate in industrial wage labor, they carry within themselves a subjective identity or an internalized 'calling' to lead their community against un-Islamic practices, interference with correct prayer or other forms of social injustice.[14] In a contradictory manner that presents an ideal example of *articulation*, the institutions that originally were created to reproduce the Muslim precapitalist society are now fully interwoven within the industrial proletariat. The strength and resilience of these institutions is such that they continue to co-exist within semi-industrial capitalism without formal hierarchy or formal organization

279

other than daily ritual, informal schooling and personalized relationships with mallams, whose prestige is earned through personal charisma and correct practice.

Though Koranic schools and mallamic networks are the Islamic institutions that register the highest degree of participation among the urban talakawa and the leburori, some workers are members of Islamic (*Sufi*) brotherhoods. Typically, brotherhood members reside in Kano for a long duration. Most were initiated before they became factory workers. Moreover, even if workers do not affiliate personally with a brotherhood, the influence of brotherhoods on non-affiliated workers is exercised through the interpretations and advice offered by their mallams, who are often affiliated with a brotherhood. I have already discussed the origins and role of brotherhoods in resisting imperialism, the penetration of western culture and, during the nationalist period, the informal identification of one brotherhood branch with the radical opposition political party (NEPU).

One must distinguish between the role of Islamic institutions at the national level and at the class level. To be sure, classes are horizontal divisions within nations. But the process of class differentiation in a peripheral capitalist society undergoing a semi-industrial transformation often directs the dominant classes toward western ideologies and styles of consumption, while the popular religions and beliefs are maintained by the lower classes and interpreted according to their class needs. In her introduction to a volume of scholarly essays on Islamic institutions, Nikki Keddie cogently argues this point:[15]

> Although ... the middle classes are far from abandoning religious institutions, a specifically Islamic ideology is less influential as one goes up the economic scale. Tacitly, the *ulema* [*mallams*] were left to deal with the bazaar petty bourgeoisie and the lower classes, whom they were expected to influence in the direction of obedience.... In practice, however, the religiosity of the masses has not proved a barrier to attacks on the upper classes.

Keddie concludes by noting that, just as in Christianity, 'Islam can easily be adapted to equalitarian and even revolutionary interpretations'.

All of the evidence indicates that among all classes and status groups of Hausa-speaking society, Islam serves as the ideological basis of regional Islamic nationalism, one that includes other northern ethnic groups. But the question that I wish to pose asks whether Islamic participation, mediated through the class experience of the talakawa and the industrial worker, articulates with the experience of proletarianization so as to advance the development of class consciousness. Clearly, the field data presented in Chapter Six suggest that Islamic culture interpreted by a mallam-worker employed at Factory C reinforced class consciousness. Yet the question remains whether this event was particular to that factory's recruitment policies, possibly because it was owned and managed by Hausa industrialists, or whether this example of the articulation between Islam and capitalism is true of all factories and of all workers sampled. In order to

280

answer this and other questions posed in the introduction to this chapter regarding the articulation of precapitalist and capitalist organizations, one must empirically examine the effect of Islamic institutional participation on class consciousness through multivariate statistical analysis.

Measuring Islamic participation

Studies of Islamic societies, such as Paden's interpretation of the role of Islamic values in the political culture of Kano, place great emphasis on the continuity of cultural values in the historical development of society. But the cultural interpretive approach poses two major problems for an empirical analysis; first, as ideal typical abstractions, values are unobservable and thus difficult to measure; second, this approach implicitly assumes that an individual's interpretation of correct behavior flowing from a particular value system does not vary significantly according to historical experience, social class or gender.[16] Moreover, by operating at a high level of abstraction when discussing the behavioral outcomes of a particular value system, such an approach is too facile, in that the abstract value is often ambiguous enough to be in agreement with mutually incompatible behavioral outcomes. Too often the proposition that a particular set of behaviors or group actions can be explained or informed by a particular set of values is tautological or non-falsifiable through empirical methods, or it fails to account for contradictory evidence. The latter occurs when members of two opposing classes cite the same cultural value system in order to justify two contradictory and antagonistic behaviors. Therefore, instead of assuming that Islamic values are unchanging and universal, or that they dictate the same behavior to all members of Kano's urban society, I prefer to focus on the effect of participation in Islamic organizations on consciousness. For, while this approach makes no assumptions about the constancy or universality of Islamic values, it does allow the empirical effect of Islamic participation on workers' consciousness to be observed and hypotheses to be verified or rejected.

An empirical and historical approach to the analysis of Islamic cultural values does not treat cultural values as Platonic essences. Rather, the way in which Muslims interpret Islamic cultural values as a motive for social or class action depends on the historical experience and material situation of the class or social group that is employing an Islamic cultural value to justify a particular collective act. Further, in contrast to the cultural interpretive approach, which assumes that Islamic culture is an unchanging and universally understood symbolic system, the relationship between participation in concrete observable Islamic social organizations and the formation of social consciousness is examined as an open empirical question. The underlying assumption here is that participation in Islamic organizations, an activity which is possible to observe and measure, reflects an individual's knowledge and capacity to interpret Islamic cultural values in a concrete social

281

Table 7.6 *Class consciousness and Islamic brotherhood participation among high urban residents*

Dimension of consciousness	Variable: participation in Islamic brotherhoods	Positive or agree	N=	Statistics
Agrees that pay is unfair	Particiaption	(21) 80.8%	(26)	Gamma = .62 P < .02 Corrected x^2 = 5.63
	No participation	(26) 50.0%	(52)	
Adebo strike support	Participation	(20) 76.9%	(26)	Gamma = .41 P < .16 Corrected x^2 = 1.94
	No participation	(32) 58.2%	(55)	
Islamic approval of fair strike	Participation	(21) 80.8%	(26)	Gamma = .51 P < .07 Corrected x^2 = 3.25
	No participation	(31) 57.4%	(54)	
Agreement with organizing at the factory level	Participation	(22) 84.6%	(26)	Gamma = .74 P < .00 Corrected x^2 = 9.54
	No participation	(24) 45.3%	(53)	
Agreement with workers engaging in politics	Participation	(16) 61.5%	(26)	Gamma = .50 P < .04 Corrected x^2 = 4.07
	No participation	(18) 34.6%	(52)	

situation. Finally, because it is assumed that Islamic cultural elements articulate with capitalist elements, this approach allows the product of articulation to emerge without assuming that Islamic culture presents its followers with norms that are universal, unchanging and non-contradictory. To this end, the effect that workers' participation in Islamic brotherhoods and Koranic schools exerts on the formation of class consciousness will be measured.

Both Islamic brotherhoods and Koranic schools are ongoing social organizations with deep roots in precapitalist society, through which Muslim culture, institutions and practices are reproduced within Kano's rapidly changing society. For these reasons, membership in Islamic brotherhoods (e.g., the Tijaniyya and Qadiriyya) and years of participation in Koranic school serve as two excellent indicators of social participation in Muslim precapitalist institutions. While the first indicator, membership in Islamic brotherhoods, was easily defined by membership, the second indicator posed some difficulty because there was uncertainty as to what weight or meaning should be attributed to a year of Koranic school attendance. To resolve this ambiguity, rather than divide the distribution at the mid-point as had been done with previous continuous variables (e.g., urban residence), the upper third of the distribution of years of Koranic schooling was taken – that is, eight years and above. This constituted *high Koranic school participation*. While evaluating this decision, it was noted that all workers reporting *mallam* as their secondary occupation were in the upper third of the distribution but not in the upper half. Let us examine Tables 7.6 and 7.7 which present class consciousness by Islamic brotherhood and by Koranic schooling respectively. Note that because only six out of thirty-three Islamic brotherhood members, i.e., 21 percent, were in the low urban residential group, Table 7.6 presents the relationship between class consciousness and Islamic brotherhood participation only among workers with high urban residential experience. For both high and low urban residential experience, see Table A.5.

Not surprisingly, a strong relationship exists between participation in Islamic institutions, that is, the institutions that reproduce the organizations and ideology of the historically antecedent precapitalist society, and the development of class consciousness. Yet there are similarities and differences between the two tables that merit consideration. First, in both tables, workers most integrated into Muslim institutions are more likely than those less integrated to favor supporting the Adebo strike and, even more strongly, to agree that Islam agrees with striking for a fair reason; that is to say, those most integrated into Muslim organizations and, presumably, the most knowledgeable are more likely to interpret Islamic values as supporting class struggle. Though urban-resident brotherhood members are significantly more likely to agree that their pay is unfair than are other urban residents, Koranic school participation exerts no such effect on the attitudes toward fairness of pay. This suggests that Islamic participation does not create new consumption needs associated with the deepening of semi-industrial capitalism.

The reader should recall an earlier finding regarding the powerful influence that urban residence exerted on the most advanced dimensions of class consciousness and the difficulty encountered in specifying exactly what concrete aspect of participation in urban social processes was responsible for increasing a worker's propensity to support factory trade unions and to favor workers' engagement in political activity. When one examines the latter two dimensions of class consciousness in Tables 7.6 and 7.7 then it is readily apparent that participation in urban Islamic organizations encour-

Table 7.7 *Class consciousness and Koranic school participation*

Dimension of consciousness	Variable: years of Koranic schooling	Positive or agree	N=	Statistics
Agrees that pay is unfair	High number of years[a]	(21) 47.7%	(44)	Gamma = .08 P < .82 Corrected x^2 = .05
	Low numbers of years[b]	(40) 44.0%	(91)	
Adebo strike support	High number of years[a]	(30) 66.7%	(45)	Gamma = .40 P < .04 Corrected x^2 = 4.29
	Low numbers of years[b]	(44) 46.3%	(95)	
Islamic approval of fair strike	High number of years[a]	(30) 66.7%	(45)	Gamma = .44 P < .02 Corrected x^2 = 5.58
	Low number of years[b]	(41) 43.6%	(94)	
Agreement with organizing at the factory level	High number of years[a]	(27) 67.5%	(40)	Gamma = .54 P < .00 Corrected x^2 = 8.36
	Low number of years[b]	(34) 38.2%	(89)	
Agreement with workers engaging in politics	High number of years[a]	(22) 51.2%	(43)	Gamma = .48 P < .01 Corrected x^2 = 6.49
	Low number of years[b]	(23) 26.7%	(86)	

[a] High=8 or more.
[b] Low=7 or less.

ages workers to support both workers' organizations at the workplace and their engagement in politics. Since urban residential experience is also correlated, let us control Koranic school experience by urban residential experience in order to see if this relationship holds true. Table 7.8 presents the four relevant indicators of class consciousness (without fairness of pay) by Koranic school participation, controlling for urban residential experience. The original relationship holds among workers with high urban

Table 7.8 *(a) Class consciousness and Koranic school participation with high urban residential experience*

Dimension of consciousness	Variable: years of Koranic schooling	Positive or agree	N=	Statistics
Adebo strike support	High number of years[a]	(22) 68.8%	(32)	Gamma = .16 P < .65 Corrected x^2 = .21
	Low number of years[b]	(30) 61.2%	(49)	Total N = 81
Islamic approval of fair strike	High number of years[a]	(24) 75.0%	(32)	Gamma = .36 P < .20 Corrected x^2 = 1.67
	Low number of years[b]	(28) 58.3%	(48)	Total N = 80
Agreement with organizing at the factory level	High number of years[a]	(23) 74.2%	(31)	Gamma = .52 P < .04 Corrected x^2 = 4.32
	Low number of years[b]	(23) 47.9%	(48)	Total N = 79
Agreement with workers engaging in politics	High number of years[a]	(19) 61.3%	(31)	Gamma = .54 P < .02 Corrected x^2 = 5.42
	Low number of years[b]	(15) 31.9%	(47)	Total N = 78

[a] High=8 or more.
[b] Low=7 or less.

experience: *there is a statistically significant relationship between Koranic school participation and the two most advanced dimensions of class consciousness (i.e., organizing at the factory and engaging in political activity), even when urban residential experience is controlled for.*

Therefore, while urban residential experience explains part of the reason why some workers develop the two most advanced dimensions of class consciousness, it is clear that participation in Islamic organizations, though reflecting participation in a precapitalist organization and ideology, articulates with the experience of urban proletarianization to raise the level of class consciousness and thus makes an independent contribution to class formation. More importantly, the greatest effect of Islamic participation is not on the tendency to engage in violent or spontaneous forms of class conflict, but rather on the tendency to form and participate in urban working class organizations. Here, the consequence of a complex articu-

Table 7.8 *(b) Class consciousness and Koranic school participation with low urban residential experience*

Dimension of consciousness	Variable: years of Koranic schooling	Positive or agree	N=	Statistics
Adebo strike support	High number of years[a]	(8) 61.5%	(13)	Gamma = .57 P < .08 Corrected x^2 = 2.97
	Low number of years[b]	(14) 30.4%	(46)	Total N = 59
Islamic approval of fair strike	High number of years[a]	(6) 46.2%	(13)	Gamma = .37 P < .38 Corrected x^2 = .78
	Low number of years[b]	(13) 28.3%	(46)	Total N = 59
Agreement with organizing at the factory level	High number of years[a]	(4) 44.4%	(9)	Gamma = .37 P < .52 Corrected x^2 = .41
	Low number of years[b]	(11) 26.8%	(41)	Total N = 50
Agreement with workers engaging in politics	High number of years[a]	(3) 25.0%	(12)	Gamma = .13 P < .94 Corrected x^2 = .01
	Low number of years[b]	(8) 20.5%	(39)	Total N = 51

[a] High = 8 or more.
[b] Low = 7 or less.

lation between precapitalist and capitalist forms of participation acts to strengthen support for working class organization and political engagement by Muslim urban workers. Hence, in the case of Kano, Islamic national consciousness appears to *reinforce* and *converge* with class consciousness among unskilled industrial workers. Such an empirical outcome contradicts the expectations of modernization theory and vulgar versions of Marxism.

ARTICULATION AND THE EMERGENCE OF REACTIVE ISLAMIC NATIONALISM

One of the paradoxes that arises from the findings of Table 7.8 is that Islam exerts its strongest influence on the class consciousness of those workers who, through extensive urban residence, have acquired the greatest exposure to the social processes of urban capitalism. Hence, the data renders implausible the simple linear interpretation that contact with urban capitalism subordinates, erodes and destroys the efficacy of all precapitalist institutions. For, if Islam were simply a backward ideology whose determining influence was limited to a precapitalist society, i.e., an ideological residual of a declining precapitalist social formation, then its influence on class consciousness would be weakest among workers with high urban residential experience and strongest among workers with low urban residential experience. The logic of this simplistic approach is one that argues that rural residence buttresses Islam as a precapitalist ideology, while urban residence erodes the influence of Islam on the consciousness of recently proletarianized workers. But as Table 7.8 indicates, contrary to this simplistic dualism, Islamic institutional participation raises the degree of support for the organizational and political dimensions of class consciousness, provided workers are resident and presumably participating in urban Islamic institutions in a semi-industrial capitalist city located at the periphery of the world economy.

Islamic institutions and urban socialization

Since Koranic school participation among workers with high urban residential experience generates support for the organizational and political dimensions of class consciousness, one must reflect on the question of *why* participation in precapitalist institutions located in a peripheral, semi-industrial capitalist city generates such support. Clearly, with the exception of support for the Adebo strike, the effect of Islamic participation among rural dwellers or recent rural migrants to the city is qualitatively different than the effect of Islamic institutional participation among workers with high urban residential experience, because urban residential experience specifies the effect that Koranic schooling has on the formation of the more advanced dimensions of class consciousness. That is to say, according to Table 7.8, the effect exerted by Koranic schooling on class consciousness is contingent upon extensive participation in the urban social processes of Kano. What is it about urban Koranic schools that explains this relationship?

Remember that to reside in a peripheral capitalist city requires workers and the urban talakawa to participate in urban social processes intensely at the level of consumption and exchange; that is, they must compete for employment, housing and the means of subsistence. Besides market forces, urban residence exposes workers to the interventions of the state on behalf of the wealthy and powerful, as in the case of land distribution for housing in Tudun Wada. And, of course, urban residence exposes workers to previously unimagined yet starkly visible accumulations of wealth that are unequally distributed, conspicuously consumed and often illegitimately acquired by the dominant classes. At the same time, the intensification of semi-industrial capitalism in urban centers not only erodes rights and privileges customarily enjoyed by the urban talakawa, but a new class of rentier capitalists manifestly accumulates wealth from the housing needs of talakawa wage earners. Placed in such a situation, where wildly inflationary prices and the commoditization of the means of subsistence create distress for both the urban-born and migrant wage earners, urban Koranic schools stand out as material and spiritual havens for the urban working class as well as for the marginally employed migrants. Koranic schools and networks not only provide food and lodging for young migrants, they also offer practical advice, social resources and psychological counseling for permanent urban workers who feel profoundly insecure in the face of their increasing dependence upon an unstable market for their livelihood.[17]

If one examines the values disseminated at the Koranic school, the informal relationship between a mallam and his students reproduces a talakawa interpretation of Islam. Thus workers not only learn about the obligations of Muslims to legitimate authority, to a way of daily life and to correct ritual, they also learn about their rights as Muslims, their charitable obligations to fellow Muslims, the commitment of Islamic principles to social and economic justice and the opposition of Islamic values to corrupt leaders. The latter aspects are important, for as Tables 7.7 and 7.8 indicate, there is a clear association between participation in Koranic schools and the belief that Islam supports 'fair strikes'. If applied to other situations, it could be argued that workers who are confident in their understanding of Islamic learning are also likely to emphasize the obligations of the wealthy and powerful toward the weak and the poor. And similarly, even ignoring the puritanical tendency of Islamic theory that emphasizes austerity, knowledgeable workers are quick to label as 'un-Islamic' conspicuous consumption or the failure of the powerful to express mercy toward the weak and the poor. Again, despite aspects of fatalism and dogmatism in Islamic doctrine, as emphasized by western 'orientalist' scholarship, urban Koranic schools teach talakawa workers about the obligations of Muslims to correct injustice, to abolish tyranny and to establish conditions of dignity for the Muslim community. For class analysis, this is the relevant ideological content of talakawa Islam as it is taught in the urban Koranic schools of Kano and as it is interpreted by class-conscious industrial workers.

But urban Koranic schools provide more than talakawa interpretations of Islam. It is important to remember that these informally organized schools are one of the few institutions, besides the family, where workers and other talakawa exert control over their immediate social environment. To follow a mallam, to become his student and to teach his students often requires that a Hausa-speaking worker meet and cooperate with Muslims from diverse ethnic groups and from distant regions (see Chapter Four). Thus, for many, urban Koranic school activity is a new social organizational experience. And for most workers, it represents their first urban organizational experience beyond the workplace. From field observations, therefore, I have no doubt that Islamic institutional participation enhances a worker's self esteem, making him more likely to demand his Islamically defined human rights and more willing to support collective solutions at the workplace. Hence, it is not simply the ideological content of Islam (i.e., cultural values) that explains the correlation between Islamic institutional participation and the organized and political dimensions of class consciousness. Rather, Koranic schools in a class-differentiated city are emerging working class institutions that are controlled by the urban lower classes. Besides serving as support and information networks, Koranic schools encourage workers to organize themselves at the workplace and to seek political solutions to problems.

Finally, the question arises whether the ideological and organizational experience of urban Koranic schools can be explained by the complex articulation of precapitalist institutions and emerging forms of capitalism alone, or whether the perceived alien qualities of an unambiguously dependent form of capitalist development – which is perceived as 'European' – plays any role in the relationship between Islamic institutional participation and class consciousness. That is to say, does the correlation between Islamic institutional participation and class consciousness arise from an Islamic nationalist reaction to the subordination of a Muslim region to a dependent position in the world division of labor?

Here it should be recalled that Hausa-speaking wage workers define wage labor for a Hausa farmer differently than for a modern industrial enterprise. Rural wage labor is called *kodago* (farm labor) but factory labor is called *aikin bature* (literally, 'working with Europeans'). Clearly, the subjective category of *aikin bature* as well as the field data presented in Chapters Four and Six suggest that workers perceive wage labor in a capitalist enterprise as alien and, if not inherently un-Islamic, certainly as a set of alien social relations introduced by European colonialism. Thus, when workers define factory labor as European work, when workers resist the timing and discipline required by capitalist production because it violates correct prayer time, and when those most integrated into Islamic institutions are much more likely to favor political action, then one must assume that Islamic nationalist sentiments are also interwoven with class consciousness.

Reactive Islamic nationalism and the world division of labor

So far, it has been argued that, contrary to linear expectations of modernization theory, the articulation of precapitalist and capitalist elements within Kano's industrial working class results in the convergence of Islamic and class consciousness.[18] This interpretation rests on the assumption that workers with the greatest degree of participation in Islamic brotherhoods and Koranic schools possess a strong commitment to Islamic national consciousness. Further, because the correlation between high Koranic school participation and the more advanced dimensions of class consciousness is contingent upon high levels of participation in the urban social processes of a semi-industrial capitalist city, this correlation cannot be attributed solely to the resistant nature of a declining precapitalist ideology held by recently urbanized workers. If this were true, workers such as commuters and recently urbanized migrants, who are most integrated into precapitalist social relations which are strongest in the countryside, should be resisting proletarianization by supporting class struggle. Why, given equivalent degrees of participation in Koranic schools, are industrial workers with the greatest degree of participation in the urban social processes of a peripheral capitalist city most likely to support the advanced dimensions of class consciousness? In responding to this question, it is argued that contact with semi-industrial capitalism in a peripheral capitalist urban center generates a *reactive form of Islamic nationalism*, one that in this instance converges with class consciousness. For it is only through residence in the peripheral capitalist city and participation in the labor process of dependent industrialization that a worker with a Muslim national consciousness becomes aware of the reality that his Islamic region plays a subordinate role in the world division of labor. Rural life tends to obscure this form of inequality. For a Hausa-speaking Muslim worker, the labeling of industrial labor as *aikin bature*, as opposed to *aikin kodago*, reflects his perception that industrial labor is alien, subordinated to foreign (i.e., Christian) control and dependent upon foreigners for management, technologies and inputs such as raw materials and spare parts. Though this Muslim worker may not be aware of the theoretical meaning of the world division of labor as defined here, he is acutely aware of the historical subordination of his nation and region to foreign control; therefore, his strong integration into Islamic organizations and his Islamic national consciousness predispose him to react against the class that controls dependent industrialization. Thomas Hodgkin states this view succinctly: 'The liberation of the Muslim community from domination by western imperialism is what Islam is all about.'[19]

The *convergence* of Islamic nationalist and class consciousness is *conjunctural* and thus rests upon the condition that Muslim workers experience proletarianization in a dependent capitalist urban situation where the subordination of their region to the dominant states and transnational corporations becomes visible. To be sure, historically both the actions of Islamic nationalists and the ideological elements of precapitalist Islamic culture can be shown to have resisted imperialism and European domination. What is valuable in the analysis that I have presented here is the argument that the structural position of a Muslim region in the world division of labor provides a structural support for the nationalist and anti-imperialist elements contained within Islamic culture. Thus class and national consciousness converge in the particular historical experience of Kano's industrial proletariat because both forms of consciousness arise from a subordinate role in the social division of labor: *class consciousness* emerges from the division of labor within the labor process of capitalist production, and *Islamic nationalist consciousness* emerges from the social division of labor within the world economy. And, of course, since the nationality of the dominant class, to whom Muslim workers are subordinated in the industrial workplace, is nearly always European, as is the system of dependent industrialization, the antagonist for both working class consciousness and Islamic nationalist consciousness appears the same: the European manager or state administrator.[20]

CLASS FORMATION AND CLASS INTEGRATION: THE PROBLEM OF ETHNICITY

Earlier, the vertical and horizontal dimensions of class formation were distinguished. It has been demonstrated that the vertical dimension of class formation and class consciousness, referring to conflict between classes representing labor and capital, is determined first by the degree of workers' participation in capitalist social relations, and second by the degree of participation in precapitalist Islamic institutions. If participation in Islamic organizations socializes workers into an urban-centered yet regionally bounded Islamic nation, which in turn reinforces class consciousness under peripheral capitalist industrialization, then the question arises as to whether the two forms of social participation – capitalist and Islamic – advance or retard the horizontal dimension of class formation and class consciousness. Clearly, the objective process of class formation is acting upon all ethnic, linguistic and religious groups that make up the urban leburori. And yet, at the same time, it is certain that an autonomous social process of Islamic national formation is going on within the urban lower classes of Kano. It is a process whereby diverse ethnic groups, usually of northern regional origin, are becoming assimilated into urban Muslim social identity. Yet, while these diverse ethnic groups are increasingly assimilated into the majority group of Hausa-speakers, each retains situationally relevant ethnic or sub-ethnic social identities derived from their ethnic, geographic, linguistic or occupational origins (*asali*).

   Again, it is critical for the reader to understand that the two processes, though interactive, maintain an autonomy from each other. Equally important is the recognition that the first – class formation – arises from the division of labor in capitalist production, while the second – the formation of a regionally bounded Islamic nation – arises from three distinct historical processes: Muslim state formation during the nineteenth century, Islamic resistance to imperialist penetration during the twentieth century and the contemporary position of the region in the international and national division of labor. Unlike class consciousness, which is determined exclusively by the division of labor within capitalist production and the urban social processes of the city, the position of the region in the international division of labor is a *secondary* structural determinant of the regionally bounded Islamic nationalist consciousness; that is, its effect is

291

contingent upon an individual's membership in the regional Muslim community.

In order to assess the nature of class formation and class consciousness among Kano's Hausa-speaking industrial workers, the problem posed by religion and ethnicity for the horizontal dimension of class consciousness must be confronted. To reiterate an earlier point, the formation of an urban working class necessitates that the researcher show empirically how a worker's loyalty to ethnic and sub-ethnic cultural and organizational patterns changes in relation to his involvement in the urban and industrial processes of capitalist development. Simply stated, the Marxist theoretical position holds that the cooperative activity involved in the labor process of capitalist production and the objective interest of all workers in opposing capitalist management create a subjective awareness of class solidarity which, over the long term, reduces antagonistic ethnic and other status differences between workers of heterogeneous social origin. Ideally, insofar as workers from diverse ethnic and social origins relate to one another primarily as workers in areas of work, residence and ultimately marriage, rather than primarily as members of distinct ethnic groups, one may conclude that ethnic integration within the working class has progressed.

To be sure, the process of horizontal integration of an urban working class does not occur within the lifetime of one generation. Rather it is a long-term historical process, one where several generations of workers need to be exposed to industrial capitalism before inter-ethnic marriage, to take the extreme example, could become commonplace. Nonetheless, there are numerous examples of situations where state intervention or political domination by one group over a second engenders bitter ethnic conflict among members of the urban working class even after each group has been exposed to industrial capitalism for several generations.[21] Despite this last caveat, my expectation is that the horizontal dimension of class formation and class consciousness will be present: the more workers are exposed to urban social processes of the peripheral capitalist city and the more they participate as wage workers in industrial production, the more likely are workers' behavior and consciousness toward diverse ethnic groups to be determined by class rather than by ethnicity. Hence, workers with the greatest degree of urban and industrial experience are expected to express greater tolerance of alien ethnic groups.

Ethnicity and class among Hausa workers

With this theoretical expectation in mind, some examples from my field work are presented which illustrate the conditions under which ethnic tolerance toward alien ethnic groups by the majority of (Muslim) Hausa workers is, like Hausa ethnicity itself, also situationally determined. Here the evidence and argument presented in Chapter Four regarding situational ethnicity in Tudun Wada should be recalled; first, Hausa speakers possess several possible ethnic and sub-ethnic identities which they invoke according to the appropriate situation and personal advantage; secondly, strict definition and maintenance of ethnic or sub-ethnic cultural practices, avoidances and preferences are constrained by market forces for work, housing and consumption and by class-defined needs to expand one's networks regardless of network members' ethnic status, especially among migrants; and thirdly, the broadest, most inclusive and most generalized ethnic category operative in Tudun Wada, and Kano in general, was defined by membership in the Muslim community. Hence, while ethnic and sub-ethnic identities continue to operate within certain situations, the combination of historical, market, class and religious forces, operating within the confines of an urban lower class stratum, creates an inclusive, open ethnic identity.

In researching the history of strikes described in Chapter Six, I found it was extremely rare for informants to invoke ethnic categories in an invidious manner toward other workers. Further, I know of no example where workers divided along ethnic lines during a strike. This is not to say that ethnicity did not operate in the minds of the workers. For example, during the Adebo affair, a strike at a furniture factory was settled by a written agreement signed by representatives of management and labor. The agreement was entrusted to a Yoruba worker. After the informant described the settlement, and because during 1971 relations between the Hausa and the Yoruba in Kano were tense, I asked if it was normal for Hausa workers to delegate trust to a Yoruba worker. The informant responded: 'It is only at work that we trust him'. Thus, despite the rivalry between the two groups for national power and competition locally for skilled jobs, ethnic rivalries did not threaten the class cohesion among workers at the furniture factory during the strike. To take a second example, in the case of Factory B when the workers there decided to strike over their Adebo payment, the striking headmen, as an informal strike committee, took account of ethnic loyalties by relieving a Nupe headman from the responsibility of leading the strike in his section though he had offered to do so, because the foreman during that shift was also Nupe. Information provided by a Hausa headman indicated that it would be a great source of personal shame for the Nupe headman in his community if he publicly humiliated the Nupe foreman. Strike leaders, therefore, recognized ethnic sensibilities, avoided shaming the headman and yet carried out the struggle against capital successfully. Thus, in each case, workers took ethnicity into account during strikes, yet it did not divide class action nor prevent the achievement of class goals.

Nigeria's recent history confirms that ethnic tensions continue to exist in northern cities between southern and northern ethnic groups. But ethnic tension, even among the most competitive groups, need not eliminate solidarity among diverse ethnic groups at the workplace. In fact, workers may segregate ethnic attitudes such as those regarding a willingness to marry or to share the same compound from a willingness to cooperate at the workplace against management as members of the leburori; that is to say, workers may be intolerant of southern or other ethnic groups in matters relating to marriage, household, community or even perceived regional nationalist interests, but, at the same time, they may accept the trust of the same ethnic group in matters limited to the workplace.

Nowhere is this tendency to segregate ethnic attitudes more clearly demonstrated than in the example of a Hausa worker from Azare who agreed to be interviewed for a final pretest of my interview schedule. When I referred to the Adebo strike (*tawaye*) in the section on class consciousness, the respondent misunderstood the question to refer to the urban communal disorders of 1966, which were directed against southerners, especially Ibos. Apparently, while living in Maidugari, the respondent had supported and participated in the urban crowds that unleashed some of the worst communal violence in Nigeria's history. He defended his action on the grounds that his ethno-national group, the northern Muslims, feared that they were losing control over the regional economy and the regional government. Nevertheless, when asked later to name a worker to head a trade union in his factory, he responded: 'Well, the only person I would trust with such a responsibility is an Ibo. There is an Ibo man in my factory whom we would nominate because we have confidence in his honesty and ability to negotiate with management.' When I asked about the apparent contradiction between supporting communal violence and his attitudes toward this ethnic group, he responded that the riots of 1966 involved issues of regional nationalism (*kasar arewa*) which he felt obligated to defend. But the leader of a factory union was a different issue because 'we are both laborers'. While this is an extreme example, it makes the point that ethnic tolerance is segregated and situational: an individual may be extremely intolerant of an ethnic group in a community or nationalist situation but express the opposite attitude with regard to a class situation. Let us return now to the problem of ethnic integration within Kano's industrial proletariat.

ETHNIC TOLERANCE AS AN INDICATOR OF CLASS INTEGRATION

The argument so far is that ethnic identities among the Hausa-speaking Muslims are situationally defined, that a regional Muslim national identity is the most inclusive identity and, further, that Hausa tolerance toward alien ethnic groups is also situationally determined. When reviewing the sociological data recorded on the Hausa-speaking industrial workers, I found that most but not all workers married within the Hausa or Fulani ethnic groups; friendships followed the same pattern; and only housing patterns, among migrants living in the Waje area, suggested fundamental changes in ethnic residential segregation patterns. One must conclude that, whatever their attitudes on ethnic tolerance and integration, there is little evidence, during the decade of the 1970s, of a major *behavioral* change in ethnic marriage, friendship and residential patterns among Kano's industrial workers. Nonetheless, the question remains whether the social experiences that advanced the vertical dimension of class consciousness (i.e., urban residence and industrial labor experience) also act to increase a Hausa-speaking worker's *subjective* level of ethnic tolerance toward minority ethnic groups residing in Kano. Furthermore, a secondary question concerns the effect of Islamic organizational experience on attitudes toward Muslim and non-Muslim ethnic groups.

Since neither the historical evolution of urban segregation patterns nor the behavior patterns of Hausa-speaking workers suggest that ethnic integration along class lines has occurred among Kano's leburori, it is appropriate to investigate whether the *subjective* attitudes of industrial workers toward alien ethnic groups change in the direction of increased tolerance as workers participate in the social relations of urban and industrial capitalism. Is there a significant correlation between the degree of urban residential experience and/or industrial labor experience and increased tolerance toward alien ethnic groups? Or, to put it in theoretical language, does the degree of horizontal class integration and class consciousness, as measured by ethnic tolerance, increase as workers participate in the urban social processes of a capitalist city and in the labor process of industrial capitalist production? If one demonstrates empirically that workers with the greatest exposure to urban-industrial capitalism are, at the same time, more tolerant of ethnic groups with whom they share the same class experiences, then one may argue that the class integrative or horizontal aspect of class formation and class consciousness is indeed occurring, though at an unknown rate toward an uncertain outcome.

Measuring class integration

In order to measure ethnic tolerance, workers were given a card with four houses painted on it. Then respondents were informed that each house represented a level of trust toward ethnic groups along the following continuum: House 1 – respondent would be willing to marry and *to give his daughter* in marriage to said ethnic group; House 2 – respondent would not marry, but would be willing to live in the same compound with said ethnic group; House 3 – respondent would not marry or share a residence with, but would be willing to work with said ethnic group; House 4 – respondents had no trust in said group, not even at work. After explaining the tolerance scale until workers understood the meaning of each level of trust, a list of ethnic groups employed in the sampled factories was presented to each worker. Then the respondent was asked to rank the group according to the amount of trust, i.e., marriage, residence, work only, or 'no trust'.

Table 7.9 presents a summary of the data describing ethnic tolerance of the leburori within my sample of industrial workers. Ethnic tolerance is correlated by years of urban residence, years of industrial experience and

Table 7.9 *Ethnic tolerance by urban residence, industrial experience and Islamic participation*

(1) Ethnic group	(2) Mean tolerance score	(3) Ethnic group as a % of total	(4) Muslims as a % of ethnic group	(5) (6) Years of urban residence		(7) (8) Years at present job		(9) (10) Years of Koranic schooling	
				r	B	r	B	r	B
Kanuri	1.35	0.9	94.4	.221	.166[c]	.143	.080	.188	.146
Nupe	2.17	1.4	96.4	.289	.277[a]	.091	.003	.112	.054
Babur	2.30	9.1	61.3	.012	−.025	.163	.178[c]	−.074	−.084
Igala	2.69	1.4	41.4	.190	.187[c]	.094	.042	−.004	−.046
Ibo	2.90	0.7	0.0	.201	.189[b]	.198	.155[c]	−.119	−.171[c]
Yoruba	2.95	3.3	39.7	−.002	.003	−.011	−.011	−.009	−.008

[a] P < .01
[b] P < .05
[c] P < .10

(with n−2 degrees of freedom)

years of Koranic schooling. Column 1 indicates each ethnic group; Column 2 records the mean score given by Hausa and Fulani workers for each ethnic group (N=125), where perfect ethnic tolerance (i.e., all respondents are willing to marry and exchange daughters with said ethnic group) would achieve a mean score of 1.00. For example, all workers identifying as Fulani were willing to marry and exchange daughters with Hausa workers, while most but not all Hausa workers were willing to marry and exchange daughters with Fulani, so that the mean tolerance score expressed by Fulanis for the Hausa is 1.00, and by Hausas for the Fulani, 1.14. Hence, the ranking of each ethnic group by its mean tolerance score indicates the willingness of Hausa and Fulani workers to associate with or to tolerate said ethnic group. Note that this score (Column 2) is the overall average score and does not take into account the effects of differential participation in capitalist or Islamic organizations on an individual worker's level of ethnic tolerance.

Column 3 presents each ethnic group as a proportion of the workforce of the three sample factories. Column 4 presents the industrial survey's (N=3,075) proportion of each ethnic group professing Islam. Column 5 presents the zero order Pearson correlation coefficient between the respondents' years of urban residence and their attitude toward each ethnic group as measured by the aforementioned ethnic tolerance scale. Column 6 presents the standardized Beta coefficient for years of urban residence and ethnic tolerance when the effects of the two following independent variables – years at present job and years of Koranic schooling – are controlled for in the multiple regression. Thus, Column 6 presents the correlation between urban residential experience and ethnic tolerance, when the effects of the two other independent variables are controlled for. Column 7 presents the zero order Pearson correlation coefficient (r) between the respondents' years at present job (i.e., degree of participation in the industrial labor process) and their attitude toward each ethnic group as measured by the ethnic tolerance scale. Column 8 presents the standardized Beta coefficient for years at present job and ethnic tolerance when the other two independent variables are controlled for in the multiple regression. Column 9 presents the zero order Pearson correlation coefficient (r) between the respondents' years of Koranic schooling and their attitude toward each ethnic group as measured by the ethnic tolerance scale. And lastly, Column 10 presents the standardized Beta coefficient for years of Koranic schooling and ethnic tolerance when the two other independent variables are controlled for.

Determinants of ethnic tolerance for three factories

What, then, does Table 7.9 tell the reader about ethnic tolerance and the horizontal integration of Kano's industrial working class? Let us begin with the information in Columns 1–4. The ordering of ethnic groups by their mean tolerance score (Column 2) indicates the overall degree of ethnic tolerance expressed by Hausa and Fulani workers for each ethnic group. Kanuris achieve nearly complete acceptance, and Yorubas score the lowest. Note that, with the exception of the Yoruba, who were the main competitors of Hausa-speaking groups for national power during the 1970s, the ranking of ethnic groups by mean tolerance score corresponds with the proportion of each group that professes Islam. The Kanuri and Nupe, for example, the two ethnic groups with the highest degree of acceptance, are over 90 percent Muslim. Both had established extensive commercial, residential and cultural ties to Kano during the precolonial period. The next two groups, ranked according to ethnic preference in Column 2, are the Babur and the Igala, minority groups within the former Northern Region, a significant proportion of whom profess Islam. Neither of these groups were incorporated into the Sokoto Caliphate during the nineteenth century. The Babur, however, quickly responded to employment opportunities offered by the advent of colonialism, so that a sizeable ethnic community of Baburs exists in Kano. In Tudun Wada, for example, a Babur ward exists as does an informal concentration of Babur residents in the Gwargarawa-Gama area of Waje. The last two groups, the Ibo and the Yoruba, were majority ethnic groups in their respective regions during the period when Nigeria was divided into three politically competitive regions. Accordingly, Ibos and Yorubas were the principal rivals of the Hausa-speaking northerners for national power. Moreover, because of their earlier incorporation into the capitalist world economy and their greater opportunities for western education, historically these two groups have dominated the control of skilled jobs in northern cities. These findings are interpreted as empirical evidence for the contention that a *regional Islamic national identity* has formed among urban workers.

To any reader familiar with ethnic relations and inter-ethnic political competition in Nigeria during the First Nigerian Republic, the findings presented in Columns 1–4 of Table 7.9 offer no surprises. Regarding northern-origin ethnic groups, Paden has argued that Islam serves to integrate diverse ethnic groups around a common, though situational, urban social identity. Moreover, despite constitutional provisions designed to reduce ethnic and regional rivalries for national power, the elections of 1979 indicate that ethnic and regional identities largely determined the outcome of the elections for Nigeria's civil government at the federal level. Therefore, given the reality of ethnic consciousness in contemporary Nigeria, one must search for social processes that alter ethnic identities and levels of ethnic tolerance if only at the level of *attitudinal* change. In this regard, one should note that Columns 1–4 present Hausa and Fulani workers' rankings of ethnic groups without regard for degree of exposure or the degree of inter-ethnic interaction. Therefore it is plausible that within these aggregates represented by Columns 1–4, workers most exposed to a common class situation, measured either by urban residence or by years at present job, will be more tolerant of alien ethnic groups than the remaining Hausa and Fulani workers. Let us examine this hypothesis.

Since I am interested in the effect of participation in capitalist and Islamic organizations on the ethnic consciousness of Hausa and Fulani workers, Columns 5–10 in Table 7.9 are of great interest. The standardized Beta coefficients in Columns 6, 8 and 10 indicate the degree to which a year of each form of social structural participation, i.e., urban, industrial or Koranic, increases or decreases ethnic tolerance on the part of Hausa or Fulani workers toward each ethnic group. To take Column 6, for example, which designates the effect of urban residential experience on ethnic tolerance, it is clear that, just as in the case of the vertical dimension of class formation and class consciousness, the most powerful determinant of class integration as measured by increased ethnic tolerance is *urban residential experience* in a peripheral capitalist city. Only the Beta coefficients for the Yoruba and the Babur remain unaffected by urban residential experience. And in the case of the Babur, increased ethnic tolerance is explained not by urban residence but by participation in the industrial labor process (see Column 8 under Babur). The effect exerted by length of time at present job (i.e., experience in the industrial labor process) is measured by the standardized Beta coefficients presented in Column 8. With the sole exception of the Yoruba, the Beta coefficients show a positive correlation between increased tolerance and the degree of participation in the industrial labor process. But only the Beta coefficients associated with the Babur and the Ibo are of any size or statistical significance. Hence urban experience, rather than industrial experience, is correlated with increased ethnic tolerance and the horizontal dimension of class consciousness.

Let us examine Column 10, which measures the effect of Islamic organizational participation (years of Koranic schooling) on ethnic tolerance. Earlier it was agreed that the processes of working class formation and regional Islamic nationalism were occurring simultaneously among urban lower class inhabitants of Kano. What effect does Islamic organizational participation have on ethnic tolerance? Since Islamic nationalism is a form of ethnic identity, one expects those most integrated into this identity to exhibit greater tolerance toward ethnic groups that are perceived as practicing Muslims and greater intolerance toward groups that are perceived as non-Islamic or marginally Islamicized. That is to say, the effect of Islamic organizational participation should specify, by positive or negative signs, greater or lesser tolerance depending on whether the ethnic group in question is Muslim or not. Hence, while Islamic nationalism reinforces the vertical dimension of class consciousness in a peripheral capitalist situation, it is possible that participation in Islamic organizations may also generate a cleavage within the urban working class, one based upon a multi-ethnic Islamic nationalist consciousness rather than upon particular ethnic identities.

Let us examine the standardized Beta coefficients presented in Table 7.9,

299

Column 10 in order to discover if Islamic nationalism divides the urban working class. The results here are mixed, and further, with the exception of the Beta coefficient referring to Ibos, all coefficients are not significant even at the .10 level. Yet the signs (+ or −) describing the direction of the correlation change from positive to negative as soon as the proportion of the ethnic group professing Islam falls below 90 percent. My field observations on patterns of ethnic social integration in the migrant working class areas of Kano suggested that Baburs would be included among the Nupe and the Kanuri.) Note that ethnic tolerance toward the Kanuri and the Nupe ethnic groups is positively correlated with Islamic organizational participation. The significant negative correlation between Islamic organizational partici-pation and tolerance toward Ibos suggests that regional Islamic nationalism, as measured by years of Koranic schooling, reacts negatively against non-Muslim ethnic groups that are perceived to threaten regional Muslim nationalist interests. But because the correlations are not significant generally, the evidence is merely suggestive. In summary then, Islamic organizational experience, overall, is negligibly correlated with ethnic tolerance in either direction.

To respond to a question posed earlier concerning the effects of Islamic organizational participation on ethnic tolerance and horizontal class inte-gration, the evidence is weak and inconsistent. True, there is a small, but statistically insignificant, positive relationship between Islamic organi-zational participation and increased tolerance among ethnic groups who profess Islam. And the only ethnic group without professed Muslims is the single group that is significantly and negatively correlated with Islamic organizational participation. But there is no consistent pattern expressed by Hausa and Fulani workers toward the six ethnic groups. To conclude, there is weak and, at best, suggestive evidence that Islamic organizational participation among Hausa and Fulani workers strengthens ethnic tolerance toward the highly Muslim, northern ethnic groups and weakens ethnic tolerance toward non-Muslim southern groups. Most importantly, the effect of Islamic organizational participation on horizontal class integration appears to be slight, especially if one considers the stronger and more consistent effect exerted on ethnic tolerance by urban residential experi-ence. Let us return now to the effect of participation in the industrial labor process on ethnic tolerance.

The effect of the industrial labor process on ethnic tolerance as measured by the standardized Beta coefficients in Column 8 of Table 7.9 appeared to be of only slight statistical significance. Before dismissing the argument that participation in industrial labor increases ethnic tolerance, however, it should be noted that the pooling of workers from three factories with heterogeneous proportions of non-indigenous ethnic groups may not allow the effect of the labor process in a single factory to be measured exactly and to manifest itself. Why? Because for an individual worker in a particular factory one is uncertain of both the degree of inter-ethnic cooperation and

Table 7.10 *Ethnic tolerance by urban residence, industrial experience and Islamic participation at Factory 'B'*

(1) Ethnic group	(2) Ethnic group as % of three factory labor force	(3) Ethnic group as % of Factory 'B'	(4) Years of urban residence		(5)		(6) Years at present job		(7)		(8) Years of Koranic Schooling		(9)	
			r	B	B		r	B	B		r	B	B	
Kanuri	0.9	0.8	.259		.197		.218		.166		.159		.085	
Nupe	1.4	2.4	.393		.350[a]		.317		.243[b]		.091		−.035	
Babur	9.3	6.9	.290		.287[b]		.304		.258[b]		−.076		−.185	
Igala	1.4	2.2	.235		.249[b]		.250		.214[c]		−.116		−.209[c]	
Ibo	0.7	0.8	.183		.162		.253		.227[c]		−.032		−.101	
Yoruba	3.3	4.8	.148		.116		.239		.218[c]		−.002		−.057	

[a] P<.01
[b] P<.05
[c] P<.10

(with n−2 degrees of freedom)

301

the degree of exposure of Hausa or Fulani workers to any single ethnic group unless a single factory with a known distribution of ethnic groups is analyzed separately. Therefore, the effect of participation in industrial labor on ethnic tolerance must be examined in individual factories where the degree of possible ethnic interaction in the industrial labor process can be estimated from the actual distribution of ethnic groups in the factory. Accordingly, Table 7.10 presents ethnic tolerance by the same three independent variables employed in Table 7.9, but only among workers employed at Factory B, the largest and most ethnically heterogeneous factory. Column 2 indicates the proportion of each ethnic group employed in the three factories as a whole, and Column 3 indicates the proportion of each ethnic group employed solely at Factory B. Except for Kanuri and Babur, each ethnic group forms a larger proportion of the labor force of Factory B than was true for the three factories as a whole. Columns 4–9 provide the same information (r and B) for the three independent variables (urban residence, industrial experience and Koranic schooling) as presented in Table 7.9 above.

The data presented in Column 7 of Table 7.10 confirm that among Hausa and Fulani workers, participation in the industrial labor process increases tolerance toward ethnic groups that cooperate in the same labor process of industrial capitalist production. With the exception of the Kanuri, participation in the industrial labor process is positively and significantly correlated with ethnic tolerance. Moreover, if one compares the size of the Beta coefficients for the relationship between participation in the industrial labor process and ethnic tolerance between Tables 7.9 and 7.10, then it appears that ethnic tolerance increases as the ethnic heterogeneity of the labor process increases (e.g., those of Table 7.10, Column 7 are consistently larger than those of Table 7.9, Column 8). That is to say, the longer a Hausa or Fulani worker participates in a labor process characterized by high ethnic heterogeneity, the more ethnic tolerance increases among these Hausa or Fulani workers. Hence, as in the determination of the vertical dimension of class consciousness, participation in the industrial labor process, acting together with urban residential experience, increases ethnic tolerance and thereby contributes to the horizontal dimension of class formation and class consciousness. To be sure, the evidence for this horizontal integration is *attitudinal* rather than behavioral, but the overall evidence indicates that participation in the industrial labor process increases ethnic tolerance and class integration.

THE STRUCTURAL DETERMINANTS OF CLASS CONSCIOUSNESS: A SUMMARY

The analysis thus far has examined the effects of participation in capitalist and Islamic organizations on the vertical and horizontal dimensions of class consciousness. Clearly, the single most important determinant of class

302

consciousness is participation in the urban social processes of a semi-industrial capitalist city as measured by urban residential experience. The peripheral capitalist city and the social processes associated with it – labor markets, class-based patterns of consumption, visible social inequality and state intervention on behalf of the wealthy and powerful – have a strong, consistent and statistically significant effect on the formation of a class-conscious industrial proletariat. Though important for certain aspects of class consciousness, participation in the industrial labor process was secondary to urban experience and contributed only partially to the organizational and political aspects of class consciousness. It was, however, shown to exert the strongest influence on ethnic tolerance, and thus on the horizontal-integrative dimension of class consciousness, within a single factory. Western literacy, treated as an attribute of participation in capitalist social relations, was also an important determinant of the vertical aspect of class consciousness, especially with regard to its organizational and political dimensions.

Participation in Islamic organizations, which are treated here as precapitalist organizations, was found to *articulate* with the class created by capitalist production, such that it reinforced the vertical or conflictual aspect of class consciousness. A notable feature of the articulation of precapitalist Islamic organizations within the industrial proletariat was that urban Islamic organizational participation enhanced the organizational and political dimensions of class consciousness even more strongly than did participation in industrial wage labor. Though urban and industrial organizational participation promoted ethnic tolerance and thus the horizontal dimension of class formation and class consciousness, Islamic organizational participation failed to have any consistent or statistically significant effect in that area. There was, however, some evidence to suggest that participation in Islamic organizations made Hausa and Fulani workers more tolerant of other northern, Muslim ethnic groups. But because this evidence was weak, the correlations inconsistent and the statistical significance levels low, this evidence is considered merely *suggestive* and is reported here only for recording purposes. Overall, the major effect of participation in Islamic organizations was to reinforce the vertical dimension of class consciousness (i.e., class struggle) rather than to frustrate the horizontal dimension (e.g., class integration).

Empirically, I have endeavored to make the case beyond the reasonable doubt of an interested or even an unsympathetic observer that class formation, class consciousness and reactive Islamic nationalism are determinant social forces in the social life of Kano's urban lower class. More importantly, since the objective social processes that have been shown to determine class struggle and class consciousness during the early years of the decade have increased dramatically by the end of the decade, one can only presume that the intensity of the struggles, the consciousness and the organizational discipline of the industrial working class have increased in rough proportion to the increase in the objective forces associated with semi-industrial urban capitalism.

8

Conclusion: the limits to populism

The last years of the 1970s witnessed the end of military rule, the election of a populist (PRP) governor of Kano State and the abolition of most of the political burdens borne by the talakawa, such as the community tax. But, by the end of 1983, despite the temporary upswing in the world petroleum market caused by the Iranian revolution, the Nigerian petroleum boom with all its associated dynamism and social contradictions was exhausted. World recession, the collapse of both prices and demand within the petroleum market, the fiscal crisis of the Nigerian state and, as a consequence, the widespread unemployment of industrial workers marked the end of the petroleum boom as well as the conjuncture that began with the Nigerian civil war. For Nigeria, as for Africa generally, the decade of the eighties promises to be radically different from the seventies when economic nationalism among the peripheral capitalist states surged forward. Industry has stagnated under the deadly weight of austerity and unresolved negotiations over the repayment of Nigeria's external debt; petroleum, the engine of growth during the seventies, has declined in price and demand beyond the most pessimistic predictions; and a new authoritarian military government has yet to demonstrate to external or internal investors a route out of the current morass. At the same time, the new military government's earnest efforts to purge and discipline the state bureaucracy, to curtail the scandalous pirate capitalism of the Second Republic and to inject, however awkwardly, a sense of productive discipline into Nigerian civil society must be acknowledged. For without a disciplined coalition around the state and a policy of creating the necessary conditions for indigenous and foreign-based accumulation, capitalist development in Nigeria will flounder only to be followed by increasing stagnation and probable anarchy. Whatever the outcome, the Nigeria of the mid-eighties lies outside the parameters of this study.

It would be superfluous to restate the central argument regarding the articulation of Islam and capitalism in northern Nigeria. Having already made this theoretical and empirical analysis, its application to the era of the Second Republic, when the populist PRP held power in Kano State, will be examined. Finally, the study concludes with an analysis of the relationship of the millenarian insurrection of the *Yan Tatsine* to the central argument developed here.

THE URBAN WORKING CLASS UNDER THE SECOND REPUBLIC

Let us begin with the social existence and consciousness of the urban *leburori*. Compared to the early 1970's, the urban working class had increased in number, awareness and tactical sophistication in waging class struggle at the workplace. The general tendencies described in Chapter Six have continued toward greater class confidence and discipline, greater demand for democratic trade unions, an increased awareness of the relationship between political power and capital and an increased tolerance of non-indigenous ethnic groups within the working class. Informants report widespread support among the industrial working class for the general strike of 1981, for the leftist faction of the Nigerian Labor Congress led by Sumono and for the policies and rhetoric of the Rimi faction of the highly fragmented PRP.[1]

With regard to the role of Islamic elements of precapitalist origin in the maturation of the working class, the available evidence suggests that, with the institutionalization of trade unions and the activity surrounding political parties, expressions of Islamic nationalist *resistance* to labor's subordination to capital are more muted than they once were. It should be noted that I was unable to verify any participation in or even mild tolerance for the millenarian *Yan Tatsine* insurrection (December 1980) on the part of industrial workers or any modern-sector wage workers. Thus, while the Islamic revival flourishes in urban Kano, and while the relationship between Islamic participation and class consciousness still holds, Muslim institutions, ideologies and clerics were less visible during civilian rule than earlier. The combination of greater class maturity, stronger trade union organization and the radical political ideology of the Rimi administration deflected the consciousness of Muslim industrial workers in some degree in a secular direction, particularly with regard to the affairs of the workplace. Yet, since the Islamic impulse toward activity is cyclical, it is fatuous to assume that Islamic nationalism has disappeared among workers.

Mention of the Rimi administration and its radical populist program raises the question of the relationship of the radical elements of the PRP to organized industrial labor. It should be noted that the radical, occasionally Marxist, anti-imperialist rhetoric emanating from the stalwarts of the Rimi administration did not generate an autonomous and politically conscious labor movement among Kano's formal-sector workers. Neither was there any significant effort on the part of the left factions of the PRP to mobilize and raise the consciousness and organization of Kano's urban working class in general, at least not as a class conscious political movement. Hence, there was a segregation of working class consciousness and action between the workplace, where militant yet *economistic* forms of class consciousness drove the NLC cadre to more militant positions, and the wider urban society where the worker's political consciousness remains attached to the class alliance of the urban talakawa. Therefore, rather than directing their political energy and political potential toward militant, politically motivated class projects, the political consciousness of the urban working class remained allied to the class-ambiguous yet nevertheless populist program of the Rimi faction of the PRP. Since the populist class alliance supporting the PRP administration was led by the property-owning petty bourgeoisie, by civil servants straddling state office and private capitalist investments, and by radical intellectuals, working class interests were subordinated to the interests of the latter group. But this bifurcation between the politics of the workplace and the politics of the populist PRP does not mean that the Rimi administration did not have a major impact on the political consciousness of the urban working class; nor does it mean that the leburori did not materially benefit from the Rimi administration.

Clearly, the thrust of the PRP ideology was directed toward the emancipation of the talakawa from extra-economic coercion, political discrimination and the corrupt greed of the sarauta and their wealthy class allies, the merchant industrial bourgeoisie. At the political level, therefore, the success of the PRP amongst workers rests on its destruction of the feudal (to use the local idiom) class and its political prerogatives. But more important than the attack on the symbols and power of the sarauta-merchant class alliance is the success of the Rimi administration in introducing a new political vocabulary into the political culture of the urban leburori. Projects like the literacy campaign (see Chapter Seven for the effect of literacy on class consciousness), the political education campaigns on television and radio and the Rimi administration's support for and public embracing of the Sumono faction of the NLC altered the way in which industrial and other wage earners viewed themselves and interpreted their situation. Further, the language of class relations expressed in the media by Marxist PRP militants entered into the vocabulary of industrial workers. This has occurred to such an extent that once naive and ignorant workers express a need for a 'revolutionary' cleaning of Nigeria's corrupt leadership; the rich are now referred to as the 'bourgeoisie' who are opposed by the 'masses'; and comparisons are made with workers elsewhere in Nigeria and even in South Africa. Hence, the beginning of a new political vocabulary, one that may stimulate an alternative vision of society, has been planted and nurtured by the Rimi administration. This is no mean feat for what is, after all, the most left-oriented administration ever to hold executive office in modern Nigeria.

Given the fact that the consciousness of the urban working class was bifurcated between the class militancy of the workplace and the populism of the talakawa class alliance, what is the legacy of the PRP for Kano's leburori? First, the bifurcation is a logical outcome of state intervention: that is to say, this division was determined by the deal struck between the leadership of the national trade union congresses and the military government, and did not arise from the conflictual social relations within civil society. At the same time, when one observed the class and educational background of the local representatives of the NLC and the 'perks' of office, such as automobile loans that flow from the automatic check-off of union dues in trade union treasuries, one cannot be optimistic about a politically conscious labor movement emerging from the NLC leadership. To a significant degree, therefore, many officials and leaders of the NLC have been 'incorporated'. In support of this view, it should be noted how, during the Second Republic, the threat of legalizing a second national trade union congress under the leadership of David Ojeli was used effectively by the NPN to dampen the militancy of the current NLC leadership. Hence any future transformation of the urban working class into a self-interested and organized political force oriented toward a radical transformation of Nigerian society must be initiated by activists whose political strength and ideology lies *outside* the trade union movement as it is presently constituted. Indeed, student efforts to organize and politicize the working class have already begun and need the support and encouragement of committed scholars. The evidence presented here argues that any cadre seeking to organize the urban working class must avoid the vulgar formulae and dogmatism presented by the classical Leninist doctrine, for Muslim industrial workers are unlikely to respond to the rigid secularism, the organizational authoritarianism and the class reductionism that invariably flow 'scientifically' from this approach.

The evidence presented here shows that the urban working class share a common social existence with independent commodity producers and even some members of the petty entrepreneurial bourgeoisie, so that strategists of any working class political movement *must* allow for shared talakawa consciousness and the continuing importance of independent commodity production in the social consciousness of industrial workers, especially as an income strategy for retired workers. Clearly, any strategy of working class politics must develop a program which, while allowing for the leading role of modern-sector labor, also relates to the political needs of independent producers and the more impoverished members of the urban talakawa: that is, labor in general. For, the continuing deluge of surplus rural population, the capital intensity of industrial production and the talakawa's deep historical attachment to independent production within the urban informal sector mean that a majority of the urban lower classes will remain *outside* the formal-sector labor force. This caveat notwithstanding, the formal-sector working class and their allies among the informal-sector wage and labor service workers are ripe for political mobilization, but they desperately need the assistance of disciplined, militant left organizers. Indeed, Kano's urban working class hungers for organization, enlightenment and disciplined political leadership, provided organizers are sensitive to Islamic nationalist issues.

The influence of precapitalist elements on working class consciousness

Let us now turn to the continuing influence of precapitalist elements in the political maturation of Kano's urban leburori. To be sure, membership in the talakawa and the common social existence shared with independent commodity producers, together with state corporativist constraints imposed on the NLC, direct modern-sector workers toward the populist class alliance. While one should not expect this alliance to dissolve but to appear during future regimes, the interests of the laboring classes in general, and especially of modern-sector workers, would be well served if the balance of forces within the alliance shifted in favor of one led by an organized urban working class that claimed to represent 'labor in general'. But here any political organizer must be careful, for the Muslim working class is already aware of the opprobrium associated with the label 'communist'. Any organizational strategy which ignores the importance of popular Islamic culture and institutions is setting the stage for a vicious and probably paralyzing attack from the right on the grounds that socialism equals atheism. More importantly, to pursue a classic Leninist strategy risks opposing the regional *nationalist* tradition that Islam represents. Lessons are to be learned from the success of the alliance between the Catholic left and the independent Marxist movements of Latin America, where a 'people's church' and a theology of liberation are a main support for the Sandinista Revolution in Nicaragua.

At the same time, even the most sympathetic observer of Islamic populist and nationalist social movements, despite the vigor contained in their anti-imperialist and radical populist ideology, cannot overlook the repressive and backward direction that the Iranian revolution has taken. For Islamic populism, like all populism, is Janus-like and thus contains a left and right face. However sympathetic one might be towards the use of Islamic institutions and ideologies to resist imperialism, to struggle against exploitation within the labor process and towards their capacity to 'make' a working class culture, recent history is a forceful and painful reminder of the authoritarian, intolerant, xenophobic and even quasi-fascist potential contained in rightist versions of Islamic populism, as reflected for example in the Muslim Brotherhood and the leadership of Iran's clerical state. But Islamic ideology, like all others, is mediated by structure and class experience so that one cannot assume that the Iranian outcome is determinant in all cases.

That radical Islamic populist ideologies exist and appear attractive to the impoverished urban masses of Muslim northern Nigeria cannot be doubted. While the *Yan Tatsine* incident was clearly millenarian and rooted in *Mahdist* traditions of the region, it is not surprising that during a period of rapid social change literally thousands of *gardi* and Koranic students engaged in an insurrection resulting in the complete breakdown of public order and thousands of casualties during the last weeks of December 1980. Since this movement is dealt with in detail elsewhere, I shall only make some observations that are germane to the central argument contained in this study.[2] As verified in the survey and qualitative data presented above, Koranic networks, rooted in the expectations of Islamic charity and interwoven within the casual labor market of Kano, present a nearly ideal-typical example of the political consequences flowing from the articulation of precapitalist and capitalist modes of production. But, by 1980, when the transition to semi-industrial capitalism had driven up food prices, when new internationalized styles of consumption generated unprecedented status and income inequalities and when state programs such as universal primary (western) education displaced the talakawa *ulema* and their peripatetic tradition, this floating population of miserable Koranic students came to be labelled as a dangerous and backward group by the upper classes. Given these material pressures, it is not surprising that the *gardi* and Koranic students were attracted to and mobilized by the ideology and insurrectionist program of a millenarian critic of the social order. The insurrection at Kano lasted ten days because the *Yan Tatsine* fortified themselves in narrow sections of the city where they held off the Nigerian police until the Nigerian Army intervened and killed their leader, Alhaji Mohammed Marwa Maitatsine. But neither his death not the banning of wandering Koranic students ended the *Yan Tatsine* insurrection, precisely because the *Yan Tatsine* reflect a deep structural contradiction within Islamic Hausa society and not an isolated incident by some fanatics. With considerable regularity during the dry season that propels the rural poor as Koranic students into the northern cities, the insurrection continued: Kaduna (1982), Bulum-Ketu, near Maidugari (1982), Jimeta, near Yola (1984) and Gombe (1985). Each insurrection involved provocations and attacks against the Nigerian police, and if measured in terms of thousands of lives lost, easily ranks as the most serious internal civil disturbance since the communal riots that presaged the Nigerian civil war. While careful research remains to be conducted, it is clear that the *Yan Tatsine* uprisings are a popular religious movement directed against the secular and religious authorities, one which is opposed to unrestrained Western consumerism and which reflects a profound social crisis arising from the destruction of a popular moral economy by a failed transition to semi-industrial capitalism. The *Yan Tatsine* provide dramatic evidence for the attractiveness of Islamic populist ideology among northern Nigeria's marginalized and dispossessed masses. In this case the movement was based upon millenarian fantasy, but given leadership and organization the articulation of Islam and capitalism may generate social movements capable of social transformation especially during the current crisis.

To conclude, Islamic nationalist ideology is not a unified, unidirectional body of thought; rather, it consists of popular and authoritarian values which are interpreted according to the situation and class or status position of a particular group. For example, the prophet Marwa (e.g., *Maitatsine*), once expelled and then returned, had been resident in Kano since the regime of military governor Bako, but the material conditions that made his ideology attractive to the floating Koranic student population existed only towards the end of the 1970's.

What, then, can one conclude about the role of Islamic nationalist institutions and ideology in the future of Muslim northern Nigeria? To begin with, one must emphasize that the *primary* contradiction and determinant of social change in the region will be rooted in the class tensions arising from the deepening and extension of a vicious, often corrupt and inexorable process of capital accumulation. As a political force, Islamic nationalism will not wither away as capitalism transforms the region. For, Islamic nationalism is the dialectical product of the encounter between Islamdom and European capitalism, a historical encounter reinforced by the dependent role played by the region in the international division of labor. Insofar as the diverse and often contradictory values within Islamic nationalism prescribed political precepts, such prescriptions are interpreted through the lens of particular class and status groups located within a historically specific phase of capitalist development.

However ironic it may be that the outcome of PRP's populist program is authoritarianism and intensified capitalism rather than a transition to socialism, it really should not be surprising to readers familiar with populist ideologies, the talakawa- and PRP-vision of society and the general level of organizational anarchy that pervades the PRP party apparatus. Indeed, the problem lies in the contradictions inherent in a populist movement whose main target is feudal privilege rather than capitalist class alliances; whose class alliance is composed of unequal members with contradictory interests; and whose ambivalence toward the disruptive exigencies of industrialization allow for neither the necessary social discipline nor the planning for a radical restructuring of society that the transition to urban based industrialization entails. Gavin Kitching's comment on populist ideas in development theory is quite appropriate to the situation of contemporary Kano, where populism has triumphed only to prepare the way for capitalism:

> For leaders and policy makers with the need or desire to change societies made up overwhelmingly of peasants and other small-scale producers, there will always be a certain attraction in a tradition of thought which suggests both that change and development is possible and that all that is conceived as best in existing institutions and practices may be maintained, and that this double objective can be achieved without creating the extremes of wealth and poverty.[3]

The failure of populism under the PRP to create an ideology, organization or movement capable of initiating an organized transition to socialism in my view marks the end of a conjuncture that began with the collapse of the First Nigerian Republic. Since then, Kano's Muslim working class has emerged as a political and economic force, and sarauta privilege has been permanently undermined. The next phase of popular struggle in northern Nigeria, however, promises to be more bitter and more extensive. And, as the state response to the *Yan Tatsine* and the Baklori insurrections suggests, popular protest is likely to be met with an unprecedented degree of ruthless force by the Nigerian security apparatus. All of which calls for a new organizational strategy by the left, one informed less by populist visions originating in the colonial era and more by a new generation of political activists devoted to constructing a new, disciplined organizational apparatus capable of inspiring and transforming the lives of workers, peasants and independent producers.

Appendix 1: Methodology

Three methods of data collection are employed in this study: comparative-historical, qualitative-field methods, and statistical-social survey methods. Each method employs distinct assumptions about reality, structure, process and meaning, as well as appropriate techniques of data collection.

The multiple method approach to data collection originates from a seminal article published by Campbell and Fisk (1956) that was applied initially to experimental psychology.[1] Drawing upon the insights contained in this approach and combining them with elements of Marxist method, the research design of this study proposes the following assumptions regarding data collection by multiple methods. Reality is assumed to be observable; hence knowledge is possible, but each technique of observation (data collection) contains its own inherent limitation. Error is inherent in each method: for example, survey methods are intrusive, and often force interviewees to respond to attitudinal items that they never considered previously. Such data are unreliable. On the other hand, qualitative methods employ the researcher as the instrument of data collection so that his/her subjective biases and unrepresentative observations are problems. To resolve these problems of reliability and, to some degree, of validity, the multi-method approach used in this study assumes that each method has a particular strength and weakness in data collection that is inseparable from the method itself. Yet, if several methods are used, then the strength of each method may be maximized while the total error may be reduced by cross-checking and comparing the findings elicited by each method. Moreover, data collected by one method may enable the researcher to understand, interpret, or reject as unreliable paradoxical findings generated by a second method. To be sure, the problem of knowledge in the social world remains a difficult one, but at least with a multiple method research design the gross errors are eliminated. More optimistically, this approach allows for the possibility of *rejecting* a researcher's most treasured ideological assumptions through constantly comparing findings from several methods of data collection.

Like theory, technical questions surrounding data collection demand that the researcher make explicit the assumptions and objectives organizing the process of data collection. The objective here is to describe and to explain the structure, consciousness, and action of a class that emerges from

312

long-term historical processes: Islamization and capitalist development. An analogy taken from photography is helpful here. To accurately analyze such a process requires a continous motion picture film; but most of the data available and/or collectable are still or snapshot photography. Given the necessity of describing and explaining a long-term historical process, I have employed three different methods of data collection so as to create the best estimate of what a motion picture account of class formation would be like if it were indeed possible.

By drawing upon secondary sources, monographs, archival materials, and similar historical situations, comparative-historical methods serve as the over-arching method of explication. Such a method allows one to trace the historical development of structural social forces such as Islamization, state formation, commodification, social class formation, and structural relations with and reactions to the world economy and state system. Two kinds of survey data are employed as snapshots of this contradictory historical process. The first is an *industrial survey* that enumerates in short interviews the social and demographic characteristics of all workers at Kano's five largest employers of industrial labor. The second survey is a sub-sample of the industrial survey in which Hausa-speaking workers were randomly selected for *structured depth interviews* based upon their urban status and urban residential experience. The former is referred to as the industrial survey: it is composed of 3,075 enumerated workers. The latter survey is referred to as a sample of depth interviews; it is composed of 140 depth interviews undertaken by the author.

Qualitative or field methods, employing participant observation, and informal interviewing techniques characteristic of social anthropology, constitute the third method of data collection. While the industrial survey was undertaken during July–August 1971, and while the depth interviews were conducted by the researcher during the months of January through May 1972, field methods were employed for over a decade: from October 1970 through June 1972, during November and December 1975, and for short visits to the 'field' during November 1978, December 1980 and September 1981. Within the decade of the 1970s, the data collected by field methods is informal and continuous, and thus falls on a continuum between snapshot photography and motion picture film accounts of the process.

COMPARATIVE-HISTORICAL METHODS[2]

This method relies on previously collected information (that is, secondary data) located in archives, unpublished and published sources, and scholarly work in general. Ideally, the comparative-historical method deals with large-scale, macro-level permanent structural processes. For example, Islamization, state formation, imperialism, merchant capitalism, semi-industrial capitalism, and working class formation are concepts that evolve in history and thus can only be described, verified, and linked to empirically

313

observable events through historical analysis. Further, one may extend one's understanding and the scientific validity of one's conclusions by comparing events, processes, and outcomes with other appropriate empirical situations, abstract models (e.g., modes of production) or ideal types in the Weberian sense of the term. The major advantage of this method lies in its long-term historical perspective, one that allows the researcher to identify in history underlying structural processes that appear repeatedly in societies under different circumstances and in distinct epochs, and thus explain empirically observable events and outcomes. On the other hand, the limitation of this method lies in its dependence upon existing archival or secondary data that are at least once removed from the researcher, the oftentimes ambiguous relationship between macro-theoretical concept and micro-level empirical indicators, the necessity of assuming that certain forms of social consciousness were held by people sharing the same structural situation, and the difficulty of comparing empirical situations with ideal types as well as generating rules for valid comparisons between two empirical situations.

Although historical and comparative methods, concepts and assumptions draw heavily upon both the Marxian and Weberian sociological traditions, the basic method employed in this study is at the macro-level of Marxian political economy. Hence, underlying structural forces and expressed empirically observable phenomena are assumed to be in a dialectical relationship with each other whereby outcomes at any moment in history are not determined by any linear processes. Furthermore, by its very nature, capitalism is assumed to generate uneven development within any society whether the units of analysis are states/regions or partners in a production relationship. Similarly, Weber's methodological assertion, which requires the researcher to relate the subjectivity of the social actor to his/her structural position through empathetic understanding, is taken seriously within this study. Whereas the two remaining methods are complementary to comparative and historical method, it is the latter that enables the researcher to interpret empirical findings in relationship to long-term historical processes and in comparison to abstract models and existing empirical studies. For it is only by comparing one's findings with some abstract or empirical standard that one *knows* the meaning and significance of one's empirical findings.

SOCIAL SURVEY METHODS[3]

Bearing in mind that this study employs two social survey methods, first as an enumeration-type industrial survey and secondly as structured depth interviews, social surveys take snapshots of social structural processes at one point in their historical development. The data are cross-sectional rather than continuous. With survey data, one obtains detailed, rigorously scientific observations about the social, demographic, and attitudinal char-

314

acteristics of the industrial working class at one particular time and at significant expense. An enumeration-type survey, furthermore, generates data from a known population which can be manipulated statistically so that latent characteristics of the population become easily visible. This allows relationships between theoretically significant categories to be explored and analyzed, and it grants the researchers some certainty concerning the objective parameters of the class under analysis, an especially valuable resource in the Nigerian case where census material is absent. To apply this method to the present study, then, workers in the five largest employers of industrial labor were enumerated. Because the factories were located geographically in each of the three industrial areas of Kano in rough proportion to the number of workers employed in each industrial area, i.e., three factories at Bompai, one at Township, and one at Fagge-Birni area, the resulting industrial survey is assumed to be representative of the population of industrial workers at the time of the survey.

From this enumeration (N = 3075), three sub-samples based upon urban residence (i.e., urbans, migrants, and commuter-peasants) were randomly selected for depth interviews. In order to increase the homogeneity and representativeness, those selected for depth interviews possessed the following characteristics: Muslim, Hausa, or Fulani ethnicity, unskilled, married, aged twenty to forty years, and lacking exposure to formal western education. After developing a listing of randomly selected workers, depth interviews were conducted personally by the researcher regarding occupational, residential and family history, residential and social relational networks, Islamic education and participation, and a bevy of attitudinal items measuring work attitudes, social equity, class consciousness, ethnic tolerance, the value of western education, occupational aspirations, and the ranking of occupations according to prestige. The role of the depth interviews was to provide high quality data on workers' consciousness and social activity which, unlike qualitative field data, were the same for each randomly selected worker, a feature that allows statistical comparison without fear of selection bias. Thus, data collected through informal participant observation methods can be compared with representative data collected from the depth interviews so as to estimate the reliability of each. Again, the data from depth interviews are exceedingly rich and detailed, yet, at the same time, remain a cross-sectional snapshot of a contradictory, long-term historical process.

FIELD METHOD[4]

The last method was employed to collect data throughout the decade and, unlike the survey methods, not just during the initial research period of 1970–2. One key advantage was continual residence in and visits to Nigeria and Tudun Wada, the oldest working class area of Kano. Chapter Four is a product of this research. Field methods assume that the researcher enters an interactive 'field' and that to some degree the researcher affects the social world that encompasses his/her field. Informal social processes that are not observable through the intervention of the survey instrument are ideally suited for field observation. Besides the advantage of observing informal social processes, illustrating, for example, how Islam and capitalism articulate in the everyday life of a first-generation working class community, field methods allow a short-term historical dimension to be integrated into the study. Once having collected formal interviews and having established field relations with workers and members of the community of Tudun Wada, data could be collected on survey topics and field topics during short research visits throughout the 1970s. Of course, the limitation of field data arises from the subjectivity of the data collection process. Unlike survey methods, there is no formal separation between the research and the instrument of data collection. Most importantly, field methods allow the researcher to understand how the popular classes – workers, craftsmen, petty traders, and service workers – experienced the transition to semi-industrial capitalism and civilian rule. Together with comparative and historical methods, this processual field perspective increased the longitudinal character of the data collected on the formation of Kano's urban working class.

Appendix 2: A natural history of multiple method research

From October 1970 to June 1971, I lived, researched and, in a marginal way, participated in the life of a workers' community called Tudun Wada, in the shadows of Bompai industrial estate. Tudun Wada was created in the 1930s as a residential area for northern Muslim migrants to Kano who worked for the government either as police and soldiers or night soil collectors; the development of Bompai industrial estate since the late 1950s had made it a densely populated community of wage workers. As such, it was considered low in status relative to the old city, but higher in status than areas such as Sabon Gari or parts of nearby Gwagwara. After establishing a residence in a new ward, I began explaining and introducing myself to the local notables and officials. During the first two months I spent most of my energy learning local concepts, personalities, vocabulary, and conducting informal life histories with the laborers who resided there and participated in the active street life. Direct observation of community life was possible because the streets and entryways of houses were public and especially active between three and nine p.m. Koranic students chanted verses; food sellers haggled over prices; workers rested and played cards; brightly dressed prostitutes emerged from houses; and children played and ran errands for their parents.

January brought a federal government-sponsored report written by the Adebo Commission recommending wage increases which, when back-dated, formed an arrears payment amounting to ten times the weekly salary of the lowest paid worker. Wage increases were recommended for the public sector but the position of the private sector was more ambiguous. This created a situation where the industrial workers employed in the private sector organized wildcat strikes and, when necessary, violent confrontations in order to receive their arrears pay. At the same time as the report's publication, the Muslim festival of *Id el-Fitr* approached, requiring significant expenses and gifts to wives and relatives. Here is an example of combined development or the articulation of two modes of production whereby the consumptive demands of fulfilling festival obligations exerted pressure on workers to demand immediate payment of their arrears pay (maximum cost per worker = ₦18). The intensity of the strike is explained by the interaction between the nineteenth-century Muslim system and the modern capitalist system.

317

From January until June, the 1964 strike, early union organizations, the failure and repression of unions (no factory unions existed in 1971–2), and the tactics used in the settlement of the 1971 Adebo strikes in several factories, formed the core of my research. By June I had collected detailed histories, sometimes hour by hour, of the strikes and the workers' efforts to create permanent workers' organizations. The data collected by informal methods was qualitatively insightful and rich in detailed personal accounts of what it meant to engage in an industrial action for both experienced and neophyte workers. But the virtual absence of statistical data meant that after nine months of field work, I had no sound or reliable knowledge of how representative of industrial workers my informants and strike participants were. Matters such as age, ethnic composition, rural-urban origins and education of the industrial labor force remained unknown. It was clear that I needed census-level material before engaging in structured interviews and especially before defining theoretically important sample categories.

After visiting many factories and observing management practices, I decided to generate a representative sample of cases from which the general socio-demographic characteristics of the industrial labor force could be ascertained; this meant that samples of workers with theoretically salient social characteristics could be randomly selected from the initial listing. In order to maximize the impact of industrial variables, the five largest employers of industrial labour were chosen. Though this sample was not representative of Kano's total factory population, it was spatially representative in that at least one firm was drawn from each of the three industrial areas of Kano with three being selected from the overwhelmingly largest area, the Bompai industrial estate. After training six local university students as enumerators, all production workers were interviewed on selected socio-demographic characteristics including: age, time in factory, housing and amenities, ethnicity and literacy. Hausa-Fulani workers were asked additional questions on land and land sales, employment history, father's occupation and social status. The socio-demographic survey took six weeks and enabled me to observe the organization, management style and process of production in each factory.

Following the enumeration, the interviews were coded and organized into broad categories that were relevant for sampling decisions. One surprise to me and my informants concerned the Hausa-Fulani. As the majority ethnic group in Kano, they accounted for just over 50 percent; but approximately one-third were rural resident commuters to the factory. Though I expected to sample by urban or rural birth, the commuters required inclusion in any final sample of structured interviews both because of their number and because their rural residence allowed a control over the effects of urban residence on workers attitudes. The existence of so many commuters provides a graphic example of how participant observation techniques lack representativeness. A second surprise concerned the vast number of ethnic groups enumerated: over 100. Because the Hausa-Fulani were the majority in our enumeration and, for a variety of political and economic reasons, are likely to increase as a proportion of the industrial labor force, they alone were selected for final interviews. I reasoned that the cost of including other ethnic groups as controls outweighed any possible gain; and further that additional samples of Hausa-Fulani such as the commuters, would yield far more interesting data. Secondly, the remaining ethnic groups were more educated and less 'conservative' or rather less dominated by authoritarian political structures than were the Hausa-Fulani. Hence, I believed that the Hausa-Fulani were least likely to exhibit 'modern' consciousness or behavior and reasoned further that any change shown among the Hausa-Fulani relative to more 'modernized' groups is even more likely to be true among the remaining groups. Finally, my resources simply did not permit elaborate sampling nor a large number of cases, and the Hausa-Fulani appeared to be the wisest investment.

The final sample called for 45–50 randomly selected interviews from each of three categories: *urbans* – life-long inhabitants of Kano city; *migrants* – rural born migrants to the city; and *commuters* – rural resident commuters to the factory. Additional controls that were designed to eliminate deviant factory workers allowed only those who were uneducated, married, Muslim, aged twenty to forty and unskilled to be included in the sample. With this sampling framework I awaited completion of the final Adebo wage review report which was scheduled for October 1971, the logic being that if its publication resulted in more strikes, the researcher should be certain to interview after the second wave of strikes. Despite this precaution, the disrupting force was not additional strikes but a trade recession which led to lay-offs in all factories and the closing down of two firms. This required a reorganization of my sample to include only three of the five original firms. Fortunately, the old city firm, having the most urban-born workers, and two large firms at Bompai remained operative and formed the basis for a new sample, yet one based exactly on the earlier sampling criteria.

Throughout the debate over the second Adebo report, compounded by a cholera epidemic and the retrenchment of workers, I continued to develop interview items for inclusion in a final interview schedule; after evaluating the ability of local interviewers, I decided to administer this myself. Not only did this increase the quality of interviewing, it allowed me to evaluate the quality of items for future data analysis. In short, it kept me close to my data and allowed me to follow-up interesting respondents for informal interviews outside the factory.

Living and conducting participant observation in the community proved to be invaluable when items were translated into Hausa. For example, my elite member translator, whom I had valued earlier as an enumerator, translated 'strike' into the Hausa word for 'riot' while the workers always used the term for 'rebellion', whereby legitimacy was inferred. Pre-testing items and especially the meaning of language choices was done individually and in groups. Workers were asked, 'what they would believe a question to mean if asked' and if they believed anyone would resist answering such a question. Actually, pre-testing the instrument was quite popular as many workers asked when their factory was to be interviewed.

Final interviews were conducted from January through May 1972. After locating the worker, who was relieved from work, the purpose and potential benefits of my research were explained, and the worker was encouraged to refuse if he could not be open or preferred not to be interviewed. Only six refusals were recorded, partly because the previous enumeration had shown that no harm occurred from being interviewed. But most important was the fact that I had been resident in the area for over fourteen months before interviewing began.

The interview schedule recorded family, residential, Islamic and occupation history in great detail because my informal research convinced me that these were influential areas of experience. Attitudinal items focused on the strike, workers' politics and organizations, adjustment and evaluation of industrial labor, ethnic tolerance, education, stratification evaluation, and aspirations. By remaining in the factories for five months, I was able to collect additional observations and notes on the management and labor process involved in production. Being an interviewer enabled me to discuss the strike with management and to gather information on how they viewed their labor force.

Table A.1 *Formal sector taxpayers (PAYE)^a by peri-urban district*

Year	Gezawa	Kumbotso	Ungogo	Total
1963/64		0.2		0.2
% PAYE	No	(24)	No	(24)
Total taxpayers	Data	(13,964)	Data	(13,964)
1966/67		1.7	0.1	0.8
% PAYE	No	(237)	(14)	(251)
Total taxpayers	Data	(14,065)	(15,721)	(29,786)
1968/69	0.1	3.7		1.7
% PAYE	(12)	(539)	No	(551)
Total taxpayers	(18,646)	(14,390)	Data	(33,036)
1969/70		0.9	1.1	1.0
%PAYE	No	(128)	(162)	(290)
Total taxpayers	Data	(13,810)	(14,568)	(28,378)
1970/71		1.2	9.9	5.8
% PAYE	No	(165)	(1,544)	(1,709)
Total taxpayers	Data	(13,907)	(15,595)	(29,502)
1971/72	0.1	3.6	9.7	4.3
% PAYE	(13)	(530)	(1,561)	(2,104)
Total taxpayers	(18,285)	(14,791)	(16,034)	(49,110)
1972/73	2.8	3.4	7.6	4.5
% PAYE	(540)	(506)	(1,237)	(2,283)
Total taxpayers	(19,061)	(15,037)	(16,201)	(50,299)
1973/74	3.0	4.6	6.4	4.6
% PAYE	(580)	(721)	(1,042)	(2,343)
Total taxpayers	(19,418)	(15,518)	(16,363)	(51,299)
1974/75	3.5	4.2	9.8	5.8
% PAYE	(704)	(666)	(1,668)	(3,038)
Total taxpayers	(19,861)	(15,824)	(16,963)	(52,648)

[a] *Pay As You Earn.*

Table A.2 *Occupational status ranking*

Sample total		Urbans (43)		Migrants (49)		Commuters (45)[a]	
Judge (alkali)	High	76.7	(33)	87.8	(43)	86.7	(39)
	Medium	23.3	(10)	12.2	(6)	13.3	(6)
	Low	0.0		0.0		0.0	
Licensed buying	High	83.7	(36)	75.5	(37)	56.8	(25)
agent (groundnuts)	Medium	16.3	(7)	22.4	(11)	40.9	(18)
	Low	0.0		2.0	(1)	2.3	(1)
Factory manager	High	72.1	(31)	75.5	(37)	65.9	(29)
	Medium	27.9	(12)	20.4	(10)	34.1	(15)
	Low	0.0		4.1	(2)	0.0	
Mallam	High	79.1	(34)	87.8	(43)	84.1	(37)
	Medium	14.0	(6)	10.2	(5)	4.5	(2)
	Low	7.0	(3)	2.0	(1)	11.4	(5)
Primary teacher	High	44.2	(19)	51.0	(25)	55.8	(24)
	Medium	48.8	(21)	46.9	(23)	32.6	(14)
	Low	7.0	(3)	2.0	(1)	11.6	(5)
Mechanic	High	9.3	(4)	16.3	(8)	27.9	(12)
	Medium	65.1	(28)	65.3	(32)	48.8	(21)
	Low	25.6	(11)	18.4	(9)	23.3	(10)
Driver	High	30.2	(13)	26.5	(13)	42.2	(19)
	Medium	60.5	(26)	59.2	(29)	48.9	(22)
	Low	9.3	(4)	14.3	(7)	8.9	(4)
Foreman	High	9.3	(4)	28.6	(14)	18.2	(8)
	Medium	76.7	(33)	53.1	(26)	63.6	(28)
	Low	14.0	(6)	18.4	(9)	18.2	(8)
Tailor	High	9.3	(4)	10.2	(5)	13.6	(6)
	Medium	81.4	(35)	77.6	(38)	63.6	(28)
	Low	9.3	(4)	12.2	(6)	22.7	(10)
Butcher	High	7.0	(3)	8.2	(4)	4.7	(2)
	Medium	67.4	(29)	46.9	(23)	44.2	(19)
	Low	25.6	(11)	44.9	(22)	51.2	(22)
Petty trader	High	2.3	(1)	6.1	(3)	0.0	
	Medium	69.8	(30)	53.1	(26)	46.7	(21)
	Low	27.9	(12)	40.8	(20)	53.3	(24)
Cart pusher	High	0.0		0.0		0.0	
	Medium	4.7	(2)	0.0		2.3	(1)
	Low	95.3	(41)	100.0	(49)	97.7	(43)
Present job	High	0.4	(0)	2.0	(1)	2.3	(1)
	Medium	20.9	(9)	16.3	(8)	15.9	(7)
	Low	79.1	(34)	81.6	(40)	81.8	(36)
People you trust	High	9.3	(4)	2.1	(1)	4.5	(2)
	Medium	44.2	(19)	18.8	(9)	22.7	(10)
	Low	46.5	(20)	79.2	(38)	72.7	(32)

[a] Due to missing data, the Commuters' total varies from 43 to 45.

Table A.3 *Tax tables of Waje*

Area of Waje	1967–8	1968–9	1969–70	1970–1	1971–2	1972–3	1973–4	1974–5
Fagge								
# of PAYE[a]	1,293	Same	1,649	1,721	1,833	1,981	2,238	2,264
% PAYE	34.1	Figures	35.0	35.8	36.3	40.3	42.3	42.2
Total # of taxpayers	3,793	as 1967–8	4,706	4,811	5,054	4,910	5,295	5,371
Gwagwarwa/Gama Tudu								
# of PAYE	780		1,007	1,123	1,437	1,568	2,115	2,289
% PAYE	26.2		30.7	32.5	35.0	35.8	41.9	42.9
Total # of taxpayers	2,981		3,285	3,459	4,108	4,377	5,051	5,339
Sabon Gari								
# of PAYE	384		312		4,000	4,030	5,000	5,645
% PAYE	54.5		23.7	No	71.7	71.0	74.6	72.6
Total # of taxpayers	704		1,317	Data	5,580	5,680	6,700	7,780[b]
Sadun Wada								
# of PAYE	753		983	1,012	1,053	1,558	1,577	2,293
% PAYE	58.8		67.3	67.6	67.0	74.5	74.1	80.1
Total # of taxpayers	1,280		1,461	1,496	1,572	2,090	2,129	2,861
Total Waje								
# of PAYE	3,210		3,951		8,323	9,137	10,930	12,491
% PAYE	36.7		36.7	No	51.0	53.6	57.0	58.5
Total # of taxpayers	8,758		10,769	Data	16,314	17,057	19,175	21,351

Pay As You Earn, i.e., wage earners

In the original documents, this total was 8,780. However, the single category accounting for the 1,000 difference, those paying personal income tax, appeared totally inconsistent for this year. When this category was last listed for Sabon Gari (1969–70), the total was 25, compared with this year's total of 1,380. This, combined with a resulting unrealistic expansion of Sabon Gari relative to the rest of Waje, made us conclude that the addition of 1,000 was an error. In either case, the indication of a general trend toward wage labor is not significantly affected.

Table A.4 *Class consciousness and urban residential experience*

Dimension of consciousness	Variable: years of urban experience	Positive or agree	N =	Statistics
Agrees that pay is unfair	High urban[a] experience	(47) 60.3%	(78)	Gamma = .65 P< .00 Corrected x^2 = 15.53
	Low urban[b] experience	(14) 24.6%	(57)	
Adebo strike support	High urban[a] experience	(52) 64.2%	(81)	Gamma = .50 P< .00 Corrected x^2 = 8.87
	Low urban[b] experience	(22) 37.3%	(59)	
Islamic approval of fair strike	High urban[a] experience	(52) 65.0%	(80)	Gamma = .59 P< .00 Corrected x^2 = 13.33
	Low urban[b] experience	(19) 32.2%	(59)	
Agreement with organizing at the factory level	High urban[a] experience	(46) 58.2%	(79)	Gamma = .53 P< .00 Corrected x^2 = 8.69
	Low urban[b] experience	(15) 30.0%	(50)	
Agreement with workers engaging in politics	High urban[a] experience	(34) 43.6%	(78)	Gamma = .48 P< .02 Corrected x^2 = 5.65
	Low urban[b] experience	(11) 21.6%	(51)	

[a] High = 6 years or more.
[b] Low = 5 years or less.

Table A.5 *Class consciousness and Islamic brotherhood participation*

Dimension of consciousness	Variable: participation in Islamic brotherhoods	Positive or agree	N =	Statistics
Agrees that pay is unfair	Participation	(25) 75.8%	(33)	Gamma = .70 P< .00 Corrected x^2 = 14.89
	No participation	(36) 35.3%	(102)	
Adebo strike support	Participation	(22) 66.7%	(33)	Gamma = .36 P< .11 Corrected x^2 = 2.62
	No participation	(52) 48.6%	(107)	
Islamic approval of fair strike	Participation	(25) 75.8%	(33)	Gamma = .61 P< .00 Corrected x^2 = 9.29
	No participation	(46) 43.4%	(106)	
Agreement with organizing at the factory level	Participation	(25) 78.1%	(32)	Gamma = .72 P< .00 Corrected x^2 = 14.63
	No participation	(36) 37.1%	(97)	
Agreement with workers engaging in politics	Participation	(19) 57.6%	(33)	Gamma = .57 P< .00 Corrected x^2 = 8.75
	No participation	(26) 27.1%	(96)	

Notes

1 Islam and class formation

1 See Keddie (1981), Fischer (1980), Said (1981) and Pipes (1980).
2 See Weber (1958), Hobsbawm (1959) and Thompson (1968).
3 Weber (1949), (1958), (1968).
4 Thompson (1968).
5 For a review of classical Marxism's theory of capitalist development and class formation, see Marx (1972), 1977), Brenner (1977), Kay (1975), Przeworski (1977) and Zeitlin (1980). For an analysis of the labor process, see Braverman (1974), Burawoy (1979a) and Blauner (1964).
6 Althusser and Balibar (1970), Meillassoux (1972, 1981), Rey (1971, 1973) and Terray (1972, 1975). For commentary and interpretation in English, see Foster-Carter (1978), Taylor (1979), Bradby (1975) and Asad and Wolpe (1976).
7 Clammer's call for 'grounding articulation in empirical reality' is relevant here, Clammer (1978), p. 252.
8 The debate over the nature of capitalism is voluminous. On commodities, see Marx (1977), Brenner (1977) and Kay (1975). The latter presents a useful comparison of merchant and industrial capital. For a critique of the classical approach, see Wallerstein (1974a and 1974b). For a general survey of the debate, see Brewer (1980) and de Janvry (1981). Note that I include dependency theory and the 'underdevelopment school' under the rubric of world systems theory: the key idea is the proposition that the external is determinant for structural social change within the internal society. See Wallerstein (1974a, 1974b, 1979), Frank (1967, 1969), Amin (1976, 1977), and Rodney (1972). For a critique of this perspective, see Palma (1978).
9 Hechter uses the term 'reactive' to describe a theory of ethnic change for the Celtic fringe of Britain and to critique the orthodox functionalist-diffusionist theory of ethnic change that explains ethnic change through the diffusion of cultural values (e.g. see Paden: 1974). According to Hechter: 'The reactive theory of ethnic change suggests that ethnicity arises from the salience of cultural distinctions in the system of stratification' (Hechter: 1975, p. 314). 'The reactive theory suggests that only when such objective cultural differences are linked to structural inequities between groups will they assume enduring significance in complex societies. For, according to this theory, it is precisely under the conditions of a cultural division of labor that ethnic boundaries are maintained, despite social interaction between groups' (Hechter: 1975, p. 326). According to Wallerstein, 'Empirically, it is obvious that within a capitalist world economy ethno-nationalist consciousness is a far more frequent phenomenon than class consciousness' (Wallerstein: 1979, p. 196.) 'The "peoples" that exist today have come into existence as a result of the development of the capitalist world-

326

economy, through which some groups (names) that were in existence before have become molded into peoples, other groups (names) have disappeared from our vocabulary, and some entirely new groups (names) have been invented. Furthermore, this *creation* of "peoples" is not a once-and-for-all happening. It is a matter of constant, if slow-moving, flux . . . The assertion of people-hood is a major political act . . . Creating a people, or remolding its definition of boundaries, is an important mechanism in shaping the world market, and in the "assignment" of different "peoples" as specific work forces in the production processes that are integrated through that market. To create and recreate peoples is to mold and remold class boundaries, and to strengthen or weaken particular processes of accumulation of capital (appropriation of surplus value). People formation is an integral *part* of class-formation' (Wallerstein: 1981, p. 50).

10 The term Islamdom is taken from Hodgson (1974): 'Islamdom . . . is the society in which Muslims and their faith are recognized as prevalent and socially dominant . . . It does not refer to an area as such, but to *a complex of social relations*, which, to be sure, is territorially more or less well-defined' (vol. I, p. 58).

11 Lubeck (1979b).

12 For elaboration, see Hodgson (1974), Weber (1968), Volume I, pp. 255–266, and B. Turner (1978, 1974). For an analysis explaining why classical Islamic societies do not correspond to Marx's model of an asiatic mode of production, see Anderson (1974), pp. 462–549.

13 See Kay (1975) and Watts (1983).

14 The quote is taken from Mabogunje (1968, pp. 94–5), who quotes R. Burton, *Wanderings in West Africa* (London, 1963).

15 Adeleye (1971), p. 120.

16 On the early history of Hausaland, see Palmer (1967), Dokaji (1958), Adeleye (1976), Last (1981), A. Smith (1976, 1970), Paden (1968), Fika (1978) and Usman (1981).

17 For a review of ecological factors in Hausaland, see Watts (1983), Buchanan and Pugh (1955) and Udo (1970).

18 A. Smith (1976), p. 192. The importance of ruling according to Islamic law (*Shari'a*) cannot be underestimated. For while Rumfa's reforms were not institutionalized, the organization of a society according to the *Shari'a* transforms societies in the spheres of polity, economy and culture. See Hodgson (1974) for a Weberian-inspired argument for the significance of 'Shari'aization' as a historical process.

19 See Palmer (1967), Last (1981, 1980, 1979), M. Smith (1981) and the citations in Last (1981). Note that the subsequent argument draws upon Last's scholarship, but he is in no way responsible for the conclusions that I have reached.

20 The literature on the *jihad* of Usman dan Fodio is vast. See Last (1967), Usman (1979), Paden (1968) and Usman (1981).

21 See Last (1974, 1967) for a description of and references for the ideologies, expectations and organization of the scholarly community known as the *jama'a*.

22 For this section, I have relied upon Fika (1978) and Paden (1968). I look forward to reading recent work by Sule Bello on nineteenth and twentieth century Kano, nearing completion for a Ph.D. dissertation for the Department of History, Ahmadu Bello University.

23 Fika (1978), p. 35. On sultanism, see Weber (1968), Lubeck (1968) and M. Smith (forthcoming). In separate and independent studies M. G. Smith and I come upon the relationship between Weber's concept of sultanism and state

centralization at Kano. I am grateful to Professor Smith for the opportunity to read his yet unpublished manuscript on the *History of Kano*.

24 See texts and references in Fika (1978), Lubeck (1968) and Watts (1983) for a complete analysis of state taxation and informal modes of surplus extraction.

25 The issue of slavery is a sensitive one, intensely debated by historians. Nigerian historians, whom I label the 'nationalist school', argue that slaves were assimilated into Hausa society whence they became *cucunawa*, while only the recent captives remained slaves, *bayi*. The national school is affronted when slavery in the Caliphate is associated with New World slavery; they believe that scholars arguing so are merely justifying imperialism since, as I shall analyze below, the abolition of slavery was the principal justification given for the British conquest. Opposed to this sanguine view are Hogendorn and Lovejoy, who, despite caveats, wish to argue that a form of 'plantation' slavery existed; that scholars should consider whether a slave mode of production is appropriate and, further, whether the division of labor within slave villages was similar to a new world plantation. It is unfortunate that the term 'plantation' was employed, for in my view this term confuses the differences between Caliphal and New World slavery and, more importantly, only obfuscates our understanding of the important role slaves played in the production process and the manner in which people of slave origin were assimilated over several generations into the Islamic Hausa nation. Lovejoy's most recent work (1981), however, appears to backtrack from many of his earlier assertions. See Lovejoy (1978, 1979, 1981), Hogendorn (1977, 1980) and Gemery and Hogendorn (1979), Adamu (1979), M. Smith (1965) and Shea (1981).

26 Marx used the concept of class for both precapitalist and capitalist situations. But he also distinguished between objective classes that play a distinct role in the social division of labor, yet lack a collective and mutually shared class consciousness toward economic and political interests, and those classes that contain both objective and subjective elements. Terray (1975), in his study of the Abron kingdom of Gyaman confronts the same problem. After reviewing Lenin's definition of class, Terray makes a point that is germane to the class issue in the Caliphate: 'Beyond the very general, abstract indication given by Lenin, it is not possible to give class a universal definition, valid for all modes of production. If class is characterized in a differential manner by its position within a determinate mode of production, it conversely follows that a specific definition of class corresponds to each particular mode of production. In other words, the question whether the concept of class is useful in studies other than those bearing on the capitalist mode of production is divested of meaning. If by "class" is understood classes such as they exist in the capitalist mode of production, then the answer is obviously no. But this does not mean that there are classes in this mode of production alone. Classes may be found in other modes of production: only then their reciprocal relations and indeed their very nature will be defined by the structure of the mode of production. For each mode of production the concept of class that is appropriate to it must be constructed.' (Terray: 1975, p. 87). To repeat, for certain purposes, such as Terray's analysis of Gyaman, classes may be defined according to the dominant precapitalist mode of production, and one can easily do so for precolonial northern Nigeria. It would, nonetheless, confuse many readers if new definitions of class appropriate to each mode of production were introduced when the theoretical object of this study is to analyze the process of working class formation in the semi-industrial, peripheral capitalist city of Kano.

27 On the importance of remaining external, see Wallerstein (1973, 1976). Accord-

ing to Wallerstein, remaining external allows strong state structures to develop and integrated economies to evolve. While the Caliphate was involved in external trade, some of which entered into the capitalist world economy during the last decades of the nineteenth century, most exchanges consisted of luxury goods rather than essentials such that the social and economic reproduction of Caliphal society did not depend on imports from capitalist states of the 'core', nor did exports from the Caliphate become essential raw materials (e.g., palm oil) for the reproduction of a capitalist world economy. Just when capitalist penetration occurred varied by location, but in Kano there is little evidence that penetration occurred prior to the actual British conquest.

28 For the data on taxation of wheat lands and the effect of market access on taxation rates, see Cargill (1908).

29 See Lubeck (1968) and Shea (1975, 1981).

30 See Tahir (1975), Lovejoy (1980), Last (1979) and A. Cohen (1969).

31 On Islamic education and labor migration, see Shea (1975, 1981) and Paden (1968).

32 On the currency system, see Lubeck (1968), Lovejoy (1974) and Johnson (1970).

33 The urban history of nineteenth century Kano remains to be written. Elements of such a history can be gleaned from Paden (1968), Frishman (1977), Shea (1975), Lovejoy (1980) and Tahir (1975). Tahir provides an interesting discussion of merchant–sarauta relations and the use of extortion (*wasau*) against the merchants.

34 For an analysis of the autonomy of Western European urban corporate groups, see Weber (1968), Vol. III. For comparison of Western Europe and the central cities of Islamdom during the Mamluke period, see Lapidus (1967).

35 For a description of the social organization of Muslim mercantile capitalism, see Tahir (1975), Lovejoy (1980), Ferguson (1973) and Baier (1980).

36 On craft production, taxation and commodity production, see Shea (1975, 1981, 1974), Jaggar (1973, 1978), Watts (1983) and Freund (N.D.).

37 Shea (1975), pp. 185–186.

38 Shea (1975), p. 161.

39 Shea (1975), Chapter Six.

40 Jaggar (1973, 1978). For evidence of a slave estate at Dorayi, Kano held as fief for the *Sarkin Makera* (Chief Blacksmith), see Hill (1977) and Shea (1981).

41 On the transformation and conquest of southern Nigeria, see Ikime (1977), Ehrensaft (1972), Herskovits-Kopytoff (1965) and Hopkins (1973). On the conquest of the Caliphate, see Adeleye (1971), Tukur (1979) and Lubeck (1979a).

42 'If we hear of any news of them (Christians) we will send it to you. Further I earnestly beseech you in God's name let no one hear a suggestion for our departure from your mouth in this land as this would mean ruin for our affairs. Our subjects and people who are within the boundaries of our land would certainly throw off their allegiance to us on hearing such news ... If circumstances indicating departure arise, let us depart.' (Blackwell: 1927, p. 74).

43 M. Smith (1960), p. 205. For a journey through the paranoid mind of the isolated colonial administrator see the appendices contained in Paden (1968) and an official document on the subject of Islamic propaganda (Tomlinson and Lethem: 1927).

44 Lugard (1970), p. 223. This view is found in the original 1906 edition of Lugard's *Political Memoranda* which, according to Shenton, was the volume that was actually used to govern Northern Nigeria and one that Lugard attempted to destroy all copies of.

45 Lugard (1970), p. 224.
46 See Rowling (1949) and M. Smith (1965).
47 White (1966), p. 179.
48 If one treats M. G. Smith's description of his relationship with the sarauta while conducting field work in the environs of Zaria during 1949–50 as a historical document, one may vividly grasp the sarauta's authoritarian domination over the talakawa. Smith informs us that the sarauta referred to the talakawa as *abincinmu* ('our food'). Smith also obtained the following succinct correspondence between two officials, which summarizes this view: 'Ka san talakawa – sai a ba su tsoro' (You know the common people – frighten them.) (M. Smith: 1950, pp. 223 ff.).
49 For details and examples of official peculation and corruption, see Shenton (1981) and M. Smith (1964).
50 Hubbard (1973), p. 305. According to Hubbard, in 1921–2 the total expenditure for a population estimated to be 10 million by the Northern Nigerian Government was only £23,708, or less than 0.3 percent of the budget. (1973) p. 62.
51 See Hogendorn (1966, 1979, 1975, 1976).
52 See Myint (1971).
53 This section relies on Watts (1983) and Shenton (1981). See Lennihan (1982) for a detailed analysis of these processes in a cotton-exporting area.
54 For a chronology of famine during the colonial period, see Watts (1983), Chapter Six.
55 See Watts (1983). By the late 1950s Vigo's study of 37 different villages and interviews of 2,400 individuals concluded: (a) that indebtedness was so widespread that the proportion of a village in debt was 'quite frequently in excess of 70 percent'; (b) that sources of credit were primarily traders and merchants (48.9 percent); (c) that farmers were forced to sell foodstuffs to clear their debts while, at the same time, 46 percent of all loans were made for food; (d) that 71 percent of all loans were made at rates of interest at or exceeding 90 percent; and (e) that, rather than remaining indebted to agents or international firms, a new creditor stratum had emerged in the countryside in the form of the rich farmer-trader-lender who also hoarded grains for speculation during the preharvest seasons (i.e., May to August). Vigo (1957).
56 For example, during 1921–2 cotton prices declined by 50 percent, but sales increased by 72 percent; similarly, '[i]n Zaria Province a decline in cotton prices of almost 50 percent between 1923 and 1926 was matched by increased sales of 140 percent' (Watts 1983). Groundnuts too followed this perverse pattern: groundnut prices declined from about £10 per ton in 1928–9 to an average of £2.7 in 1934. Nevertheless, exports between those same years increased from 135,000 to 244,866 tons. Shenton (1981), p. 183.
57 On the social organization and decline of *gandu*, see M. Smith (1950), Hill (1972), Buntjer (1970) and Goddard (1969, 1973).
58 See Watts (1983), Hill (1972) and Wallace (1979).
59 For an analysis of changing urban hierarchies and organization under colonialism, see Home (1974), Lubeck and Walton (1979), Mabogunje (1968) and Frishman (1977).
60 For the urban history of colonial Kano, see Tahir (1975), Paden (1968), Frishman (1977), Hogendorn (1966, 1979) and Greenhill (1972).
61 Frishman (1977), p. 106. Frishman provides the best description and analysis of ideological assumptions underlying British colonial urban planning, racial and ethnic segregation planning and British efforts to block an urban market from

evolving. Yet, despite the efforts of the British to inhibit an urban land market, Resident Rowling noted in 1949: 'Though in theory illegal, the sale of rights is known by everyone to be universal and common'.

62 The merchant class is described in Tahir (1975) and Hogendorn (1979). The import-export trade is described in Bauer (1959) and Helleiner (1966).

63 For an analysis of the role played by the merchant class in the NPC, see Tahir (1975), also Dudley (1968), Whitaker (1970) and Sklar (1963).

64 Sharwood-Smith (1969). This is a valuable source for understanding the role played by the British in encouraging the alliance between the sarauta and the merchants as well as the hostility expressed toward NEPU, the talakawa's populist political party.

65 See Tahir (1975) and Paden (1968, 1974).

66 For a history and analysis of the Tijaniyya, see Abun Nasr (1965), Martin (1976), Paden (1968, 1974) and Tahir (1975). See Weber (1958). Note that in contrast to Weber's analysis of Calvinism, membership in the Tijaniyya is assumed to bring economic success, which is analogous to Calvinist membership in 'the elect', but the Calvinist injunction to abstain from ostentatious consumption is absent in the Tijaniyya case.

67 For population growth, spatial form and urban demography of Kano, see Frishman (1977, Chapter Eleven) and Trevaillion (1966).

68 On NEPU, see Paden (1974), Dudley (1968), Sklar (1963), Post (1964) and Whitaker (1970). I am grateful for the use of Professor Ken Post's unpublished notes on NEPU.

69 For a biography of Aminu Kano, see Feinstein (1973).

70 Whitaker (1970), p. 393.

71 The expression 'supporter of the heart' was used ubiquitously by informants when describing their support for NEPU in the face of severe N.A. repression (see Chapter Four in this volume).

2 The political economy of urban Kano

1 For the civil war and military rule, see Stremlau (1977), Panter-Brick (1970), Kirk-Greene (1971), Oyediran and Gboyega (1979), Kirk-Greene and Rimmer (1981), Williams and Turner (1978), Arnold (1977), Luckham (1971) and Miners (1971).

2 For a thorough analysis of state intervention and state production, see Forrest (forthcoming).

3 For the best overview of allocation of state revenue, see Rimmer (1981) and articles by L. Rupley in *West Africa* (1 July and 8 July, 1974, and 6 January, 1975). For analyses of the federal civil service and relationships between states and the federal center, see *Quarterly Journal of Administration*.

4 For a selection of critics' views, see T. Turner (1976), Williams (1980) and Collins (1977).

5 For a discussion of the Murtala government and the 1973 census, see Kirk-Greene and Rimmer (1981), p. 6. The complete statistics of the 1973 census were not disclosed, rather only the summaries by state were announced.

6 For the most detailed analysis of the decline in the quality of urban life in Nigeria, see the report on basic needs edited by the International Labor Office mission on Nigeria, under the authority of Dudley Seers (ILO: 1981).

7 For an analysis of petroleum revenues in the Nigerian economy and state revenue system, see Rimmer (1981), Kirk-Greene and Rimmer (1981) and

publications of the Central Bank of Nigeria, *Annual Reports* and *Economic Financial Review*.

8 Revenue statistics are taken from *Kano State Statistical Yearbook – 1977* (Kano State: 1978, p. 47). See Frishman for additional analysis (Frishman: 1977, p. 195).

9 See Oyediran and Gboyega (1979).

10 For an analysis of the impact of the petroleum boom on rural incomes and welfare, see Watts (1983, Chapter Eight) and Bienen and Diejomaoh (1981).

11 Despite the absence of the of reliable statistics on real income changes during the petroleum boom, my observations and the evidence presented in Table 3.1 suggest that, even ignoring the quality of life, real income declined for the majority of Kano's population during this period. Rimmer also makes the same point from macro-level statistical evidence: 'Real private consumption per capita was projected to grow at no less than 10.5 percent per annum under the Third Plan, "so that the average Nigerian would experience a marked improvement in his standard of living". But the national accounts show total private consumption at current prices increasing less fast between 1970/71 and 1976/77 than the recorded rate of inflation in consumer prices; and it would appear that real private consumption per capita was falling in this period.' (Rimmer: 1981, p. 57.) Note that the official consumer price index, in Rimmer's opinion, actually underestimates the rise in prices. Hence the decline in real private consumption per capita, a statistic that ignores the distribution of income, was worse than his estimate.

12 For Zaria, see Mortimore (1970). For Kaduna, see Seymour (1978) and Medugbon (1976).

13 For a description and analysis of KRP, see Wallace (1979).

14 See Jackson (1979).

15 These figures are drawn from World Bank press releases. The financing of the Kano Agricultural Development Project depends on equal shares from the World Bank, the Federal Government and the Kano State Government. Total expenditure for the project statewide was projected to reach ₦500 million over five years, but, almost certainly, the economic crisis will require reductions.

16 See Beckman (1981a), Wallace (1980) and Stryker (1979).

17 See *Directory of Industrial and Commerical Establishments, Kano State, 1980*, Statistics Division: Governor's Office.

18 For the best summary of this debate, see de Janvry (1981) and Palma (1978). For an orthodox Marxist approach arguing that industrial development is occurring, see Warren (1980). For an application of the Warren position to Nigeria, see Beckman (1981b and 1982).

19 See Osoba (1979), Hoogvelt (1979) and Biersteker (forthcoming).

20 For a clear statement of this position, see Kitching (1982).

21 Beckman (1982).

22 For an analysis of the indigenization decrees, see Hoogvelt (1979), Biersteker (forthcoming) and Beckman (1982).

23 See Rimmer (1981), p. 56, and Forrest (forthcoming).

24 See *West Africa*, 'Accounts to be Settled' (9 November, 1981). Both *West Africa* and the *Business Times* of Lagos are excellent sources of information on state economic activity and public investigations.

25 These figures are taken from Rimmer (1981), pp. 55–57.

26 See Castells (1977), Chapter Five.

27 Marx (1977), Vol. I, p. 777.

28 Marx (1977), Vol. I, p. 779.

29 Lojkine (1976), p. 119.
30 Lojkine (1976), p. 120.
31 Pickvance (1976), p. 18.
32 Lojkine (1976), p. 121.
33 See Marx (1977), Vol. I, Chapters One and Two.
34 See Frishman (1977).
35 See Frishman (1977), p. 308. I have relied on Frishman for the empirical material contained in this section. Yet virtually all informed members of Kano's middle and upper classes acknowledge that this process is occurring and most either have obtained some land or feel threatened by not doing so. Mediation by the state means that large amounts of land have been acquired by politically influential individuals, but it is difficult to gain access to records of land transfer and registration. Recently, fires at two sources of records at the state survey office and the planning board have destroyed the records of land registration and land transfers. Such 'spontaneous' fires that destroy evidence, in the opinion of my informants, are mere covers for evidence-destroying arson.
36 Hill (1977), p. 77.
37 Frishman (1977), p. 361.
38 For an analysis and review of the literature on food production and hunger in Nigeria, see Watts (1983).
39 Castells (1978), p. 20.
40 Castells (1978), p. 20.
41 Bienen and Diejomaoh (1981).
42 Cited in Frishman (1981), p. 13, who in turn cites an unpublished World Bank study by R. Sarly (1981), *Urban Development Strategy in Metropolitan Kano*.
43 The tension generated by the internationalization of consumption in a situation of increasing income inequality may become clearer when one examines the increase in private motor car registrations; for no single consumption item differentiates the wealthy and dominant classes from the poor and laboring classes more than motor car ownership. Between 1970 and 1976 new registrations of motor vehicles increased from 693 in 1970, or 18.2 percent of all vehicle registrations, to 5,595 in 1976, or 24.8 percent of all vehicle registrations. Not only have new motor car registrations increased by 707.4 percent but such registrations have increased their share of all new vehicle registrations. (Frishman: 1981, p. 12.)
44 For a discussion of approaches to social class, see footnote 18, Chapter Two. Terray (1975), Zeitlin (1980), Post (1978, Parts I and II) and Marx (1963).
45 See Althusser and Balibar (1970), Poulantzas (1973a and 1973b) and Taylor (1979).
46 Zeitlin (1980), p. 3.
47 Thompson (1968), p. 11.
48 If examined against the lifestyle expectations of the traditional sarauta role models, the new entrepreneurial capitalists from sarauta origin appear quite contradictory. For example, despite *ulema* hostility to films, a major officeholder now is the owner of a majority of Kano's cinemas. Further, one encounters businessmen whose business cards list both their titled office and the international firm that they represent, as well as a list of the commodities offered for sale.
49 I am employing the structuralist concept 'class fraction' to distinguish groups within a single class. Taylor uses the term to indicate that 'within a particular class (whose limits are defined economically, politically and ideologically), there are groups who are capable of becoming autonomous (politically or

economically) form other groups in that class in particular conjunctures'. (Taylor: 1979, p. 286). The key is the degree of autonomy experienced by one group (fraction), which distinguishes them from other members of the same class. For economic and political reasons, for example, Kano's industrial workers from a distinct class fraction of the working class and federal bureaucrats form a distinct class fraction of the state bourgeoisie.

50 For a discussion of the widening gap in income distribution and inequality, see Bienen and Diejomaoh (1981), ILO (1981), Frishman (1981) and Rimmer (1981).

51 This term is taken from Tumin and Feldman (1961).

3 The leburori within urban talakawa

1 See Thompson (1968). Besides illustrating how urban workers consciously 'make' their own history and, through empirical analysis, how precapitalist practices, statuses, traditions and institutionalized ideologies articulate with elements of semi-industrial capitalism, my purpose is to demonstrate the relationship between objective experience and subjective evaluation among urban workers.

2 The 'possible class alliance' that I have in mind is one where a disciplined, politically conscious and well organized labor movement acts in the interest of 'laboring people in general'. Such a movement would organize informal- and formal-sector wage workers as well as independent commodity producers who participate directly as workers in the labor process of producing a good or service.

3 For a discussion and description of the informal sector and its application to independent commodity producers, see Walton and Portes (1981), Roberts (1978, Chapter Five), Bromley and Gerry (1979), Arrighi (1970) and Sandbrook (1982). For a valuable evaluation and critique of the concept of informal sector, see Portes (1982).

4 This section relies on Frishman (1979a).

5 For an example of efforts on the part of Kano's blacksmiths to form a modern industry, see Jaggar (1978).

6 Within the popular culture of the urban talakawa, cart-pushing is an invidious labor category because the cart pushers often take drugs (e.g., amphetamines) to increase their endurance and strength, and because the labor process requires them to wear rags or merely a loincloth. Further, while competing with motor vehicles for space in Kano's crowded streets, the cart pushers (Hausa: *'yan kura*) often curse and insult those who block the movement of their overflowing carts which lack brakes. The dominant and intermediate classes refer to them as *'Yan iska* (literally: sons of the wind) or hooligans or lumpenproletarians. Many informants believe that drug-taking and moral depravity allowed cart pushers to be manipulated as aggressors in the communal riots against southern Nigerians that occurred in 1966.

7 See Frishman (1981), p. 12.

8 For a detailed description of levels of hierarchy among trading networks and the role of the *ulema* in mediating credit and commercial transactions, see Tahir (1975) and Yusuf (1975).

9 See A. Cohen (1969) and Last (1979).

10 The position of labor service workers in the urban class structure illustrates a case in point for the debate between the structuralist definition of class (i.e., according to a role in a mode of production) and the historical definition of class

(according to how particular historical experiences define class boundaries and identities). Labor service workers are only indirectly linked to capital and thus do not share the wage relationship as do industrial workers. But the articulation of membership in a precapitalist status group, together with the homogenizing effects of common career, familial and community relations – a common social existence – means that this occupational category identifies with and participates politically as a member of the urban talakawa and oftentimes as a member of the urban leburori. Unskilled industrial workers, moreover, relate to labor service workers as members of the leburori.

11 Peter Waterman has completed an excellent study that compares the labor process and trade union organization among state and private sector labor within the cargo-handling industry of Lagos port. See Waterman (1979, 1983).

12 For a comparison of the twelve-state system with the contemporary nineteen-state system, see Kirk-Greene and Rimmer (1981), p. 10.

13 For the clustering of ethnic groups I have relied on Paden, Morrison, Mitchell and Stevenson (1972) and Murdock (1959).

14 For a more detailed analysis of the industrial labor survey, see Lubeck (1983).

15 See Lubeck (1981), Lubeck (1985) and Lubeck (forthcoming).

16 For a description of the ethnic origins of merchant groups, see Lovejoy (1973, 1980).

17 Note that the intention is to blame the sarauta and the administrators of the N.A. and not the NEPU leaders such as Aminu Kano who campaigned and published materials advocating western education for both men and women.

18 See, for example, Mantoux (1961).

19 Here I am following the analysis first suggested by Meillassoux (1972), subsequently elaborated by Wolpe (1972) for the South African case, which argues that precapitalist peasant households subsidize the cost of producing and reproducing labor power for the industrial capitalist sector. That is to say, because commuters utilize household-organized farming and petty commodity income sources, part of the cost of maintaining workers, reproducing the next generation of workers, and the social security for aged, infirm and injured workers is borne by the precapitalist peasant household. If the industrial capitalist had to pay for the full cost of sustaining, reproducing and providing social security for necessary labor power, the wage rate would have to be increased.

20 By passive I mean that the semi-industrial city forces them to become proletarians, rather than, as in the case of the migrants, making an active choice to enter the urban labor market. And further, I know of at least several cases where the peri-urban peasantry, once dispossessed of their land by the state, resisted appropriation of their means of production by destroying the buildings constructed by rentier capitalists who obtained their land.

21 Here I am speculating about the possible articulation of slave status within industrial proletarianization. As described by Hill (1977) for Dorayi, and as is well known by historians, many of the villages in the peri-urban area originated as royal or sarauta slave estates: e.g., Panisau, Gandun Albasa and Gandun Nassarawa. M. G. Smith (1965) argues that slave owners continued to extract surplus labor from former slaves on the eve of national independence. Hence there is every reason to believe that former owners continue to exploit and certainly intimidate the descendants of their former slaves and that this relationship may contribute to the consciousness of the commuters.

22 See Bendix (1977), Chapter II.

23 The tendency toward three-generational families and away from extensive

kinship relations of lineages appears to be correlated with Islamization. Non-Muslim Hausa tend to live in larger and more extensive kinship networks than do the Muslim Hausa. Hodgson (1974) interprets this tendency as one arising from the process of *Shari'a*ization whereby the deepening of Islamization requires the application of *Shari'a* rules of inheritance which do not recognize rights other than the immediate family.

24 While I do not intend to offer the theoretical and empirical critique that Hill's analysis of Dorayi certainly deserves, I believe that one has an obligation to caution the reader against accepting uncritically many of Hill's assertions about the ruralness of Dorayi, the degree of dependence of urban income and the degree of rural-urban integration during the precolonial and colonial periods. For a stimulating review of Hill's study of Dorayi that recomputes occupational data provided by Hill to disprove her own thesis of rural isolation from urban Kano, see Frishman's review (Frishman: 1979b).

25 For a definition and elaboration of 'labor commitment', see Feldman and Moore (1960). It should be noted that Professor Feldman has recanted and now rejects the concept as managerial ideology.

26 On clientage, see Tahir (1975), M. Smith (1950, 1955), Yusuf (1975), Lloyd (1974), A. Cohen (1969) and Aronson (1971).

27 As applied to Africa, the labor aristocracy thesis argues that modern-sector wage laborers are isolated from and form a distinct stratum from semi-proletarianized workers and the peasantry. Obviously, because of talakawa status, unequal access to state patronage and a common social existence, there is no labor-aristocratic cleavage among formal- and informal-sector workers in Kano. Nor, according to Peace (1975), does it exist in Lagos. For additional debate, see Arrighi (1970), Peace (1975), Saul (1975) and Waterman (1975).

4 Tudun Wada

1 This definition of requirements for a class to exist is taken from Marx's empirical studies of French politics (Marx: 1963).

2 I want to emphasize that the evidence for increased horizontal integration of workers from diverse ethnic groups and religions within the compounds of migrants living in Waje was collected in 1972. Since then the pressure from market forces toward increased cohabitation among diverse ethnic groups and religions has intensified, and my qualitative data collected since 1972 confirm that ethnic segregation patterns have continued to decline in favor of increased class segregation patterns in the Waje areas.

3 For a discussion of the planning of industrial estates, see Frishman (1977).

4 For a discussion of the 1953 riots, see Paden (1970) and Frishman (1977). Paden provides some useful census materials and definitions of ethnic identities from a Parsonian theoretical perspective.

5 The trend toward gentrification whereby the shelter needs of the working class are subordinated to market forces and the consumption needs of the upper classes provides a clear example of the deepening of semi-industrial capitalism in urban Kano. For a stimulating discussion of urban property that elaborates upon F. Engels's *The Housing Question*, see Lamarche (1976).

6 According to an article in the *New York Times*: 'A recent Government-sponsored study at the Stanford Research Institute International Center for Research on Stress and Health found that workers who moved from shift to shift suffered severe disruption of their "physical and psychological well-being". They had more accidents than other workers, consumed more alcohol and sleeping

pills, and reported more digestive difficulties, menstrual disorders, colds, nervousness and fatigue. They also complained of less satisfactory domestic and social lives' (*New York Times*: 31 December 1978, p. E7.)

7 I wish to acknowledge the contribution of Deborah Phillips Lubeck with regard to conducting the Tudun Wada housing survey, as well as for informal observations collected within secluded compounds.

8 Here I am arguing that while individuals originating from diverse ethnic groups form a regional Muslim nation, and while the language and customs of this nation are disproportionately Hausa, each class within this nation interprets moral and political obligations, to a significant degree, according to class position and class interests.

9 For a discussion of situational ethnicity, see Paden (1970).

10 An exception is found among the Yoruba, who are not accepted as part of the regional Islamic nation, allegedly because of continuing syncretist practices and because *Shari'a* law is not applied within the community.

11 On mallams as an occupational group, see Paden (1968) and Chamberlin (1975). For a fascinating biography of a Kano mallam, see Skinner (1977).

12 Kirk-Greene's pamphlet *Mutumin Kirkii* (1974) provides interested readers with an idealized conception of the 'good man' in Hausa society.

13 The ideal for the Muslim Hausa, like Arabs, is a parallel cousin marriage: e.g., ego marries his father's brother's daughter.

14 In 1980 Nigeria sent over 100,000 pilgrims on the *hajj*, thereby surpassing all others in number. Sincere Muslims are concerned with the increase in corrupt practices such as drug smuggling and the manipulation of foreign exchange laws by merchants who provide free transportation and fees for the impoverished in exchange for the latters' willingness to bring back expensive consumer goods which the merchant then sells for a high profit. This practice allows the merchant to avoid foreign exchange controls on the importations of luxury goods, as the *hajj* costs are paid in naira.

15 As one might expect, since Tsoho's death and the return of his son from military service, his house has become the local headquarters for the National Party of Nigeria – the party representing sarauta privilege and capitalist classes.

5 Industrial labor and the labor process

1 On the concept of the labor process, see Braverman (1974), Blauner (1964), Edwards (1979) and Marx (1977, Vol. I). For a creative synthesis of structuralist and classical Marxist interpretation of the labor process that I have found valuable for this section, see Burawoy (1979, Chapter Two).

2 In applying the concept of alienation to Kano's industrial workers I have relied on Marx (1977, Vol. I), Ollman (1971), Blauner (1964) and Meszaros (1970).

3 For a description of the Hausa household and relations of clientage, see M. Smith (1955), Tahir (1975), Hill (1972), Watts (1983) and A. Cohen (1969).

4 The comparison with Kaduna and Lagos is based upon the author's field work and several unpublished World Bank studies. There is no up-to-date study of Nigerian manufacturing industry. See Teriba, Edozien and Kayode (1981) for the latest Nigerian study and Kirk-Greene and Rimmer (1981) for an overview.

5 Schatzl (1973), p. 201.

6 Kano State, Ministry of Finance and Development (1978), pp. 79–92.

7 See Hoogvelt (1979). For the standard description of industrial dependence and underdevelopment, see Dos Santos (1970) and Akeredolu-Ale (1975).

8 The distinction between entrepreneurial and rational bureaucratic styles of

management follows from Weber's theory of rational bureaucratic administration, where formal written rules, separation of person (e.g., owner) from office and a concern for motivation of the workforce are typical features of bureaucratic management. See Burawoy (1979b) for a review of the literature on bureaucratic and motivation studies of industrial organization.

9 See Kirk-Greene (1974) for cultural material explaining master-servant relations and the importance of avoiding public humiliation of servants according to Hausa cultural norms.

10 For elaboration on supervisors' manipulation of trade unions which caused many workers to be hostile to trade unions in general at this factory, see my article (Lubeck: 1975) in Cohen and Sandbrook (1975).

11 Note here that the supervisor's interest in selling jobs renders problematic any interpretation of turnover rates in the labor force. Certainly, the turnover rate does not reflect an absence of commitment to industrial labor.

12 See Tahir (1975) for some valuable material describing the positive feelings associated with this industrial venture among Kano's merchant capitalist class.

13 Much of the demand originated from the Nigerian military, and thus orders declined at the end of the Nigerian civil war (1970).

14 One of the interesting anomalies of industrial capitalism in Kano is that during an era when much of the world economy is in crisis and when new microelectronic technologies are transforming production in Southeast Asia and the core economies, a process Marx termed 'relative surplus value', the indigenous bourgeoisie of Nigeria is practising accumulation by 'absolute surplus value' by extending the working day and by paying illegal wage rates.

15 See Inkeles and Smith (1974). Nigeria (Lagos and Ibadan regions) was one of the case studies for this six-nation study.

16 Marx's observation regarding the American case is taken from Dahrendorf (1965), p. 73.

17 See Lloyd (1977). This thesis is argued also in his recent work where he devotes an entire book to questioning the reality of a third world proletariat (Lloyd: 1982). The problem with his approach is that it takes classes in a 'strict', virtually ideal typical sense, and then, by comparing real empirical examples, Lloyd attempts to 'prove' that class is an inappropriate concept for analyzing third world laboring people. No empirical example can ever achieve the purity of the ideal type: thus the comparison is flawed methodologically. Furthermore, in selecting definitions of class from the Marxist literature, Lloyd emphasizes the more abstract and dogmatic interpretations of class rather than the historical approaches exemplified in the work of Thompson or Zeitlin, or even Marx. I agree with Lloyd that the process of class formation will be different at the periphery from what was the case at the core for historically specific reasons and, further, that the international division of labor arising from a capitalist world economy may reinforce ethno-national consciousness. But these differences do not deny the value of class analysis for the method of Marxist class analysis acknowledges the importance of historical, cultural and conjunctural specificity. For example, in a classic passage from *Capital*, where Marx defines the relationship between the direct producers and the owners of the means of production as determining social structure (i.e., class structure), he goes on to state: 'This does not prevent the same economic basis – the same from the standpoint of its main conditions – due to innumerable different empirical circumstances, natural environment, racial relations, external historical influences, etc. from showing infinite variations and gradations in appearance which can be ascertained only by analysis of the empirically given circumstances'. (Marx: 1972, pp. 791–792).

18 On labor commitment, see Feldman and Moore (1960).
19 Chinoy (1955) and Taira (1969).
20 Touraine and Rangazzi (1961).
21 Stearns (1975), pp. 336–337.
22 Thompson (1968), p. 914.
23 For a discussion of Weber's empirical field work on the resistance of small-holders, see Bendix (1977, Chapter Two).
24 Though the problem cannot be resolved here, the situation in peripheral capitalist societies is clearly one where informal-sector workers and independent commodity producers will remain a majority of the urban lower stratum. Thus the question of class alliances and the relationship of the latter to the proletariat emerges as a crucial theoretical question for theorists and practitioners of progressive social change.

6 The process of class struggle

1 For a discussion of trade unions during the late 1960s and early 1970s, see Lubeck (1975), Peace (1974, 1975) and R. Cohen (1974).
2 O'Connor (1973), p. 6.
3 For an analysis of regional semi-peripheral states, see Wallerstein (1979, Chapters Four and Five).
4 See Touraine and Pecaut (1967).
5 For the 1964 general strike, see Morgan (1964) and Melson (1971).
6 See the First (Adebo) Report (1970), p. 9.
7 For a discussion of the political negotiations between labor, capital and state, see Peace (1974 and 1979).
8 See, for instance, *The New Nigerian*, 22 February 1971, p. 17.
9 Hobsbawm (1964), p. 9.
10 One of those to be laid off was Ahmadu, the factory worker whose life is described in Chapter Four.
11 See *The Main Report of the Public Service Review Commission* (Udoji: 1974) and relevant issues of *West Africa* (1974) for descriptions, analyses and commentaries on the report.
12 Lubeck (1975).
13 Adebiyi Report (1977). Sources for the material here are taken from *West Africa* and interviews that I conducted with Nigerian trade union leaders during December 1978 and December 1980.
14 Moore (1978), p. 188.

7 Class consciousness

1 Lubeck (1979b).
2 In formulating, interpreting and applying the concept of class consciousness to the leburori of Kano, I have relied on Foster (1974), Hazelrigg (1973), Meszaros (1971b), Post (1978) and Mann (1973).
3 This statement by Marx is from *The Poverty of Philosophy*, as quoted in Meszaros (1971b, p. 106). Mann (1973) suggests a similar definition and sequence regarding class consciousness.
4 Meszaros takes the position that in order for the proletariat to be a class *for itself* rather than merely *in itself*, it must favor the abolition of class society, and in that sense the proletariat becomes the universal 'mediator' in the Hegelian-Marxist interpretation of class consciousness. I find this position quite idealistic and

inappropriate for the analysis of Kano's leburori at its present stage of development. (Meszaros: 1971b, pp. 106–107.)

5 Marx (1977), Vol. I, p. 799.

6 Marx (1933), p. 33.

7 Methodological note: Because politics had ended over six years earlier and because I wanted to be certain that those workers responding knew what 'participating in politics' involved, I asked each worker to comment on the possible return to politics in order to judge whether the respondent comprehended the question. Some did not, and thus they became missing cases on this dimension.

8 Cabral (1969), p. 51.

9 Lenin (1970).

10 The statistical analysis described here for 'Adebo strike support' is available in my Ph.D. dissertation. (Lubeck: 1975b).

11 For comparative purposes note that Cornelius (1975, pp. 64–72) reports that urban-born and literates are more politically aware and cynical about authority than their migrant and illiterate counterparts in Mexico City.

12 See references and discussion of articulation in Chapter One.

13 Though hostile to structuralist theory and the concept of articulation, E. P. Thompson describes the articulation of precapitalist religious elements within the English working class as well as the traditions of the freeborn Englishman. His interpretation is appropriate for Kano: 'No ideology is wholly absorbed by its inherents: it breaks down in practice in a thousand ways under the criticism of impulse and of experience: the working class community injected into the chapels its own values of mutual aid, neighborliness and solidarity.' (Thompson: 1968, p. 431).

14 For a discussion of the concept of a 'calling', see Weber (1958) and Bendix (1977).

15 Keddie (1972), pp. 13–14.

16 For a review of the cultural interpretative approach, see Geertz (1963, 1973). For a review and application to Kano, see Paden (1968, 1974).

17 For an analysis of Koranic school networks and the millenarian *Yan Tatsine* movement, see Lubeck (1981), which was written before the millenarian revolt of December 1980, Lubeck (forthcoming) in Burke and Lapidus and especially Lubeck (1985).

18 For a review of modernization theory's expectations regarding changes in consciousness, see Inkeles and Smith (1974) and Kahl (1968).

19 Hodgkin (1980), p. 79.

20 This fact raises the question of whether, once Nigerianization of industry takes effect, and Nigerian rather than European managers control Muslim Hausa-speaking laborers, workers will continue to define industrial wage labor as *aikin bature* or whether they will perceive the subordination of their nation and region to a peripheral role in the international division of labor as antagonistic. My guess is probably yes. Why? Because even after national independence educated Nigerian administrators are referred to as *bakin bature* (Black Europeans), for the system introduced by the Europeans is perceived as unchanged.

21 If, for example, as in the case of Northern Ireland, the American South and cities, political representatives of the dominant class manipulate ethnic and racial stereotypes and introduce legal mechanisms to force one ethnic group against the other, then ethnic antagonisms will continue indefinitely within the industrial working class.

8 Conclusion

1 For an analysis of the NLC's relationship to the state and the general strike of 1981, see Otobo (1981 and 1982).
2 Lubeck (1985).
3 Kitching (1982), p. 63.

Appendix 1

1 Campbell and Fisk (1956).
2 For a review of comparative historical methods, see Vallier (1971), Smelser (1976), Armer and Grimshaw (1973) and Przeworksi and Teune (1970).
3 For a review of survey methods, see Babbie (1973) and Davis (1971).
4 For a review of field methods/qualitative methods, see McCall and Simmons (1969) and Strauss and Schatzman (1973).

Bibliography

Abun Nasr, J. 1965. *The Tijaniyya*. London; Oxford University Press.

Adamu, M. 1979. 'The Delivery of Slaves from the Central Sudan to the Bight of Benin in the 18th and 19th Centuries.' In *The Uncommon Market*, ed. Gemery and Hogendorn. New York: Academic Press.

Adamu, M. 1979. 'Distribution of Trading Centres in the Central Sudan in the 18th and 19th Centuries.' In *Studies in the History of the Sokoto Caliphate*, ed. Y. B. Usman. Zaria: Ahmadu Bello University.

Adebiyi Report. 1977. *Report of the Tribunal of Inquiry into the Activities of Trade Unions*. Lagos: Federal Ministry of Information.

Adebo (Interim) Report. 1970. *First Report of the Wages and Salaries Review Commission*. Lagos: Federal Ministry of Information.

Adebo (Final) Report. 1971. *Second and Final Report of the Wages and Salaries Review Commission*. Lagos: Federal Ministry of Information.

Adeleye, R. 1971. *Power and Diplomacy in Northern Nigeria*. Ibadan, Nigeria: Ibadan University Press.

1976. 'Hausaland and Borno 1600–1800.' In *History of West Africa*, Vol. I, ed. J. Ajayi and M. Crowder. New York: Columbia University Press.

Ajayi, J. and Crowder, M. 1976. *History of West Africa*. New York: Columbia University Press.

Akeredolu-Ale, E. 1975. *The Underdevelopment of Indigenous Entrepreneurship in Nigeria*. Ibadan, Nigeria: Ibadan University Press.

Al-Hajj, M. 1966. 'The Sudanese Mahdiyya and the Niger-Chad Region.' In *Islam in Tropical Africa*, ed. I. Lewis. Oxford: Oxford University Press.

Al-Hajj, M. 1971. 'Hayatu B. Sa'id: 'A Revolutionary Mahdist in the Western Sudan'. In *Sudan in Africa*, ed. Y. Hasan. Khartoum.

Althusser, L. and Balibar, E. 1970. *Reading Capital*. London: New Left Books.

Amin, S. 1976. *Unequal Development*. London: Harvester.

1977. *Imperialism and Unequal Development*. New York: Monthly Review Press.

Anderson, P. 1974. *Lineages of the Absolutist State*. London: New Left Books.

Armer, M. and Grimshaw, A. 1973. *Comparative Social Research*. New York: Wiley.

Arnold, G. 1977. *Modern Nigeria*. London: Longman.

Aronson, D. 1971. 'Ijebu Yoruba Urban-Rural Relationships and Class Formation.' *Canadian Journal of African Studies* 5 (1971): 263–79.

Arrighi, G. 1970. 'International Corporations, Labor Aristocracies and Economic Development in Tropical Africa.' *Journal of Modern African Studies* 6: 141–69.

Asad, T. and Wolpe, H. 1976. 'Concepts of Modes of Production.' *Economy and Society* Vol. 5, No. 4 (1976): 470–506.

Babbie, E. 1973. *Survey Research Methods*. Belmont, CA: Wadsworth.

Baier, S. 1980. *An Economic History of the Central Sudan*. London: Oxford University Press.

342

Barbour, K. M., Oguntoyinbo, J. S., Onyemelukwe, J. O. C., Nwafor, J. C. (eds) 1982, *Nigeria in Maps*. New York: Africana Publishing Co.

Barth, H. 1965. *Travels and Discoveries in North and Central Africa, 1849–1855* (in three volumes). London: Frank Cass.

Bauer, P. 1959. *West African Trade*. Cambridge: Cambridge University Press.

Beckman, B. 1981a. 'The World Bank and the Nigerian Peasantry.' Unpublished paper, presented to AKUT Group, Stockholm.

1981b. 'Imperialism and the National Bourgeoisie.' *Review of African Political Economy*, No. 22.

1982. 'Whose State: State and Capitalist Development in Nigeria.' *Review of African Political Economy*, No. 23.

Beetham, D. 1974. *Max Weber and the Theory of Modern Politics*. London: Allen and Unwin.

Bendix, R. 1977. *Max Weber*. Berkeley: University of California Press.

Bienen, H. and Diejomaoh, V., eds. 1981. *The Political Economy of Income Distribution in Nigeria*. New York: Holmes and Meier.

Biersteker, T. 1978. *Distortion or Development? Contending Perspectives on the Multi-national Corporations*. Cambridge, MA: MIT Press.

Forthcoming. 'Indigenization and the Nigerian Bourgeoisie.' In *The African Bourgeoisie: Capitalist Development in Nigeria, Kenya and the Ivory Coast*, ed. P. Lubeck.

Blackwell, H. 1927. *The Occupation of Hausaland: 1900–1904*. Lagos: The Government Printer.

Blauner, R. 1964. *Alienation and Freedom*. Chicago: University of Chicago Press.

Bloch, M. 1975. *Marxist Analysis and Social Anthropology*. New York: John Wiley and Sons.

Bradby, B. 1975. 'The Destruction of Natural Economy.' *Economy and Society* IV, 2: 127–61.

Braverman, H. 1974. *Labor and Monopoly Capital*. New York: Monthly Review Press.

Brenner, R. 1977. 'The Origins of Capitalist Development: A Critique of Neo-Smithian Marxism.' *New Left Review*, No. 104 (July–August): 25–92.

Brewer, A. 1980. *Marxist Theories of Imperialism*. London: Routledge and Kegan Paul.

Bromley, R. and Gerry, C., ed. 1979. *Casual Work and Poverty in Third World Cities*. New York: John Wiley.

Buchanan, K. and Pugh, J. 1955. *Land and People in Nigeria*. London: University of London Press.

Bull, M. 1963. 'Indirect Rule in Northern Nigeria, 1906–1911.' In *Essays in Imperial Government*, ed. K. Robinson et al. Oxford: Basil Blackwell.

Buntjer, B. 1970. 'Rural Society: The Changing Structure of Gandu.' In *Zaria and Its Region*, ed. M. Mortimore. Zaria: Ahmadu Bello University, Department of Geography.

Burawoy, M. 1979a. *Manufacturing Consent*. Chicago: University of Chicago Press.

1979b. 'The Anthropology of Industrial Work.' *Annual Review of Anthropology*, Vol. 8: 231–66.

Cabral, A. 1969. *Revolution in Guinea: An African People's Struggle*. London: Stage 1.

Campbell, D. and Fisk, D. 1956. 'Convergent and Discriminant Validation by the Multitrait-Multimethod Matrix.' *Psychology Bulletin* 56.

Cardoso, F. 1973. 'Associated Dependent Development.' In *Authoritarian Brazil*, ed. A. Stepan. New Haven: Yale University Press.

Cargill, F. (Resident) 1908. 'Report on Assessment in Madaki's District. 7179/' *Kano Province Economic Survey, 1909*. National Archives, Kaduna. (I am indebted to Professor John Paden for access to this document.)

Castells, M. 1977. *The Urban Question*. London: Edward Arnold.

1978. *Class, City and Power*. London: Macmillan.

Chamberlin, J. 1975. 'Koranic Schools in Kano.' Ph.D. thesis, Columbia University.

Chinoy, E. 1955. *Automobile Workers and the American Dream*. New York: Doubleday.

343

Bibliography

Clammer, J. 1978. *The New Economic Anthropology*. New York: St. Martin's Press.

Cohen, A. 1969. *Custom and Politics in Urban Africa*. Berkeley: University of California Press.

Cohen, R. 1974. *Labour and Politics in Nigeria 1945–1974*. London: Heinemann.

Cohen, R. and Sandbrook, R., eds. 1975. *The Development of an African Working Class*. London: Longmans.

Collins, P. 1977. 'The State and Dependent Capitalist Development: The Nigerian Experience.' *Journal of Commonwealth and Comparative Political Studies* 15, 2.

Cornelius, W. 1975. *Politics and the Migrant Poor in Mexico City*. Stanford, CA: Stanford University Press.

Dahrendorf, R. 1965. *Class and Class Conflict in Industrial Society*. Stanford, CA: Stanford University Press.

Davis, J. 1971. *Elementary Survey Analysis*. Englewood Cliffs, NJ: Prentice Hall.

de Janvry, A. 1981. *The Agrarian Question and State Reformism in Latin America*. Baltimore: Johns Hopkins University Press.

Dokaji, A. 1958. *Kano ta Dabo Cigari*. Zaria: Gaskiya.

Dos Santos, T. 1970. 'The Structure of Dependence.' *American Economic Review* LX, 2.

Dudley B. 1968. *Parties and Politics in Northern Nigeria*. London: Cass.

Edwards, R. 1979. *Contested Terrain*. New York: Basic Books.

Ehrensaft, P. 1972. 'The Political Economy of Informal Empire in Pre-Colonial Nigeria, 1807–1884.' *Canadian Journal of African Studies*, Vol. 6, No. 3: 451–90.

Federal Ministry of Information. 1974. *The Main Report of the (Udoji) Public Service Review Commission*. Lagos.

Feinstein, A. 1973. *African Revolutionary*. New York: Quadrangle Books.

Feldman, A. and Moore, W. 1960. *Labor Commitment and Social Change in Developing Areas*. New York: Social Science Research Council.

Ferguson, D. 1973. 'Nineteenth Century Hausaland, being a description by Iman Imoru.' Ph.D. dissertation, University of California, Los Angeles.

Fika, M. 1978. *The Kano Civil War and British Over-Rule (1882–1940)*. Ibadan: Oxford University Press.

Fischer, M. 1980. *Iran: From Religious Dispute to Revolution*. Cambridge, MA: Harvard University Press.

Forrest, T. Forthcoming. 'State Capital, Capitalist Development and Class Formation in Nigeria.' In *The African Bourgeoisie: Capitalist Development in Nigeria, Kenya and the Ivory Coast*, ed. P. Lubeck.

Foster, J. 1974. *Class Struggle and the Industrial Revolution*. New York: St. Martin's Press.

Foster-Carter, A. 1978. 'The Modes of Production Controversy.' *New Left Review* 107 (Jan–Feb 1978).

Frank, A. 1967. *Capitalism and Underdevelopment in Latin America*. New York: Modern Reader Paperbacks.

1969. *Latin America: Underdevelopment or Revolution*. New York: Monthly Review Press.

Freund, W. (N.D.), 'Tin Commodity Production in the Sokoto Caliphate.' Unpublished manuscript.

Frishman, A. 1977. 'The Spatial Growth and Residential Location Pattern of Kano, Nigeria.' Ph.D. thesis, Northwestern University.

1979a. 'Small-Scale Industry in Metropolitan Kano, Nigeria.' *A Report for the World Bank* (June, 1979).

1979b. A Review of *Population, Prosperity and Poverty: Rural Kano, 1900 and 1970* by P. Hill (Cambridge: Cambridge University Press, 1977). *African Studies Association Review of Books*, Vol. 5: 39–43.

1981. 'Urban Transport Decisions in Kano, Nigeria.' Manuscript. Geneva, New York: Hobart and William Smith Colleges.

344

Geertz, C., ed. 1963. *Old Societies and New States*. New York: Free Press.

　　1973. *The Interpretation of Cultures*. New York: Basic Books.

Gemery, H. and Hogendorn, J. 1979. *The Uncommon Market: Essays in the Economic History of the Atlantic Slave Trade*. New York: Academic Press.

Giddens, A. 1972. *Politics and Sociology in the Thought of Max Weber*. London: Macmillan.

Goddard, A. 1969. 'Are Hausa Family Structures Breaking Up?' *Samaru Agricultural Newsletter* 11: 34–47.

　　1973. 'Changing Family Structures Among the Hausa.' *Africa*, Vol. 43, No. 3: 207–218.

Greenhill, C., ed. 1972. 'The Kurmi Market Study.' Report for the Kano Metropolitan Planning and Development Board.

Hazelrigg, L. 1973. 'Aspects of the Measurement of Class Consciousness.' In *Comparative Social Research*, ed. M. Armer and A. Grimshaw. New York: John Wiley.

Hechter, M. 1975. *Internal Colonialism*. Berkeley: University of California Press.

Helleiner, G. 1966. *Government and Economic Growth in Nigeria*. Homewood: Yale University Press.

Herskovits-Kopytoff, J. 1965. *A Preface to Modern Nigeria*. Madison: University of Wisconsin Press.

Hill, P. 1972. *Rural Hausa: A Village and a Setting*. London: Cambridge University Press.

　　1977. *Population, Prosperity and Poverty: Rural Kano 1900–1970*. London: Cambridge University Press.

Hobsbawm, E. 1959. *Primitive Rebels*. New York: Norton.

　　1964. *Labouring Men*. New York: Anchor Book.

Hodgkin, T. 1980. 'The Revolutionary Tradition in Islam.' *Race and Class*, Vol. 21, No. 3.

Hodgson, M. 1974. *The Venture of Islam* I, II, III. Chicago: University of Chicago Press.

Hogendorn, J. 1966. 'The Origins of the Groundnut Trade in Northern Nigeria.' Ph.D. dissertation, London University.

　　1975. 'Economic Initiative and African Cash Crop Farming: precolonial origins and early colonial developments.' In *Colonialism in Africa*, ed. L. Gann and P. Duignan, Vol. 4, pp. 87–103. London: Cambridge University Press.

　　1976. 'The Vent-for-Surplus Model and African Cash Agriculture to 1914'. *Savanna*, Vol. 5, No. 1 (June).

　　1977. 'The Economics of Slave Use on Two Plantations in Zaria Emirate, Hausaland.' *International Journal of African Historical Studies*, Vol. 6: 369–83.

　　1979. *Nigerian Groundnut Exports*. Zaria: Ahmadu Bello University Press.

　　1980. 'Slave Acquisition and Delivery in Precolonial Hausaland.' In *West African Culture Dynamics: Archeological and Historical Perspectives*, ed. B. Schatz and R. Dumett. The Hague: Mouton Press.

Home, R. 1974. 'The Influence of Colonial Government upon Nigerian Urbanization.' Ph.D. dissertation, University of London.

Hoogvelt, A. 1979. 'Indigenization and Foreign Capital: Industrialization in Nigeria.' *Review of African Political Economy*, No. 14.

Hopkins, A. 1973. *An Economic History of West Africa*. London: Longman.

Hubbard, J. 1973. 'Education Under Colonial Rule: A History of Katsina College, 1921–1942.' Ph.D. thesis, University of Wisconsin, Madison.

Ikime, Obaro. 1977. *The Fall of Nigeria: The British Conquest*. London: Heinemann.

Inkeles, A. and Smith D. 1974. *Becoming Modern*. Cambridge, MA: Harvard University Press.

International Labour Office. 1981. 'First Things First.' Report to the Government of Nigeria. Addis Ababa.

Jackson, S. 1979. 'Hausa Women on Strike.' *Review of African Political Economy*, No. 13.

Jaggar, P. 1973. 'Kano City Blacksmiths: Precolonial Distribution, Structure and Organization,' *Savanna*, Vol. 2, No. 1.

Bibliography

1978. 'The Blacksmiths of Kano City.' M.A. thesis, London University, School of Oriental and African Studies.

Jessop, B. 1977. 'Recent Theories of the Capitalist State.' *Cambridge Journal of Economics*, Vol. I, No. 4: 353–73.

Johnson, M. 1970. 'The Cowrie Currencies of West Africa (Parts I and II).' *Journal of African History* XI, 1 and 3.

Kahl, J. 1968. *The Measurement of Modernism*. Austin: University of Texas Press.

Kano State. 1978. *Statistical Yearbook, 1977*. Kano: Statistics Unit, Ministry of Finance and Development.

Kano State. 1980. *Directory of Industrial and Commercial Establishments*. Government Printer.

Kay, G. 1975. *Development and Underdevelopment*. London: Macmillan.

Keddie, N. 1981. *The Roots of Revolution*. New Haven: Yale University Press.

ed. 1972. *Scholars, Saints and Sufis: Muslim Religious Institutions Since 1500*. Berkeley: California University Press.

Kirk-Greene, A. 1971. *Crisis and Conflict in Nigeria*, 2 Vols. Oxford: Oxford University Press.

1974. *Mutumin Kirki: The Concept of the Good Man in Hausa*. African Studies Program. Bloomington: Indiana University Press.

Kirk-Greene, A. and Rimmer, D. 1981. *Nigeria Since 1970*. London: Hodder and Stoughton.

Kitching, G. 1982. *Development and Underdevelopment in Historical Perspective*. New York: Methuen Publishers.

Lamarche, F. 1976. 'Property Development and the Economic Foundation of the Urban Question' in C. Pickvance. *Urban Sociology*. London: Metheun Publishers.

Lapidus, I. 1967. *Muslim Cities in the Later Middle Ages*. Cambridge: Harvard University Press.

Last, M. 1967. *The Sokoto Caliphate*. London: Longman.

1974. 'Reform in West Africa: The Jihad Movements of the Nineteenth Century.' In *History of West Africa*, eds. A. Crowder and J. Ajayi. London: Longman.

1979. 'Some Economic Aspects of Conversion in Hausaland (Nigeria).' *Conversion to Islam*, ed. N. Leviton. New York, London: Homes and Meier Publishers, Inc.

1980. 'Historical Metaphors in the Kano Chronicle.' *History in Africa*, No. 7. Waltham, MA: African Studies Association.

1981. 'From Sultanate to Caliphate: Kano 1450–1800.' Conference on History of Kano, Bayero University.

Lenin, V. 1970. *What is to be Done?*. Moscow: Progress Publishers.

Lennihan, L. 1982. 'The Origins and Development of Agricultural Wage Labor in Northern Nigeria, 1886–1980.' Ph.D. dissertation, Columbia University.

Lloyd, P. C. 1974. *Power and Independence: Urban Africans' Perceptions of Social Inequality*. Routledge and Kegan Paul.

1977. His Review of: The Development of an African Working Class: Studies in Class Formation and Action, ed. Sandbrook and Cohen. And of: Nigeria: Economy and Society, ed. Williams. In the *Times Higher Education Supplement*, April 1, 1977: 24.

1982. *A Third World Proletariat?* London, MA: Allen and Unwin.

Lojkine, J. 1976. 'Contribution to a Marxist Theory of Capitalist Urbanization.' In *Urban Sociology*, ed. C. G. Pickvance. London: Methuen.

Lovejoy, P. 1973. 'The Kambarin Beriberi: A Specialized Group of Hausa Kola Traders.' *Journal of African History*, Vol. XIV: 633–651.

1974. 'Interregional Monetary Flows in the Pre-Colonial Trade of Nigeria, *Journal of Africa History*, Vol. XV, No. 4.

1978. 'Plantations in the Economy of the Sokoto Caliphate.' *Journal of African History*, Vol. XIX: 341–368.

1979. 'The Characteristics of Plantations in the Nineteenth Century Sokoto Caliphate.'

American Historical Review, Vol. 84, No. 5, December.

1980. *Caravans of Kola: The Hausa Kola Trade, 1700–1900*. Zaria: Ahmadu Bello University.

1981. 'Slavery in the Political Economy of the Sokoto Caliphate.' In *The Ideology of Slavery in Africa*, ed. Lovejoy. Beverly Hills: Sage Publications.

Lovejoy, P. and Hogendorn, J. 1979. 'Slave Marketing in West Africa.' *The Uncommon Market*, ed. Gemery and Hogendorn. New York: Academic Press.

Lubeck, P. 1968. 'The Revenue System of Pre-Colonial Kano Emirate.' Unpublished manuscript. Evanston, Illinois: Northwestern University.

1975a. 'Unions, Workers and Consciousness in Kano, Nigeria.' *The Development of an African Working Class*, ed. R. Sandbrook and R. Cohen. London: Longman.

1975b. 'Early Industrialization and Social Class Formation Among Factory Workers in Kano.' Ph.D. thesis, Northwestern University.

1977. 'Contrasts and Historical Continuity in a Dependent City: The Case of Kano, Nigeria.' *Third World Urbanization*, ed. J. Abu-Lughod and C. Hay. Chicago: Maaroufa Press.

1979a. 'Islam and Resistance in Northern Nigeria.' *The World System of Capitalism*, ed. W. Goldfrank. Beverly Hills: Sage Publications.

1979b. 'The Value of Multiple Methods in Researching Third World Strikes. *Development and Change* No. 10, 2.

1981. 'Islamic Networks and Urban Capitalism: An Instance of Articulation From Northern Nigeria.' *Cahiers D'Etudes Africaines*, Vol. XXI, No. 1–3, 1981–83: 67–79.

1983. 'Industrial Labor in Kano in B. Barkindo.' *A History of Kano*. Ibaden: Heinemann.

1985. 'Islamic Protest Under Semi-Industrial Capitalism: Yan Tatsine' Explained.' *Africa: Journal of the International African Institute*, Vol. 55, No. 4.

(forthcoming). 'Islamic Political Movements in Northern Nigeria: The Problem of Class Analysis.' Forthcoming in E. Burke and I. Lapidus, *Islamic Political Movements*.

Lubeck, P. and Walton, J. 1979. 'Urban Class Conflict in Africa and Latin America: Comparative Analyses From a World Systems Perspective.' *International Journal of Urban and Regional Research*, Vol. 3, No. 1: 3–29.

Luckham, R. 1971. *The Nigerian Military*. Cambridge: Cambridge University Press.

Lugard, L. 1970. *Political Memoranda*. London: Frank Cass.

Mabogunje, A. 1968. *Urbanization in Nigeria*. London: The University Press.

Mann, M. 1973. *Consciousness and Actions Among the Western Working Class*. London: Macmillan.

Mantoux, P. 1961. *The Industrial Revolution in the Eighteenth Century*. New York: Harper and Row.

Martin, B. 1976. *Muslim Brotherhoods in the 19th Century*. Cambridge: Cambridge University Press.

Marx, K. 1933. *Wage Labor and Capital*. New York: International Publishers.

1963. *The Eighteenth Brumaire of Louis Bonaparte*. New York: International Publishers.

1972. *Capital*, Vol. III. London: Lawrence and Wishart.

1977. *Capital*, Vol. I. New York: Vintage (Translation by B. Fowkes).

Marx, K. and Engels, F. 1970. *The German Ideology*. New York: International Publishers.

McCall G. and Simmons J. 1969. *Issued in Participant Observation*. MA: Addison-Wesley.

Medugbon, A. K., 1976. 'Kaduna, Nigeria: The Vicissitudes of a Capital City, 1917–1975.' Ph.D. dissertation, University of California, Los Angeles.

Meillassoux, C. 1972. 'From Reproduction to Production.' *Economy and Society*, Vol. I, No. 1.

1981. *Maidens, Meal and Money*. Cambridge: Cambridge University Press.

Melson, R. 1971. 'Ideology and Inconsistency: The Cross Pressured Nigerian Worker.' *Nigeria: Modernization and the Politics of Communalism*, ed. Melson and Wolpe. Lansing: Michigan State University.

347

Bibliography

Meszaros, I. 1970. *Marx's Theory of Alienation*. London: Merlin Press.

    1971. 'Contingent and Necessary Class Consciousness.' In his, *Aspects of History and Class Consciousness*. London: Merlin Press.

Miliband, R. 1969. *The State in Capitalist Society*. New York: Basic Books.

Miners, N. 1971. *The Nigerian Army*. London: Methuen.

Moore, B. 1978. *Injustice: The Social Bases of Obedience and Revolt*. New York: Sharpe.

Morgan Report. 1964. 'Report of the Commission on the Review of Wages, Salaries and Conditions of Service of the Junior Employees of the Governments of the Federation and in Private Establishments, 1963–1964.' Lagos: Federal Ministry of Information.

Mortimore, M., ed. 1970. *Zaria and Its Region*. Department of Geography, Zaria: Ahmadu Bello University.

Murdock, G. 1959. *Africa: Its Peoples and Their Cultural History*. New York: McGraw Hill.

Myint, H. 1971. *Economic Theory and Underdeveloped Countries*. London: Oxford University Press.

O'Connor, J. 1973. *The Fiscal Crisis of the State*. New York: St Martin's Press.

Ollman, B. 1971. *Alienation: Marx's Conception of Man in Capitalist Society*. Cambridge: Cambridge University Press.

Osoba, S. 1979. 'The Deepening Crisis of the Nigerian Bourgeoisie.' *Review of African Political Economy*, No. 13.

Ossowski, S. 1963. *Class Structure in the Social Consciousness*. New York: Free Press.

Otobo, D. 1981. 'The Nigerian General Strike of 1981.' *Review of African Political Economy*, No. 22.

    1982. 'The Political Clash in the Aftermath of the 1981 Nigerian General Strike.' *Review of African Political Economy*, No. 25.

Oyediran, O. and Gboyega, E. 1979. 'Local Government and Administration.' In O. Oyediran, ed., *Nigerian Government and Politics Under Military Rule, 1966–1979*. London: Macmillan.

Paden, J. 1968. 'The Influence of Religious Elites on Political Culture and Community Integration in Kano' Unpublished Ph.D. dissertation, Department of Government, Harvard University.

    1970. 'Urban Pluralism, Integration, and Adaptation of Communal Identity in Kano, Nigeria.' In R. Cohen and J. Middleton, *From Tribe to Nation in Africa*. Scranton, PA: Chandler.

    1971. 'Communal Competition, Conflict and Violence in Kano.' *Nigeria Modernization and the Politics of Communalism*, ed. Melson and Wolpe. Lansing: Michigan State University Press.

Paden, J. 1974. *Religion and Political Culture in Kano*. Berkeley: University of California Press.

Paden, J., Morrison, D., Mitchell, R., and Stevenson, M. 1972. *Black Africa*. New York: The Free Press.

Palma, G. 1978. 'Dependency: A Formal Theory of Underdevelopment or a Methodology For the Analysis of Concrete Situations of Underdevelopment?' *World Development*, Vol. 6: 881–924.

Palmer, H. 1967. *Sudanese Memoires*, Vol. III. London: Cass.

Panter-Brick, S. (ed.) 1970. *Nigerian Politics and Military Rule*. London: Athlone Press.

Parsons, T. 1968. *The Structure of Social Action*. Glencoe: The Free Press.

Peace, A. J. 1974. 'Industrial Protest at Ikeja, Nigeria.' In G. Williams and E. deKadt, *Sociology and Development*. London: Tavistock Publications.

    1975. 'The Lagos Proletariat: Labour Aristocrats or Populist Militant?' In Sandbrook, R. and Cohen, R. (ed.), *The Development of an African Working Class*. Longmans.

    1979. *Choice, Class and Conflict*. New Jersey: Humanities Press.

Pickvance, C. G. 1976. *Urban Sociology: Critical Essays*. London: Tavistock/Methuen.

348

Pipes, D. 1980. 'This World is Political. The Islamic Revival of The Seventies.' *Orbis*, Vol. 24, No. 1, Spring 1980.

Portes, A. 1982. 'The Informal Sector: Definition, Controversy and Relations.' Paper prepared for the Third Seminar of the Working Group on Latin American Organization, Mexico.

Post, K. 1963. *The Nigerian Federal Election of 1959*. London: Oxford University Press.

1964. 'The Northern Elements Progressive Union.' N.I.S.E.R. Conference Proceedings 1963. Ibaden.

1978. *Arise Ye Starvelings*. The Hague: Nijhoff.

Poulantzas, N. 1973a. *Political Power and Social Classes*. New Left Books and Sheed and Ward. First French edition 1968.

1973b. 'On Social Classes.' *New Left Review*, Vol. 78: 27–55.

Przeworski, A. and Teune, H. 1970. *The Logic of Comparative Social Inquiry*. New York: John Wiley.

1977. 'Proletariat Into a Class: The Process of Class Formation from Karl Kautsky's, The Class Struggle to Recent Controversies.' *Politics and Society*, Vol. 7, No. 4: 343–402.

Rey, P. 1971. *Colonialisme, Neo-Colonialisme et Transition au Capitalisme*. Paris: Maspero.

1973. *Les Alliances de Classes*. Paris: Maspero.

Rimmer, D. 1981. 'Development in Nigeria: An Overview.' In H. Bienen and V. Diejomaoh, *The Political Economy of Income Distribution in Nigeria*. New York: Homes and Meier.

Roberts, B. 1978. *Cities of Peasants*. Beverly Hills: Sage Publications.

Rodinson, M. 1978. *Islam and Capitalism*. Austin: University of Texas Press.

Rodney, W. 1972. *How Europe Underdeveloped Africa*. London: Bogle-L'ouverture.

Rowling, G. 1949. *Report on Land Tenure, Kano Province*. Kaduna: Government Printer (Nigeria).

Said, E. 1981. *Covering Islam*. New York: Pantheon.

Sandbrook, R. 1982. *The Politics of Basic Needs*. Toronto: University of Toronto Press.

Saul, J. 1975. 'The Labour Aristocracy Thesis Reconsidered.' In the *Development of an African Working Class*, ed. R. Sandbrook and R. Cohen. London: Longman.

Schatzl, L. 1973. *Industrialization in Nigeria: A Spatial Analysis*. Munich: Weltforum Verlag.

Schatzman, L. and Strauss, L. 1973. *Field Research*. New Jersey: Prentice Hall.

Seymour, T. 1978. 'Housing Conditions in Towns of Northern Nigeria: A Review of Existing Data.' Zaria: Ahmadu Bello University.

Sharwood-Smith, B. 1969. *But Always as Friends*. London: Allen and Unwin.

Shea, P. 1974. 'Economies of Scale and the Dying Industry of Pre-colonial Kano.' *Kano Studies*, (new series), Vol. I, No. 2.

1975. 'The Development of an Export Oriented Dyed Cloth Industry in Nineteenth Century Kano Emirate.' Ph.D. dissertation, University of Wisconsin.

1981. 'Approaching the Study of Production in Rural Kano.' Conference on the History of Kano, Bayero University.

Shenton, R. 1981. 'Studies in the Development of Capitalism in Northern Nigeria.' Unpublished, Ph.D. dissertation, History, University of Toronto.

Skinner, N. (ed.) 1977. *Alhaji Mahmudu Koki*. Zaria: Ahmadu Bello University Press.

Sklar, R. 1963. *Nigerian Political Parties*. Princeton: Princeton University Press.

Smelser, N. 1976. *Comparative Methods in the Social Sciences*. Englewood Cliffs: Prentice Hall.

Smith, A. 1970. 'Some Considerations Relating to the Formation of States in Hausaland.' *Journal of the Historical Society of Nigeria*. Vol. V., No. 3, December.

1976. 'The Early States of The Central Sudan.' In *History of West Africa*, Vol. I, ed. J. F. Ajayi and M. Crowder. New York: Columbia University Press.

Smith, M. F. 1965. *Baba of Karo: A Woman of the Muslim Hausa*. London: Faber and Faber.

Bibliography

Smith, M. G., 1950. 'Social and Economic Change Among Hausa Communities, Northern Nigeria.' Ph.D. dissertation, University of London.

1955. 'The Economy of Hausa Communities in Zaria.' *Colonial Research Studies*, No. 16, London. HMSO.

1960. *Government in Zauzau*. London: Oxford University Press.

1964. 'Historical and Cultural Conditions of Political Corruption Among the Hausa.' *Comparative Studies in Society and History VI*: 164–194.

1965. 'Hausa Inheritance and Succession.' In *Studies in the Laws of Succession in Nigeria*, ed. J. D. M. Derret. London: Oxford University Press.

(forthcoming). *A History of Kano*.

1981. 'The Kano Chronicle.' Paper presented at History of Kano Conference. Bayero University Kano.

Stearns, P. N. 1975. *Lives of Labor: Work in a Maturing Society*. New York: Homes and Meier.

Stremlau, J. 1977. *The International Politics of the Nigerian Civil War*. Princeton: Princeton University Press.

Stryker, R. 1979. 'The World Bank and Agricultural Development.' *World Development*, Vol. 7, No. 3.

Tahir, I. 1975. 'Scholars, Sufis, Saints and Capitalists in Kano, 1904–1974; A Pattern of a Bourgeois Revolution in an Islamic Society.' Ph.D. dissertation, Cambridge University.

Taira, K. 1969. 'Industrial Revolution and Factory Labor in Japan.' Paper for the Research Center in Economic Growth. Stanford University.

Taylor, J. G. 1979. *From Modernization to Modes of Production*. New York: MacMillan Press.

Teriba, O. Edozien, E. C. and Kayode, M. O. 1981. *The Structure of Manufacturing Industry in Nigeria*. Ibadan: Ibadan University Press.

Terray, E. 1972. *Marxism and Primitive Societies*. New York: Monthly Review Press.

1975. 'Classes and Class Consciousness in Abron Kingdom of Gyaman.' In ed. M. Bloch, *Marxist Analyses and Social Anthropology*. New York: John Wiley.

Thompson, E. 1967. 'Time, Work-disciple and Industrial Capitalism.' *Past and Present*, No. 36, December 1967: 56–97.

1968. *The Making of the English Working Class*. Harmonsworth: Pelican.

Tomlinson, G. and Lethem G. 1927. *History of Islamic Propaganda in Nigeria*. London: Waterlow.

Touraine, A. and Rangazzi, O. 1961. 'Ouvriers d'Origine Agricole.' Laboratoire De Sociologie Industrielle De L'ecole Pratique des Hautes Etudes. Paris.

Touraine, A. and Pecaut, D. 1967. 'Working Class Consciousness and Economic Development in Latin America.' *Studies in Comparative International Development*, Vol. 3, No. 4: 65–94.

Trevaillion, B. 1966. *Metropolitan Kano Report on the Twenty Year Development Plan 1963–1983*. Kano, Greater Kano Planning Authority.

Tukur, M. M. 1979. 'The Imposition of British Colonial Domination of the Sokoto Caliphate.' Ph.D. dissertation, 2 vols. Zaria: Ahmadu Bello University.

Tumin, M. and Feldman, A. 1961. *Social Class and Social Change in Puerto Rico*. Princeton: Princeton University Press.

Turner, B. 1974. *Weber and Islam*. Boston: Routledge and Kegan Paul.

1978. *Marx and the End of Orientalism*. Boston: Allen and Unwin.

Turner, T. 1976. 'Multinational Corporations and the Nigerian State.' *Review of African Political Economy*, No. 5.

Udo, R. K. 1970. *Geographical Regions of Nigeria*. Berkeley: University of California Press.

Usman, Y. B. 1979. *Studies in the History of the Sokoto Caliphate*. Zaria: Ahmadu Bello University.

350

1981. *The Transformation of Katsina, 1400–1883*. Zaria: Ahmadu Bello University Press.

Vallier, I. (ed.) 1971. *Comparative Methods in Sociology*. Berkeley: University of California.

Vigo, A. H. 1957. 'A Survey of Agricultural Credit in the North of Nigeria.' Mimeograph. Ministry of Agriculture. Kaduna.

Wallace, T. 1979. 'Rural Development Through Irrigation: Studies in a Town on the Kano River Project.' Centre for Social and Economic Research. Zaria: Ahmadu Bello University.

1980. 'Agricultural Projects and Land in Northern Nigeria.' *Review of African Political Economy*, No. 17.

Wallerstein, I. 1973. 'Africa in a Capitalist World.' *Issue*, Vol. 3, No. 3.

1974a. 'The Rise and Future Demise of the World Capitalist System: Concepts for Comparative Analysis.' *Comparative Studies in Society and History*, Vol. XVI: 387–415.

1974b. *The Modern World System*. New York: Academic Press.

1976. 'The Three Stages of African Involvement in the World-Economy.' In I. Wallerstein and P. Gutkind ed. *The Political Economy of Contemporary Africa*. Beverly Hills: Sage Publications.

1979. *The Capitalist World-Economy*. Cambridge: Cambridge University Press.

1981. 'Race is Class? Some Reflections on South Africa Inspired by Magubane.' *Monthly Press*, Vol. 32, No. 10.

Walton, J. and Portes, A. 1981. *Labor, Class, and the International System*. New York: Academic Press.

Warren, B. 1980. *Imperialism, Pioneer of Capitalism*. London: Verso.

Waterman, P. 1975. 'The Labor Aristocracy in Africa: Introduction to a Debate.' *Development and Change*, Vol. 6, No. 3.

1979. 'Consciousness, Organization and Action Amongst Lagos Portworkers.' *Review of African Political Economy*, No. 13.

1983. 'Aristocrats and Plebeians in African Trade Unions? Lagos Port and Dock Worker Organization and Struggle.' Ph.D. dissertation, University of Nijmegen.

Watts, M. 1983. *Silent Violence*. Berkeley: University of California Press.

Wearmouth, R. 1972. *Methodism and the Working Class Movements of England*. Clifton, New Jersey.

Weber, M. 1949. *The Methodology of the Social Science*. Glencoe: The Free Press.

1958. *The Protestant Ethic and the Spirit of Capitalism*. New York: Scribner.

1968. *Economy and Society*. New York: Bedminster Press.

Whitaker, Jr., C. S. 1970. *The Politics of Tradition, Continuity and Change in Northern Nigeria*. Princeton: Princeton University Press.

White, S. 1966. *Dan Bana*. New York: Heinemann.

Williams, G. 1980. *State and Society in Nigeria*, Afrografika Publishers, Idanre, Ondo State.

Williams, G. and Turner, T. 1978. 'Politics in Nigeria'. In J. Dunn, ed. *West African States: Failure and Promise*. Cambridge University Press.

Wolpe, H. 1972. 'Capitalism and Cheap Labor-Power in South Africa: From Segregation to Apartheid.' *Economy and Society*, Vol. I, No. 4.

Yusuf, A. B. 1975. 'Capital Formation and Management Among the Muslim Traders of Kano, Nigeria.' *Africa*, Vol. XLV: 167–182.

Zeitlin, M. 1980. 'On Classes, Class Conflict and the State: An Introductory Note.' In M. Zeitlin, ed., *Classes, Class Conflict and the State*. Cambridge, MA: Winthrop.

351

Index

Index